Keys to Growth

Meditations on the Acts of the Apostles

Will Vaus

Keys to Growth
Meditations on the Acts of the Apostles

Copyright © 2012 Will Vaus

Barnabas Books
a division of Winged Lion Press
Hamden, CT

All rights reserved. Except in the case of quotations embodied in critical articles or reviews, no part of this book may be reproduced or transmitted in any form or by any means, electronic or mechanical, including photocopying, recording, or by any information storage or retrieval system, without written permission of the publisher.
For information, contact Winged Lion Press www.WingedLionPress.com

Unless otherwise noted Scripture references are taken from the HOLY BIBLE, NEW INTERNATIONAL VERSION ®. Copyright © 1973, 1978, 1984 International Bible Society.
Used by permission of Zondervan. All rights reserved.

Winged Lion Press titles may be purchased for business or promotional use or special sales.

10-9-8-7-6-5-4-3-2-1

Barnabas Books

ISBN-13 978-1-936294-19-0

Dedicated to

the congregations

I have been blessed to serve in

California, South Carolina,

Pennsylvania & West Virginia

CONTENTS

Introduction	1
Jesus	3
Prayer	9
The Holy Spirit	16
Devotion	24
Healing	31
Suffering	38
Community	45
Honesty	52
Perseverance	58
Vision	65
Evangelism	73
Reproduction	81
Confrontation	88
Mission	95
God's Person	103
Church Planting	110
Problems	117
Mentoring	124
Providence	132
Women	138
Attitude	145
Trouble Making	152
Seeking Truth	159

Be a Transformer	167
Growing Relationships	175
Crises	182
Passing the Torch	190
Claiming the Power of the Name	197
Recognizing the Way	205
Encouragement	212
Worship	218
Leadership	225
Tenacity	233
Compromise	239
Closed Doors	245
God's Sovereignty	252
Holy Boldness	260
A Living Savior	267
Telling Your Story	275
Stormy Weather Faith	283
Preaching	290
Conclusion	299
Acknowledgements	300
Select Bibliography	301

INTRODUCTION

I still remember the first time I read *The Acts of the Apostles* for myself. I was sixteen years old. My parents allowed me to travel by myself that summer from our home in San Diego to New York City where I stayed for one week in a hotel off of Times Square in order to tour the Big Apple. Yes, it was daring on my parents' part to allow me to do that. However, one of my brothers lived a relatively short distance away, in Philadelphia, and my parents had other friends in the vicinity of New York to call on for help if I ran into trouble.

One thing I remember from that trip is feeling very alone the first night in the hotel. There were countless people, at all hours of the night, milling about outside my window in Times Square. Still, I felt very alone.

That night I picked up my Bible, and for some reason, I began reading Acts. Even though the story of the first followers of Jesus was about nineteen centuries and thousands of miles distant from my experience sitting in that New York hotel room, suddenly I didn't feel so all alone. I could relate to the people Acts was talking about. It has been a favorite biblical book of mine ever since.

As a pastor, I have preached through the entire book of Acts at least four times to four different congregations in three states, besides preaching single sermons from this book countless other times in many locations over the past 25 years. Whether anyone else learned anything or not, *I* learned something new each time.

The "meditations" presented in this book are based upon those sermons. Each chapter is adapted from a single sermon and adjusted to the medium of the printed page. However, I believe the power of God's Word is the same, whether it is conveyed through a live sermon or through a book.

J. B. Philips, a pastor in England in the mid twentieth century who wrote a rather popular translation of the New Testament, once said that as he was translating the Scriptures he felt like an electrician re-wiring an old house with the electricity on. I have felt something similar as I have read again and edited these meditations for the purpose of this book. Acts is an electric book and I have felt fresh power coming into my life through this renewed study. I hope the same will be true for you—that you will receive from the reading of this book a new jolt of grace from our Triune God.

However, let me offer one caution at the outset. There is so much spiritual truth to meditate on in the book of Acts that if we try to take it in all at once, we will be overwhelmed. Therefore, I recommend taking these mediations in small doses. Try reading one chapter per week, or at the most—one chapter per day. Take time to think about what you are reading and ask the Lord how he wants you to apply it in your life. I believe the book of Acts is well worth spending a month, or even a year on. In fact, it is a book so filled with the power of the Holy Spirit, that we could meditate on it for our entire lives and never come to the end of its power. May God bless you as you tap into that power, whether it be for a month, a year, or a lifetime….

JESUS

My eldest son, James, brought two pumpkin plants home from school one day when he was about thirteen years old. When he brought the plants home they were small, perhaps an inch or so in height. He planted them in two clay pots with good soil, rich in nutrients, and he placed the pots by the window in our living room. Every day James continued to pay attention to those plants. He checked their soil to see how dry they were. If they needed water, he watered them. When we went away for a few days we left the light on the table where the plants were located so that they would be certain to get plenty of light. It was interesting to watch the pumpkin plants grow. They stretched out toward the window, toward the light, in a dramatic way. Eventually the plants got so big, James stuck a pencil in each pot and attached the pumpkin vines to the pencils to help them grow up straight and strong. Eventually, the plants got too big for the pots and too big to keep indoor. Thus, James cleared out an old, overgrown flower bed, put some good top soil down in it and planted his pumpkin plants outside. Unfortunately, it was at that point that the plants didn't survive very well. Perhaps the soil and the sunlight were not quite right to produce healthy pumpkins, despite the fact that James did his best with the project.

What would have happened to those plants if James hadn't given them good soil to grow in at all? What would have happened if he hadn't watered them? What would have happened if he hadn't put the plants near a good source of light? What would have happened if he hadn't given them room to grow? What would have happened to those pumpkin plants without a gardener like James? It's obvious; those plants would have died even sooner.

Every living thing or person requires certain ingredients in order to grow. And if a thing or person is not growing, it is dying. What is true in the physical realm is also true in the spiritual realm. In order to grow spiritually, individual Christians, and the whole Church in fact needs certain fundamental ingredients.

Acts is a book that is all about growth. In at least ten places in this book growth is specifically mentioned or inferred:

1. "In those days Peter stood up among the believers (a group numbering about a hundred and twenty)." Acts 1:15

2. "Those who accepted his message were baptized, and about three thousand were added to their number that day." Acts 2:41
3. "But many who heard the message believed, and the number of men grew to about five thousand." Acts 4:4
4. "Nevertheless, more and more men and women believed in the Lord and were added to their number." Acts 5:14
5. "So the word of God spread. The number of disciples in Jerusalem increased rapidly, and a large number of priests became obedient to the faith." Acts 6:7"
6. Then the church throughout Judea, Galilee and Samaria enjoyed a time of peace. It was strengthened; and encouraged by the Holy Spirit, it grew in numbers, living in the fear of the Lord." Acts 9:31
7. "But the word of God continued to increase and spread." Acts 12:24
8. "So the churches were strengthened in the faith and grew daily in numbers." Acts 16:5
9. "In this way the word of the Lord spread widely and grew in power." Acts 19:20
10. "Boldly and without hindrance he preached the kingdom of God and taught about the Lord Jesus Christ." Acts 28:31

We see from these verses that the spiritual growth of individual Christians and of the Church as a whole manifested itself in physical ways. With this in mind, let's begin our examination of Acts with the first eleven verses in the first chapter, and see what they have to tell us about how to grow as Christians.

> In my former book, Theophilus, I wrote about all that Jesus began to do and to teach until the day he was taken up to heaven, after giving instructions through the Holy Spirit to the apostles he had chosen. After his suffering, he showed himself to these men and gave many convincing proofs that he was alive. He appeared to them over a period of forty days and spoke about the kingdom of God. On one occasion, while he was eating with them, he gave them this command: "Do not leave Jerusalem, but wait for the gift my Father promised, which you have heard me speak about. For John baptized with water, but in a few days you will be baptized with the Holy Spirit."
>
> So when they met together, they asked him, "Lord, are you at this time going to restore the kingdom to Israel?"
>
> He said to them: "It is not for you to know the times or dates the Father has set by his own authority. But you will receive power when the Holy Spirit comes on you; and you will be my witnesses in Jerusalem, and in

all Judea and Samaria, and to the ends of the earth."

After he said this, he was taken up before their very eyes, and a cloud hid him from their sight.

They were looking intently up into the sky as he was going, when suddenly two men dressed in white stood beside them. "Men of Galilee," they said, "why do you stand here looking into the sky? This same Jesus, who has been taken from you into heaven, will come back in the same way you have seen him go into heaven."

Acts is the second book in a two volume work which began with the Gospel of Luke, written by the traveling companion of Paul. The first key ingredient to Christian growth which Luke reveals to us in this second book is, simply, Jesus, reigning in our lives. Luke writes, "In my former book, Theophilus," which means lover of God, "I wrote about all that Jesus *began* to do and to teach." This statement implies that Luke's second volume is going to teach us about all that Jesus *continued* to do and to teach. Acts shows us all that Jesus continued to do and teach in the Church through the work of the Holy Spirit. By application, I believe this book will teach us what Jesus can continue to do in our lives through the Holy Spirit, how Jesus can help us to grow. Jesus is the "not-so secret" ingredient to growth in the Christian life.

Now, if we want Jesus to help us grow in our Christian lives then there are three pre-requisites mentioned by Luke. First of all, we must become convinced of his resurrection. We read that after Jesus' suffering, "he showed himself to these men and gave many convincing proofs that he was alive. He appeared to them over a period of forty days . . ."

There was once a man named Frank Morison, a respected British lawyer, who believed that the bodily resurrection of Jesus didn't really happen. He began writing a book to disprove the resurrection. But in the course of studying the evidence he came to the conviction that Jesus really did rise bodily from the grave. The one question which led him to faith was: "Who moved the stone?" He could not conceive of why the Roman guards would have moved the stone covering Jesus' tomb. Morison could not conceive that the disciples would have moved the stone and stolen the body. So he came to the conclusion that the resurrection of Jesus happened the way the Gospels told it. He titled the book which resulted from his research: *Who Moved The Stone?*

The bodily resurrection of Jesus is what brought hope to his disciples. It is part of the good news, along with Jesus' death for our sins, which those same disciples proclaimed to the world. Belief in the resurrection is what helped them to grow in faith. And it will help us grow too.

Secondly, if Jesus is going to help us grow, we must learn about his kingdom plans. Over a period of forty days, between the resurrection and the ascension, Jesus spoke about the kingdom of God to his disciples. Jesus' teaching even raised questions for the disciples. On one occasion they asked him, "Are you at this time going to restore the kingdom to Israel?" You see, the disciples still had in mind that Jesus was going to establish a political, earthly kingdom for Israel. In answer to their question, Jesus taught his disciples that the kingdom of God is:

- spiritual in character,
- international in its membership and
- gradual in its expansion.

The kingdom of God is all about bringing the will of God to bear in our lives on earth just as it is done in heaven.

Thirdly, if we want Jesus to help us grow spiritually, we must wait on him to do his work in his perfect time. Jesus told his disciples, "Do not leave Jerusalem, *but wait* for the gift my Father promised, which you have heard me speak about. For John baptized with water, but in a few days you will be baptized with the Holy Spirit."

Waiting for growth is often hard for us to do as human beings. My son James couldn't wait to see his pumpkin plants full grown. Perhaps that is one reason why he *didn't* get to see them full-grown. Maybe he tried to rush the growing process.

Children sometimes can't wait to be grown up. Teenagers often can't wait to drive a car. College students are often anxious to be done with school. Singles can't wait to be married. Some married people can't wait to have kids. Then once they have kids they can't wait until they are grown up!

Just so, we sometimes have a hard time waiting for the spiritual growth that Jesus wants to bring about in our lives. But we have to wait, because spiritual growth, like most other types of growth, doesn't happen instantly.

Orin L. Crain once wrote this wonderful prayer:

> Slow me down, Lord.
> Ease the pounding of my heart by the quieting of my mind.
> Steady my hurried pace with a vision of the eternal reach of time.
> Give me, amid the confusion of the day, the calmness of the everlasting hills.
> Break the tensions of my nerves and muscles with the soothing music of the singing streams that live in my memory.
> Teach me the art of taking minute vacations—of slowing down to look at a flower, to chat with a friend, to pat a dog, to smile at a child, to read a few lines from a good book.
> Slow me down, Lord, and inspire me to send my roots deep into the soil of life's enduring values, that I may grow toward my greater destiny.

> Remind me each day that the race is not always to the swift; that there is more to life than increasing its speed.
> Let me look upward to the towering oak and know that it grew great and strong because it grew slowly and well.

Jesus, reigning in and through our lives, is *the* key to spiritual growth. However, to see that growth happen, we must believe in his resurrection, understand his kingdom plan, and wait on his timing.

Luke also tells us in these verses that growth will occur as we *continue* to be Jesus' witnesses. The theme verse of this book is Acts 1:8,

> But you will receive power when the Holy Spirit comes on you; and you will be my witnesses in Jerusalem, and in all Judea and Samaria, and to the ends of the earth.

This verse acts as a sort of Table of Contents for the whole book of Acts. Chapters 1-7 talk about the witness in Jerusalem. Chapters 8-12 talk about the witness in Judea and Samaria. And chapters 13-28 talk about the Christian witness to the ends of the earth.

In this one verse Jesus tells us some very important things:

- The power for witness comes from the Holy Spirit living in us.
- Witness is a team effort, the activity of the whole Church working together.
- If you are a Christian then you are a witness.

Witness is something you *are* more than something you *do*. A number of years ago Harvard University commissioned a study on communication. They discovered no less than 700,000 different ways of communicating without words. That statistic says to me that if I try to communicate the Gospel by words alone, I am going to be out-numbered by 700,000 to 1!

After H. M. Stanley found David Livingston in Central Africa and had spent some time with him, he said, "If I had been with him any longer I would have been compelled to be a Christian and he never spoke to me about it at all." I wonder: is the Christian witness of our life, as well as our words, irresistible?

We must also recognize that we are called to point people to Jesus, not call attention to ourselves.

My mother once told me that a short while before my father died he told her he felt that he had spent too much of his life telling *his story* to other people, and not enough time telling *Jesus' story*.

That is important to keep in mind. There is a time for telling people our story, of what Jesus means to us and has done for us. But we must always lead out of our story to draw people's attention to Jesus as pre-eminent.

We also need to recognize that being a witness will require sacrifice. The word for witness in Greek is the same as the word for "martyr". It reminds us of the fact that many of the first Christian witnesses laid down their lives for Jesus. We must be willing to do the same, while recognizing that he may call us to lay down our lives *daily* over a lifetime of seventy years or more, rather than simply laying our physical lives down in one day, though he may call us to do that as well.

A final essential thing Luke tells us about growth in these opening verses of the book of Acts is that growth is assured because Jesus reigns. Jesus' ascension into heaven means that he is reigning on the throne. Psalm 68:18 says, "When you ascended on high, you led captives in your train." And Psalm 47:5,8 say, "God has ascended amid shouts of joy . . . God reigns over the nations; God is seated on his holy throne." And in Ephesians 2:6 Paul says, "And God raised us up with Christ and seated us with him in the heavenly realms in Christ Jesus."

Because Jesus is risen and reigning on his throne we, who are believers in Jesus, are also reigning with him. We can extend his kingdom reign over the whole earth by acting as his witnesses in the world. And the success of our witness is assured because he reigns. The gates of hell shall not prevail against the Church of Jesus Christ.

On the way home from church one Sunday a mother asked her young son what he learned about in Sunday School. The boy said, "Our teacher taught us about the book of Revelation." The mother, surprised that a child so young was being taught such a complicated biblical book asked, "So what did you learn about the book of Revelation?" The boy responded, "Oh, it's simple Mom. We learned that the book of Revelation means that Jesus is going to win in the end."

I think that is the message of Revelation, and of the ascension. Jesus is on the throne. He is sovereign. That means our growth, unlike my son's pumpkin plants, is assured. Our labor for the Lord is never in vain. Our witness for him will be successful if we are trusting in God. Jesus is definitely going to win in the end. And we can win with him.

Prayer

To: Jesus, Son of Joseph,
Woodcrafters Shop
Nazareth

From: Jordan Management Consultants
The Solomon Building
Jerusalem

Thank you for submitting the resumes of the 12 men you have picked for management positions in your new organization. All of them have now taken our battery of tests, and we have not only run the results through our computer but also have arranged personal interviews for each of them with our psychologist and vocational aptitude consultant.

The profiles of all the tests are included, and you will want to study each of them carefully. As part of our service and for your guidance, we make some general comments. These are given as a result of staff consultations and come without additional fee.

It is the staff opinion that most of your nominees are lacking in background, education, and vocational aptitude for the type of enterprise you are undertaking. They do not have the team concept. We would recommend that you continue your search for persons of experience in managerial ability and proven capability.

Simon Peter is emotionally unstable and given to fits of temper. Andrew has absolutely no qualities of leadership. The two brothers, James and John, the sons of Zebedee, place personal interest above company loyalty. Thomas demonstrates a questioning attitude that would tend to undermine morale. We feel that it is our duty to tell you that Matthew has been blacklisted by the Greater Jerusalem Better Business Bureau. James, the son of Alphaeus, and Thaddeus definitely have

> radical leanings, and they both registered a high score on the manic depressive scale.
>
> One of the candidates, however, shows great potential. He is a man of ability and resourcefulness, meets people well, has a keen business mind and has contact in high places. He is highly motivated, ambitious and responsible. We recommend Judas Iscariot as your controller and right hand man. All the other profiles are self-explanatory.
>
> We wish you every success in your new venture.

Thankfully Jesus did not take the advice of the Jordan Management Consultants when it came to selecting his first twelve disciples.

How did Jesus go about it? Luke 6:12-13 tells us:

> One of those days Jesus went out to a mountainside to pray, and spent the night praying to God. When morning came, he called his disciples to him and chose twelve of them, whom he also designated apostles . . .

Persistent prayer is one of the essentials of the Christian life, in fact it is one of the keys to growth in Christ. And we see the pattern of Jesus' commitment to prayer repeated in the life of his disciples after he departed from them. Acts 1:12-26 tells us more about this....

> Then they returned to Jerusalem from the hill called the Mount of Olives, a Sabbath day's walk from the city. When they arrived, they went upstairs to the room where they were staying. Those present were Peter, John, James and Andrew; Philip and Thomas, Bartholomew and Matthew; James son of Alphaeus and Simon the Zealot, and Judas son of James. They all joined together constantly in prayer, along with the women and Mary the mother of Jesus, and with his brothers.
>
> In those days Peter stood up among the believers (a group numbering about a hundred and twenty) and said, "Brothers, the Scripture had to be fulfilled which the Holy Spirit spoke long ago through the mouth of David concerning Judas, who served as guide for those who arrested Jesus—he was one of our number and shared in this ministry."
>
> (With the reward he got for his wickedness, Judas bought a field; there he fell headlong, his body burst open and all his intestines spilled out. Everyone in Jerusalem heard about this, so they called that field in their language Akeldama, that is, Field of Blood.)
>
> "For," said Peter, "it is written in the book of Psalms,
>
> "'May his place be deserted; let there be no one to dwell in it,' and,

"'May another take his place of leadership.'

Therefore it is necessary to choose one of the men who have been with us the whole time the Lord Jesus went in and out among us, beginning from John's baptism to the time when Jesus was taken up from us. For one of these must become a witness with us of his resurrection."

So they proposed two men: Joseph called Barsabbas (also known as Justus) and Matthias. Then they prayed, "Lord, you know everyone's heart. Show us which of these two you have chosen to take over this apostolic ministry, which Judas left to go where he belongs." Then they cast lots, and the lot fell to Matthias; so he was added to the eleven apostles.

We see two things in this passage about prayer as a key to Christian growth and Church growth. First of all, prayer brings about growth of the individual Christian and the whole Church when we all join together constantly in prayer. In verse 14 we read that "They all joined together constantly in prayer . . ." Let's examine this verse word by word.

Who were "they" who joined together constantly in prayer? It was the apostles and the women, including Mary, the mother of Jesus. The group of praying people also included Jesus' brothers. These were the ones who didn't believe in Jesus as the Messiah during his earthly life. But they became convinced that Jesus was the Messiah when he rose from the dead. Paul tells us specifically in 1 Corinthians 15:7 that Jesus appeared to James, that is to his brother James, after he rose from the dead.

However, I think we may also assume that the "they" who prayed included the 120 believers whom we just read about Peter speaking to. Verse 24 specifically suggests that *all* the believers joined together in prayer. This teaches us that powerful prayer is not the prerogative of a few elite Christians but it is the privilege of every member of the Body of Christ.

The next key phrase we see in this verse is: *joined together*. Luke uses one of his favorite words here. In fact he uses it ten times in Acts and it appears only one other time in the New Testament outside of Acts. The word is ὁμοθυμαδὸν and it means "with one mind". Prayer is only effective when we pray in unity. When people in the church are back-biting, forming factions, angry with each other, prayer is just a pretense. But the converse is also true, when we get down on our knees and seriously begin to pray together, division cannot last for long.

What do most Christians pray every Sunday in The Lord's Prayer? "Forgive us our trespasses as we forgive those who trespass against us." If we are *honestly* praying these words together every Sunday then division cannot last. We cannot harbor grudges any longer. We must forgive, we must let the past go, if we want to be forgiven by our Lord.

I wonder: do we realize what dramatic promises Jesus makes to Christians who dwell in unity? In Matthew 18:19-20 Jesus says,

> Again, I tell you that if two of you on earth agree about anything you ask for, it will be done for you by my Father in heaven. For where two or three come together in my name, there am I with them.

Jesus promises that where only two or three of us truly gather together in the unity of his name, he is present with us! And if only two of us, who are gathered in his name to accomplish his purpose, agree about anything we ask for, our Father in heaven will do it. That is a promise seldom claimed by Christians. But if we gather together in unified prayer, seeking the Lord's will, we can claim such promises.

The next key word we see in Acts 1:14 is the word: *constantly*. The word is προσκαρτεροῦντες and it means to be earnest towards, to persevere, to be constantly diligent. Could those words be used of our prayer life?

Paul commands us, in 1 Thessalonians 5:17, to "pray without ceasing". Now obviously this doesn't mean that we are all supposed to be down on our knees in our bedroom every moment of every day, or that we are supposed to gather together in church to pray every hour of every week. If we did either of those things we would have to forsake obedience to many of God's other commands in Scripture.

To me, praying without ceasing, means cultivating the habit of "practicing the presence of God" in my everyday life. It means lifting up prayers to him as we walk along the road, as we sit in our offices, as we go to school, even as we drive in the car. I remember saying to a friend once, as I was driving him along in my car and an important matter came up in conversation, "Let's pray about that right now." And then I added, "Don't worry. I won't close my eyes or bow my head. But you can!" He laughed.

We need to practice the presence of God in our everyday lives. But we also could probably stand to come together more often as a church just for the purpose of prayer. What is prayer, after all? The word that is used here can literally mean "to pour out". Prayer is pouring out our hearts before the Lord. But the word as it is used here with the definite article "the" may have reference to the specific stated times of prayer in the Jewish temple. So what Luke may be telling us is that the disciples devoted themselves to going to the temple to pray at the specific Jewish times for prayer. I think we would benefit as a church if we had more times to come together just for the purpose of prayer.

On some occasion, Charles Spurgeon, the great London preacher of the 19th century, was showing some visitors his church building. After visiting the large, impressive sanctuary he said, "Come, I want to show you the heating system for the church." The visitors thought this was a strange thing for

Spurgeon to want to show them, but they complied, expecting to see some newly installed furnace. They were surprised then when Spurgeon took them to a room underneath the pulpit where more than four hundred members of the church were kneeling in prayer.

The power of the church flows through the prayers of God's people. It always has, and it always will.

Secondly, we see in this passage that prayer brings about growth for the individual Christian and for the entire church when we pray about specific decisions which are before us. When presented with two men to fill the place of Judas, who had abandoned his apostleship, we read:

> Then they prayed, "Lord, you know everyone's heart. Show us which of these two you have chosen to take over this apostolic ministry, which Judas left to go where he belongs."

Some people think that the disciples made a mistake by casting lots to choose the twelfth apostle. They say that Paul should have taken that place and if the church had only waited they would have seen God's will. But people who say this forget a few important facts. As Peter states, the twelve were those who had been with Jesus from the time of his baptism until his ascension. Specifically, each of the twelve were witnesses of Jesus' bodily resurrection. Paul did not fulfill these qualifications, though he did have a vision of the risen Lord and was an apostle in a broader sense.

However, the qualifications for the twelfth apostle suggest some marks of true Christians in a more general sense. The real mark of a true Christian is not that he or she knows *about* Jesus, but that he or she *knows* Jesus as a living presence. And secondly, the real Christian is one who lives *with* Jesus day by day, in a spiritual sense, just as the Twelve lived with Jesus day by day in a physical sense.

I love the moment in the movie *Fiddler on the Roof* where Tevye sings to his wife of many years. He sings the question: Do you love me? Her reply is to list all she has done for him—cooking meals, cleaning the house, washing clothes, raising children. Still, Tevye persists with his question: But do you love me? Tevye doesn't want just a faithful, dutiful, obedient wife. He wants a lover.

I think God wants us to be more than faithful, dutiful, obedient servants. He wants lovers. He wants us to love him and trust him supremely. That is the mark of the true Christian, just like it is the mark of a true apostle: one who knows Jesus intimately as a living presence, one who lives with that presence day in and day out, one who loves Jesus passionately.

Getting back to how Matthias was chosen, it should be recognized that making decisions "by lot" was a common practice within Judaism at that time.

That was how people were selected for jobs in the Temple. So this was not an inappropriate way for the disciples to make a decision about who should fill Judas' place.

Thirdly, Bible commentators who reject the choice of Matthias as the twelfth apostle fail to recognize the prayer that went before this choice. The disciples were praying together constantly and they prayed specifically about this choice. They allowed themselves to be guided by Scripture and by reason. Then they left the final decision in God's hands by casting lots.

Now, we are not instructed anywhere else in Scripture to continue using lots to determine God's will. But the rest of the disciples' pattern for discerning the divine will *is* valid for today:

- Study Scripture
- Use your reason.
- Pray.

It is amazing when we consider who was selected by this method to be one of the Twelve: Matthias. He must have been an "ordinary guy" because we never hear anything more about him. In fact all the first disciples were ordinary people. The raw materials God uses to build his kingdom are not usually the impressive metals of this world. Jesus called fishermen to be his spokesmen. If God could use them, then maybe there is hope for us.

The three who were closest to Jesus–Peter, James and John–were fishermen–common, hard-working, earthy people. Yet God enjoyed entrusting his good news to them. As someone once said, two thousand years ago God decided that human flesh was a good conductor for his Spirit, and he hasn't changed his mind since.

As we shall see further on in Acts, people were astonished that unschooled, ordinary human beings would be so bold as to risk their lives for what they believed. Yet this was recognized as a mark of their having been with Jesus (Acts 4:13). Later on we will read about the martyrdom of James who died by the sword of Herod Agrippa.

The Bible doesn't tell us what happened to the rest of the twelve apostles. But tradition tells us that Peter went to Rome and was crucified. Peter told his executioners that he did not deserve to die in the same manner as his Lord so they turned the cross upside down with Peter on it. John was exiled to Patmos. Thomas is said to have died by the spear. Bartholomew is said to have been flayed alive for his testimony. Tradition says that James the son of Alphaeus was clubbed to death. Simon the Zealot was martyred in Egypt.

Later we will read of one of the first deacons, Stephen, who was stoned to death because of his faith in Jesus. What motivated common people to go to the ends of the Roman Empire to proclaim the message of Christ? It was supernatural power which they received through prayer. God became a living presence in their lives. The love of Christ compelled them.

What about us? Have we discovered Jesus Christ as a living presence in our life? Do we know him, or just know about him? Do we live with him day by day? I believe Jesus asks us today, "Do you love me?" Will we answer him through a devoted life of prayer: "Yes I love you!"

THE HOLY SPIRIT

One New Year's Day, in the Rose Parade in Pasadena, California, a beautiful float suddenly sputtered and quit. It was out of gas. The whole parade was held up until someone could get a can of fuel. The amazing thing was that the float which ran out of gas was sponsored by the Standard Oil Company.

Unfortunately, the same thing often happens to us as Christians. We run out of juice by which to power our lives. Someone who is a pillar of the church suddenly quits, leaves, and is never heard from again. A pastor falls, by some indiscretion, and the movement he had sought to propel comes to a screeching halt. The choir director and the organist get into a fight, and the following Sunday the music in church no longer sounds so beautiful.

What's the problem? The difficulty is that all of us as Christians have a resource of unlimited power, but we fail to tap into it. We fail to fill our tanks. And so, suddenly, in the middle of the parade we sputter to a standstill, embarrassed.

In Acts 2:1-41 we read about the Christian's source of unlimited power....

> When the day of Pentecost came, they were all together in one place. Suddenly a sound like the blowing of a violent wind came from heaven and filled the whole house where they were sitting. They saw what seemed to be tongues of fire that separated and came to rest on each of them. All of them were filled with the Holy Spirit and began to speak in other tongues as the Spirit enabled them.
>
> Now there were staying in Jerusalem God-fearing Jews from every nation under heaven. When they heard this sound, a crowd came together in bewilderment, because each one heard them speaking in his own language. Utterly amazed, they asked: "Are not all these men who are speaking Galileans? Then how is it that each of us hears them in his own native language? Parthians, Medes and Elamites; residents of Mesopotamia, Judea and Cappadocia, Pontus and Asia, Phrygia and Pamphylia, Egypt and the parts of Libya near Cyrene; visitors from Rome (both Jews and converts to Judaism); Cretans and Arabs--we hear them declaring the wonders of God in our own tongues!" Amazed and perplexed, they asked one another, "What does this mean?"

Some, however, made fun of them and said, "They have had too much wine."

Then Peter stood up with the Eleven, raised his voice and addressed the crowd: "Fellow Jews and all of you who live in Jerusalem, let me explain this to you; listen carefully to what I say. These men are not drunk, as you suppose. It's only nine in the morning! No, this is what was spoken by the prophet Joel:

> " 'In the last days, God says,
>   I will pour out my Spirit on all people.
> Your sons and daughters will prophesy,
>   your young men will see visions,
>   your old men will dream dreams.
> Even on my servants, both men and women,
>   I will pour out my Spirit in those days,
>   and they will prophesy.
> I will show wonders in the heaven above
>   and signs on the earth below,
>   blood and fire and billows of smoke.
> The sun will be turned to darkness
>   and the moon to blood
>   before the coming of the great and glorious day of
>   the Lord.
> And everyone who calls on the name of the Lord will be
>   saved.'

"Men of Israel, listen to this: Jesus of Nazareth was a man accredited by God to you by miracles, wonders and signs, which God did among you through him, as you yourselves know. This man was handed over to you by God's set purpose and foreknowledge; and you, with the help of wicked men, put him to death by nailing him to the cross. But God raised him from the dead, freeing him from the agony of death, because it was impossible for death to keep its hold on him. David said about him:

> " 'I saw the Lord always before me.
>   Because he is at my right hand,
>   I will not be shaken.
> Therefore my heart is glad and my tongue rejoices;
>   my body also will live in hope,
>   because you will not abandon me to the grave,
>   nor will you let your Holy One see decay.
> You have made known to me the paths of life;

you will fill me with joy in your presence.'

"Brothers, I can tell you confidently that the patriarch David died and was buried, and his tomb is here to this day. But he was a prophet and knew that God had promised him on oath that he would place one of his descendants on his throne. Seeing what was ahead, he spoke of the resurrection of the Christ, that he was not abandoned to the grave, nor did his body see decay. God has raised this Jesus to life, and we are all witnesses of the fact. Exalted to the right hand of God, he has received from the Father the promised Holy Spirit and has poured out what you now see and hear. For David did not ascend to heaven, and yet he said,

" 'The Lord said to my Lord:

> "Sit at my right hand
> until I make your enemies
> a footstool for your feet." '

"Therefore let all Israel be assured of this: God has made this Jesus, whom you crucified, both Lord and Christ."

When the people heard this, they were cut to the heart and said to Peter and the other apostles, "Brothers, what shall we do?"

Peter replied, "Repent and be baptized, every one of you, in the name of Jesus Christ for the forgiveness of your sins. And you will receive the gift of the Holy Spirit. The promise is for you and your children and for all who are far off—for all whom the Lord our God will call."

With many other words he warned them; and he pleaded with them, "Save yourselves from this corrupt generation." Those who accepted his message were baptized, and about three thousand were added to their number that day.

I believe the greatest unused power in the history of the world may be the power of the Holy Spirit. But in Acts 2 we see what can happen when that power is tapped.

Pentecost, the feast of harvest for the Jews, became a day when a harvest of people were brought into the church. Can you imagine what that would be like? The church in Jerusalem multiplied in size by 26 times.

Why were so many people gathered into the church on one day? It was because on this particular Pentecost feast day the new covenant ministry of the Holy Spirit was inaugurated.

We should never imagine that the Holy Spirit didn't exist before Pentecost. We see evidence of the Spirit of God at work from creation, through Noah, Abraham, Moses, Joshua, in the Judges, in David and many of the good kings of Israel and Judah. We see the Holy Spirit at work in the life of Jesus and even in his disciples, prior to Pentecost.

So what was new about the work of the Holy Spirit on Pentecost? J. I. Packer once described it this way. He was on his way one winter evening to preach at a church. Suddenly, as he rounded a street corner the floodlights came on the church at the head of the street and the church architecture was illuminated in all of its glory.

What happened on Pentecost was something like that. Suddenly God the Father turned the floodlight of the Holy Spirit on the completed work of his Son Jesus Christ. That light was shining through the 120 believers who were part of the first church in Jerusalem. They came under the full influence and control of the Holy Spirit.

Is that same light of the Holy Spirit shining through us today? Have we tapped into his power? What will happen when we do?

When we are filled with the Holy Spirit I believe one thing that will happen is that we will be communicating the good news of Jesus Christ. Certainly there were other signs of the Holy Spirit evident on that first Pentecost after the resurrection and ascension of Jesus. There was something like the sound of the wind, there was what appeared to be tongues of fire that came and rested on each of the believers. These are traditional symbols of the Holy Spirit. But we never really hear of them again after that Pentecost. But this result of the believers being filled with the Holy Spirit we *do* read about again. "All of them were filled with the Holy Spirit and began to speak in other tongues as the Spirit enabled them." In other words, those 120 believers were enabled to speak in the languages of the many Jews who were gathered in Jerusalem for the feast of Pentecost.

Furthermore, Peter preached a riveting sermon with brilliance and boldness. It was a sermon that was personal and immediate. It answered the questions his audience was asking. It was a sermon with a clear purpose. It was filled with Scripture. And most importantly, Peter pointed people to Jesus and offered them hope–the hope of forgiveness, one of the greatest needs of the human heart.

The great news is that the Holy Spirit can enable us, today, to speak in words that non-Christians will understand. I'm not talking about suddenly having the gift of speaking French or Spanish or some other language without having taken a class. That might be helpful in certain missionary situations. However, what I'm talking about is the fact that sometimes Christians tend to speak in a language all their own. We use words like salvation, redemption, atonement, Lordship, and a host of other terms that non-Christians today just can't relate to. But when the Holy Spirit is filling us, he will be creating opportunities for us to share our faith with others, and he will give us the words to speak, words that others can understand. I'm not talking about preaching a sermon like Peter. Some are called to do that. Most Christians aren't.

I think the following story captures what all Christians are called to do. Christian singer, songwriter, and author John Fischer, tells the following story about riding in the middle seat, 11B, on a cross-country flight:

> As I boarded the already-crowded plane, I noticed 11C was standing by patiently at his seat. Obviously a frequent flyer, he knew he would eventually have to get up for two people, so he chose to stand and wait.
>
> We made eye contact and he moved away to let me pack my carry-ons in the overhead bin and enter my assigned cubicle. "Welcome to Sardine Airlines," he said. Well, at least he has a sense of humor, I thought. We stood next to each other, waiting for 11A to show up, and carried on typical small talk.
>
> Suddenly his eyes widened and I followed his studying gaze to a very attractive woman who was making her way up the aisle toward us. When she passed, he sighed, "How come they never end up next to me? Some guys get all the luck."
>
> "Well, thanks a lot!" I replied.
>
> Seconds later, however, she was back. "Excuse me. I think that's my seat," she said, nodding toward 11A, and 11C and I eagerly scrambled out to let her in. As we did, I stole a glance at him and found his eyebrows in a raised position. "Some guys get all the luck," he repeated in a whisper, indicating that stock in 11B had suddenly shot up in value.
>
> The woman next to me let us know right away that she was up for conversation.
>
> I say "us" because from the start I had 11C hanging over my right shoulder making sure I never had one private moment with the brunette in 11A.
>
> For the next three hours, I leaned my seat back, and 11A and C leaned into a lively exchange that had my head rotating like a lawn sprinkler. Three hours trapped in 11B between two bright and captivating people. I kept my seat belt fastened the whole flight.
>
> Those three hours went a long way toward changing my concept of what Christians commonly call "witnessing". Believe me, when you're strapped into a 600-mile-an hour conversation in 11B at 30,000 feet, all those neat books and seminars on "How to Share Your Faith" go flying out the airplane window. If I could re-write those seminars and books, I would try something like, "How to Be Normal", or "How to

Enjoy People", or "How to Be a Part of What's Happening Around You".

Half an hour into the flight and halfway into finding out what each of us did for a living, the flight attendant came by with beverages.

"I'd like a beer," said 11C, leaning for his wallet.

"White wine, please," said 11A, reaching for her purse.

"I'm buying," said 11B, pushing back both the wallet and the purse. I can't believe I'm doing this, I thought. Is this anything like the wine at the wedding, Jesus? Something tells me you won't find this part in the witnessing book.

We had already found out that 11A represented an interior design firm that specialized in decorating corporate offices. Now we discovered that 11C represented a furniture company that specialized in furnishing corporate offices, which immediately set off a mad exchange of business cards, brochures, and ideas. My neck felt as if someone had turned up the water pressure on the sprinkler.

"And what do you do?" they asked inevitably.

I knew it was coming, but there was no way I could have been prepared.

"Uh ... music. I write and perform my own music. I have a couple of books published as well."

No, I didn't tell them I wrote Christian music or Christian books. It was difficult, but I found ways around it. I wasn't ready to tell them I was a Christian. Not when they were just starting to like me, and not when I was finding out I could actually carry on normal conversations with normal people.

We followed my lead into discussing music, writing, and the arts, then on to a brief dip into politics, and finally the subject of religion came up. Halfway through the flight, my moment came. 11C set me up perfectly.

"Would you believe the uncanny luck I have?" he said. "It seems as if almost every flight I'm on, I end up sitting next to some minister who wants to talk to me about God!"

"Well, brace yourself," I said, "Cause it happened again!"

(Rule #1 in John Fischer's book on how to witness: Be a knowledgeable person. Have something to talk about. Don't just read Christian books and Christian magazines. It's a big world out there, and the Lord is the

Lord of it all. If Jesus is the way, the truth, and the life, you should be able to start anywhere and end up with Him. Paul did this in Athens. He started with an idol to an unknown god and ended up with the resurrected Christ.

Rule #2: Don't tell them you're a Christian too soon; they might just happen to like you. And then when you finally do tell them you're a Christian, they might decide to like you anyway, which means that because of you, they will have to reexamine their whole idea of Christianity in the first place.

In this case, they had to like me because we were all having too much fun.)

"No! You're a minister and you bought the drinks?"

"Ever hear of the first miracle of Jesus?" I asked.

"Wasn't that when He changed the water to wine at a wedding?" asked 11A.

"Yes. How'd you know that?"

"I used to be a Baptist." And we were off.

For the next hour and a half we talked about miracles, Christians, TV evangelists, Catholicism, Baptists, faith, family, relationships, living together, life, death, Jesus Christ, and 11A's boyfriend who was waiting for her in San Francisco–the one she couldn't decide about because she left one in Dallas, too. (We understood how this could happen.)

By the time we landed at San Francisco airport, there wasn't one thing that I wanted to say about the Gospel of Jesus Christ that I hadn't said. Yet none of it was forced, planned, rehearsed, or manipulated. And none of what I said was received as a sermon.

I'll never forget saying goodbye and walking away from baggage claim realizing that I had just been the best witness I could be by simply fastening my seat belt in 11B and going along for the ride. For in the energy, excitement, and sensuality that was flying around row 11, there was also a Holy Spirit very alive and well in the middle of it all.[1]

I believe the Holy Spirit can be alive and well in our lives too. He can empower us to love other people to Jesus. All we have to do is give him permission to use us.

Power can be used in at least two ways: it can be unleashed, or it can be harnessed.

---

1 Fisher, John, *True Believers Don't Ask Why*, Minneapolis: Bethany House, 1989, pp. 118-121.

The energy in a ten gallon can of gasoline can be released explosively by dropping a lighted match into the can. Or that same power can be channeled through a car engine in a controlled burn and used to transport people for many miles.

The Holy Spirit works both ways too. At Pentecost he exploded on the scene; his presence was like tongues of fire. Thousands were affected by one burst of God's power. But the Holy Spirit wants to also work through us, perhaps not so explosively, but over the long haul, day in and day out, as we point people by our life and by our words to Jesus.

DEVOTION

Dr. Richard C. Halverson, former Chaplain of the U. S. Senate, once made this statement about the church in an address to the General Assembly of the Presbyterian Church:

> In the beginning the church was a fellowship of men and women centering on the living Christ. Then the church moved to Greece, where it became a philosophy. Then it moved to Rome, where it became an institution. Next it moved to Europe where it became a culture, and, finally, it moved to America where it became an enterprise.

Perhaps we need to get back to the church as a fellowship centered on the living Christ. I think Acts 2:42-47 shows us how....

> They devoted themselves to the apostles' teaching and to the fellowship, to the breaking of bread and to prayer. Everyone was filled with awe, and many wonders and miraculous signs were done by the apostles. All the believers were together and had everything in common. Selling their possessions and goods, they gave to anyone as he had need. Every day they continued to meet together in the temple courts. They broke bread in their homes and ate together with glad and sincere hearts, praising God and enjoying the favor of all the people. And the Lord added to their number daily those who were being saved.

If there is one word that characterized the first church in Jerusalem, the word *devoted* would be a good candidate. As we move through this text together, I have six questions that I want us to ask ourselves which will help us determine how we are measuring up to the devotion of the early church. The first question is this: are we devoting ourselves to the apostles' teaching? That was the first mark of devotion in the church at Jerusalem. All the believers who were added to the church on Pentecost, plus the original 120, devoted themselves to the apostles' teaching.

A pastor was asked the perennial question: "What's the size of your congregation?" The pastor's answer was unique. He said, "Twenty-five miles wide and one inch deep."

That is a danger for many churches. It was certainly a potential danger for the first church in Jerusalem. The most important question in terms of church growth is not: "How many people do we have?" but rather: "Are we growing deeper in a spiritual relationship with Jesus Christ?"

The primary way we grow deeper in a relationship with Jesus Christ is by devoting ourselves to the apostles' teaching, by devoting ourselves to the hearing, reading, studying, memorizing, meditating and obeying of God's Word given to us especially in the New Testament.

How are we doing at devoting ourselves to the apostles' teaching on a personal basis? Do we spend time, daily, reading God's Word in the Bible for ourselves?

How about as families? Do we take any time as a family to read God's Word together? Do we read God's Word with our children? There are many resources available to help us with a personal or family time in studying and applying God's Word to our lives, but we have to take advantage of the resources available. We are far from perfect at doing this in my own family. However, when our children were young, we read the Bible to them and prayed together at bed time. In more recent years, we have shared devotional times around the dinner table.

How is your church doing when it comes to devoting itself to the apostles' teaching? If our devotion to God's Word stops in the sanctuary, then we are in trouble. James 1:22-25 says,

> Do not merely listen to the word, and so deceive yourselves. Do what it says. Anyone who listens to the word but does not do what it says is like a man who looks at his face in a mirror and, after looking at himself, goes away and immediately forgets what he looks like. But the man who looks intently into the perfect law that gives freedom, and continues to do this, not forgetting what he has heard, but doing it–he will be blessed in what he does.

A former park ranger at Yellowstone National Park tells the story of a ranger leading a group of hikers to a fire lookout. The ranger was so intent on telling the hikers about the flowers and animals that he considered the messages on his two-way radio distracting, so he switched it off. Nearing the tower, the ranger was met by a nearly breathless lookout, who asked why he hadn't responded to the messages on his radio. A grizzly bear had been seen stalking the group, and the authorities were trying to warn them of the danger.

Any time we tune out the message God has sent us through the Scriptures, we put at peril not only ourselves, but also those around us. How important it is that we never turn off God's saving communication, but rather that we take every opportunity to hear what he has to say to us.

The second question raised by Acts 2:42 is: are we devoting ourselves to the fellowship? Many churches are filled with people who care about one another and that is good. As Jack R. Van Ens has said, "People join churches more because they want warmth than light. We like to think it's our stunning proclamation of the truth that keeps them in the pews. Sermons may get them into the church the first time, but what keeps them coming are friendships that foster inward awareness and support."

I hope that in your church you never draw a circle that says, "Us four and no more!" The first church in Jerusalem didn't do that. Think of the tremendous job those first 120 believers had following Pentecost. They had to welcome 3000 new people into the church. Are we open to welcoming new people into our fellowship?

I also hope our fellowship as Christians is more than Sunday-deep. As Kent Hughes has said, "Fellowship is not just punch and cookies." Fellowship means sharing in common. One way I have seen Christians grow in fellowship is by inviting each other over for meals or dessert in their homes. We read in Acts 2:47 that the first Christians "broke bread in their homes and ate together with glad and sincere hearts." They showed hospitality to one another, and so their fellowship with one another grew deeper.

Small groups provide an organized way for the church to grow deeper in fellowship. There was no way that all the people at the first Church in Jerusalem could get to know each other just by worshiping together in the temple. There were too many of them. That's one reason why they met in homes, in addition to their worship time in the temple.

Are we giving to others as they have need? That's another part of fellowship. The story is told of two boys trying to ride the same tricycle at the same time. One boy said to the other: "You know, if one of us would get off I could have a lot more fun."

That's the way some of us go through life. We put ourselves first. If your wants and needs conflict with my wants and needs, it's my wants and needs that are going to be met first.

That was not the attitude of the first Christians in Jerusalem. "All the believers were together and had everything in common. Selling their possessions and goods, they gave to anyone as he had need." This was not an early form of communism. These first disciples maintained private property. But as there were needs in the church, people in the church would sell their property and bring it to the apostles to distribute to those in need. These early Christians had fantastic attitudes. We read in Acts 4:32, "All the believers were one in heart and mind. *No one claimed that any of his possessions was his own, but they shared everything they had.*" Growing churches live by the motto: "Find a need and fill it. Find a hurt and heal it."

Chuck Colson says that the second most dramatic event in his life (the first was his introduction to Jesus Christ) happened while he was serving time in prison after the Watergate scandal. During that period his family was having some serious problems. So the 18th ranking member of the House of Representatives, a former political opponent but a member of Colson's prayer group, came up with a way to solve the problem. The man asked permission from the President of the United States to serve out Colson's term in prison for him. At that point Colson knew he belonged to a new kind of society. That's fellowship.

Can we say, like the early church: "What I have is yours. Let me give you what I have to give, whatever you need"?

Let me ask another question: are we devoting ourselves to Holy Communion?

When Luke says that the first Christians in Jerusalem devoted themselves to the breaking of the bread, he was talking about Communion, the Lord's Supper, the Eucharist.

Why do we need to be devoting ourselves to Communion? Because the Lord commanded it. He said, "Do this in remembrance of me." (Luke 22:19) Because when we partake of the Lord's Supper, trusting in Christ alone to save us from our sin, the Lord's Supper spreads the life of Christ to us by the power of the Holy Spirit. Through the Eucharist, Christ feeds us supernaturally, the spiritual food of his body and blood in a way we can't fully put into words.

We need to devote ourselves to Communion because in it we are reminded of Christ's forgiveness for our sins bought by his body broken and his blood shed on the cross. In Communion we are offered a time for a regular spiritual check-up in which we have the opportunity to turn away from our sins in a fresh way and get right with God and others.

How are we to devote ourselves to Communion? We do that by preparing for it. Next time before you have Communion in your church, take some time to examine your life. Ask God to turn the search light of his Word upon your heart and show you any sin that is in your life. Then confess that sin to the Lord. Ask him to forgive you through Christ. Ask him for the grace to change your ways. Then come to the Lord's Supper ready to receive the tokens of the Lord's forgiveness.

But more than anything I think that understanding WHAT Communion is will really transform our experience of it. I love what J. B. Phillips once said about Holy Communion:

> . . . we have in it something which is alive in itself . . . it is unique in that the other end of it is, so to speak, *alive*, intimately joined to the very life of the Son of God Himself.

Phillips invites us to imagine what it would be like if we possessed some of Jesus' actual clothes, or a lock of his hair or a piece of furniture he made. If we had such, they would be relics of enormous historical value. But our attention would be drawn only to the *past*, not to Christ's living presence with us *today*. In Communion we have so much more than a dead relic,

> we have a living life-line, stretching unbroken to Christ himself . . .
> we are given an evergreen memorial which says in effect, '*This is what He touches now.*'

When we come to the Lord's Table we need to be prepared to be touched by the hand of Christ. And if we really realize it is his hand which touches us, we will naturally devote ourselves to Communion.

Another question we must ask is this: are we devoting ourselves to prayer? When Luke says that these early Christians devoted themselves to prayer, the word for prayer that he uses is in the plural. *They were continually devoting themselves to the prayers.* Luke is probably talking about the stated times for corporate prayer in the temple. In Acts 3 we see an example of the apostles going up to the temple at the time for corporate or group prayer, public prayer.

Jim Cymbala has written, "The Christian church was born not in a clever sermon but in a prayer meeting." In Acts 1:14 we read that the disciples "all joined together constantly in prayer."

This is an area where most churches need to grow. Many of us are committed to praying by ourselves and that is wonderful. Prayer in the regular worship services of the church is essential. But these times of prayer are not enough. I believe there need to be times where the church gathers just to pray, nothing else.

Prayer meetings often have the lowest attendance of any meetings in the church because prayer is hard work. It is hard work to concentrate and to pray for an hour, especially in our pragmatic society. It is hard for us to see the value of prayer because it is so spiritual in nature and we seldom see immediate material results from prayer. Perhaps that is why Jesus said to his disciples, "Watch and pray so that you will not fall into temptation. The spirit is willing, but the body is weak." (Mark 14:38)

In *Total Eclipse* Annie Dillard writes:

> The Ring Nebula, in the constellation Lyra, looks, through binoculars, like a smoke ring. It is a star in the process of exploding. Light from its explosion first reached the earth in 1054; it was a supernova then, and so bright it shone in the daytime. Now it is not so bright, but it is still exploding. It expands at the rate of seventy million miles a day. It is interesting to look through binoculars at something expanding seventy million miles a day. It does not budge. Its apparent size does not increase. Photographs of the Ring Nebula taken fifteen years ago

seem identical to photographs of it taken yesterday.

Huge happenings are not always visible to the naked eye—especially in the spiritual realm. How often it is that this nebula resembles the process of prayer. Sometimes we pray and pray and seemingly see no change in the situation. But that's only true from our perspective. If we could see from heaven's standpoint, we would know all that God is doing and intending to do in our lives. We would see God working in hearts in ways we cannot know. We would see God orchestrating circumstances that we know nothing about. We would see a galaxy of details being set in place for the moment when God brings the answer to fulfillment.

When we look at prayer that way—does it make us want to be more devoted?

What about worship? Are we devoting ourselves to worship? We can't just answer this question by the numbers, by answering how many people were in church last Sunday. We also have to ask: *are we filled with awe in our worship?* We read in Acts 2:43 that the first Christians were all filled with awe at what the Lord was doing in their lives.

Are we truly praising God with joy? Luke tells us that the first Christians ate together with *glad* and sincere hearts, praising God! But as Kent Hughes has said about contemporary Christians, some of us look like someone put Clorox in our coffee when we come to worship.

Bruce Larson has written about these first Christians that: "They were praising the Lord—not because they had no problems, and not because there was no persecution. Not at all. Gladness and joy are the gifts of God, and those early Christians, who had at least as many problems as we do, were known for their joy and their gladness. . . . I would not trust a dreary saint. Grimness is not a Christian virtue."

If we are running low on the joy of the Lord in our lives, maybe we need to ask him to give us a new injection of gladness that will overflow into worship. He is the source of joy; he is the joy-giver. I wonder sometimes why we do not simply ask him for more joy.

Finally, let me ask this question: are we devoting ourselves to outreach? We read about that first Church in Jerusalem that they were "enjoying the favor of all the people. And the Lord added to their number daily those who were being saved." (Acts 2:47)

The Lord is the One who can give us a good reputation with outsiders and he is the one who will add to our number. Only God can make someone a Christian and give him or her the desire to get involved in his Church. We can't do that. We can pray for people. We can share Jesus with them. We can invite them to a worship service. But we can't make them Christians and we can't grow the Church. Jesus said, "I will build my Church." (Matthew 16:18) It is God who adds people to the Church. Our job is to welcome those whom he adds. As Paul says in Romans 15:7, "Accept one another, then, just as Christ accepted you, in order to bring praise to God." There was a time when each of us were outsiders to a new congregation. Someone reached out to accept us, or else we wouldn't be part of the Church at all. Now it's our turn to reach out and accept someone else who is new. As Gary Harrison has said, "No matter how much the church wants to reach out, growth will not happen if the building and the people fail to say 'Welcome!'"

The best definition of evangelism I have ever heard is that evangelism is overflow! If we are devoting ourselves to the apostles' teaching, to the fellowship, to the breaking of bread and to prayer, then we will be so filled up with Jesus that he will naturally flow out of us every day.

It's like a glass of water. If I carry around with me a glass of water, filled up to the brim, then when I go through life and bump into other people, the water will naturally overflow. In the same way, if we are filled up with Jesus, through devotion to the Word, prayer, fellowship, worship, then Jesus will flow out of our lives to others, and Jesus will draw into his Church those whom we are touching with his love.

Devotion to the apostles' teaching, to fellowship, to Communion, to prayer, to worship, to outreach–all of these are essential to Christian and church growth. But the bottom line is this: none of us can be devoted to God in our own power. Unless Christ is at the center, living in us through the Holy Spirit, we will fail.

HEALING

What would you say to a beggar? There are millions of them on the streets of America today. You cannot go into any major city, anywhere in the world, without encountering one or more.

C. S. Lewis, upon encountering a beggar near his home in Oxford, England, gave the needy person some money. Lewis's friend immediately protested, "Jack, you know that man is just going to go and blow that money on drink!" To which C. S. Lewis responded, "Well, if I kept the money *I* would just blow it on drink!"

Tertullian, one of the early church fathers, once said: "It is our care for the helpless, our practice of loving kindness, that brands us in the eyes of many of our opponents. 'Look!' they say. 'How they love one another! Look how they are prepared to die for one another.'"

So what would you say to a beggar? I don't know what you would say. I don't even know what I would say in certain circumstances. But we do know what the first Christians said. Let us read their story in Acts 3....

> One day Peter and John were going up to the temple at the time of prayer—at three in the afternoon. Now a man crippled from birth was being carried to the temple gate called Beautiful, where he was put every day to beg from those going into the temple courts. When he saw Peter and John about to enter, he asked them for money. Peter looked straight at him, as did John. Then Peter said, "Look at us!" So the man gave them his attention, expecting to get something from them.
>
> Then Peter said, "Silver or gold I do not have, but what I have I give you. In the name of Jesus Christ of Nazareth, walk." Taking him by the right hand, he helped him up, and instantly the man's feet and ankles became strong. He jumped to his feet and began to walk. Then he went with them into the temple courts, walking and jumping, and praising God. When all the people saw him walking and praising God, they recognized him as the same man who used to sit begging at the temple gate called Beautiful, and they were filled with wonder and amazement at what had happened to him.
>
> While the beggar held on to Peter and John, all the people were

astonished and came running to them in the place called Solomon's Colonnade. When Peter saw this, he said to them: "Men of Israel, why does this surprise you? Why do you stare at us as if by our own power or godliness we had made this man walk? The God of Abraham, Isaac and Jacob, the God of our fathers, has glorified his servant Jesus. You handed him over to be killed, and you disowned him before Pilate, though he had decided to let him go. You disowned the Holy and Righteous One and asked that a murderer be released to you. You killed the author of life, but God raised him from the dead. We are witnesses of this. By faith in the name of Jesus, this man whom you see and know was made strong. It is Jesus' name and the faith that comes through him that has given this complete healing to him, as you can all see.

"Now, brothers, I know that you acted in ignorance, as did your leaders. But this is how God fulfilled what he had foretold through all the prophets, saying that his Christ would suffer. Repent, then, and turn to God, so that your sins may be wiped out, that times of refreshing may come from the Lord, and that he may send the Christ, who has been appointed for you—even Jesus. He must remain in heaven until the time comes for God to restore everything, as he promised long ago through his holy prophets. For Moses said, 'The Lord your God will raise up for you a prophet like me from among your own people; you must listen to everything he tells you. Anyone who does not listen to him will be completely cut off from among his people.'

"Indeed, all the prophets from Samuel on, as many as have spoken, have foretold these days. And you are heirs of the prophets and of the covenant God made with your fathers. He said to Abraham, 'Through your offspring all peoples on earth will be blessed.' When God raised up his servant, he sent him first to you to bless you by turning each of you from your wicked ways."

In this story we see healing flowing along two pathways. First of all we see that healing comes through the giving of the self.

Peter and John were on their way to the Temple to pray at three o'clock in the afternoon. We have seen already in Acts how important prayer is to the life of the Christian and the life of the Church. Peter and John were on their way to do a good thing. But they were suddenly interrupted.

Their plans were interrupted by a man with a birth defect–a man who was paralyzed and apparently unable to work. And so this man sat at the Temple every day to beg money from the religious people who were entering. Just as he did every day, this man asked Peter and John for money.

And what did Peter and John do? Did they look the other way? Did they brush him off? Did they give him money? None of the above. Peter got the man's attention and then said, "Look, we don't have any money to give you, but we have something better: in the name of Jesus Christ of Nazareth, walk!" Then Peter took the man by the hand, helped him up, and the beggar was immediately healed.

It would have been a lot easier for Peter and John to have done one of two things: either not get involved at all, or just give the man money. As we will see in the next chapter, what Peter and John did do, cost them a lot more.

What do you do when confronted with someone in need? Do you count it an interruption and try to get on with your own business as quickly as possible? What we count as interruptions are, from God's perspective, just the daily events of our lives as he sends them to us. The question is: what are we going to do with those interruptions? Are we going to give of ourselves? Or withhold ourselves? Healing flows through the giving of the self.

It is interesting to note the result of tests run by psychologists and psychiatrists trying to determine the type of counseling most helpful to people in need. When comparing the effect of different types of therapy, doctors always set up a control group with counselors made up of ordinary people. Invariably the control group consisting of non-professionals often gets the same results as professional therapy. Why? Bruce Larson gives the answer. "Power for healing is released when you and I simply focus on somebody else unhurriedly, taking him or her seriously and listening. The problem is that we are all so focused on our own concerns we don't take time do this."

Dr. Seymour Diamond did some research on family problems. He maintains, based upon that research, that today's average American father gives undivided attention to his children thirty-eight seconds a day. The average father gives partial attention to his children twenty minutes per day while he is doing something else: watching TV or working on a project. If we are to really love our children and heal the problems we have in our own families then we, as Christian parents, must give significant time every day, focusing on our children and listening to them. We have to give of ourselves.

Sometimes we hesitate to give of ourselves because we feel like we have nothing to give. This is where spending time alone with the Lord, every day, comes in. He is the One who can best fill our tanks so that we have something to give out to others.

Peter and John gave what they had. They didn't give what they didn't have. They didn't have money they could give to help others. Maybe you do. I don't think I have the gift of healing like Peter had. Some people have that gift. I don't have that gift to give away. But I can listen. I can pray for people. I can offer wisdom from God's Word. What do you have to give? George Sweeting has said: "When the church stops giving, it loses its power. When the church stops serving, it almost always starts swerving–into the wrong lane."

During World War II, a church in Strasbourg, France, was destroyed. Little remained but rubble. When the rubble was cleared, a statue of Christ was found still standing. It was unharmed except for the hands of Christ which were missing.

In time the church was rebuilt. A sculptor offered to carve a new statue of Christ, one with hands. The leaders of the church considered this. They decided to keep the old statue and they put a sign at the foot of it which read: "He has no hands but yours."

The real Jesus does have hands today. He reigns in heaven and can work from there with or without us. But he chooses to work with us, through our hands, by his Holy Spirit, to help other people, just as he worked through Peter and John. The healing of Jesus flows through us when we offer our hands in his service, as we give of ourselves for his cause.

The second pathway for healing which we see in this passage is through the preaching of Jesus. The healing of the man in Acts 3 drew a crowd in response. Everyone who went to the temple knew this beggar. They knew he had been paralyzed, but here he was walking around, even leaping and praising God. What had happened? The crowd wanted to know. And so Peter took the opportunity to explain to them that this miracle had been performed by the power of Jesus and not the power of Peter.

The preaching of Jesus in the apostolic church had certain very definite characteristics. First of all, it focused on the crucifixion of Jesus. Peter made it clear that the sins of his hearers put Jesus on the cross. That is no less true today than it was 2,000 years ago. Ours sins, yours and mine, put Jesus on the cross. But it was also God's purpose that his Son would suffer for our sins. As Paul later said, "Christ died for our sins according to the Scriptures." The wages of sin is death, but Jesus paid that death penalty for us.

Secondly, the apostolic preaching focused on the resurrection of Christ. God vindicated Jesus by raising him from the dead. Without the resurrection, the Church never would have come into being. But the resurrection was the proof of Christ's indestructible life.

This leads to the third point of apostolic preaching: *there is power in the name of Jesus and the faith that comes through him*. It was by the name of Jesus that this man was healed. It is in the name of Jesus that healing continues to happen today–whether that healing is physical, emotional, or primarily spiritual. So long as we think of what *we* can do and what *we* can be, in and of ourselves, there will be nothing but failure and frustration and fear in our lives. But when we think, "not I, but Christ in me" then there flows from us healing, peace and power.

The fourth essential ingredient of apostolic preaching was the *call to repentance.* Repentance is a change of mind which results in a change in direction. Apart from Christ we are turned 180 degrees away from God. We must do an about-face, by the power of the Holy Spirit, and turn to God and start walking his way. We must change our minds about sin and about Christ and start walking in his footsteps.

Once we do that, at least three results will follow. Repentance has consequences on the past the present and the future. First of all, when we repent *our sins are wiped out.* The word for "wiped out" is a vivid one. William Barclay tells us:

> Ancient writing was upon papyrus, and the ink used had no acid in it. It therefore did not bite into the papyrus as modern ink does; it simply lay upon the top of it. To erase the writing a man might take a wet sponge and simply wipe it away. So God wipes out the sin of the forgiven man.

Evangelist Luis Palau tells the story of being invited to meet with the secretary of the Communist Party in Ecuador. The woman arrived at Luis' office promptly at 9:30 the next morning. After checking Palau's office for hidden microphones she launched into the most vicious tirade Luis had ever heard. For more than twenty minutes she berated everything that stood for Christ, including Luis himself. Bitterness gushed from her and left Luis speechless.

When she finally stopped to catch her breath Luis asked, "Madam, what is your name?"

"Why do you want to know?" she demanded.

Luis replied, "Well, you've said a lot of things here and I don't even know you."

After some thought she announced that she was Maria Benitez-Perez. Then, for the next three hours, without pause or interruption, she told Luis her violent, pathetic life story. It sounded like the plot of a B movie, reeking with sin and guilt.

Finally, she paused and asked, "Palau, supposing there is a God, would he accept a woman like me?"

"Look Maria," Luis replied, "Don't worry about what I think; look at what God says." And he opened to Hebrews 10:17 and turned the Bible so she could see.

"But I don't believe in the B–"

"But we're just supposing there's a God, right?" Luis interjected.

"Let's just suppose the Bible is his word. He says, 'Their sins and lawless acts I will remember no more.'"

She waited, as if there had to be more. Luis said nothing.

"But listen, I've been an adulteress, married three times, and in bed with a lot of different men."

Luis repeated, "Their sins and lawless acts I will remember no more." And he began counting the number of times he repeated that verse.

Seventeen times he responded to Maria's objections and confessions with that verse. It was past lunch time. Luis was tired and weak. He had no more to offer. "Would you like Christ to forgive all that you've told me about and all the rest I don't even know?"

Maria was quiet. Finally she spoke softly. "If he could forgive me and change me, it would be the greatest miracle in the world."

Within ten minutes Luis witnessed that miracle as Maria Benitez-Perez confessed her sins, asked for forgiveness and received Christ. Today Maria is actively serving the Lord.

When we repent, God forgives all of our sin. Our sins are wiped out. He forgives our sin and remembers our wickedness no more!

A second result of repentance happens in the present. Repentance brings times of refreshing. Into our lives comes a power that will be a strength in weakness and a rest in weariness. As the hymn-writer, George W. Robinson put it:

> Heaven above is softer blue
> Earth around is sweeter green
> Something lives in every hue
> Christ-less eyes have never seen.
> Birds with gladder songs o'er-flow
> Flowers with deeper beauties shine
> Since I know as now I know
> I am His and He is mine.

A third result will flow from our repentance in the future. Peter says, "Repent, then, and turn to God, so that your sins may be wiped out, that times of refreshing may come from the Lord, and *that he may send the Christ, who has been appointed for you—even Jesus. He must remain in heaven until the time comes for God to restore everything, as he promised long ago through his holy prophets.*"

What is the connection between repentance and the Second Coming of Christ? C. S. Lewis explains it this way. He asks:

> Why is God landing in this enemy-occupied world in disguise and starting a sort of secret society to undermine the devil? Why is He not landing in force, invading it? Is it that He is not strong enough? Well, Christians think He is going to land in force; we do not know when. But we can guess why He is delaying. He wants to give us the chance of joining His side freely. I do not suppose you and I would have thought

much of a Frenchman who waited till the Allies were marching into Germany and then announced he was on our side. God will invade. But I wonder whether people who ask God to interfere openly and directly in our world quite realise what it will be like when He does. When that happens, it is the end of the world. When the author walks on to the stage the play is over. God is going to invade, all right: but what is the good of saying you are on His side then, when you see the whole natural universe melting away like a dream and something else–something it never entered your head to conceive–comes crashing in; something so beautiful to some of us and so terrible to others that none of us will have any choice left? For this time it will be God without disguise; something so overwhelming that it will strike either irresistible love or irresistible horror into every creature. It will be too late then to choose your side. There is no use saying you choose to lie down when it has become impossible to stand up. That will not be the time for choosing: it will be the time when we discover which side we really have chosen, whether we realised it before or not. Now, today, this moment, is our chance to choose the right side. God is holding back to give us that chance. It will not last for ever. We must take it or leave it.[2]

---

2   C. S. Lewis. *Mere Christianity*. New York: Macmillan, 1984, pp. 65-66.

SUFFERING

Evangelist Leighton Ford, who lost his son Sandy to a rare heart disease at the age of 21, once made this statement:

> I have become deeply convinced of the place of suffering and death in God's plan. When we plan our strategies for missions and evangelism—or any part of our life and work—we don't program an element of suffering. Nor should we, it would be morbid. There is no way we can plan for a young man's death, or his mother's grief-spawned eye spasms and lost weight, or his girlfriend's shattered dreams, or the loneliness of his mourning friends. Yet suffering is fertile ground for the Gospel. The seed must fall into the ground and die.³

There was much suffering in the life of the early church, there continues to be so among Christians today. As Leighton Ford says, we should not, nor can we plan an element of suffering into our lives. But suffering and persecution do attend the lives of all Christians. The question is: how are we going to respond when the suffering or persecution comes?

Acts 4 shows us how to respond, as we see the response of Peter and John to their first taste of persecution in the days of the early church....

> The priests and the captain of the temple guard and the Sadducees came up to Peter and John while they were speaking to the people. They were greatly disturbed because the apostles were teaching the people and proclaiming in Jesus the resurrection of the dead. They seized Peter and John, and because it was evening, they put them in jail until the next day. But many who heard the message believed, and the number of men grew to about five thousand.
>
> The next day the rulers, elders and teachers of the law met in Jerusalem. Annas the high priest was there, and so were Caiaphas, John, Alexander and the other men of the high priest's family. They had Peter and John brought before them and began to question them: "By what power or what name did you do this?"

---

3   Ford, Leighton, *Sandy: A Heart for God*, Downer's Grove, Illinois: Intervarsity Press, 1985, p. 168

Meditations on the Acts of the Apostles

Then Peter, filled with the Holy Spirit, said to them: "Rulers and elders of the people! If we are being called to account today for an act of kindness shown to a cripple and are asked how he was healed, then know this, you and all the people of Israel: It is by the name of Jesus Christ of Nazareth, whom you crucified but whom God raised from the dead, that this man stands before you healed. He is

> " 'the stone you builders rejected,
> which has become the capstone.'

Salvation is found in no one else, for there is no other name under heaven given to men by which we must be saved."

When they saw the courage of Peter and John and realized that they were unschooled, ordinary men, they were astonished and they took note that these men had been with Jesus. But since they could see the man who had been healed standing there with them, there was nothing they could say. So they ordered them to withdraw from the Sanhedrin and then conferred together. "What are we going to do with these men?" they asked. "Everybody living in Jerusalem knows they have done an outstanding miracle, and we cannot deny it. But to stop this thing from spreading any further among the people, we must warn these men to speak no longer to anyone in this name."

Then they called them in again and commanded them not to speak or teach at all in the name of Jesus. But Peter and John replied, "Judge for yourselves whether it is right in God's sight to obey you rather than God. For we cannot help speaking about what we have seen and heard."

After further threats they let them go. They could not decide how to punish them, because all the people were praising God for what had happened. For the man who was miraculously healed was over forty years old.

On their release, Peter and John went back to their own people and reported all that the chief priests and elders had said to them. When they heard this, they raised their voices together in prayer to God. "Sovereign Lord," they said, "you made the heaven and the earth and the sea, and everything in them. You spoke by the Holy Spirit through the mouth of your servant, our father David:

> " 'Why do the nations rage
> and the peoples plot in vain?
> The kings of the earth take their stand
> and the rulers gather together
> against the Lord and against his Anointed One.'

Indeed Herod and Pontius Pilate met together with the Gentiles and the people of Israel in this city to conspire against your holy servant Jesus, whom you anointed. They did what your power and will had decided beforehand should happen. Now, Lord, consider their threats and enable your servants to speak your word with great boldness. Stretch out your hand to heal and perform miraculous signs and wonders through the name of your holy servant Jesus."

After they prayed, the place where they were meeting was shaken. And they were all filled with the Holy Spirit and spoke the word of God boldly.

As Christians, how should we respond to persecution and suffering? We see here in the example of Peter that we need to be filled with the Holy Spirit. When Peter and John were arrested and brought before the Sanhedrin, the Jewish ruling council, and asked by what power or name they had healed the man at the beautiful gate, we are immediately told by Luke that Peter was filled with the Holy Spirit before he responded.

What does it mean to be filled with the Spirit? This seems to be a favorite phrase of Luke, who uses it about 9 times in his Gospel and in the book of Acts. He may have learned this terminology from Paul, who in Ephesians 5:18 says: "Do not get drunk on wine, which leads to debauchery. Instead, be filled with the Spirit." Being filled with the Spirit is thus contrasted with being filled with wine. When we are filled with alcohol we come under its influence. When we are filled with the Holy Spirit we come under the influence of God. So the real question is: are we driving under the influence of the Holy Spirit, or something else?

Of what we allow ourselves to come under the influence is a matter of life and death. In the aftermath of the tragic auto accident that killed Princess Diana in 1997 it was discovered that the chauffeur of the car had three times the legal limit of alcohol in his bloodstream. Furthermore, police estimated the car had been going as fast as 120 miles per hour when the crash occurred in the Paris tunnel. This one tragic incident reminded the world of something we all know: being filled with alcohol can lead to death, whether it is over the long haul or as the result of one night's bad choices.

By contrast, being filled with the Holy Spirit leads to life in all its fullness. Pastor and teacher Stephen Olford reports that his most memorable encounter with God happened shortly after World War II when he was serving as an Army Scripture Reader in Great Britain. Olford writes that at this point in his spiritual journey he became increasingly aware of a deep inner dissatisfaction. Olford witnessed the power of the Holy Spirit at work through the life of a little known pastor-evangelist in Wales. He yearned to see the same power at work in his own ministry. He read about D. L. Moody and F. B. Meyer's unique encounters with the Spirit and he wanted to experience the same. What Olford saw, read and felt led him to action. He cleared his schedule for a period of two weeks and retreated to a little cottage on the south coast of Wales. While there he studied key New Testament passages on the Holy Spirit. He discovered in Ephesians that "all the blessings of the Spirit are *already* given to us in Christ." From Ephesians 5:18 he learned that the Holy Spirit is "essentially a Person, and to be filled with Him is to come under His CONTROL." This led Olford to study 2 Corinthians 3:17 where Paul tells us that "the Lord is the Spirit and where the Spirit of the Lord is there is liberty". This verse can also be translated: "Where the Spirit *is Lord*, there is liberty." Upon reading that verse Olford realized he needed to surrender to the Lordship of the Holy Spirit in his life as well as the Lordship of Jesus. He later wrote:

> Without reading further, I dropped to my knees and yielded everything to the reign and rule of the *indwelling* Spirit. No glory filled the room, no vision filled my eyes, and no tongues were uttered; but I knew, there and then, that *I was set free!* The fetters and frustrations were gone. I hadn't to wait to preach to know that I was liberated! There were tears in my eyes, but peace in my soul!
>
> I turned to the Scripture again, only to confirm that the initial acceptance of the Spirit's control must be matched by *the continual dependence on the Spirit's control.* The verb indicates a continuous experience–"Be ye being filled with the Spirit." To maintain this fullness of the Spirit, there must be a daily repentance of sin–"Grieve not the Holy Spirit" (Eph. 4:30), and there must be a daily obedience to Scripture, for God gives the Holy Spirit "to them that obey him" (Acts 5:32), and the net result is that "where the Spirit is Lord, there is liberty."

Finally, Olford concluded: " . . . liberty in the Holy Spirit is not freedom to do what I want, but power to do what I ought." It is that power which enables you and me to handle times of suffering and persecution in the Christian life.

In Acts 4 Luke also shows us that being filled with the Spirit leads to being a courageous witness. Being filled with the Spirit, Peter boldly told the Sanhedrin that the paralyzed man at the Beautiful Gate had been healed in the name of Jesus. The Sadducees, who were the priestly rulers of the Temple, didn't like the fact that Peter was healing people in the name of Jesus and proclaiming the resurrection of Jesus, because they, quite simply, didn't believe in the resurrection of the body. They didn't want some upstart preacher going around teaching what they thought was false doctrine and drawing crowds away from them. But Peter was not deterred by their strong-arm tactics. He was as bold in preaching to the Sanhedrin as he was in the temple courts. We read that when the Sadducees "saw the courage of Peter and John and realized that they were unschooled, ordinary men, they were astonished and they took note that these men had been with Jesus." The same will be true for us, when we respond to suffering and even persecution with bold witness, people will take note that we have been with Jesus.

Such courageous witness in the face of persecution *cannot be explained*. The bold witness of these "uneducated and untrained men" shocked the religious establishment of first century Palestine. The same has been true all down through history. "Martin Luther was a despairing monk, William Carey a cobbler, D. L. Moody a shoe salesman. Yet Luther became a great church reformer, Carey a mighty missionary, and Moody an evangelist." (Sweeting) How do we explain such things? We can't in the natural. The only explanation is a supernatural one: people who spend time with Jesus have their lives transformed and in turn become transformers themselves.

Courageous witness in the face of persecution also *cannot be argued with*. The Sanhedrin debated how to respond to Peter and John. "'What are we going to do with these men?' they asked. 'Everybody living in Jerusalem knows they have done an outstanding miracle, and we cannot deny it.'" As George Sweeting has said, "A man with an argument is always at the mercy of a man with a genuine experience." Are we having trouble convincing non-Christians of the truth of Christianity? Then we need to tell them our story. People cannot argue with a changed life.

"Take, for example, the conversion of Charles Colson, former special counsel to President Nixon, convicted and sent to prison for his Watergate activities in the mid-1970's. The press handled his conversion story with suspicion. People were skeptical about whether his conversion was genuine or not. Many thought that his work with prisoners after being released from jail was a tactic to win sympathy. By the 1980's the critics changed their tune. Cynicism was gone. A major news magazine simply called him 'the founder of Prison Fellowship and a lay Christian minister.' His life speaks for itself. It cannot be argued with." (Sweeting)

We also see in Acts 4 that a courageous witness, empowered by the filling of the Holy Spirit, *cannot be intimidated*. The Sanhedrin commanded Peter and John not to speak anymore in the name of Jesus. Peter and John responded by saying, "Judge for yourselves whether it is right in God's sight to obey you rather than God. For we cannot help speaking about what we have seen and heard."

"Joe Butts went out as a pioneer missionary to the mountain village of El Carman, Colombia. He founded an elementary school and began a Bible study. Hostility in the village grew and he was forced to leave the area. Ten years later

Joe returned to El Carman, where there had been no missionary for over a decade. There he found several churches with fifty to one hundred members each, and many smaller congregations in the surrounding countryside. Though persecution existed, the holy life of the believers could not be constrained." (Sweeting)

How should we respond to suffering and persecution? Luke tells us we need to be filled with the Holy Spirit. We need to be courageous witnesses. And thirdly, we need to be prayerful.

The Sanhedrin couldn't decide what to do with Peter and John. So many people in Jerusalem were singing the disciples' praises because of this miraculous healing that the Sanhedrin was afraid to punish Peter and John. Perhaps they were afraid that if they did so they would have a riot on their hands. So after further threats they let them go.

When Peter and John returned to the other disciples, how did they all respond to this report of persecution? They prayed. And what did they pray for? They didn't pray for an end to their suffering. They prayed for more boldness! They prayed for more miracles to be done like this one that got them into trouble in the first place! Incredible!! One mark of being filled with the Spirit is that we can't stop praying. These first Christians were filled with the Spirit and couldn't stop praying. In turn they prayed to be filled even more with the Spirit – and they were! It was an endless life-giving cycle that had been started.

Did you know that the Christian missionary effort in Korea was begun a little over a hundred years ago by Presbyterians? At that time there were no Christians in Korea. Today there are millions. In fact, there are more Presbyterians in Korea than in all of the United States put together. I think I discovered why that is the case when I was in seminary. My first year at Princeton Seminary I roomed in Alexander Hall, the first building built in the United States for the training of Presbyterian ministers. My room was on the first floor. Every morning during term time the Korean seminary students would get up before the break of day and have a prayer meeting in the basement of Alexander Hall. How do I know? Because my room was right above them and I could hear them praying as I was trying to sleep! That's why the church in Korea has grown by leaps and bounds.

Here's another reminder of the power of prayer...."Warren Wiersbe says that one of the most moving experiences of his life came when he stepped from John Wesley's bedroom in his London home into the little adjacent prayer room. Outside the house was the traffic of the city road, but inside was the hush of God. Its only furnishings were a walnut table that held a Greek New Testament, a candlestick, a small stool, and a chair. When he was in London, Wesley entered that room early each morning to read God's Word and pray. The guide said to Dr. Wiersbe, 'This little room was the powerhouse of Methodism.'"

What is the powerhouse of our life? How do we respond to suffering and persecution for being Christians? Do we respond like the first Christians, by being prayerful, being filled with the Holy Spirit, being a courageous witness? Have we ever known any persecution or suffering on account of our Christian faith? Perhaps the main problem of the church in America today is that it is so much like the world that no one can tell the difference. Thus there is no persecution.

We cannot program any persecution into the life of the church, nor should we. But perhaps it is time for us to start living lives which, like the lives of the first Christians, demand an explanation.

COMMUNITY

Chad Reuter, a reserve catcher for the Chicago White Sox back in the mid 90's, severely dislocated and fractured his left shoulder on a play at home base. He underwent surgery, and the White Sox placed him on the 60-day disabled list. That's the kind of thing that makes a backup player feel even less like a part of the team.

But Chad did not feel left out. Apparently his teammates had a strong liking for him; each player put Chad's number 12 on his ball cap to show support. Chad was a member of the team whether he played or not.

As you can imagine, that meant a lot to Chad. Later in the season when he was able to play again, he showed his appreciation by putting the numbers of all his teammates on his own ball cap.

All for one and one for all. That is what makes a team, and that is also what makes the community of Christ known as the Church.

We read about the activities of that community in Acts 4:32-37....

> All the believers were one in heart and mind. No one claimed that any of his possessions was his own, but they shared everything they had. With great power the apostles continued to testify to the resurrection of the Lord Jesus, and much grace was upon them all. There were no needy persons among them. For from time to time those who owned lands or houses sold them, brought the money from the sales and put it at the apostles' feet, and it was distributed to anyone as he had need.
>
> Joseph, a Levite from Cyprus, whom the apostles called Barnabas (which means Son of Encouragement), sold a field he owned and brought the money and put it at the apostles' feet.

In these brief verses we learn about two essential activities of Christian community. One is sharing and the other is encouragement.

Richard Leakey, famous archeologist who worked in northern Kenya, commented in his book *People of the Lake* about what separates human beings from apes. He said it is not our intelligence, but our generosity. Our ability to share sets us apart.

We are created in God's image, a step above the animals. Being made in God's image we have a capacity for generosity because our God is a giving person.

Jesus Christ came to make us truly human; he came to give back to us the true humanity we have lost. We often slip back into being nothing more than apes. Human beings often act as though "survival of the fittest" was the only rule of life. But Jesus can make us whole people, generous people. In Christian community we are meant to share with each other and with the world.

Acts 4:32-37 expands our knowledge of what the early Christian community was like and builds upon the picture in Acts 2:42-47. The early Christians had a radical attitude which led to sacrificial action. Their radical attitude was that all of them were one in heart and mind. They didn't consider any of their possessions to be their own. In other words, they understood that everything they had was given to them by God—in trust, to be used for his glory. It is for that reason they shared everything they had with those who were in need.

I don't know if you have ever heard of The Stradivari Society, but "The Stradivari Society of Chicago performs an important role in the music world. The society entrusts expensive violins into the hands of world-class violin players who could never afford them on their own.

"Top-flight violins made by 17th and 18th century masters like Antonio Stradivari produce an incomparably beautiful sound and now sell for millions of dollars each. Their value continues to climb, making such violins highly attractive to investors. But 'great violins are not like great works of art,' writes music critic John von Rhein. 'They were never meant to be hung on a wall or locked up under glass. Any instrument will lose its tone if it isn't played regularly; conversely, an instrument gains in value the more it is used.'

"And so it is that those who own the world's greatest violins are looking for first-rate violin players to use them. The Stradivari Society brings them together, making sure that the instruments are preserved and cared for. One further requirement made by investors in such violins: the musician will give the patron at least two command performances a year.

"Like the Stradivari Society, God also entrusts exquisite 'violins' into the care of others. He gives us gifts, talents and resources which remain his property. He wants those resources to be used. He delights to hear beautiful music from our lives. And he wants us to play for him."

We need to have the same attitude toward the gifts, talents or resources God has entrusted to us which the early Christians had. We need to have the radical attitude the church in Jerusalem had and not regard these possessions as our own, but as something to be used for God's glory and the help of others. As George Sweeting has written, "We own nothing. It is on loan to us. It is loaned for a purpose: to serve others in Jesus' name."

The result of this sharing in the first church in Jerusalem was that people were more and more attracted to the message of the first Christians. It has been well and truly said, "Nobody cares how much you know until they know how much you care." Once others in Jerusalem saw how much the followers of Jesus cared for those in need they were much more interested in hearing what the Christians had to say. That is why the apostles were able to testify with great power to the resurrection of Jesus. Communication is a two-way street. You can speak with all the power in the world, but what difference does it make if no one is listening? The first Christians in Jerusalem had earned the right to be heard by caring for those in need.

My father learned this principle early on in his ministry in New York City. After reading an article in *Life* magazine about the teen gang problem in New York in the late 1950's my father felt called to reach these troubled youth with the Gospel of Jesus Christ. Having been a juvenile delinquent and former member of organized crime, my father felt that God might be able to use him to reach teen gang members.

So, Dad moved into a storefront in Spanish Harlem. He got names of key gang leaders from the police department. He set about trying to find the living quarters of these teens, but at each tenement he was told: "No one here by that name." The residents of Hell Gate Station, New York, figured my father was a cop because all white men in Spanish Harlem were police officers.

Finally, in desperation, my father approached the administration of the local junior high school and asked if he might put on an electronics show for the student body. After discussions with three key members of the administration he was granted the opportunity to lead a school assembly. On the appointed day my father single-handedly unloaded two tons of electronic equipment and set it up on the stage of the school auditorium. The students entered the assembly with "show-me" expressions on their faces, but within minutes they were entranced by my father sending bolts of electricity through fellow students' bodies to light up light bulbs. He used black-light to reveal the hidden glories of rocks. And he shook the auditorium with the sound of a steam-engine locomotive which ripped through the center of the crowd with startling reality, all due to a then little known device called stereophonic recording and amplification.

The next week my father had a crowd of students show up at his club to learn about electronics, where before he had been all alone. He even had to issue membership cards to limit the crowd in his small storefront operation. Over time, through building friendships and meeting needs in the Harlem community, he earned the right to share the good news about Jesus Christ.

The same principle which worked in Jerusalem in the first century and in Harlem in the 20th century still works today: we earn the right to share the Gospel by caring for those in need. "Nobody cares how much you know until they know how much you care."

A second result of the sharing of the first church in Jerusalem was that there were no needy persons among them. Can you imagine that? Many people have dreamed of ending poverty. The Greeks of the first century looked back to a golden age in their culture when all property was public and Pythagoras is said to have practiced the kind of sharing which later went on in the church of Jesus Christ. Plato later incorporated this ideal in his vision of a utopian republic.

The Jewish historian Josephus tells us that the Essenes of the Qumran Community sought to practice the same kind of sharing as the Pythagoreans. However, the Essenes' inspiration for this kind of common life came from the Hebrew Scriptures. Centuries before the Essenes even existed, it was stated in the law (Deuteronomy 15:4) "there should be no poor among you." But when had anyone ever fulfilled this utopian vision? Did the Essenes really fulfill it?

I believe it required the coming of God in human flesh to live out this ideal in his own person. The Gospel of the kingdom, which Jesus preached and lived, was good news for the poor. I believe that only as Jesus changes us from the inside-out can we really have the radical attitude about our possessions which leads to sacrificial action.

Even Karl Marx was borrowing a Christian principle when he said: "From each according to his abilities, to each according to his needs." That comes right out of the book of Acts.

Fredrich Engels, a collaborator with Marx, criticized religion because it supposedly did nothing to help the plight of the needy. He claimed that D. L. Moody and the Salvation Army in his own day were ineffective in dealing with social need.

It has been over a hundred years since the days of Marx and Engels. What has happened to the socialist and communist experiments? The socialist and communist experiments have proved that real sharing cannot be effectively legislated. There are still needy persons in the world today. I believe the only way that is going to change is not by people becoming more like Marx and Engels, but by our hearts being changed through a relationship with Jesus Christ. As William Barclay has said, "It is not when the law compels us to share, but when the heart moves us to share, that society becomes really Christian. The charity of legislation can never be a substitute for the charity of the heart."

John Wesley proclaimed that there is "no holiness but social holiness . . . to turn Christianity into a solitary religion is to destroy it."

Leonard Ravenhill once said, "The greatest miracle that God can do today is to take an unholy man out of an unholy world and make him holy . . . and then put him back into that unholy world, and keep him there."

If our hearts have been changed by Jesus Christ then we will make a difference in the world where we live. We will be living by the motto: "Find a need and fill it."

In his book *I Was Wrong* former PTL president and television personality Jim Bakker, who was sent to prison for fraud writes:

> Not long after my release from prison, I joined Franklin Graham and his family at his parents' old log mountain home for dinner. Ruth Graham (Billy's wife) had prepared a full-course dinner. We talked and laughed and enjoyed a casual meal together like family.
>
> During our conversation, Ruth asked me a question that required an address. I reached into my back pocket and pulled out an envelope. My wallet had been taken when I went to prison. I had not owned a wallet for over four-and-a-half years.
>
> As I fumbled through the envelope, Ruth asked tenderly, "Don't you have a wallet, Jim?"
>
> "This is my wallet," I replied.
>
> Ruth left the room, returning with one of Billy's wallets. "Here is a brand-new wallet Billy has never used. I want you to have it," she said.
>
> I still carry that wallet to this day. Over the years I have met thousands of wonderful Christian men and women, but never anyone more humble, gracious, and in a word, 'real' than Ruth Graham and her family.

Sharing with those in need does not have to be extravagant in order to give glory to God and mean a lot to the person on the receiving end.

The first essential activity we see in the first Christian community is sharing. But the second activity is just as important: encouragement.

We are introduced here to a key person in the early church. His name is Joseph. He is a Levite from the island of Cyprus. But the man also has connections in Jerusalem. As a Levite he would have served in the Temple. And we later learn that his nephew is John Mark, later to be the author of the Gospel which bears his name.

Joseph was so beloved by the apostles in Jerusalem that he was given a nickname–Barnabas. And we are told the meaning of the nickname–Son of Encouragement. Barnabas was one who encouraged people by what he did– like selling a field he owned and bringing the money to the apostles to be used for people in need. But Barnabas also encouraged people by who he was, what he said, and the way he was with people. Barnabas is the one who, later in the book of Acts, will introduce Saul/Paul to the apostles when all the other Christians are afraid to get near him. The Greek word for encouragement which is used to describe Barnabas, παρακλήσεως, literally means "one who comes alongside". Barnabas was one who came alongside of other people like Saul who would become Paul; Barnabas put his arm around people like that and encouraged them by his words and by his actions. The same word which is used of Barnabas is also used of the Holy Spirit, the Paraclete. For the Holy Spirit is the one who ultimately comes alongside, puts the arm of God around us, and encourages us with God's good news.

Coach Earl Toler was a Barnabas, a Paraclete, in my life. Toler was my seventh grade physical education teacher in public school in La Jolla, California. When I entered Toler's class he called me a "La Jolla fat boy". And I was! But that man inspired me to get into better physical shape. He gave extra points in class to students who would do some jogging outside of class time. So I started getting up early every morning to jog two miles. I earned an "A" in Toler's class, and I will never forget how Coach Toler helped me to beat an 8-minute mile–yes–8 minutes! I was the slowest runner in class; I was at the back of the pack with another "La Jolla fat boy"! Toler got me to run the mile in less than 8 minutes by his sheer encouragement. Every time I would run a lap I had to go past the coach and he would yell out some form of encouragement–"Come on Vaus you can do it! Pick up the pace!!" Then when I was coming in for the home stretch–"Get going Vaus–move those buns! You're doing great!! You can make it!!! Your best time yet!!!" And I clocked in at just under 8 minutes. It may not sound like much, but considering I started out the class running the mile in over 10 minutes time, it was quite an achievement for me.

Somehow I found out that Coach Toler was a Christian. At that time my father used to speak to the visiting professional baseball teams through a ministry called Pro Athletes' Outreach. So I invited Coach Toler to join us for Baseball Chapel one Sunday and he attended the baseball game with me afterwards. Toler was duly impressed by the opportunity to meet many of the players on the Los Angeles Dodgers' team. And I was impressed by the way Toler took time to explain to me more about baseball as we later sat watching the game together. Earl Toler was a great encouragement in my young life. He taught me by his example that Christianity could be muscular–that it isn't for wimps. And he set me an example of encouragement which I have tried to model in my own life.

I hope you have had a Barnabas, a Coach Toler, in your life. But even if you haven't, you can become a Barnabas, a Paraclete, for someone else by God's grace. Who is there in your life whom you could encourage this week. Maybe it would be the encouragement of a phone call, a hug, a prayer shared together, or "letter-lifter"–a note of encouragement. I keep almost every encouraging note that people write to me. I often re-read them years later and they continue to bring encouragement. You never know just what tremendous impact a "letter-lifter" may have in the life of someone else.

Maybe the way you can encourage someone this week isn't through a letter, or a word so much as through meeting a need. Maybe there is some money you can give to someone you know in financial deprivation. Giving to meet such a need can also be a Barnabas act.

Sharing and encouragement are two of the essential activities of Christian community. But we need Jesus Christ, living through us, to enable us to effectively carry out these activities. Jesus is the greatest encourager and sharer who ever lived; he can empower us to be Paracletes, ones who come alongside others to lift them up in a time of need.

HONESTY

The Civil War in England came to a bloody conclusion when King Charles I had his head chopped off and Oliver Cromwell became, for a brief time, the Lord Protector. Cromwell was well known, among other things, for a number of unsightly warts on his face. On one occasion a portrait painter, seeking to please his important client, painted Cromwell *without* the warts. To Cromwell's credit, when he saw the portrait he said, "Take it away and paint me warts and all."

It is to the credit of Luke that in the Book of Acts he paints a picture of the early church, "warts and all". The story which we are about to read in Acts 5:1-11 is one which demonstrates the almost stubborn honesty of the Bible. It is a story which some authors might well have thought to leave out, because it reveals that, as wonderful as the first church in Jerusalem was, it wasn't perfect.

It has been well said that if you are looking for a perfect church, and if you find it, you shouldn't join it because then it wouldn't be perfect anymore! The fact is: there is no perfect church on planet earth. There never has been and never will be, until Jesus returns. The story in Acts 5 confirms this truth and hints, in a backhanded sort of way, how we are to handle living as imperfect Christians in an imperfect church and an imperfect world….

> Now a man named Ananias, together with his wife Sapphira, also sold a piece of property. With his wife's full knowledge he kept back part of the money for himself, but brought the rest and put it at the apostles' feet.
>
> Then Peter said, "Ananias, how is it that Satan has so filled your heart that you have lied to the Holy Spirit and have kept for yourself some of the money you received for the land? Didn't it belong to you before it was sold? And after it was sold, wasn't the money at your disposal? What made you think of doing such a thing? You have not lied to men but to God."
>
> When Ananias heard this, he fell down and died. And great fear seized all who heard what had happened. Then the young men came forward, wrapped up his body, and carried him out and buried him.
>
> About three hours later his wife came in, not knowing what had

happened. Peter asked her, "Tell me, is this the price you and Ananias got for the land?"

"Yes," she said, "that is the price."

Peter said to her, "How could you agree to test the Spirit of the Lord? Look! The feet of the men who buried your husband are at the door, and they will carry you out also."

At that moment she fell down at his feet and died. Then the young men came in and, finding her dead, carried her out and buried her beside her husband. Great fear seized the whole church and all who heard about these events.

What was the sin of Ananias and Sapphira? Quite simply, their sin was one of dishonesty. Last week we read of Barnabas who sold a piece of property and brought the proceeds to the apostles to be used to help the needy. Now we read that Ananias and Sapphira sold a piece of property, kept back part of the proceeds for themselves, and laid the rest at the feet of the apostles.

Somehow Peter found out what Ananias and Sapphira were up to. Either he found out supernaturally, in other words–God revealed it to Peter, or he found out, somehow, by natural means. We are not told how Peter knew what was going on. But he knew. He did not accuse Ananias and Sapphira of lack of generosity. He did not accuse them of not fulfilling an obligation. No. He told Ananias: "Look, you have lied to the Lord. You had every right to keep your property to yourself. You were under no obligation to give all of the money to the church. Your sin is that you have given part, while trying to make out that you have given all. You have been dishonest Ananias."

Money has a strange effect on people. Former heavyweight boxing champion Joe Louis once said, "I don't like money, actually, but it quiets my nerves." Perhaps we can all relate to that.

In and of itself, money is neutral; it is neither good nor evil. The Bible is often misquoted as saying that money is the root of all evil. But the Bible doesn't say that. 1 Timothy 6:10 says, "For the *love* of money is *a* root of all kinds of evil." Money isn't evil in and of itself. But because of a kink in our own souls we have a way of trusting money, rather than God, to quiet our nerves.

Ananias and Sapphira wanted to have it both ways. They wanted to have their money and it seems they wanted to have the praise of people for giving their money away.

A Sunday School teacher was telling her children the story from Luke 16 about the rich man and Lazarus. She explained how poor Lazarus had very little in life but he was rich in faith. So when he died he was taken to the bosom of Abraham. The rich man had everything in this life but faith. In the end the rich man died and he was separated from God.

When she finished the story, the Sunday School teacher asked her students, "Now which person would you like to be?" One very honest child spoke up and said, "I would like to be the rich man while he lived and Lazarus when he died."

In our heart of hearts that is probably what all of us would like. But Jesus tells us life doesn't work that way. "No servant can serve two masters. Either he will hate the one and love the other, or he will be devoted to the one and despise the other. You cannot serve both God and Money." (Luke 16:13)

Ananias and Sapphira tried to cut life against the grain. They tried to serve both God and money, but it ended up killing him. Ananias and Sapphira were killed by their own dishonesty. They claimed to be serving God completely, but they were in actuality hedging their bet.

This leads to another interesting question: Who killed Ananias and Sapphira? Did God kill Ananias and Sapphira? I think the answer is both yes and no.

Suppose you try to prove the existence of God to a friend by jumping off the roof of a twenty story building saying: "God will catch me." You will certainly plummet to your death. But did God kill you? Yes and no. God created the world to function according to the law of gravity. And the law of gravity took over when you stepped off that building. So in a sense, God's law killed you. But did God kill you, directly, for your presumption? No.

I think Bruce Larson has rightly pointed out that Ananias and Sapphira were killed by three things: stress, loneliness and judgment. Let me explain.

One of the greatest killers today is *stress*. Doctors agree that stress is one factor in a number of diseases. Psychologist Archibald Hart, the author of *Adrenalin and Stress*, has written:

> Good stress (also called 'eustress,' from the Latin *eu*, meaning good) is positive and helpful only because it is *not experienced continuously*. It excites, but then it lets the system go back to normal quickly. If a moment never comes when all the demand for stress is passed - if the body *never* returns to a state of rest and recovery - the result will be bad stress (or 'distress,' from the Latin *dis*, meaning bad), no matter what originally produced the arousal. . . . TOO MUCH *stress* - especially stress that is not relieved by times of rest and renewal - can harm us physically, mentally and spiritually.

We put ourselves under a great deal of stress when we try to act like something we aren't. The Greeks had a word for this: hypocrisy. The word literally means: to wear a mask. Actors in Greek theater were called hypocrites because they wore masks. To be a hypocrite is to play a part, to act like something you really aren't, to pretend.

That's what Ananias and Sapphira were doing: pretending. And the stress of their pretense contributed, I think, to their deaths.

A second contributing factor to Ananias' and Sapphira's deaths was *loneliness*. Loneliness is not the same as being alone. One can be alone and find great peace in spending time with God, reading, doing any number of things. Loneliness happens when we feel cut off from others. It is what you feel when abandoned by a spouse, or when you are betrayed by a friend or business partner.

For Ananias and Sapphira the church had to be a very important source of relationship. Yet they were wearing masks in the presence of those with whom they ought to have been most intimate and honest. The fear of being found out, and then suddenly being discovered, by people who really mattered to them, may have been enough to kill Ananias and Sapphira.

The story is told of one occasion when Edward the Confessor, King of England, blazed in anger against one of his courtiers and the man died on the spot. This man loved the king but had failed him. The king's approval was so important to this courtier that the man dropped dead when he received the king's anger instead.

A third contributing factor to Ananias' and Sapphira's deaths was Peter's *judgment* of them. Peter lowered the boom on this dishonest couple and he didn't mince words. Combine stress, a sense of being cut off, and judgment being declared by the leader of the church—no wonder Ananias and Sapphira died.

Some Bible commentators have noted that they think Peter's attitude was all wrong. The more I have grown as a Christian I think they are right. Peter's attitude toward these sinners was so unlike Jesus' attitude. How did Jesus respond to the woman caught in the act of adultery? He said to the religious leaders who wanted to judge her: "If any one of you is without sin, let him be the first to throw a stone at her." And then Jesus said to the woman, "Neither do I condemn you. Go now and leave your life of sin."

I think Peter got it wrong. But we shouldn't be surprised at that. Luke is showing us the church, warts and all. One possible title for the book of Acts might be: The Mistakes of Peter and Paul. I don't think we are meant to use this story in Acts 5 as a model for the way to treat dishonest people in the church. If all dishonest people were judged and condemned like Ananias and Sapphira, our church buildings would probably be empty on Sunday mornings.

That leads me to the question: How do we get out of spiritual stress, loneliness and judgment? If Peter's way of handling dishonesty in the church was the wrong way, what is the right way to handle sin? I think the right way is through confession.

In a sense, Peter may have given Ananias and Sapphira a chance to confess and repent, but he didn't give them much of one. We need to leave room, we need to give ample opportunity to our brothers and sisters in Christ to confess sin and turn. Jesus is the model, not Peter. We all need to have the same attitude toward sin that Jesus had. We need to offer the same message to our brothers and sisters in Christ: "Neither do I condemn you. Go now and leave your life of sin."

Pulitzer Prize winning author Alice Walker tells of the following experience she had as a little girl:

> When I was a little girl, I accidentally broke a fruit jar. Several brothers and a sister were nearby who could have done it. But my father turned to me and asked, "Did you break the jar, Alice?"
>
> Looking into his large, brown eyes, I knew he wanted me to tell the truth. I also knew he might punish me if I did. But the truth inside of me wanted badly to be expressed. "I broke the jar," I said.
>
> The love in his eyes rewarded and embraced me. Suddenly I felt an inner peace that I still recall with gratitude to this day.

Confession, agreeing with our heavenly Father about our sin, is the way to handle the Ananias and Sapphira syndrome.

The key is honesty. We have to be willing to come clean. We have to replace hypocrisy with truth-telling. And we need to create an environment in the church conducive to people taking off their masks. We have to let people know, by our words and actions, that if they confess sin in the context of church fellowship they are not going to be condemned but rather nurtured towards a life of greater health, greater truth, greater love.

A number of years ago I was confronted about an area in my life where I needed to change. However, my brothers and sisters in Christ didn't know the whole story. I had a choice. I could make a halfway confession, or I could come clean about all that was going on in my heart and life.

It was just at that juncture that I read something in Rick Warren's book, *The Purpose Driven Life*, that was indeed life-changing. Warren writes:

> I must choose to be honest with God. The first building block of a deeper friendship with God is complete honesty—about your faults and feelings. God doesn't expect you to be perfect, but he does insist on complete honesty. None of God's friends in the Bible were perfect. If perfection was a requirement for friendship with God, we would never be able to be his friends. Fortunately, because of God's grace, Jesus is still the "friend of sinners." . . . God listens to the passionate words of his friends; he is bored with predictable, pious clichés. . . . Every time you trust God's wisdom and do whatever he says, even

when you don't understand it, you deepen your friendship with God. . . . We are often challenged to do "great things" for God. Actually, God is more pleased when we do small things for him out of loving obedience. . . . Great opportunities may come once in a lifetime, but small opportunities surround us every day. Even through such simple acts as telling the truth . . . we bring a smile to God's face. . . You are as close to God as you choose to be. Intimate friendship with God is a choice, not an accident. You must intentionally seek it. Do you really want it–more than anything? What is it worth to you? Is it worth giving up other things? . . . You may have been passionate about God in the past but you've lost that desire. That was the problem of the Christians in Ephesus–they had left their first love. . . . Your problems are not punishment; they are wake-up calls from a loving God. God is not mad at you; he's mad about you, and he will do whatever it takes to bring you back into fellowship with him. But there is an easier way to reignite your passion for God: Start asking God to give it to you, and keep on asking until you have it. Pray this throughout your day: "Dear Jesus, more than anything else, I want to get to know you intimately." . . . There is nothing–absolutely nothing–more important than developing a friendship with God.

When I read those words I knew I needed to come clean with God and others. I knew I needed to be totally honest. That stark honesty cost me a lot at the time. But the dividends it has paid ever since have been worth it.

Where are you at in your relationship with God? Are you trying to be like Ananias and Sapphira? Are you trying to straddle the fence and serve two masters? If so, it is time to get right with God, to be honest with him and take off your mask. Don't put off the decision any longer–the stress, the loneliness, the judgment you will feel for playing the hypocrite can kill you. And God doesn't want that. He wants to give you life in all its fullness.

PERSEVERANCE

Winston Churchill spoke the following words on 29 October 1941 to the boys at Harrow School, the institution where Churchill felt he had failed miserably as a child:

> Never give in–never, never, never, never, in nothing great or small, large or petty, never give in except to convictions of honour and good sense. Never yield to force; never yield to the apparently overwhelming might of the enemy.

That's perseverance and it is the next key to growth we learn about in Acts 5:12-42....

> The apostles performed many miraculous signs and wonders among the people. And all the believers used to meet together in Solomon's Colonnade. No one else dared join them, even though they were highly regarded by the people. Nevertheless, more and more men and women believed in the Lord and were added to their number. As a result, people brought the sick into the streets and laid them on beds and mats so that at least Peter's shadow might fall on some of them as he passed by. Crowds gathered also from the towns around Jerusalem, bringing their sick and those tormented by evil spirits, and all of them were healed.
>
> Then the high priest and all his associates, who were members of the party of the Sadducees, were filled with jealousy. They arrested the apostles and put them in the public jail. But during the night an angel of the Lord opened the doors of the jail and brought them out. "Go, stand in the temple courts," he said, "and tell the people the full message of this new life."
>
> At daybreak they entered the temple courts, as they had been told, and began to teach the people.
>
> When the high priest and his associates arrived, they called together the Sanhedrin—the full assembly of the elders of Israel—and sent to the jail for the apostles. But on arriving at the jail, the officers did not find them there. So they went back and reported, "We found the jail securely locked, with the guards standing at the doors; but when

we opened them, we found no one inside." On hearing this report, the captain of the temple guard and the chief priests were puzzled, wondering what would come of this.

Then someone came and said, "Look! The men you put in jail are standing in the temple courts teaching the people." At that, the captain went with his officers and brought the apostles. They did not use force, because they feared that the people would stone them.

Having brought the apostles, they made them appear before the Sanhedrin to be questioned by the high priest. "We gave you strict orders not to teach in this name," he said. "Yet you have filled Jerusalem with your teaching and are determined to make us guilty of this man's blood."

Peter and the other apostles replied: "We must obey God rather than men! The God of our fathers raised Jesus from the dead—whom you had killed by hanging him on a tree. God exalted him to his own right hand as Prince and Savior that he might give repentance and forgiveness of sins to Israel. We are witnesses of these things, and so is the Holy Spirit, whom God has given to those who obey him."

When they heard this, they were furious and wanted to put them to death. But a Pharisee named Gamaliel, a teacher of the law, who was honored by all the people, stood up in the Sanhedrin and ordered that the men be put outside for a little while. Then he addressed them: "Men of Israel, consider carefully what you intend to do to these men. Some time ago Theudas appeared, claiming to be somebody, and about four hundred men rallied to him. He was killed, all his followers were dispersed, and it all came to nothing. After him, Judas the Galilean appeared in the days of the census and led a band of people in revolt. He too was killed, and all his followers were scattered. Therefore, in the present case I advise you: Leave these men alone! Let them go! For if their purpose or activity is of human origin, it will fail. But if it is from God, you will not be able to stop these men; you will only find yourselves fighting against God."

His speech persuaded them. They called the apostles in and had them flogged. Then they ordered them not to speak in the name of Jesus, and let them go.

The apostles left the Sanhedrin, rejoicing because they had been counted worthy of suffering disgrace for the Name. Day after day, in the temple courts and from house to house, they never stopped teaching and proclaiming the good news that Jesus is the Christ.

I believe one of the major keys to growth in the early church is the fact that the disciples never gave up. They did not give in to despair because of the sin of Ananias and Sapphira in their midst. They did not give up when persecuted from without, by the Sanhedrin.

I think we need to take notice of at least three things about the church and their meetings from this passage. First of all, note where the church met. "And all the believers used to meet together in Solomon's Colonnade." In other words, the first Christians met openly in the temple courts despite the fact that they were warned not to teach any longer in the name of Jesus.

Why did they continue to meet openly? Obviously because they felt compelled by their Lord to do so. Also because they felt compelled by the needs of unbelievers. The Temple was the place where they were most likely to meet the most people who might be receptive to the Gospel. They could not contain the Good News about Jesus Christ. It simply had to be spoken.

One of the joys of my life was the opportunity to start three C. S. Lewis book discussion groups in three different states at different times in my life. When I started my first group in Columbia, South Carolina a woman called my church to tell me that she thought it was a bad idea for a Christian to hold a meeting in a secular bookstore where they sell Gay & Lesbian and New Age books. My response to that woman was to say that I thought that was exactly where Christians should be hanging out. We've got to go where "the fish are biting". The Lord has called us all to be fishers of men, not aquarium keepers. Or, to use another metaphor, we are called to be the salt of the world, and if we are going to be the salt of the world then we've got to get out of the salt-shaker.

So let me ask you: do you frequent places where non-Christians hang out? Do you try to take advantage of the opportunities the Lord might be giving you to share Christ with others?

The second thing I think we need to note about this passage is *how* the church met. They met *in the power of the Holy Spirit*. "The apostles performed many miraculous signs and wonders among the people. . . . As a result, people brought the sick into the streets and laid them on beds and mats so that at least Peter's shadow might fall on some of them as he passed by. Crowds gathered also from the towns around Jerusalem, bringing their sick and those tormented by evil spirits, and all of them were healed." Perhaps if we recovered more of the power of the Holy Spirit in our own day then more people would be attracted to the church.

C. S. Lewis and Joy Davidman, the woman who became Lewis's wife, had such an unusual relationship that a movie was made about them called *Shadowlands*. Davidman was a secular American Jewish woman who was led to faith in Christ partly through reading Lewis's books. She wrote to Lewis in England thanking him for his books and a pen friendship began. Then in

1952, as her marriage to Bill Gresham was falling apart, Joy decided to travel to England for a break and to meet her spiritual mentor, Lewis. Joy subsequently divorced her husband, who was a compulsive adulterer, and moved with her two boys to England. Joy and Lewis met frequently and their friendship deepened. Then in 1956 the British Home Office refused to renew Joy's visa; they were ready to deport her back to America. At that point C. S. Lewis agreed to marry Joy in a civil ceremony, extending to her and her boys his British citizenship. The two were married in law but continued to live apart as friends. Later that same year, Joy was diagnosed with cancer and it was at that point, as the sword of Damocles hung over Joy's head, that Jack Lewis realized he was in love with Joy Davidman. Joy was only expected to live for a matter of days or weeks; her body was riddled with cancer. But Jack wanted to marry her in an ecclesiastical ceremony nonetheless. The problem was that the Anglican Church at that time did not approve of the remarriage of divorcees under any circumstances. The Bishop of Oxford could not approve of the marriage, though he was sympathetic. So C. S. Lewis called on a former student of his, Peter Bide, and asked if he would perform the marriage ceremony. Bide agreed, and the two were married at Joy's hospital bedside. Now it was known that Peter Bide had, in the past, prayed for various people and witnessed some miraculous healing. So Lewis asked Bide if he would lay hands on his wife. Bide did. And Joy Lewis, whose body was shot through with cancer, who wasn't expected to live but a couple of days, recovered. The cancer went into remission and she lived another three years. Jack and Joy went on honeymoon together to Ireland and, in the last months of Joy's life, took a dream trip to Greece together.

Years later, when Bide was asked about his healing gift, he said, "the Lord Jesus Christ sometimes chooses to heal people when I pray for them." What a wonderful, humble way to put it! Perhaps if we prayed more for people, expecting the Lord to heal and perform miracles, we would see more of the power of the Holy Spirit in the church today.

The third thing I think we should notice from this passage in Acts 5 is the *result* of the church meeting. The results were three-fold.

First of all, some were afraid to join these first Christians and make a profession of faith. "No one else dared join them, even though they were highly regarded by the people." Perhaps the reason why some were afraid to join was because they had witnessed what had happened to pretenders like Ananias and Sapphira. Perhaps they were afraid to join because they realized that Jesus asked for a total commitment. As Dietrich Bonhoeffer once wrote in his book, *The Cost of Discipleship*, "When Christ calls a man he bids him come and die." Or as C. S. Lewis wrote in *Mere Christianity*:

Christ says 'Give me All. I don't want so much of your time and so much of your money and so much of your work: I want You. I have not come to torment your natural self, but to kill it. No half-measures are any good. I don't want to cut off a branch here and a branch there, I want to have the whole tree down. I don't want to drill the tooth, or crown it, or stop it, but to have it out. Hand over the whole natural self, all the desires which you think innocent as well as the ones you think wicked—the whole outfit. I will give you a new self instead. In fact, I will give you Myself: my own will shall become yours.'[4]

A second result of the church meeting in Solomon's Colonnade was that *many did join the church*. "Nevertheless, more and more men and women believed in the Lord and were added to their number."

There was a famous arctic explorer who once ran an advertisement in a major newspaper asking for people to join in his endeavor. The ad ran something like this:

Wanted: men and women for dangerous arctic exploration. Little pay, long hours and many months separated from family. Extremely uncomfortable conditions to be expected. Possibility of no return. Reward if successful: worldwide renown.

The explorer received hundreds of responses to his advertisement. That just goes to show that people are looking for something that will make their lives significant.

Jesus issues a similar invitation:

Wanted: Men, women, boys and girls for a difficult lifelong mission in building the kingdom of God. Total devotion required around the clock. Leaving family behind will sometimes be necessary. Persecution to be expected. Participants may have to sacrifice their very lives in the end. Little or no remuneration. Reward in case of success: eternal glory.

Jesus continues to attract people to his mission to this very day, despite the difficulties attached to it, because following Jesus gives significance to human life as nothing else does. As someone once said, "Jesus promises four things: Peace, Power, Purpose and Trouble." And it is because Jesus promises the first three that people are willing to brave the fourth.

A third result of the church meeting was that *some people, outside the church, became jealous and persecuted the church*. "Then the high priest and all his associates, who were members of the party of the Sadducees, were filled with jealousy. They arrested the apostles and put them in the public jail."

Of course, when you have God on your side, that kind of persecution is not necessarily an obstacle. During the night an angel opened the prison doors

---

4   *Mere Christianity*, p. 167.

and let the apostles out, commanding them to continue telling the message of this new life in the temple courts.

The apostles obeyed the angelic command and were arrested once again for their labors. When asked why they were still teaching in the name of Jesus when they had been commanded not to, the apostles replied: "We must obey God rather then men!"

When the Sanhedrin heard this, many of its members were furious and wanted to put the apostles to death. But Gamaliel counseled caution. "If this work is of men it will eventually die out. But if it really is of God then we don't want to be opposing Him."

So the Sanhedrin called the apostles back in. They had them flogged and ordered them once again not to speak in the name of Jesus.

What was the response of the apostles to this first taste of physical suffering for the cause of Christ? They rejoiced because God had counted them worthy to suffer disgrace for the name of Jesus. And they continued to teach and proclaim the good news that Jesus is the Christ wherever they went.

Senator John McCain served as a Navy pilot during the Vietnam War. He was shot down by a North Vietnamese missile on October 26, 1967. For nine days McCain received no treatment for the injuries he sustained when he parachuted into a North Vietnamese mob: two broken arms, a shattered knee, a shattered shoulder and bayonet wounds in his ankle and groin. He survived in captivity for the next five and a half years under constant and extreme torture.

The truly amazing part of McCain's story is that he suffered all of this voluntarily. McCain belongs to a distinguished military family; his father and grandfather were both admirals, and his father was commanding the bombing of Hanoi at the time McCain's Navy fighter was shot down. The North Vietnamese planned for their famous POW to violate US military policy, which dictated that prisoners return in the order they had arrived. McCain's early release might have demoralized American troops. So McCain refused to go along with the plan. For five and a half years the North Vietnamese tortured McCain and for five and a half years he refused to go home.

McCain later explained that he had no choice in the matter. To accept early release would have brought dishonor, not only to himself, but to his family. He just couldn't do that.

There are times when the only way to escape suffering is unworthy of who we are. Those who are persecuted for their faith in Christ may face that choice. The apostles knew and we must learn that the only path worthy of a Christian is at all costs to continue proclaiming the good news that Jesus is the Christ.

The only way that the apostles could keep on preaching Christ despite persecution, the only way that any of us can take such a stand, is by the presence and power of the Holy Spirit in our lives. The church empowered by the Holy Spirit is unstoppable!

VISION

Proverbs 29:18 says, "Where there is no vision, the people perish." One of the keys to growth in the life of the individual Christian and in the Church is vision. If you don't have a vision of where you want to go in life, you aren't going to get there. As the saying goes, "Even God can't steer a parked car!" But when an individual Christian or a group has a vision of what the Lord wants them to do–then growth towards the realization of that vision can occur.

In Acts 6:8-8:1 we read about a real man of vision whose life and death prepared the early church to achieve exponential growth....

> Now Stephen, a man full of God's grace and power, did great wonders and miraculous signs among the people. Opposition arose, however, from members of the Synagogue of the Freedmen (as it was called)—Jews of Cyrene and Alexandria as well as the provinces of Cilicia and Asia. These men began to argue with Stephen, but they could not stand up against his wisdom or the Spirit by whom he spoke.
>
> Then they secretly persuaded some men to say, "We have heard Stephen speak words of blasphemy against Moses and against God."
>
> So they stirred up the people and the elders and the teachers of the law. They seized Stephen and brought him before the Sanhedrin. They produced false witnesses, who testified, "This fellow never stops speaking against this holy place and against the law. For we have heard him say that this Jesus of Nazareth will destroy this place and change the customs Moses handed down to us."
>
> All who were sitting in the Sanhedrin looked intently at Stephen, and they saw that his face was like the face of an angel.
>
> Then the high priest asked him, "Are these charges true?"
>
> To this he replied: "Brothers and fathers, listen to me! The God of glory appeared to our father Abraham while he was still in Mesopotamia, before he lived in Haran. 'Leave your country and your people,' God said, 'and go to the land I will show you.'

"So he left the land of the Chaldeans and settled in Haran. After the death of his father, God sent him to this land where you are now living. He gave him no inheritance here, not even a foot of ground. But God promised him that he and his descendants after him would possess the land, even though at that time Abraham had no child. God spoke to him in this way: 'Your descendants will be strangers in a country not their own, and they will be enslaved and mistreated four hundred years. But I will punish the nation they serve as slaves,' God said, 'and afterward they will come out of that country and worship me in this place.' Then he gave Abraham the covenant of circumcision. And Abraham became the father of Isaac and circumcised him eight days after his birth. Later Isaac became the father of Jacob, and Jacob became the father of the twelve patriarchs.

"Because the patriarchs were jealous of Joseph, they sold him as a slave into Egypt. But God was with him and rescued him from all his troubles. He gave Joseph wisdom and enabled him to gain the goodwill of Pharaoh king of Egypt; so he made him ruler over Egypt and all his palace.

"Then a famine struck all Egypt and Canaan, bringing great suffering, and our fathers could not find food. When Jacob heard that there was grain in Egypt, he sent our fathers on their first visit. On their second visit, Joseph told his brothers who he was, and Pharaoh learned about Joseph's family. After this, Joseph sent for his father Jacob and his whole family, seventy-five in all. Then Jacob went down to Egypt, where he and our fathers died. Their bodies were brought back to Shechem and placed in the tomb that Abraham had bought from the sons of Hamor at Shechem for a certain sum of money.

"As the time drew near for God to fulfill his promise to Abraham, the number of our people in Egypt greatly increased. Then another king, who knew nothing about Joseph, became ruler of Egypt. He dealt treacherously with our people and oppressed our forefathers by forcing them to throw out their newborn babies so that they would die.

"At that time Moses was born, and he was no ordinary child. For three months he was cared for in his father's house. When he was placed outside, Pharaoh's daughter took him and brought him up as her own son. Moses was educated in all the wisdom of the Egyptians and was powerful in speech and action.

"When Moses was forty years old, he decided to visit his fellow Israelites. He saw one of them being mistreated by an Egyptian, so he went to his defense and avenged him by killing the Egyptian. Moses thought that his own people would realize that God was using him to rescue them, but they did not. The next day Moses came upon two Israelites who were fighting. He tried to reconcile them by saying, 'Men, you are brothers; why do you want to hurt each other?'

"But the man who was mistreating the other pushed Moses aside and said, 'Who made you ruler and judge over us? Do you want to kill me as you killed the Egyptian yesterday?' When Moses heard this, he fled to Midian, where he settled as a foreigner and had two sons.

"After forty years had passed, an angel appeared to Moses in the flames of a burning bush in the desert near Mount Sinai. When he saw this, he was amazed at the sight. As he went over to look more closely, he heard the Lord's voice: 'I am the God of your fathers, the God of Abraham, Isaac and Jacob.' Moses trembled with fear and did not dare to look.

"Then the Lord said to him, 'Take off your sandals; the place where you are standing is holy ground. I have indeed seen the oppression of my people in Egypt. I have heard their groaning and have come down to set them free. Now come, I will send you back to Egypt.'

"This is the same Moses whom they had rejected with the words, 'Who made you ruler and judge?' He was sent to be their ruler and deliverer by God himself, through the angel who appeared to him in the bush. He led them out of Egypt and did wonders and miraculous signs in Egypt, at the Red Sea and for forty years in the desert.

"This is that Moses who told the Israelites, 'God will send you a prophet like me from your own people.' He was in the assembly in the desert, with the angel who spoke to him on Mount Sinai, and with our fathers; and he received living words to pass on to us.

"But our fathers refused to obey him. Instead, they rejected him and in their hearts turned back to Egypt. They told Aaron, 'Make us gods who will go before us. As for this fellow Moses who led us out of Egypt—we don't know what has happened to him!' That was the time they made an idol in the form of a calf. They brought sacrifices to it and held a celebration in honor of what their hands had made. But God turned away and gave them over to the worship of the heavenly bodies. This agrees with what is written in the book of the prophets:

> " 'Did you bring me sacrifices and offerings
>   forty years in the desert, O house of Israel?
> You have lifted up the shrine of Molech
>   and the star of your god Rephan,

the idols you made to worship.
Therefore I will send you into exile' beyond Babylon.

"Our forefathers had the tabernacle of the Testimony with them in the desert. It had been made as God directed Moses, according to the pattern he had seen. Having received the tabernacle, our fathers under Joshua brought it with them when they took the land from the nations God drove out before them. It remained in the land until the time of David, who enjoyed God's favor and asked that he might provide a dwelling place for the God of Jacob. But it was Solomon who built the house for him.

"However, the Most High does not live in houses made by men. As the prophet says:

> " 'Heaven is my throne,
>   and the earth is my footstool.
> What kind of house will you build for me?
> says the Lord.
>   Or where will my resting place be?
> Has not my hand made all these things?'

"You stiff-necked people, with uncircumcised hearts and ears! You are just like your fathers: You always resist the Holy Spirit! Was there ever a prophet your fathers did not persecute? They even killed those who predicted the coming of the Righteous One. And now you have betrayed and murdered him—you who have received the law that was put into effect through angels but have not obeyed it."

When they heard this, they were furious and gnashed their teeth at him. But Stephen, full of the Holy Spirit, looked up to heaven and saw the glory of God, and Jesus standing at the right hand of God. "Look," he said, "I see heaven open and the Son of Man standing at the right hand of God."

At this they covered their ears and, yelling at the top of their voices, they all rushed at him, dragged him out of the city and began to stone him. Meanwhile, the witnesses laid their clothes at the feet of a young man named Saul.

While they were stoning him, Stephen prayed, "Lord Jesus, receive my spirit." Then he fell on his knees and cried out, "Lord, do not hold this sin against them." When he had said this, he fell asleep.

And Saul was there, giving approval to his death.

On that day a great persecution broke out against the church at

Jerusalem, and all except the apostles were scattered throughout Judea and Samaria.

Stephen was a man of vision. In Acts 6:5 we read that Stephen was a man full of faith and the Holy Spirit. That is why he was chosen to oversee the distribution of food in the Jerusalem church. Then in Acts 6:8 we read that Stephen was a man full of God's grace and power. He performed many miracles among the people.

One of the key things we see in this part of Acts is that people of vision are often persecuted. There was something about Stephen that disturbed people who were stick-in-the-muds, people who didn't want to change, people who lacked vision. Some of the Jews began to argue with Stephen but they could not stand up against his wisdom or the Spirit by whom he spoke. These Jews didn't like the fact that Stephen seemed to be promoting changes in their religion as they wanted to practice it.

All of us have a hard time handling change—in little things as well as in big things. I am one of those people who has a hard time handling change. Yet God has also called me to be a change agent in certain situations.

In one of the churches I served the Lord blessed us with numerical growth. Over the course of six years we saw our church grow from an attendance of 50 to having two Sunday morning worship services with 200 people in attendance. Along the way this growth necessitated changes in our building. By God's grace I was able to lead that church to refurbish their whole facility from top to bottom, adding additional classroom space among other things.

My wife Becky sat in on some of the initial meetings of the refurbishment committee. In one of those meetings she suggested that my office should be moved from one side of the building to the other so that the nursery could be relocated to a better position. I was against the idea from the start. I told Becky my opinion before she brought up her idea in the meeting. When she brought it up anyway I was ready to kick her under the table but my leg wouldn't reach! I didn't want to move my office, especially my library consisting of hundreds of books. But in the end I had to give in because everybody else liked the idea so much. And I had to admit, after the fact, that the move was the best thing for the church and especially for the nursery ministry. But I didn't want to change.

That, in a microcosm, is our dilemma as human beings. God has called us to a life of change, but we don't like it. We resist it. In fact, God has called us to be visionaries, to be change agents like Stephen, but we are often like the Jews of old, resisting that role to which God has called us.

The second thing we need to notice in this passage is the essence of Stephen's vision. Stephen saw five things very clearly.

First of all, Stephen saw that the people who played a really great part in the history of Israel were people of faith. They were people willing to follow

God anywhere in the adventure of faith.

Abraham was the classic example of this. God called Abraham to leave his country and his people and go to the land he was going to show him. Abraham obeyed God's command even though he didn't know where he was going.

Leslie Newbigin was originally from Scotland and became a bishop in the Church of South India. In leading the Church of South India Newbigin often found the progress of the church being held up by people who would demand to know where such and such a step might lead. In the end he had to say to these overly cautious people: "A Christian has no right to ask where he is going!" We are called to be like Abraham who "went out, not knowing whither he went." (Hebrews 11:8)

Secondly, Stephen saw very clearly that God could be worshiped anywhere by anyone. He pointed out to the Sanhedrin that God was worshiped long before there was a Temple and that God does not live in houses made by human beings.

To the Jew, the Temple was the most sacred of places, especially for the Sadducees who were the ruling priestly class. Their entire lives were devoted to the Temple. They could not imagine the Temple ever being done away with. They didn't like the talk of anyone who suggested that the Temple was no longer necessary.

Stephen also had a vision for taking the Good News of Jesus to the Greeks. He was a Hellenized Jew, a Grecian Jew who spoke Greek fluently. That is why when the Grecian Jews complained that they were being overlooked in the distribution of food in the Jerusalem Church, Stephen was one of the ones selected to oversee the distribution. The church figured if Grecian Jews were complaining then who better to oversee the distribution than one of their own number.

But the Jews did not like Stephen's universal vision of the scope of God's salvation. They saw it as a rejection of God's law and God's temple. That's why they opposed Stephen so violently.

This may sound strange to you. But have you ever known anyone who identified God's purposes so much with a church building that they couldn't stand to see any change in it? Some of the greatest fights in the church arise over changes to church facilities. For some, who have labored long in the church, buildings become even more important than people. That is not right.

John Stott has written,

> Change is painful to us all, especially when it affects our cherished buildings and customs, and we should not seek change merely for the sake of change. Yet true Christian radicalism is open to change. It knows that God has bound himself to his church (promising that he

will never leave it) and to his word (promising that it will never pass away). But God's church means people not buildings, and God's word means Scripture not traditions. So long as these essentials are preserved, the buildings and the traditions can if necessary go. We must not allow them to imprison the living God or to impede his mission in the world.

Thirdly, Stephen saw clearly that visionaries are often persecuted. Joseph was persecuted by his brothers for articulating his dreams. Moses was rejected by the Israelites, both before his call in the wilderness and later on when he was leading those same Israelites through the wilderness. Many of the Old Testament prophets were also persecuted for speaking the truth to God's people. The Sanhedrin even killed Jesus, the Son of God, and the greatest visionary who ever lived. Stephen probably anticipated the persecution he himself was going to receive at the hands of the Sanhedrin.

Fourthly, Stephen saw with great clarity that following Jesus is more important than anything else. Stephen was committed to following Christ no matter the cost. Even when the Sanhedrin was ready to stone him, Christ was at the center of Stephen's vision–not the maddening crowd. "But Stephen, full of the Holy Spirit, looked up to heaven and saw the glory of God, and Jesus standing at the right hand of God."

Finally, because Jesus was at the center of Stephen's vision Stephen saw clearly that forgiveness of one's persecutors is imperative. While the elders of Israel were stoning him, Stephen prayed just like his Master on the cross and said, "Lord, do not hold this sin against them."

One of the indelible images from the Vietnam War is the photograph of a nine-year-old girl named Phan Thi Kim Phuc. During a battle between North and South Vietnamese troops, an American commander ordered South Vietnamese aircraft to drop napalm bombs on Kim's tiny village. Two of her brothers were killed, and she was burned badly. Wearing no clothes, she fled up the road toward a cameraman. The photographer caught a shot of Kim, arms held out in pain and mouth open in a cry of agony.

Kim Phuc suffered third degree burns over fifty percent of her body, but she lived. She endured fourteen months of painful rehabilitation and countless skin grafts. It was so painful to have her wounds washed and dressed that she would often lose consciousness when touched.

Since that time Kim has married, emigrated to Canada and become a Christian. Despite her past suffering she accepted an invitation from several Vietnam veteran groups to join in Veterans' Day ceremonies held at the Vietnam Veterans Memorial in Washington, D. C. where she laid a wreath and spoke words of forgiveness.

"I have suffered a lot from both physical and emotional pain," she told an audience of thousands who greeted her with two standing ovations.

"Sometimes I could not breathe. But God saved my life and gave me faith and hope. Even if I could talk face to face with the pilot who dropped the bombs, I would tell him, 'We cannot change history, but we should try to do good things for the present and for the future to promote peace.'"

I wonder: is there someone in your life whom you need to forgive? I believe that those who have Jesus at the center of their vision in life are the most forgiving people.

The last thing I think we need to see in this passage is that: The non-visionaries killed the visionary but they could not kill the vision. The Sanhedrin put Stephen to a brutal death. But that was not the end of Stephen's Christian vision. Stephen's martyrdom led to the expansion of the church beyond Jerusalem, as we will see in coming chapters. And even as Stephen was being stoned, the witnesses laid their garments at the feet of a young man named Saul who would one day carry on Stephen's vision and take the Good News of Jesus Christ to many Jews *and* Gentiles throughout the Roman Empire. The blood of the martyrs truly is the seed of the church.

Joseph Tson was a pastor in Romania. On one occasion he was arrested by the secret police for publishing a sermon calling for the churches to refuse to submit to the communist government's demand for control over their ministries. When an official told Tson he must renounce his sermon, Tson refused.

The official, surprised that anyone would respond so forcefully to the secret police, asked: "Aren't you aware that I can use force against you?"

Tson replied, "Sir, let me explain that to you. You see, your supreme weapon is killing. My supreme weapon is dying. . . . You know that my sermons are spread all over the country on tapes. When you kill me, I will only sprinkle those tapes with my blood. Those sermons will speak ten times louder after my death because everyone will say: 'That preacher meant what he said because he sealed it with his blood.' So go on, sir, kill me. When you kill me, I win the supreme victory."

The secret police released Tson, knowing his martyrdom would be far more of a problem than his sermon. You can kill the Christian visionary, but you can't kill the vision of Jesus Christ.

EVANGELISM

A Mercedes Benz TV commercial years ago showed a Mercedes colliding with a cement wall during a safety test. In the commercial someone asks the company spokesman why they do not enforce their patent on the Mercedes Benz energy-absorbing car body, a design evidently copied by other companies because of its success.

The company spokesman replies matter-of-factly, "Because some things in life are too important not to share."

The energy-absorbing car body of the Mercedes Benz does not always prevent people from getting killed. But Christians have a message to share about a life-saving device that works 100% of the time. Some things in life, like the Good News about Jesus, are too important not to share. Sharing the Good News, what is also called evangelism, is the next key to growth we see in Acts 8….

> On that day a great persecution broke out against the church at Jerusalem, and all except the apostles were scattered throughout Judea and Samaria. Godly men buried Stephen and mourned deeply for him. But Saul began to destroy the church. Going from house to house, he dragged off men and women and put them in prison.
>
> Those who had been scattered preached the word wherever they went. Philip went down to a city in Samaria and proclaimed the Christ there. When the crowds heard Philip and saw the miraculous signs he did, they all paid close attention to what he said. With shrieks, evil spirits came out of many, and many paralytics and cripples were healed. So there was great joy in that city.
>
> Now for some time a man named Simon had practiced sorcery in the city and amazed all the people of Samaria. He boasted that he was someone great, and all the people, both high and low, gave him their attention and exclaimed, "This man is the divine power known as the Great Power." They followed him because he had amazed them for a long time with his magic. But when they believed Philip as he preached the good news of the kingdom of God and the name of Jesus Christ, they were baptized, both men and women. Simon himself believed and

was baptized. And he followed Philip everywhere, astonished by the great signs and miracles he saw.

When the apostles in Jerusalem heard that Samaria had accepted the word of God, they sent Peter and John to them. When they arrived, they prayed for them that they might receive the Holy Spirit, because the Holy Spirit had not yet come upon any of them; they had simply been baptized into the name of the Lord Jesus. Then Peter and John placed their hands on them, and they received the Holy Spirit.

When Simon saw that the Spirit was given at the laying on of the apostles' hands, he offered them money and said, "Give me also this ability so that everyone on whom I lay my hands may receive the Holy Spirit."

Peter answered: "May your money perish with you, because you thought you could buy the gift of God with money! You have no part or share in this ministry, because your heart is not right before God. Repent of this wickedness and pray to the Lord. Perhaps he will forgive you for having such a thought in your heart. For I see that you are full of bitterness and captive to sin."

Then Simon answered, "Pray to the Lord for me so that nothing you have said may happen to me."

When they had testified and proclaimed the word of the Lord, Peter and John returned to Jerusalem, preaching the Gospel in many Samaritan villages.

Now an angel of the Lord said to Philip, "Go south to the road—the desert road—that goes down from Jerusalem to Gaza." So he started out, and on his way he met an Ethiopian eunuch, an important official in charge of all the treasury of Candace, queen of the Ethiopians. This man had gone to Jerusalem to worship, and on his way home was sitting in his chariot reading the book of Isaiah the prophet. The Spirit told Philip, "Go to that chariot and stay near it."

Then Philip ran up to the chariot and heard the man reading Isaiah the prophet. "Do you understand what you are reading?" Philip asked.

"How can I," he said, "unless someone explains it to me?" So he invited Philip to come up and sit with him.

The eunuch was reading this passage of Scripture:
> "He was led like a sheep to the slaughter,
>   and as a lamb before the shearer is silent,
>   so he did not open his mouth.

> In his humiliation he was deprived of justice.
> Who can speak of his descendants?
> For his life was taken from the earth."

The eunuch asked Philip, "Tell me, please, who is the prophet talking about, himself or someone else?" Then Philip began with that very passage of Scripture and told him the good news about Jesus.

As they traveled along the road, they came to some water and the eunuch said, "Look, here is water. Why shouldn't I be baptized?" And he gave orders to stop the chariot. Then both Philip and the eunuch went down into the water and Philip baptized him. When they came up out of the water, the Spirit of the Lord suddenly took Philip away, and the eunuch did not see him again, but went on his way rejoicing. Philip, however, appeared at Azotus and traveled about, preaching the Gospel in all the towns until he reached Caesarea.

This passage offers us several pointers for effective sharing of the Good News about Jesus Christ. The first is that: God can use us in unexpected places.

Jesus had commanded his followers to make disciples of all nations, but up to this point the first Christians were not taking the Gospel very far outside of Jerusalem. It took the martyrdom of Stephen and the fear of possible death to get some of the disciples to move out and start taking the message of Jesus where it needed to go. Philip and the others probably didn't want to go to Samaria with the Gospel, initially. But once they were there in that awkward situation, God used them.

Bruce Larson tells the following story. . . .

> A few years ago, while we were living in Florida, a friend called and said, "Bruce, I've been reading your books and I understand you believe in spiritual healing." I said, "I sure do. I've seen God's miracles." Then he mentioned the very sick young daughter of some mutual friends in town. "I have been told she's dying," he said, "and I just called the family to ask if you and Hazel and my wife and I could come over tomorrow and pray for her healing." I was less than eager. The whole scheme seemed a little pushy. "Don't you believe in healing?" he asked. I told him we'd be there.
>
> The next day we went. Now this man is a manufacturer of heavy machinery and not exactly a "spiritual type," but he is a man full of the Holy Spirit. My friend announced our intentions right off to the young woman. "We came to pray for you. We believe Jesus wants to make you well." As we prayed, I confess I mostly felt uncomfortable and somewhat of an intruder. But within a month the young woman began to improve. The point is that even when we get into those places

we wouldn't have chosen, we can expect God to use us there. Instead of asking, "What am I doing here?" we can say, "Lord, there's a need here. I'm going to proclaim Good News."

God can use us in unexpected places, just as he used Bruce Larson, and just as he used the Christians who were scattered outside Jerusalem.

The second pointer in this passage is that: God calls all of us to be evangelists. "Those who had been scattered preached the word wherever they went." Those who were scattered were not the apostles. They were not the official preachers and teachers of the church. Philip was a deacon, not an elder or a pastor. But he preached the word wherever he went. There is no gift of evangelism mentioned in the Bible, though there is the gift of the evangelist. God gives certain persons to the Body of Christ to equip the whole Body for the work of evangelism. But we can all play a part in the work of evangelism, regardless of our gifts. Some evangelize through serving, some through helping, others through healing (as Philip did), some evangelize through leading, some through teaching. As St. Francis is reported to have said, "Preach the Gospel at all times, in all places. If necessary, use words!"

I think my wife Becky is a great evangelist. She would never claim to be a preacher or teacher of any sort. But when we lived in South Carolina she spent a great deal of time building a friendship with one of our unchurched neighbors. One day after we had moved away Becky got a call from our old neighbor, Lucretia. She wanted to let Becky know that she was going to be joining a church on Easter Sunday and that she owed a lot of her newfound faith to Becky's influence and example.

The same thing happened when we were living in Pennsylvania. Becky built a relationship with our next door neighbor Anne. Becky also worked gently at being a witness to her hairdresser, Lindy. Both of these women made professions of faith in Christ as a result of Becky's friendship.

You don't have to be a teacher or preacher to be used in the work of evangelism. You just have to love people to Jesus by the power of the Holy Spirit. All you have to do is make yourself available for the Lord to use.

A third pointer from this passage is that: Not everyone who makes a profession of faith is a true believer. Simon Magus made a profession of faith but he was not a true believer. Our job is to preach and let God deal with the results.

The example of Simon Magus shows us that evangelism is needed in the church as much as anywhere else. Simon became a church member but he didn't have Christ in his heart. He needed to hear the Gospel all over again.

I have probably preached the Gospel more in churches than anywhere else. And I have seen countless people in churches make decisions for Christ—many of them who have spent their whole lives in churches. The danger of growing up in the church is that we tend to think being born in a Christian home, being born into the church, makes us Christians. But if that were so then it would follow that being born at McDonald's would make you a Big Mac. It just doesn't work that way. In order to truly be a Christian you have to receive the Spirit of Jesus Christ into your heart.

A fourth pointer about evangelism which we learn here is that: Sometimes God's evangelism plan doesn't make sense. An angel of the Lord took Philip away from a massively successful evangelistic campaign reaching crowds of people in order to talk to just one man about Jesus. How much sense does that make? It doesn't make much sense at all to our human way of thinking. But God's ways are not our ways. In fact, his thoughts are higher than our thoughts. And through this seemingly illogical move, the Gospel traveled to a whole new continent: Africa! Even though some of God's plans may not make sense to us–the important thing is that we should obey like Philip did.

When my father went to New York City in 1957 to try and reach teen gangs with the Gospel, that move didn't make a whole lot of sense. Up to that time he had been traveling and speaking to crowds numbering in the hundreds and thousands. Now he was giving it all up to try to reach a few teenagers in a place no one else wanted to touch. My father left our family temporarily on the West Coast. He didn't even have enough money to make the initial trip across country. But God provided for his needs. He rented a store front in Hell Gate Station, New York City, and he slept in the back of the store front. He tried to meet up with key gang leaders but was unsuccessful. It was not until he put on an electronics show at the local junior high school that he was able to attract youth to his club. But after that initial show he had handfuls of kids showing up at 2110 Second Avenue.

Out of the first nine youth my father worked with, all of them accepted Christ as their leader and forgiver. All but one of them are still alive today, so far as I know. All went on to lead exemplary lives in the community. In fact, the young man who led the largest gang of over 900 members went on to be a vice-president with Chase Manhattan Bank.

God's evangelism plan doesn't make much sense to us sometimes. But ours is not to reason why. Ours is simply to obey.

A fifth pointer from this passage is that: The Gospel is for all people. The Jews didn't like the Samaritans because they were half-breed Jews who did not follow all the teaching of the Old Testament. But God wanted the Good News of his Son to go to the Samaritans, and Philip took the news to them. The eunuch on the road to Gaza belonged to another nation. But Philip knew the Gospel was for him. The eunuch was of a different socioeconomic class; but the Gospel was for him. The eunuch was black; but the Gospel was for him. The Good News of Jesus Christ is for everyone! As Paul says in Galatians

3:28 the Gospel creates a whole new community, a whole new world– "There is neither Jew nor Greek, slave nor free, male nor female, for you are all one in Christ Jesus."

A sixth pointer from this passage is that if you are going to be a good evangelist then: you need to depend upon the Holy Spirit. The Spirit told Philip: Go to that chariot and stay near it. And Philip obeyed.

I remember when I first became a Christian I thought I literally had to share the Gospel with everyone I met. I felt guilty if I didn't. This compulsion, which I am convinced was of human origin, made me rather obnoxious in my approach. And it made me rather nervous because I thought it was all up to me.

But the more I grew as a Christian I came to realize that God is sovereign in the area of evangelism. He is the one who initiates salvation. Our job is just to depend on him and do his will in this area. Having this outlook has made me much more relaxed about evangelism. I try to be sensitive to the nudges of the Holy Spirit and simply walk through the doors that he opens.

A seventh pointer from this passage is that if you are going to be a good evangelist then: It is helpful to become a good question-asker! Philip began his evangelism with the Ethiopian eunuch by asking a good question: Do you understand what you are reading? One very broad question you can ask people to bring the conversation around to Jesus is: what has your spiritual journey been like? After listening to the other person's story it gives you an opportunity to share your own journey with Christ.

The eighth pointer for effective evangelism is: Begin where people are. Another good thing about what Philip did was that he began where the Ethiopian eunuch was. Philip began with the passage of Scripture the man was reading and preached Christ to him. Every Sunday I give a children's sermon using something called The Mystery Box. I invite one of the children in the congregation to put something different in the box every week and then I talk about the object, relating it to some spiritual lesson. The only rules are that the object must fit inside the box, and it must not be alive or dead! One thing I have learned from doing this for many years is that it is possible to begin a conversation just about anywhere and end up with Jesus.

The ninth pointer about evangelism we see in this passage is that: When the fruit is ripe it falls off the tree. The Ethiopian eunuch was ripe for the kingdom. He was ready to begin a relationship with Christ. When someone is ready to be responsive to the Gospel then you don't have to be pushy. The Ethiopian was the one pushing to be baptized, not Philip.

This story reminds me of a young woman I met while looking for an apartment one day in San Diego, California. Her name was Jennifer and she was the manager of an apartment complex. One of the first things she asked me was: "What do you do for a living?"

I reluctantly said, "I'm a pastor." The reason I was reluctant to reveal this information was because usually when I tell people I am a pastor, the conversation turns down a dark alley. Most people don't like talking to a pastor; for some reason it makes them feel guilty. In this situation, I didn't have any choice but to fess up. I was cornered.

To my surprise, Jennifer expressed interest in our church and she came for a visit. I followed up with Jennifer by inviting her over to dinner at our home. After dinner Becky and I asked Jennifer if she wanted to learn more about Jesus by studying the Bible with us. Again, I was hesitant, but Jennifer was enthusiastic in her response: "I'd love to study the Bible with you."

We met with Jennifer every week and read a chapter of the Gospel of John together and talked about it. Then one day when Jennifer was house-sitting for us she tumbled into the Kingdom. She was all alone, but she was ready to ask Jesus to come into her life, and so she did. What was true in the situation with the Ethiopian eunuch has been true down through the ages: When the fruit is ripe, it falls off the tree!

Finally, the example of Philip shows us: There are many ways to be a good evangelist. Philip evangelized in at least three ways:

- He preached to the masses.
- He shared Christ one-on-one.
- He also shared Christ in the home.

The next time we hear of Philip he is in his own home in Casarea with four unmarried daughters who prophesy (Acts 21:8-9). How did Philip's daughters come to know the Lord? I'm sure it was through Philip who shared the Gospel with them.

Every parent has the tremendous opportunity to share the Gospel with their children when they are growing up. "Train up a child in the way he should go and when he is old he will not depart from it." Maybe your children are grown and now you have grandchildren. You can share the Gospel with them.

The essence of the Gospel is not hard to communicate. Paul sums it up this way in 1 Corinthians 15:1-5,

> Now, brothers, I want to remind you of the Gospel I preached to you, which you received and on which you have taken your stand. By this Gospel you are saved, if you hold firmly to the word I preached to you. Otherwise, you have believed in vain.
>
> For what I received I passed on to you as of first importance: that Christ died for our sins according to the Scriptures, that he was buried, that he was raised on the third day according to the Scriptures, and that

he appeared to Peter, and then to the Twelve.

That is the essence of the Gospel we have to communicate. In addition to this, I often tell people that becoming a Christian is as simple as A, B, C, D....

- **A**dmit that you are a sinner.
- **B**elieve that Jesus died on the cross and rose again from the dead.
- **C**onfess your faith in Christ publicly.
- **D**ecide to turn from your sin and follow Christ in the fellowship of the Church.

Latin American evangelist Luis Palau tells the story of how he first started out communicating the Good News to non-Christians. Luis was working in a bank in Argentina. He had been a Christian since about age 12. However, Luis' mother felt very strongly that God was calling Luis to be an evangelist. She would constantly say to Luis, "Why don't you go to such and such a city and preach the Gospel in the streets there." And Luis would respond, "But Mama, I'm waiting for the call." This went on for quite some time until Luis' mother finally got fed up with his response. The last time Luis Palau said, "But Mama, I'm waiting for the call," his mother responded, "Luis, the call went out 2,000 years ago; God is waiting for the answer."

And that is true not just for Luis Palau, not just for Billy Graham, but also for you and for me. God calls some of us to preach to the masses. He calls others to talk to strangers, one on one, like Philip did. He calls others of us to share the Good News of Jesus with people we know in our family, our neighborhood, our workplaces. All we have to do is make ourselves available to the Holy Spirit, pray for opportunities, then love people to Jesus. The call to share Christ with the world went out 2,000 years ago. Jesus is waiting for our response.

REPRODUCTION

What is the purpose of the Church of Jesus Christ? Is it to build great buildings, like the beautiful cathedrals in Europe? Is it primarily to feed the hungry, heal the sick, alleviate poverty, or promote peace around the world? Though these are all part of the work of the Church I do not think they strike at the primary purpose of the Church. I believe the church's basic job is to reproduce Christians by the power of God. If we are doing that, all else follows. The Christians who are reproduced will feed the hungry, care for the poor, promote peace and carry out all the other functions of the Church. But our basic job as a Church is to reproduce Christians.

How does one go about reproducing Christians? Dawson Trotman once said that just as human beings are born to reproduce physically, so Christians are born to reproduce spiritually. But how? That is the question which Acts 9 answers for us....

> Meanwhile, Saul was still breathing out murderous threats against the Lord's disciples. He went to the high priest and asked him for letters to the synagogues in Damascus, so that if he found any there who belonged to the Way, whether men or women, he might take them as prisoners to Jerusalem. As he neared Damascus on his journey, suddenly a light from heaven flashed around him. He fell to the ground and heard a voice say to him, "Saul, Saul, why do you persecute me?"
>
> "Who are you, Lord?" Saul asked.
>
> "I am Jesus, whom you are persecuting," he replied. "Now get up and go into the city, and you will be told what you must do."
>
> The men traveling with Saul stood there speechless; they heard the sound but did not see anyone. Saul got up from the ground, but when he opened his eyes he could see nothing. So they led him by the hand into Damascus. For three days he was blind, and did not eat or drink anything.
>
> In Damascus there was a disciple named Ananias. The Lord called to him in a vision, "Ananias!"
>
> "Yes, Lord," he answered.

The Lord told him, "Go to the house of Judas on Straight Street and ask for a man from Tarsus named Saul, for he is praying. In a vision he has seen a man named Ananias come and place his hands on him to restore his sight."

"Lord," Ananias answered, "I have heard many reports about this man and all the harm he has done to your saints in Jerusalem. And he has come here with authority from the chief priests to arrest all who call on your name."

But the Lord said to Ananias, "Go! This man is my chosen instrument to carry my name before the Gentiles and their kings and before the people of Israel. I will show him how much he must suffer for my name."

Then Ananias went to the house and entered it. Placing his hands on Saul, he said, "Brother Saul, the Lord—Jesus, who appeared to you on the road as you were coming here—has sent me so that you may see again and be filled with the Holy Spirit." Immediately, something like scales fell from Saul's eyes, and he could see again. He got up and was baptized, and after taking some food, he regained his strength.

Saul spent several days with the disciples in Damascus. At once he began to preach in the synagogues that Jesus is the Son of God. All those who heard him were astonished and asked, "Isn't he the man who raised havoc in Jerusalem among those who call on this name? And hasn't he come here to take them as prisoners to the chief priests?" Yet Saul grew more and more powerful and baffled the Jews living in Damascus by proving that Jesus is the Christ.

After many days had gone by, the Jews conspired to kill him, but Saul learned of their plan. Day and night they kept close watch on the city gates in order to kill him. But his followers took him by night and lowered him in a basket through an opening in the wall.

When he came to Jerusalem, he tried to join the disciples, but they were all afraid of him, not believing that he really was a disciple. But Barnabas took him and brought him to the apostles. He told them how Saul on his journey had seen the Lord and that the Lord had spoken to him, and how in Damascus he had preached fearlessly in the name of Jesus. So Saul stayed with them and moved about freely in Jerusalem, speaking boldly in the name of the Lord. He talked and debated with the Grecian Jews, but they tried to kill him. When the brothers learned of this, they took him down to Caesarea and sent him off to Tarsus.

Then the church throughout Judea, Galilee and Samaria enjoyed a time of peace. It was strengthened; and encouraged by the Holy Spirit, it grew in numbers, living in the fear of the Lord.

In this chapter we get a detailed picture, in the story of Saul's conversion, of how a Christian is reproduced. There are at least three stages to this process. There is a before, a during, and an after.

Let's look at the **BEFORE**. What was Saul like *before* he became a Christian? What sort of state was he in? One might say that he was *without the light*.

Saul was about as much against Christ and the Church as a person could be. He gave approval to the death of Stephen (Acts 8:1). He was breathing out murderous threats against the Lord's disciples (Acts 9:1). He was going to the high priest and asking him for letters to the synagogue in Damascus, so that if he found any who belonged to the Way (that is Christians), whether men or women, he might take them as prisoners to Jerusalem (Acts 9:2).

Saul had all the credentials of a faithful Israelite, and then some. Can you imagine what it would be like to be totally sold out to your religion, to your people, to your cause, and then wake up one day and suddenly realize you had been all wrong? That's what happened to Saul. His whole world fell apart. And it all started to happen because of a person he met–a person who was a real fire-brand. That person's name was Stephen.

Jim Elliot, the missionary who gave his life trying to reach the Auca Indians of South America, was the same sort of fire-brand as Stephen. Elliot once said that he wanted to be a "fork in the road" to everyone he met. He wanted everyone, upon meeting him, to have to decide for or against Christ. Stephen was that kind of fire-brand, that kind of fork in the road. And as such, Saul couldn't get him out of his mind.

Saul could not forget standing in Stephen's presence, while the man was being stoned, and hearing him say things like: "Lord Jesus, receive my spirit." and "Lord, do not hold this sin against them." Watching a Christian die can be a powerful experience–a tremendous motivator for getting one's life right with God. Stephen's death did not immediately motivate Saul to become a Christian, but I'm sure that Stephen's example ate away at Saul's outward bravado. Stephen's life and death brought Saul under *conviction*.

Malcolm Muggeridge, the atheistic British journalist, became a Christian at age 79. When asked to explain his conversion, Muggeridge said he could resist all the great books and great sermons. But when he saw Mother Teresa serving the dying poor of Calcutta he said, "If this is Christianity, I've got to have it." Mother Teresa was Muggeridge's Stephen. She was an artesian well, bubbling over with the Holy Spirit; a person whom Muggeridge could not forget.

Who was or is the Stephen in your life? Who was the person whose example led you to become a Christian? More importantly–to whom can you be a Stephen, maybe even this coming week?

Secondly in this passage we see the **DURING** of Saul's conversion. This is the time of Saul *under the light*, the time of Saul's *acceptance* of Jesus Christ as leader and forgiver.

We read in Acts 9:3, "As he neared Damascus on his journey, suddenly a light from heaven flashed around him. He fell to the ground and heard a voice say to him, 'Saul, Saul, why do you persecute me?'

"'Who are you, Lord?' Saul asked.

"'I am Jesus, whom you are persecuting,' he replied. 'Now get up and go into the city, and you will be told what you must do.'"

The men who were traveling with Saul did not know what to say. They heard the sound of Saul's voice speaking to someone, but they didn't see or hear that someone.

In a sense, our conversion is impossible to explain to anyone else. A transaction so intimate takes place that no one else can fully share in it. "Worldlings" will never understand your relationship with Jesus. Only the Christian can begin to share with another Christian all that conversion really means.

Few of us have had the kind of lightening experience Saul had. Few if any of us have ever been blinded by a vision of Jesus and so overcome that we could not eat or see for days. Few if any of us saw a physical light at the time of our conversion. But that doesn't mean we are any less spiritually enlightened than Saul.

Only those who live in the country know what real physical darkness is. I remember a time at a Christian camp in the mountains of Southern California. I went outside one night to talk to a friend. We walked so far away from the lights of the buildings that we could not see each other, even though we sat down with our faces inches away from one another.

Saul had walked so far away from God, that he no longer knew up from down, left from right, right from wrong. He was persecuting God's people and didn't even realize it . . . until that voice came to him out of the darkness and made him realize there was Someone right next to him, someone whom he had been persecuting, and that Someone was the Lord of glory. An electric light was switched on in the pitch blackness.

Jesus' words to Saul are rather enlightening aren't they? Jesus tells Saul that by persecuting the Church, individual Christians, Saul has been persecuting himself. We are the Body of Christ. If anyone hurts the Body he hurts the Head, Jesus himself. If any one part of the Body is honored, Jesus is honored.

At the moment of Christian conversion we become a part of Christ's body. We begin a special relationship, not only with God through Jesus Christ, but also with the Church. We become part of a family. Jesus told Saul to go into the city because it was in the city that Jesus was preparing the man who would welcome Saul into the family, into the Body of Christ.

That man was Ananias. The Lord told Ananias to go to the house where Saul was staying and place his hands on him so that Saul might have his sight restored. Ananias argued with the Lord, "God don't you know who that man is? He has been harming your people?"

And the Lord said, "Ananias, I know all about Saul. And he is my chosen instrument to take my name before the Gentiles and their kings and the people of Israel. He too will suffer just as the rest of the saints have suffered."

So Ananias went to the house. He placed his hands on Saul and called him "brother". What a welcome word that must have been to Saul! He had family. He was no longer alone in the dark. The scales fell from Saul's eyes. He rose up and was baptized.

Who was or is the Ananias in your life? Who was the one who played mid-wife at your new birth? For me it was Robert Schuller.

I grew up in a Christian home. My mother helped me memorize John 3:16 at a young age. I heard my father's testimony of coming to living faith through the preaching of Billy Graham countless times. However, I did not understand the Gospel or take it on board until one Sunday morning when my mother and I were listening to Robert Schuller on television. He explained very simply that Jesus had died on the cross so that I could be forgiven of all my sin. He also said that when Jesus forgives, he forgets. When he buries the axe, he doesn't leave the handle sticking above the ground.

That was welcome news to me. Before that Sunday morning God seemed distant to me. I felt guilty about certain things I had done and thought in my young life. I couldn't forget my sin. I felt unloved, not by my parents surely, but by peers at school, and perhaps unloved in some cosmic sense. Now here was a man telling me that Jesus loved me and died for me, that my sin was forgiven and forgotten by God. I welcomed the good news with tears and an open heart.

Who was your Ananias? To whom might you be an Ananias, even this week?

The Swiss psychiatrist Paul Tournier once told the story of going back to medical school to visit his favorite old professor. Tournier had just written his first book and he wanted to read it to his mentor. As they sat in the gathering gloom of a Swiss winter afternoon, Paul Tournier read his new book to his aging teacher. When Tournier finished reading, he looked up and saw tears in the old man's eyes and his teacher said, "Oh Paul, that's a wonderful book. Every one of us Christians should read that."

Paul was surprised. "I didn't know you were a Christian, professor. When did you become one?"

"Just now, as you read your book." Paul Tournier was the Ananias for his beloved teacher–and he didn't even know it until afterwards.

Finally, let us look for a moment at what Saul's life was like **AFTER** he met Christ. Saul began to live his life *in the light*. And his new life in the light was characterized by *confession of faith*.

In Acts 9:20 we read, "At once he [Saul] began to preach in the synagogue that Jesus is the Son of God."

I have thought for some time that new Christians are always the best witnesses because no one has told them yet that they aren't supposed to evangelize! You see, the longer we are Christians the more we get accustomed to our holy huddle, the less we have relationships with unbelievers, the more muted we get in our approach to sharing the good news of Christ. Saul was bold in going forth to preach Jesus. And we need such a holy boldness in the Church and in the world today.

Notice, Saul did not go through an evangelism training course. He didn't go to seminary. Not that there is anything wrong with seminary or evangelism training courses. They are wonderful. But if you have begun a relationship with Jesus Christ then you are already equipped to help someone else do the same.

Saul grew more and more powerful in testifying to Christ. You and I can always learn more about how to be better witnesses for Jesus. But the moment you become a Christian, you are a witness, and you have everything you need to lead others into the kingdom.

It was at this point in time that a third pivotal person came into Saul's life. That person was Barnabas. Because of his courageous witness, Saul's opponents were violently against him. Saul went from persecutor to persecuted. He had to be ushered out of Damascus in a basket through a window in the wall of the city.

Not only did Saul have a hard time with his opponents, he also had a hard time receiving acceptance from fellow followers of the Way, fellow saints of God. When he went to Jerusalem he tried to join the disciples but they were all afraid of him and ran in the other direction! They knew his former reputation and had a hard time believing he was really changed.

Barnabas means "son of encouragement". We read about him in Acts 4 and how he sold a piece of property and gave the money to the apostles to meet the needs of others in the church. Now we see Barnabas again in Jerusalem. He sees the trouble Saul is having, not being welcomed into the Church. So he puts his arm around Saul and ushers him into the presence of the apostles– "Meet brother Saul. Jesus changed his life on the road to Damascus. He has preached Christ without fear since then. I think we ought to welcome him into our fellowship." The apostles followed Barnabas' lead and did just that.

Who was or is the Barnabas in your life–the person who has encouraged, discipled and welcomed you into the family of God? There have been a number of Barnabases in my life. As I mentioned to you, I became a Christian through hearing a preacher on television. My family did not attend church at that time. The way I got into church was through another young man like myself. The young man's name was Jeff. He lived down the street from me. I can remember him following me home from school one day. He had a friend with him. They pitched little stones at me and called me names. Well, somehow Jeff and I met on neutral turf and became friends. We found out that we both watched Robert Schuller on television and could recite the Possibility Thinker's Creed from memory—an amazing thing for two 13 year olds! Jeff invited me to his youth group. Eventually I accepted. The first night I went to youth group at La Jolla Presbyterian Church was the first night they had a new youth pastor—Sonny Salsbury. I loved Sonny, I loved the youth group, and so I started attending regularly. Eventually I started attending Sunday morning services at the church and became a member—all because of two Barnabases in my life—Jeff Vida and Sonny Salsbury.

Who was your Barnabas and to whom can you be a Barnabas? Who is there in your sphere of influence who may need some encouragement this week, or even an invitation to come to church? The whole purpose of the Church is to reproduce Christians. You can be part of that reproduction ministry by being a Stephen, or an Ananias or a Barnabas to someone else.

As C. S. Lewis once said, ". . . the Church exists for nothing else but to draw men into Christ, to make them little Christs. If they are not doing that, all the cathedrals, clergy, missions, sermons, even the Bible itself, are simply a waste of time. God became Man for no other purpose." (*Mere Christianity*, pp. 169-170)

If that is the case, then we better get busy being reproducers for Jesus, whether it is as a Stephen, an Ananias, or a Barnabas.

CONFRONTATION

No one likes confrontation. The *Chicago Tribune Magazine* told a story of conflict and confrontation that may inspire a knowing nod if you have ever had a difficult neighbor.

"When Mr. Palmer moved into his new house, he and his new neighbor got along just fine. They would smile broadly and wave when they saw each other in the driveway. There was no fence between their yards, and it appeared they would never need one.

"The problems began when Palmer's children began stepping in dog droppings in their yard, though they themselves didn't own a dog. The neighbor had two poodles, and Palmer was sure they were the culprits, so one day Palmer brought up the delicate subject. The neighbor denied the poodles were the problem, and before long the two neighbors descended into a messy spiral of antagonism. Droppings were thrown from lot to lot. Angry words were exchanged. Signs were posted. Eventually the dogs disappeared, but the damage had been done.

"In Palmer's mind, the conflict reached its low point when another issue surfaced. One day he received a note from the hostile neighbor suggesting that the dead elm tree that stood squarely on the lot line between them should be cut down. Palmer didn't like the idea of splitting the costs involved and ignored the letter. A few months later he and his wife suddenly heard the sound of a chain saw outside. They looked out their window and watched the dead elm on the lot line as it was sawn vertically down the middle, leaving half of a grotesque dead elm standing on his property. He left it standing for a few years as a conversation piece, then finally cut it down."

That is an example of a bad kind of confrontation. But there is a good kind. When the Gospel of Jesus Christ confronts situations, there is always a good result. In the next section of the book of Acts, from Acts 9:32-12:25, Luke focuses on the ministry of Peter. And he shows us the Gospel confronting four negative situations: disease, death, prejudice and political oppression. In each situation there is a positive result of the confrontation: healing, new life, love, deliverance.

First of all, what happens when the Gospel confronts disease? When the Gospel confronts disease there is healing. As Peter traveled around Palestine he went to visit the Christians in a town called Lydda, sort of in the middle of Palestine. There was a man there named Aeneas. He was a paralytic and had been bedridden for eight years. Following the example of Jesus and attributing all the power to the Lord, Peter said to Aeneas: "Jesus Christ heals you. Get up and take care of your mat." Immediately Aeneas got up. All those who lived in that area saw the miracle which had been performed, and as a result they turned to the Lord.

In 1993 the late author and church leader John Wimber found he had inoperable cancer and underwent radiation treatments. The cancer went into remission. In his book *Living with Uncertainty* Wimber wrote about going without a miraculous healing for himself even though he had seen others dramatically healed by God.

> "I was speaking in South Africa at a large conference. A friend, John McClure, was with me, and we were asked to go to the home of a lady of the church. She was dressed beautifully but was very emaciated, weighing only 85 pounds. She had been sent home from the hospital to die. Her body was full of cancer. Her only hope of survival was divine intervention.
>
> "We prayed for her, but not with great fervency. John had confidence that she would be healed. I felt nothing.
>
> "That night she woke up with a vibrant, tingling feeling throughout her body. For the next four hours her body was full of intense heat. She tried to call out to her husband in the next room but couldn't raise her voice loud enough for him to hear.
>
> "Alone and frightened, she crawled into the bathroom, her body racked with pain. At the time she thought, 'O my God. My body is coming apart and I'm dying.' Without knowing it, she eliminated from her body a number of large tumors. Finally, exhausted from the night's events, she fell back asleep. She didn't know if she'd wake up.
>
> "But half an hour later she woke up incredibly refreshed. Later her husband woke up to the smell of freshly brewed coffee. 'What are you doing?' he asked, astonished to see his wife on her feet and preparing breakfast.
>
> "She replied with sudden understanding: 'God healed me.'
>
> "Two days later she reported to her doctors, who gave her a clean bill of health. They couldn't find a cancer in her body. God had completely delivered her of all of it."
>
> "Without much energy to pray on our part and without any desperation or faith on her part, the Lord chose to heal this woman's cancer-infested

body through divine means. That's God, and that is sometimes how he does it."

John Wimber, himself, later died of cancer.

How are we to explain this? Why does God heal in one situation and not in another? Why does God leave one person on earth and take another– perhaps one who had family who especially needed him or her?

We don't have answers to a lot of our "why" questions. I was asking a lot of those questions in 2005 after my brother died from cancer complications at the age of 49, leaving behind a wife and two young boys. "Why God?" And do you know what God told me? He said, "Will, you are not seeing the whole picture. You will not understand this until you do."

We don't see the whole picture here on earth. We don't know why God heals in one situation and not in another. But here is what I do know: God has the power to heal any disease, whether supernaturally, or naturally through normal medical means. God wants us to pray for healing, following the example of Jesus and Peter and many others. Sometimes God answers our prayers with a "yes", sometimes with a "wait" and sometimes with a "no". But regardless of his answer he is always working with the best interest of his children in mind. "And we know that in all things God works for the good of those who love him, who have been called according to his purpose." (Romans 8:28)

I heard a Mennonite pastor at a memorial service say something wonderful. The deceased had once asked the pastor what it means in Psalm 23 when God promises to prepare a table for us in the presence of our enemies. The pastor, after meditating on the question, told the dying woman that he thought that meant, in her case, that God was going to prepare a table for her in the presence of her cancer.

I love that. No matter what we go through in life, God prepares a table in the presence of our trials and tribulations. He enables us, by his Holy Spirit, to rejoice regardless of the circumstances.

So, God has power to heal. God wants us to pray for healing. Sometimes God answers no. But even in those situations he enables us to rejoice. And finally, we need to recognize that the ultimate healing is to go to heaven where we can be in the presence of God.

The second thing we see in the ministry of Peter is what happens when the Gospel confronts death. When the Gospel confronts death there is always new life.

In the town of Joppa, on the Mediterranean coast not too far from Lydda, there was a disciple named Tabitha. Here was someone who was always doing good for others, helping the poor. But she became sick and died.

To our human way of thinking that doesn't make sense. Why would God take such a person?

Well, when some of the followers of Christ in Joppa heard that Peter the healer was in Lydda, not too far away, they sent two men who urged him to come to Joppa at once. When Peter got there all the widows were standing around, crying and showing Peter the clothing Tabitha had made while she was alive.

Here were a bunch of women who had gone through tremendous loss in their own lives. And now they had another loss to endure. They must have been asking: Why God?

But Peter sent them out of the room. He got down on his knees and prayed. Turning to the dead woman, and following the example of Jesus, he said: "Tabitha, get up." And the woman opened her eyes and sat up. Peter took her by the hand and helped her to her feet. Peter called all the widows together, and you can imagine the rejoicing that went on. This miracle became known all over Joppa and many people came to believe in the Lord as a result.

Stories like this make me ask the question: Why did God raise this person from death? It's hard enough dying once, but having your dying to do all over again—that's really hard. C. S. Lewis often said that he thought Lazarus ought to be considered the first martyr because he had his dying to do all over again!

And therein lies the point of this healing. I think God used Peter to raise Tabitha from death, not for Tabitha's sake. She would have been better off in heaven. And I don't think the Lord did it just for the sake of the grieving widows. I think the Lord raised up this woman because of the witness it would be to everyone around. As a result of this woman being raised from the dead, many came to believe in the Lord.

And that should teach us something. It doesn't matter so much what happens to us in this life—as long as we use what happens to us to exalt the Lord Jesus Christ. And there is nothing that will ever happen to us, there is no situation we will ever be in, where we cannot lift up Jesus Christ.

My brother used his cancer as an opportunity to witness to everyone he came in contact with in the hospital. His witness was so powerful we had a nurse all the way from the hospital in Charlottesville come to his memorial service in the little village of Head Waters, Virginia; that's a seventy mile distance.

The Apostle Paul wrote in Philippians 1:20-21, "I eagerly expect and hope that I will in no way be ashamed, but will have sufficient courage so that now as always Christ will be exalted in my body, whether by life or by death. For to me, to live is Christ and to die is gain."

When the Gospel confronts death there is always new life. In Tabitha's case, the Gospel confronting her death brought new life for her, for an extended period of time here on earth. It also brought new spiritual life to those who heard of her being raised from the dead. In my brother's case I believe the Gospel as it met his death brought new life for my brother in heaven, and renewed spiritual life for many left on earth who saw his witness. To live is Christ. To live on this earth is to have continual opportunity to be a witness for Jesus. But to die is to gain heaven.

The third situation which we see the Gospel confronting through the ministry of Peter is the situation of prejudice. When the Gospel confronts prejudice there is love, love that breaks down barriers. One of the greatest bits of prejudice which had to be overcome in the early church was the prejudice that Jewish believers in Jesus had against Gentiles, or non-Jews.

William Barclay reminds us of the first century Jewish attitude toward Gentiles. He writes, "The Jew believed that for the Jews alone God had any use and that other nations were quite outside the mercy and the privileges of God. The really strict Jew would have no contact with a Gentile or even with a Jew who did not observe the Law. Two things in particular the strict Jew would not do. He would never have as a guest nor would he ever be the guest of, a man who did not observe the Law."

With that in mind we see what tremendous barriers the Gospel breaks down in Acts 10 and 11. At Caesarea, a Roman town on the Mediterranean coast of Palestine, there was a man named Cornelius. He was a Roman centurion; that is, he was in charge of a hundred soldiers. His group was known as the Italian Regiment.

Cornelius was a God-fearer. That means he had attached himself to the Jewish religion but he was not willing to go all the way with it and become circumcised. So Cornelius was seeking after God.

One day he has a vision of an angel who tells him to send to Joppa and have Peter come to his house. So Cornelius follows the angel's instructions and sends men to collect Peter.

While this is going on Peter also has a vision. He sees the sky opened and something like a large sheet being let down to the earth with all sorts of animals on it which would be unclean for a Jew to eat. A voice tells him to kill the animals and eat them. Peter, as a good Jew, protests. But the voice speaks to him a second time and says, "Do not call anything impure that God has made clean."

While Peter is wondering about the meaning of the vision, Cornelius' men arrive to collect Peter. While the men are at the gate of the house where Peter is staying, the Spirit says to Peter, "Don't hesitate to go with these men for I have sent them."

The men tell Peter their story. And amazingly, Peter invites them into the house as guests. This is something that no good Jew would do. But Peter does it because God is beginning to change his prejudice against Gentiles.

The next day Peter goes with the men to the house of Cornelius in Caesarea. Cornelius gathers all his relatives and close friends together to hear what Peter has to say to them. And Peter's message is this: "You are well aware that it is against our law for a Jew to associate with a Gentile or visit him. But God has shown me that I should not call any man impure or unclean." Peter has understood the meaning of the vision God gave him. Then he goes on to explain the good news about Jesus to Cornelius and those who are gathered in his house. He tells them that those who put their trust in Jesus receive forgiveness of sins through his name.

While Peter is speaking, the Holy Spirit comes on all those who hear his message. They all start speaking in tongues, just like the Jewish believers in Jesus did on Pentecost. Peter's response is to ask, "Can anyone keep these people from being baptized with water? They have received the Holy Spirit just as we have." And so Cornelius and all those in his household are baptized.

This is such an important turning point in the history of the Church that the whole story is re-told by Peter to the apostles and believers in Jerusalem, and re-told by Luke in Acts 11. The bottom line is that when the Gospel confronts prejudice there is love and a breaking down of barriers. The Jewish believers in Jesus come to realize that the Gospel of Jesus Christ is for all people, Jew and Gentile alike. And a person does not have to become a Jew first in order to be a follower of Jesus in good standing.

Are there areas of prejudice in your life which the Gospel needs to confront? In a church I led in South Carolina we had two white families who had adopted black children. I remember visiting one of the elderly white members in the congregation who told me she thought that was wrong. I told her, as gently as I could, that I thought she was wrong.

We have other friends, a black man and a white woman, who attended a college in the South many years ago. They got married while in college and had to face the hostility of people around them who didn't think that was right.

These kind of attitudes need to change in the Church of Jesus Christ. And I know they are changing. The Good News of Jesus Christ is for everyone–black, white, Hispanic, Asian–it doesn't matter. And as Christians we need to have love for all people. The barriers between the races ought to come down in the Church of Jesus Christ more than anywhere else. But those barriers can only come down as Christ works love in our hearts for all people.

The final thing we see the Gospel confronting through the ministry of Peter is political oppression. And the result is deliverance.

In Acts 12 Herod arrests some who belong to the church, intending to persecute them. He even has James, the brother of John, put to death by the sword, thus making James the second martyr of the infant Church.

Herod has Peter arrested and put in jail, handing him over to be guarded by four squads of four soldiers each. But as the Church earnestly prays for Peter he is, once again, released from prison by the intervention of an angel. In the end, Herod, rather than Peter, is struck down by an angel of the Lord, is eaten by worms and dies. When the Gospel confronts political oppression and persecution the result is deliverance. The Word of God cannot be held down. It continues to increase and spread.

Once again we see that one of the Lord's servants is taken to heaven. The other is left to carry on the work of the Gospel. At one point the persecutor, Herod, seems to be winning. But then Herod is struck down. Overall what we need to see is that God buries his messengers, eventually, but the message carries on. When the Gospel confronts persecution and political oppression, the Gospel wins out, eventually. There may be setbacks here and there. But in the end, the Gospel triumphs.

When the army of Julian the Apostate, the Roman emperor from 361-363, was on the march to Persia some of the soldiers got hold of a Christian man to torment him. After they got tired of torturing this man, they looked into his eyes and asked with great scorn, "Where now is your carpenter God?"

The prisoner looked up through the blood and agony, and he said, "Where now is my carpenter God? He is building a coffin for your emperor."

Interestingly enough, the dying words of Julian the Apostate were, "You have conquered, Galilean."

Jesus always has been and always will be the victor. When the good news of Jesus Christ confronts disease, there is healing. When it confronts death, there is new life. When it confronts prejudice, there is love and a breaking down of barriers. And when Jesus confronts the rulers of this world, even the principalities and powers–there is always deliverance, and the good news goes forth to conquer.

MISSION

What is your mission in life? What are you put here for? John Knox, the Christian preacher whose life set fire to the Reformation in Scotland prayed, "Give me Scotland, or I die!" Is there anything for which you are willing to give your life?

What is it that God wants you to be and to do? And what is the unique way that he has for you to be and do it, that only you can be and do?

These are the big questions of life, the questions we seldom pause to consider and to answer. But these are the essential questions. And if we don't answer them, we will miss life itself.

In this chapter, we are going to examine what the mission of every Christian should be, what we are put on this earth to accomplish. Now each Christian will accomplish this same mission in a different way. The vision for each of our lives is unique, though our mission is the same. Your vision must necessarily be different than my vision because the Lord has given you unique gifts, a unique background, unique opportunities that are different than mine. But our mission is and must be the same. We see that mission written across the lives of a group of people that the Bible tells us about in Acts 11, a group of people who came to be known as the church at Antioch. Let's read about this group of rascal saints who made a difference for Christ and his kingdom because they understood the mission to which he had called them.

> Now those who had been scattered by the persecution in connection with Stephen traveled as far as Phoenicia, Cyprus and Antioch, telling the message only to Jews. Some of them, however, men from Cyprus and Cyrene, went to Antioch and began to speak to Greeks also, telling them the good news about the Lord Jesus. The Lord's hand was with them, and a great number of people believed and turned to the Lord.

The first thing that we need to see in this passage is that the Lord has called us to love people to Christ. Those believers who had been scattered away from Jerusalem on account of the persecution related to the martyrdom of Stephen knew what they were about. They had a clear summons given to them by the Lord Jesus when he said:

Keys to Growth

All authority in heaven and on earth has been given to Me. Therefore go and make disciples of all nations, baptizing them in the name of the Father, and of the Son, and of the Holy Spirit, teaching them to obey everything I have commanded you. And surely I am with you always, to the very end of the age (Matthew 28).

These first disciples of Jesus understood that he wanted them, wherever they went, to love people to Christ by word and deed. It took the death of Stephen and the subsequent persecution of the church to get them to spread the good news of Christ's love beyond Jerusalem. But after that, they went on with the mission of Christ like gang-busters. And the Lord wants us to do the same.

The Lord wants us to love people to Christ by telling non-Christians the good news about him. It is vital that we build relationships with non-Christians as a platform for sharing the Gospel with them. But we also need to communicate the love of Christ in words as well as in deeds. The failure of much friendship evangelism today is seen in the fact that it is long on friendship and short on evangelism. There is no such thing as a silent witness. To be witnesses of Jesus Christ it is essential that we *tell* others the Good News of Jesus' life, his death for sinners and his resurrection.

The importance of speaking to others about Christ is wonderfully illustrated in Joe Bayly's parable entitled *I Saw Gooley Fly*. Herb Gooley, as Bayly describes him, was a college student,

> an ordinary sort of guy until the night he stepped out of his third floor dorm window and flew away into the wild blue yonder.
>
> Up until Christmas break his junior year, Gooley had been distinguished by only one thing - the knack of tripping over his own feet. But when he got back from Christmas vacation, his astonished fellow students found he was actually able to fly - fly his own body, that is, not an airplane.
>
> His roommate told how it happened. After studying late one night, Gooley decided to go down the street for a hamburger. His roommate reminded him that the hamburger place would close in just three minutes, to which Gooley replied matter-of-factly, "I'll fly down."
>
> He went over to the window, lifted it up, and stepped out. Jerry, his roommate, thought he had gone crazy and ran around telling everybody that Gooley had jumped out the window. But when they looked outside, no one was there.
>
> The whole campus buzzed. They would see Gooley walking along, and all of a sudden he would be airborne. The library was besieged with

requests for books on aerodynamics and anything else that had to do with flying. Everyone wanted to learn to fly like Gooley, but nobody would actually admit to envy. The administration was embarrassed by this flight freak, so they invited a specialist to give lectures for a "Flight Emphasis Week". The hall was packed until the students found out the lecturer couldn't fly. The crowd suddenly dropped off.

The parable ends as follows:

> You know, I've always been surprised that Gooley didn't tell us how to do it, or at least how he did it. He couldn't help knowing how interested we all were. But he kept his mouth shut. So none of us learned to fly.
>
> It's a funny thing, but I still have a sense of loss at not learning Gooley's secret. And other grads have confessed the same thing to me.
>
> What happened to Gooley? I've often wondered about that. He transferred that fall to another college where, they say, all the students know how to fly.

We are a lot like Gooley. We have a secret that could transform the lives of others if we would only share it with them. We know how to fly, spiritually speaking. How can we keep the wonderful secret of Christ's love to ourselves?

Who is there in your life who needs to hear the Good News? Look at the people with whom these first disciples built relationships. They weren't simply people "like them". No, these first disciples became willing to cross cultural gaps to share the Good News about Jesus, because they became convinced that this Good News was meant for all types of people; this Good News was meant for the world.

It is one thing to communicate the Gospel to people who are "like us"; it is quite another thing to communicate the Gospel to someone who is very different from you. The story is told of a cultured woman who found herself among people of a strange language and race with many varied customs. While she was there she became a close friend of a devoted missionary. One day she said, "I was troubled by an experience with those quarreling, difficult people, and I related my grievances to my missionary friend. 'They are so self-interested,' I complained. 'So self-absorbed, so soft on themselves, so violent with others, so unreasoning, so totally difficult,' and when I had finished rehearsing their faults as I saw them my friend smiled a little and said something I have never forgotten–'That's why they need us.'"

The Lord wants us to communicate Jesus not only to people who are "like us", but he may also send us to people who are very much *not* like us, to people who are difficult to love. Perhaps the thing that will help us most when faced with communicating the Gospel to someone whom we find "unlovable" is to remember that we are like them, we too are difficult to love.

We also read about these first missionaries that: "The Lord's hand was with them, and a great number of people believed and turned to the Lord." It was due to the Lord's hand, the Lord's power, the Lord's presence in their efforts, that the labor of these missionaries brought the result of people becoming Christians. As we go about building relationships and gossiping the Gospel to non-Christians we need to remember that it is the Lord alone who can bring people into a relationship of love with him. He alone can change their hearts by the power of the Holy Spirit. The Lord alone can make someone a Christian. So we must remember to rely on him to bring the results. Jesus said: "No one can come to me unless the Father who sent me draws him..." (John 6:44) and "Apart from me, you can do nothing." (John 15:5) It is very encouraging to remember that when it comes to evangelism, what the Lord wants from us is faithfulness; he will provide the success.

But loving other people to Jesus is only the beginning of our mission; the Lord also wants us to *grow people in Christ*. Let us read on in Acts 11. . . .

> News of this reached the ears of the church at Jerusalem, and they sent Barnabas to Antioch. When he arrived and saw the evidence of the grace of God, he was glad and encouraged them all to remain true to the Lord with all their hearts. He was a good man, full of the Holy Spirit and faith, and a great number of people were brought to the Lord.
>
> Then Barnabas went to Tarsus to look for Saul, and when he found him, he brought him to Antioch. So for a whole year Barnabas and Saul met with the church and taught great numbers of people. The disciples were called Christians first at Antioch.

The disciples were called "Christians" first at Antioch. The word "Christian" means "a little copy of Christ". Non-Christians first used this name for the disciples with a derogatory tone: "O you little copies of Christ—you think you're so great don't you?"

But it was a name that stuck. And it is an appropriate one. To be a Christian is to be a Christ-in person, a person in whom Christ lives by the Holy Spirit. And that is what we are.

So how do you grow a Christian? The New Testament tells us that we do it primarily through teaching. To disciple someone in Christ means essentially to teach them about how to have a growing relationship with Christ. It means to teach them to obey everything that Jesus commanded.

Now you may be thinking, "I am not a teacher; how am I going to disciple other people? How am I to grow other people in Christ?" I believe that Colossians 3:16 gives us the answer: "Let the word of Christ dwell in you richly as you teach and admonish one another with all wisdom..."

Meditations on the Acts of the Apostles

As we get God's Word into our minds and hearts, his Word is naturally going to overflow and be of benefit to others. Sometimes teaching and admonishing one another is as simple as sharing a Scripture verse that you read recently with someone. Perhaps a Christian brother or sister shares with you how they have been struggling with worry. You tell them of your own struggle with worry and how Philippians 4:6-7 helps you to overcome worry. "Do not be anxious about anything, but in everything, by prayer and petition with thanksgiving, let your requests be made known to God. And the peace of God which transcends all understanding will guard your hearts and your minds in Christ Jesus."

Growing people in Christ involves encouraging them like Barnabas did. Barnabas was one who always came alongside of others to encourage them. When there were needs in the church at Jerusalem, Barnabas sold a field and brought the money to the apostles so that they could distribute it to meet the need. After Saul's conversion, Saul came to Jerusalem and tried to join the disciples but they were all still afraid of him; they didn't believe that Saul had really become a Christian and so they were afraid that he was going to haul them off to jail as he had done in the past. It was Barnabas who took Saul, put his arm around him, and brought him to the apostles. He told the apostles about Saul's conversion. As a result, the apostles accepted Saul into their company and Saul began to speak boldly in the name of the Lord.

We can each be like Barnabas as we get to know others in the Body of Christ. We can come alongside of others in the church, especially younger Christians. We can encourage one another. We can show the love of Christ to each other.

I remember a story from a sermon I heard when I was twelve years old, a sermon that led me to accept Christ's love and forgiveness for my sin. It was a story about a young boy whose family was always criticizing him. One afternoon, the family was at it again. One after another the father, the mother, the brothers and sisters all made cutting remarks about this boy, right to his face. Finally, he got up and ran out of the room; he couldn't take it any longer. But as he ran down the hallway to his bedroom, there was someone standing in the way. It was his grandmother. And this wonderful grandmother put her arms around her grandson, looked him in the eyes and said: "I've heard everything that they have been saying about you. And I just want you to remember one thing: I believe in you."

That experience was so powerful, it changed that young man's life. And it was that same kind of encouragement which made Saul into the apostle Paul; Barnabas came along and said, "Saul, I believe the Lord is going to use you to reach others." "Saul, come and help me teach these new believers in Antioch." Barnabas' encouragement of that one man, changed the course of the church, and the course of history as we know it.

Who is there in the Church, perhaps someone on the fringes, or someone at the core, whom you can encourage this week? Maybe you can call that person up and pray with them, or get together with them for a breakfast or lunch, or write them an encouraging note. Whatever it is that you can do to encourage one another, that action will go a long way toward fulfilling your mission and the church's mission, the mission of growing people in Christ.

Finally, we see from this passage of Scripture that our mission is not complete with just loving people to Christ and growing people in Christ in our own neighborhood. No, the Lord also wants us to *send and be sent for Christ*. Certainly the Lord wants us to be missionaries where we are. Just because we cannot go around the world for Christ, that does not excuse us from going across the street for him. But where we cannot go, God wants us to send others with our prayers and with our giving and with our encouragement. We read in Acts 11, 12 and 13...

> During this time some prophets came down from Jerusalem to Antioch. One of them, named Agabus, stood up and through the Spirit predicted that a severe famine would spread over the entire Roman world. (This happened during the reign of Claudius.) The disciples, each according to his ability, decided to provide help for the brothers living in Judea. This they did, sending their gift to the elders by Barnabas and Saul....
>
> When Barnabas and Saul had finished their mission, they returned from Jerusalem, taking with them John, also called Mark....
>
> In the church at Antioch there were prophets and teachers: Barnabas, Simeon called Niger, Lucius of Cyrene, Manaen (who had been brought up with Herod the tetrarch) and Saul. While they were worshiping the Lord and fasting, the Holy Spirit said, "Set apart for me Barnabas and Saul for the work to which I have called them." So after they had fasted and prayed, they placed their hands on them and sent them off.

What a variety of people there were in the church at Antioch! Barnabas was from the island of Cyprus; Simeon was called Niger, probably because he was of dark complexion. Lucius was from Cyrene, the capital of Libya; Menaen was a foster-brother of Herod Antipas, one of the key rulers in Palestine; and then there was Saul, the persecutor of Christians turned herald of Christ.

There was a variety of people in the church at Antioch, but they were united by a common mission, a common vision. The believers in Antioch were ignited by the Lord's mission and vision; they could not rest content with reaching Antioch alone for Christ. No, they were moved by the Holy Spirit to have a vision for the world.

Where did they get this vision? They got it while they were worshiping the Lord, fasting and praying. We cannot develop a heart-desire to see the world come to Christ from listening to just one sermon, or from just one prayer meeting. No, you and I need to log hours in prayer; we need to fast and pray. We need to get out of ourselves and start seeing the world the way the Lord sees the world. Like Bob Pierce, the founder of World Vision, we need to let "our hearts be broken by the things that break God's heart". As someone once said, "A missionary is one who never gets used to the sound of non-Christian foot-beats on their way to a Christ-less eternity."

Why is prayer and fasting and worshiping the Lord so essential to getting the Lord's vision for his Church? Because the Holy Spirit is the one who must initiate and sustain the mission of the church. "Unless the Lord builds the house, those who build labor in vain." (Psalm 127:1) We can have a great vision for the Church written down on paper, but if it is not the Lord's vision, and if he does not empower us to fulfill it, then we will fail.

Are we willing to spend sacrificial time in prayer for the evangelization of the world? Are we willing to ask the Lord to send us anywhere he wants us to go, to share the Gospel with anyone to whom he wants us to speak?

When Robert Moffat, Scottish missionary to South Africa, came back to recruit helpers in his homeland, he was greeted by the fury of a cold British winter. Arriving at the church where he was to speak he noted that only a small group had braved the elements to hear his appeal. What disturbed him even more was that there were only ladies in attendance that night, for he had chosen as his text Proverbs 8:4, "Unto you, *O men* I call."

In his consternation Moffat failed to notice one small boy in the loft who had come to work the bellows of the organ. Dr. Moffat felt hopeless as he gave the message, realizing that few women could be expected to undergo the rigorous experiences they would face in the undeveloped jungles of the continent where he labored. But God works in mysterious ways to carry out his wise purposes. Although no one volunteered, the young fellow assisting the organist was thrilled by the challenge, deciding that he would follow in the footsteps of this pioneer missionary, he went on to school, obtained a degree in medicine, and then spent the rest of his life ministering to the unreached tribes of Africa. His name: David Livingstone!

Perhaps there is one person reading this story today whom the Lord wants to use to reach many for Christ. The Lord is speaking to you and he is calling you today to lay down your life for him and to serve him in getting the Gospel out. Will you respond to God's call and fulfill your mission of loving people to Christ, growing people in Christ and sending people for Christ wherever God leads?

GOD'S PERSON

I once heard the pastor of a large church in San Diego say that the key to church growth is the right person in the right place at the right time with the right plan. Dawson Trotman, founder of the international Christian ministry, The Navigators, once said that God blesses the person, not the institution. Or as someone else once said, God decided 2,000 years ago that a human being was a good conductor for his Spirit and he hasn't changed his mind since!

Whatever you may think of that, it is evident that God used Saul of Tarsus in a powerful way to reach the Roman Empire with the Good News of Jesus Christ. Today I want to examine with you: *God's Person*, Paul–his pattern, power, preaching and parish, based upon Paul's first missionary journey recorded in Acts 13....

> The two of them [Barnabas and Saul], sent on their way by the Holy Spirit, went down to Seleucia and sailed from there to Cyprus. When they arrived at Salamis, they proclaimed the word of God in the Jewish synagogues. John was with them as their helper.

First of all, it was Paul's *pattern* to proclaim the word of God first in the Jewish synagogues in the towns he visited. Why? Paul says in Romans 1:16,

> I am not ashamed of the Gospel, because it is the power of God for the salvation of everyone who believes: first for the Jew, then for the Gentile.

Paul recognized that he was part of an ongoing story. The good news of God did not begin with him. He did not invent it. The story began with God's chosen people Israel and so they should be the first to receive the next installment of the continuing story. As N. T. Wright has written:

> The earliest apostolic preaching was neither a standard Jewish message with Jesus added on at the end, nor a free-standing announcement of a new religion cut off from its Jewish roots, but rather the story of Jesus *understood* as the fulfillment of the Old Testament covenant narrative, and thus as the *euangelion*, the good news or "Gospel"–the creative force which called the church into being and shaped its mission and life (*The Last Word*, p. 47).

If Jesus was the fulfillment of a Jewish story then, Paul figured, the Jews had first dibs on hearing the completion of that story. This in no way denies that the story of Jesus as the fulfillment of the Old Covenant is a story for the whole world. Paul was quick to recognize that, as the continuation of his first missionary journey reveals.

Why too, we may ask, did Barnabas and Saul go first to Cyprus to spread the good news? The text does not reveal the answer. But perhaps it was because Barnabas had a concern for his own country; he was from Cyprus, after all. And this reveals, doesn't it, that we each need to have a concern that our own nation, our own neighbors in fact, should hear the good news of Jesus Christ. Barnabas was never able to let go of this concern for his fellow Cypriots. In fact, when he and Paul parted company in Acts 15:39 we read that Barnabas took Mark and sailed for Cyprus once again. That was part of Barnabas' pattern, a concern for those near to home, while Paul had a concern for the world. In fact, a new pattern for Paul emerges once he parts company with Barnabas; he begins to focus on the major cities of Greek culture and of the Roman Empire: Philippi, Thessalonica, Athens, Corinth, Ephesus, and finally Rome itself. As I hinted in the last chapter, we each need to have a bit of Barnabas in us, as well as a bit of Paul. We need to be concerned for those closest to us that they should hear the good news of Jesus; and we need to be concerned for the world, we need to send and be sent for Christ wherever he wants us to go.

The second thing we see on this first missionary journey is something about Paul's *power*. Let us read on in Acts 13:6-12. . . .

> They traveled through the whole island until they came to Paphos. There they met a Jewish sorcerer and false prophet named Bar-Jesus, who was an attendant of the proconsul, Sergius Paulus. The proconsul, an intelligent man, sent for Barnabas and Saul because he wanted to hear the word of God. But Elymas the sorcerer (for that is what his name means) opposed them and tried to turn the proconsul from the faith. Then Saul, who was also called Paul, filled with the Holy Spirit, looked straight at Elymas and said, "You are a child of the devil and an enemy of everything that is right! You are full of all kinds of deceit and trickery. Will you never stop perverting the right ways of the Lord? Now the hand of the Lord is against you. You are going to be blind, and for a time you will be unable to see the light of the sun."
>
> Immediately mist and darkness came over him, and he groped about, seeking someone to lead him by the hand. When the proconsul saw what had happened, he believed, for he was amazed at the teaching about the Lord.

Here we are told Saul's Greek name for the first time: Paul. In fact this becomes the name by which Luke refers to him throughout the rest of Acts. This signals a change from the Hebrew Saul focusing primarily on ministry to the Jews, to the visionary Paul who has a heart for the whole world to come to Christ.

What was the source of Paul's power? How was it that Paul could look a powerful magician, Elymas, in the eye and tell him he was going to be blind, and then have it happen? The source of Paul's power is the same as your source and mine: the Holy Spirit.

Jesus confronted evil in the same power. In Luke 4:1 we read that Jesus was "full of the Holy Spirit". It was only by the Spirit's power that he was able to handle the temptation in the desert.

What about us? How do we handle the devil, temptation, evil? You say, "Well I've never had to face an evil magician!" Maybe not. But evil is not just a force outside of us, operative in strange and magical ways. Evil is also a force that can move in our own hearts tempting us to go astray from God's way. We need the power of the Holy Spirit as much as Paul or Jesus did, to face seemingly ordinary evil in our everyday lives.

Did you ever hear about Satan's lawn sale? He decided to sell some of the old worn-out tools he had used over the millennia. One avid bargain-hunter was sorting through all of Satan's stuff and came across an implement that was really worn out and ragged, almost falling apart. On the side of that tool, do you know what was inscribed? One word: discouragement.

Discouragement and depression are two of Satan's most oft-used weapons. He tries to get us down. He whispers to us that our lives don't really matter in the long run. This life is just one pain and problem after another. Nothing will ever be different. Our life is just a sordid tale, full of sound and fury, signifying nothing.

That's the kind of garbage Satan tries to sell some people every day of their lives. How are we going to respond to his sales pitch? Are we going to buy it? Or are we going to respond in the power of the Holy Spirit and say: Be gone Satan! Jeremiah 29:11 says: "'For I know the plans I have for you,' declares the Lord, 'plans to prosper you and not to harm you, plans to give you hope and a future.'"

We all need the power of the Holy Spirit working through God's Word on a daily basis, in order to confront the evil that tries to worm its way into our hearts and minds. Thank God we have the same power the Apostle Paul had! Praise God we have the same power Jesus had! We have the power of the Holy Spirit to comfort and encourage us every day!

The third thing we see about Paul on his first missionary journey is something about his *preaching*. Here is the continuing story from Acts 13:13-41. . . .

From Paphos, Paul and his companions sailed to Perga in Pamphylia, where John left them to return to Jerusalem. From Perga they went on to Pisidian Antioch. On the Sabbath they entered the synagogue and sat down. After the reading from the Law and the Prophets, the synagogue rulers sent word to them, saying, "Brothers, if you have a message of encouragement for the people, please speak."

Standing up, Paul motioned with his hand and said: "Men of Israel and you Gentiles who worship God, listen to me! The God of the people of Israel chose our fathers; he made the people prosper during their stay in Egypt, with mighty power he led them out of that country, he endured their conduct for about forty years in the desert, he overthrew seven nations in Canaan and gave their land to his people as their inheritance. All this took about 450 years.

"After this, God gave them judges until the time of Samuel the prophet. Then the people asked for a king, and he gave them Saul son of Kish, of the tribe of Benjamin, who ruled forty years. After removing Saul, he made David their king. He testified concerning him: 'I have found David son of Jesse a man after my own heart; he will do everything I want him to do.'

"From this man's descendants God has brought to Israel the Savior Jesus, as he promised. Before the coming of Jesus, John preached repentance and baptism to all the people of Israel. As John was completing his work, he said: 'Who do you think I am? I am not that one. No, but he is coming after me, whose sandals I am not worthy to untie.'

"Brothers, children of Abraham, and you God-fearing Gentiles, it is to us that this message of salvation has been sent. The people of Jerusalem and their rulers did not recognize Jesus, yet in condemning him they fulfilled the words of the prophets that are read every Sabbath. Though they found no proper ground for a death sentence, they asked Pilate to have him executed. When they had carried out all that was written about him, they took him down from the tree and laid him in a tomb. But God raised him from the dead, and for many days he was seen by those who had traveled with him from Galilee to Jerusalem. They are now his witnesses to our people.

"We tell you the good news: What God promised our fathers he has fulfilled for us, their children, by raising up Jesus. As it is written in the second Psalm:

> "'You are my Son;
> today I have become your Father.'

The fact that God raised him from the dead, never to decay, is stated in these words:

"'I will give you the holy and sure blessings promised to David.'

So it is stated elsewhere:

"'You will not let your Holy One see decay.'

"For when David had served God's purpose in his own generation, he fell asleep; he was buried with his fathers and his body decayed. But the one whom God raised from the dead did not see decay.

"Therefore, my brothers, I want you to know that through Jesus the forgiveness of sins is proclaimed to you. Through him everyone who believes is justified from everything you could not be justified from by the law of Moses. Take care that what the prophets have said does not happen to you:

"'Look, you scoffers,
   wonder and perish,
for I am going to do something in your days
   that you would never believe,
   even if someone told you.'"

There are three crucial elements to the preaching of Paul. First of all, he set the Jesus story in the context of Israel's story. This seems very strange to many of us today who are so far removed from Israel's story itself. But if Paul had not done this it would be like a preacher today standing up and trying to explain about Jesus without telling a story to tie Jesus' story into our contemporary story. So that's the first important aspect of Paul's preaching. When he was in the synagogue he related Jesus' story to Israel's story and showed how Jesus was the fulfillment of various themes in the Old Testament narrative.

Secondly, Paul in his preaching focused upon the crucifixion and resurrection of Jesus. He tied together the Old Testament themes of Messiah and Suffering Servant and showed how both of these were fulfilled in Jesus of Nazareth.

Thirdly, Paul proclaimed the result of Jesus' life, death and resurrection, namely that we can be forgiven of our sins. If we trust in Jesus we can be justified, declared righteous in God's sight. This is something which the Law of Moses could not accomplish for us because we have not obeyed it.

Do you see how bold Paul is in his preaching? He is not ashamed to name the name of his crucified and risen Savior. He is not afraid to tell the Jews where they are wrong and how they can get right.

Anglican evangelist John Guest was asked to pray at a Rotary Club on one occasion. Before he got up to speak one of the officials with the Rotary

Club cautioned him not to use the name of Jesus in his prayer. So when John Guest got up to pray he prefaced his prayer with this statement: "Before I pray let me take a moment to explain pluralism to you. We live in a pluralistic society. This means that there are diverse ethnic, racial, religious and social groups who are pursuing their unique beliefs and lifestyles within the confines of our common civilization. What that works out to in practice is that if you invite a Buddhist to pray at your Rotary Club you should expect him or her to pray a Buddhist prayer. If you invite a Muslim to pray he will pray an Islamic prayer. If you invite a Jew to pray she should pray a Jewish prayer. I am a Christian so I will now lead us in a prayer in the name of Jesus Christ."

That's boldness! And that's the way we should all conduct our Christian lives in this pluralistic society.

A fourth thing we should notice about Paul is his *parish*. John Wesley once said, "The world is my parish." The Apostle Paul could have said the same thing. But what I really want you to notice about Paul's parish is that it was divided. Listen to how the people reacted to Paul's sermon in Acts 13:42-52.

> As Paul and Barnabas were leaving the synagogue, the people invited them to speak further about these things on the next Sabbath. When the congregation was dismissed, many of the Jews and devout converts to Judaism followed Paul and Barnabas, who talked with them and urged them to continue in the grace of God.
>
> On the next Sabbath almost the whole city gathered to hear the word of the Lord. When the Jews saw the crowds, they were filled with jealousy and talked abusively against what Paul was saying.
>
> Then Paul and Barnabas answered them boldly: "We had to speak the word of God to you first. Since you reject it and do not consider yourselves worthy of eternal life, we now turn to the Gentiles. For this is what the Lord has commanded us:
>
> " 'I have made you a light for the Gentiles,
> that you may bring salvation to the ends of the earth.'"
>
> When the Gentiles heard this, they were glad and honored the word of the Lord; and all who were appointed for eternal life believed.
>
> The word of the Lord spread through the whole region. But the Jews incited the God-fearing women of high standing and the leading men of the city. They stirred up persecution against Paul and Barnabas, and expelled them from their region. So they shook the dust from their feet in protest against them and went to Iconium. And the disciples were filled with joy and with the Holy Spirit.

Paul's parish was divided. Some of the Jews wanted Paul to keep on preaching. They wanted to hear more about this Jesus. The service didn't go on long enough for them. After they were dismissed they followed Paul and Barnabas out of the synagogue and continued to discuss spiritual matters with them.

But when Paul came back to the synagogue on the next Sabbath some of the Jews were jealous because Paul was attracting such a big crowd. So they spoke abusively about Paul's message.

Paul's response was to turn to the Gentiles with the message. As we noticed at the beginning of this chapter, Paul felt it only right to go to the synagogue first and tell them how Israel's story was fulfilled in Jesus. But when the Jews rejected his message he always turned to the Gentiles; he found a platform for speaking outside of the synagogue. We read that the Gentiles welcomed Paul's message with gladness "and all who were appointed for eternal life believed".

Some of the Jews stirred up even more trouble for Paul and Barnabas. So much so that Paul and Barnabas could not remain in their region. So they shook the dust from their feet in protest against the Jewish rejection of the Gospel and moved on to greener pastures in Iconium.

The Gospel has continued to garner the same results down through history. The Anglican Church a couple hundred years ago was so upset by John Wesley's message that Wesley had to take to the fields, the highways and the byways to preach the Gospel. A whole new movement of Christians was formed out of that rejection of the Gospel. We know them as the Methodists today.

The Good News of Jesus Christ will always be offensive to some people because the Good News contains the Bad News that we are all sinners bound for hell apart from the salvation available in Jesus Christ alone. "Salvation is found in no one else, for there is no other name under heaven given to men by which we must be saved" (Acts 4:12).

The message of Jesus Christ is itself divisive because it sees every person as either a missionary or a mission field. The all-important question is: Which one are you?

CHURCH PLANTING

In A. D. 532, Emperor Justinian I set out to build a magnificent Church in Constantinople, modern-day Istanbul. The Church was to be called Hagia Sophia or St. Sophia. Justinian summoned the most gifted architects of his day to plan and superintend the project. Ten thousand workers were employed. Twelve different kinds of marble were brought from around the world. 320,000 pounds of gold were spent on the enterprise, which practically emptied the emperor's treasury. Silver, ivory and various precious stones were used for decorative ornamentation. Provincial governors were called upon to send their finest relics to the new Church.

Justinian pushed his workers relentlessly to finish the project in almost six years. By December 537 the construction was complete. To celebrate the event, the emperor led a solemn procession into the great Church. Once inside, Justinian stepped up to the pulpit, raised his hands and cried: "Glory be to God who has thought me worthy to accomplish so great a work! O Solomon! I have vanquished you!"

For years, St. Sophia was known as "the great Church". Its builder, Justinian, was honored for his monumental achievement. But what, really, did Justinian achieve? A material work of gold, marble and other elements. Hagia Sophia eventually became an Islamic mosque and today is a museum.

The apostles of Jesus also built churches, but not with gold or silver or marble. The elements the apostles used to plant and build up churches were seemingly more humble, but also more enduring. Let's look at Acts 14 and see what Paul and Barnabas used to plant and build churches throughout Asia Minor in the first century, because church-planting today is still a key to growth for the Church of Jesus Christ. . . .

> At Iconium Paul and Barnabas went as usual into the Jewish synagogue. There they spoke so effectively that a great number of Jews and Gentiles believed. But the Jews who refused to believe stirred up the Gentiles and poisoned their minds against the brothers. So Paul and Barnabas spent considerable time there, speaking boldly for the Lord, who confirmed the message of his grace by enabling them to do miraculous signs and wonders. The people of the city were divided;

some sided with the Jews, others with the apostles. There was a plot afoot among the Gentiles and Jews, together with their leaders, to mistreat them and stone them. But they found out about it and fled to the Lycaonian cities of Lystra and Derbe and to the surrounding country, where they continued to preach the good news.

In Lystra there sat a man crippled in his feet, who was lame from birth and had never walked. He listened to Paul as he was speaking. Paul looked directly at him, saw that he had faith to be healed and called out, "Stand up on your feet!" At that, the man jumped up and began to walk.

When the crowd saw what Paul had done, they shouted in the Lycaonian language, "The gods have come down to us in human form!" Barnabas they called Zeus, and Paul they called Hermes because he was the chief speaker. The priest of Zeus, whose temple was just outside the city, brought bulls and wreaths to the city gates because he and the crowd wanted to offer sacrifices to them.

But when the apostles Barnabas and Paul heard of this, they tore their clothes and rushed out into the crowd, shouting: "Men, why are you doing this? We too are only men, human like you. We are bringing you good news, telling you to turn from these worthless things to the living God, who made heaven and earth and sea and everything in them. In the past, he let all nations go their own way. Yet he has not left himself without testimony: He has shown kindness by giving you rain from heaven and crops in their seasons; he provides you with plenty of food and fills your hearts with joy." Even with these words, they had difficulty keeping the crowd from sacrificing to them.

Then some Jews came from Antioch and Iconium and won the crowd over. They stoned Paul and dragged him outside the city, thinking he was dead. But after the disciples had gathered around him, he got up and went back into the city. The next day he and Barnabas left for Derbe.

They preached the good news in that city and won a large number of disciples. Then they returned to Lystra, Iconium and Antioch, strengthening the disciples and encouraging them to remain true to the faith. "We must go through many hardships to enter the kingdom of God," they said. Paul and Barnabas appointed elders for them in each church and, with prayer and fasting, committed them to the Lord, in whom they had put their trust. After going through Pisidia, they came into Pamphylia, and when they had preached the word in Perga, they went down to Attalia.

> From Attalia they sailed back to Antioch, where they had been committed to the grace of God for the work they had now completed. On arriving there, they gathered the church together and reported all that God had done through them and how he had opened the door of faith to the Gentiles. And they stayed there a long time with the disciples.

There are at least six crucial elements that Paul and Barnabas used to plant and build up churches in Asia Minor. The first element was *preaching*. In order to plant churches, Paul and Barnabas sowed the seed of the Word of God.

Jesus talked about this in his Parable of the Sower (Luke 8:5-15). A farmer went out to sow his seed. As he was scattering it, some fell along a path. Some fell on rock. Some seed fell among thorns. Other seed fell on good soil. Jesus said that the seed in his story represented the Word of God. Each one of us are like different types of soil. So were Paul and Barnabas' first listeners like different types of soil–some rejected the seed of the Word, others accepted it and produced a crop of other followers of Jesus who eventually formed churches.

In the previous chapter we saw how Paul preached in the Jewish synagogue on Cyprus. Now we again see Paul and Barnabas preaching in the synagogue. We are not told exactly what they preached in the synagogue in Iconium, which today is Turkey's fourth largest city, but we can imagine their preaching had the same elements whenever addressing a Jewish crowd. They would begin with Israel's story, show how Jesus' story was the fulfillment of Israel's story and focus particularly on Jesus' crucifixion and resurrection. Finally, they would give their Jewish brothers the application of the story, namely that we can be forgiven of sin through Jesus' death and resurrection.

The interesting thing in Acts 14 is that we get a snippet of Paul's preaching to the Gentiles which started out a bit different than his preaching to the Jews. We do not have a full-dress sermon in Acts 14. What we do have is Paul's response to the people in Lystra who wanted to offer sacrifices to Paul and Barnabas because Paul had healed a man lame from birth. Notice that with these Gentiles Paul begins his message not with Israel's story, which would *not* have been interesting to them, but with creation. Paul urges the people of Lystra to turn from idols "to the living God, who made heaven and earth". Paul talks about things the people of Lystra could relate to. He talks about how God has shown them kindness by giving them rain from heaven and crops in their seasons and plenty of food. When we get to Acts 17 and Paul's sermon on Mars Hill in Athens, there we will see how Paul starts with creation and ends up with Jesus.

The point is this: when we are communicating the Gospel to other people we have to relate it to their world. If someone you know is struggling with worry, talk with them about how Jesus helps you overcome anxiety. If you are talking with a business person, you might talk about business principles you have learned from the Bible. The bottom line is that you should be able to start from any topic and end up with Jesus, for as Paul says in Colossians 1:17, "He is before all things, and in him all things hold together."

A second element Paul and Barnabas used to plant and build the church in Asia minor was the *power* of the Holy Spirit. As I have already mentioned, Paul healed a man lame from birth. But Paul didn't do this by his own power. As he points out to the people of Lystra, he is human just like them. No, it is by the power of the Holy Spirit that Paul performed this miracle.

As mentioned in the last chapter: you and I have the same power Paul had, if we are trusting in Jesus Christ for our salvation. We have the power of the Holy Spirit living in us. To be a Christian is to be a "Christ-in" person, someone in whom Christ lives by the Holy Spirit.

But just because we have the power of the Holy Spirit in our lives that doesn't mean everything is going to be perfect. Life wasn't perfect or easy for Paul, and it won't be for us either.

In *Discipleship Journal* author Mack Stiles tells the story of how he led a young man from Sweden named Andreas to Christ.

Andreas said to Stiles, "I've been told if I decide to follow Jesus, He will meet my needs and my life will get very good."

This seemed to Andreas to be a point in Christianity's favor. But Stiles faced a temptation—to make the Christian life sound easier than it is.

"No, Andreas, no!" said Stiles.

Andreas blinked his surprise.

"Actually, Andreas, you may accept Jesus and find that life goes very badly for you."

"What do you mean?" he asked.

"Well, you may find that your friends reject you, you could lose your job, your family might oppose your decision—there are a lot of bad things that may happen to you if you decide to follow Jesus. Andreas, when Jesus calls you, He calls you to go the way of the cross."

Andreas stared at Mack Stiles and asked the obvious question: "Then why would I want to follow Jesus?"

Sadly, this is the question that stumps many people today. But Mack Stiles gave Andreas the right answer: "Andreas, you should follow Jesus because He is true."

The power of the Gospel, the power of the Holy Spirit, is the power of the truth, not a power to make everything perfect in this life.

That leads to a third element God used to plant and build the church in Asia Minor—*persecution*. We don't like to think of persecution as an element in

God's plan for building the church. And I don't for one minute think that God *sends* persecution and suffering into our lives. But when human beings cause other human beings to suffer, out of an exercise of their own free will, God *uses* that suffering to bring about his purposes.

We have seen already throughout our study of the book of Acts how the blood of the martyrs was the seed of the church. In Paul and Barnabas' case God used the persecution of the Jews to drive them from city to city. In Lystra Paul was stoned, dragged outside of the city and left for dead. But he had such God-given courage and power that he got up again and went back into the city! Can you imagine it? It was this kind of courage displayed in the midst of persecution which won to the Lord people like Timothy, who we will read about later on in Acts.

Whenever we suffer we naturally ask God: "Why?" Instead we should be asking God: "What are you going to do with this suffering? What do you want me to do with it? How do you want me to handle it? How can I be a witness in the midst of my suffering?"

Look what Paul and Barnabas did with their suffering: "they returned to Lystra, Iconium and Antioch, strengthening the disciples and encouraging them to remain true to the faith. 'We must go through many hardships to enter the kingdom of God,' they said."

In 2 Corinthians 1:3-4 Paul writes, "Praise be to the God and Father of our Lord Jesus Christ, the Father of compassion and the God of all comfort, who comforts us in all our troubles, so that we can comfort those in any trouble with the comfort we ourselves have received from God."

Joe Bayly, the author of that parable we read in an earlier chapter, *I Saw Gooley Fly*, was the author of many books and was, at one time, the vice president of David C. Cook Publishing Company. Joe Bayly lost his young daughter through death; out of that experience he wrote a book which has helped many grieving parents. That must be one of the most hard-to-bear sufferings in life–losing a child. And yet, God used that suffering in Joe Bayly's life to encourage others.

Whatever suffering we are going through, we can experience God's comfort. And we can turn around and be a comfort to others who are going through tough times.

A fourth element or action Paul and Barnabas used in planting and building the Church in Asia Minor was *passing the baton*. They realized that they couldn't do all the work of the Church themselves. So Paul and Barnabas appointed others in the Church to take over where they left off. These others they called elders, following the pattern of Israel in the Old Testament.

Do you remember the story of Moses in the wilderness? He was listening to the Israelites complain morning, noon and night. They were all coming to

Moses with their cases for him to judge. Moses' father-in-law, Jethro, saw this and realized Moses was going to die of fatigue if he didn't do something about this. So he told Moses:

> Listen now to me and I will give you some advice, and may God be with you. You must be the people's representative before God and bring their disputes to him. Teach them the decrees and laws, and show them the way to live and the duties they are to perform. But select capable men from all the people—men who fear God, trustworthy men who hate dishonest gain—and appoint them as officials over thousands, hundreds, fifties and tens. Have them serve as judges for the people at all times, but have them bring every difficult case to you; the simple cases they can decide themselves. That will make your load lighter, because they will share it with you. If you do this and God so commands, you will be able to stand the strain, and all these people will go home satisfied.

Paul and Barnabas followed this same "Jethro-principle". And the Church of Jesus Christ has been following this principle ever since. It is not the job of the pastor to do all the ministry of the Church, but rather to teach and equip the people, especially the elders, to do the work of the ministry.

A fifth element that Paul and Barnabas used to plant and build the Church in Asia Minor was *prayer*. We read that "Paul and Barnabas appointed elders for them in each church and, *with prayer and fasting*, committed them to the Lord, in whom they had put their trust." Paul later tells his protege Timothy that prayer should be the first priority in the local church.

> I urge, then, first of all, that requests, prayers, intercession and thanksgiving be made for everyone—for kings and all those in authority, that we may live peaceful and quiet lives in all godliness and holiness (1 Timothy 2:1-2).

Is prayer the first priority in your church? When you seek to select new leaders for the Church do you do so in prayer and fasting? Or do you simply take whatever able body comes along and is nominated by the nominating committee? If we want the Lord to bless the work of the Church then we have to get back to his methods for planting and building up the Church. After all, this is his work, not merely a human organization.

A sixth and final element Paul and Barnabas used to plant and build the churches in Asia Minor was *partnership*. From the beginning of their first missionary journey Paul and Barnabas worked together as partners. Their very relationship served as a witness of Jesus Christ to all who met them. But they also had the partnership of the Church in Antioch. And when they were finished with their first missionary journey, which may have lasted as much as two or three years, they returned to the Church at Antioch and reported to the

Church what "God had done through them and how he had opened the door of faith to the Gentiles".

That leads me to ask: "What missionaries does your church support?" and "Do you support church-planting efforts?" It doesn't matter how small your church is or how little money you have. The Church at Antioch wasn't large to start with. Neither were the churches which Paul and Barnabas planted. But soon we will see those newly planted churches supporting the missionary effort of the Church out of their meager supply. "Little is much when God is in it." And God wants to take our little bit and use it to plant churches and spread the Gospel of Jesus Christ around the world, if we will let him do so.

The great 19th century evangelist D. L. Moody once said that he had no interest in being remembered by monuments of stone. They will crumble. The only monument he wanted was the lives of men and women who would carry the Gospel to the ends of the earth.

Moody's concerns are a distant echo of Jesus' thoughts on church building. Jesus predicted that the temple in Jerusalem would be destroyed. But the temple of Jesus' body, the Church, endures.

We are part of that body, if we have put our faith in Jesus Christ. And we can be part of planting and building churches just as Paul was—not churches made of bricks and mortar—but people won to Christ and built up in Christ and sent for Christ through the giving of our time, our talent and our treasure.

PROBLEMS

M. Scott Peck opened his inimitable best-selling book *The Road Less Traveled* with these simple but powerful words: *Life is difficult.* We begin our exploration of the next section of Acts with some similar bad news: problems are inevitable. Problems are a part of life which none of us can really avoid. So it is best to learn how to handle problems with God's grace.

One key to handling problems is the ability to recognize when it's going to be a bad day. Someone put together the following list. *You know it's going to be a bad day when . . .*

- You see a *60 Minutes* news team in your office.
- You call the Suicide Prevention Hotline and they put you on hold.
- You turn on the news and they're showing emergency routes out of your city.
- Your twin sister forgot your birthday.
- Your car horn goes off accidentally and remains stuck as you follow a group of Hell's Angels down the highway.
- Your boss calls you into his office and tells you not to bother to take off your coat.
- Your income tax check bounces.
- You put both contact lenses in the same eye.
- You wake up in the hospital all trussed up and your insurance agent tells you that your accident policy covers falling off the roof, but not hitting the ground.

We all have bad days like that sometimes, don't we? What we need in the midst of the bad days is some encouragement, and sometimes some humor to help us through. Most of all, we need God's Word to remind us that problems are inevitable but defeat is optional.

I think Acts 15 is one of the great chapters in the Bible which reminds us of this fact. In this chapter we read about two great problems faced by the Early Church and how those problems were actually a key to growth in the life of the Church....

Keys to Growth

Some men came down from Judea to Antioch and were teaching the brothers: "Unless you are circumcised, according to the custom taught by Moses, you cannot be saved." This brought Paul and Barnabas into sharp dispute and debate with them. So Paul and Barnabas were appointed, along with some other believers, to go up to Jerusalem to see the apostles and elders about this question. The church sent them on their way, and as they traveled through Phoenicia and Samaria, they told how the Gentiles had been converted. This news made all the brothers very glad. When they came to Jerusalem, they were welcomed by the church and the apostles and elders, to whom they reported everything God had done through them.

Then some of the believers who belonged to the party of the Pharisees stood up and said, "The Gentiles must be circumcised and required to obey the law of Moses."

The apostles and elders met to consider this question. After much discussion, Peter got up and addressed them: "Brothers, you know that some time ago God made a choice among you that the Gentiles might hear from my lips the message of the Gospel and believe. God, who knows the heart, showed that he accepted them by giving the Holy Spirit to them, just as he did to us. He made no distinction between us and them, for he purified their hearts by faith. Now then, why do you try to test God by putting on the necks of the disciples a yoke that neither we nor our fathers have been able to bear? No! We believe it is through the grace of our Lord Jesus that we are saved, just as they are."

The whole assembly became silent as they listened to Barnabas and Paul telling about the miraculous signs and wonders God had done among the Gentiles through them. When they finished, James spoke up: "Brothers, listen to me. Simon has described to us how God at first showed his concern by taking from the Gentiles a people for himself. The words of the prophets are in agreement with this, as it is written:

> " 'After this I will return
>   and rebuild David's fallen tent.
> Its ruins I will rebuild,
>   and I will restore it,
> that the remnant of men may seek the Lord,
>   and all the Gentiles who bear my name,
> says the Lord, who does these things'
>   that have been known for ages.

"It is my judgment, therefore, that we should not make it difficult for the Gentiles who are turning to God. Instead we should write to them, telling them to abstain from food polluted by idols, from sexual immorality, from the meat of strangled animals and from blood. For Moses has been preached in every city from the earliest times and is read in the synagogues on every Sabbath."

Then the apostles and elders, with the whole church, decided to choose some of their own men and send them to Antioch with Paul and Barnabas. They chose Judas (called Barsabbas) and Silas, two men who were leaders among the brothers. With them they sent the following letter:

The apostles and elders, your brothers,

To the Gentile believers in Antioch, Syria and Cilicia:

Greetings.

We have heard that some went out from us without our authorization and disturbed you, troubling your minds by what they said. So we all agreed to choose some men and send them to you with our dear friends Barnabas and Paul—men who have risked their lives for the name of our Lord Jesus Christ. Therefore we are sending Judas and Silas to confirm by word of mouth what we are writing. It seemed good to the Holy Spirit and to us not to burden you with anything beyond the following requirements: You are to abstain from food sacrificed to idols, from blood, from the meat of strangled animals and from sexual immorality. You will do well to avoid these things.

Farewell.

The men were sent off and went down to Antioch, where they gathered the church together and delivered the letter. The people read it and were glad for its encouraging message. Judas and Silas, who themselves were prophets, said much to encourage and strengthen the brothers. After spending some time there, they were sent off by the brothers with the blessing of peace to return to those who had sent them. But Paul and Barnabas remained in Antioch, where they and many others taught and preached the word of the Lord.

Some time later Paul said to Barnabas, "Let us go back and visit the brothers in all the towns where we preached the word of the Lord and see how they are doing." Barnabas wanted to take John, also called Mark, with them, but Paul did not think it wise to take him, because he had deserted them in Pamphylia and had not continued with them in the work. They had such a sharp disagreement that they parted company. Barnabas took Mark and sailed for Cyprus, but Paul chose Silas and left, commended by the brothers to the grace of the Lord. He went through Syria and Cilicia, strengthening the churches.

The first problem mentioned in Acts 15 is that of *legalism*. Legalism happens whenever someone tries to maintain that we are justified in God's sight by keeping God's law, or when someone tries to add to God's law something God hasn't specifically required. In this case some men came down from Judea to Antioch and were teaching the Christians there: "Unless you are circumcised, according to the custom taught by Moses, you cannot be saved."

This sent Paul and Barnabas into hysterics. They had just come back from preaching the Gospel all over Asia Minor. Many Gentiles had come to faith in Jesus Christ and been added to the Church. Now some Jewish Christians from Judea were teaching that the Gentiles basically had to become Jews first, in order to be saved. As far as Paul and Barnabas were concerned, the very Gospel was at stake. It was due to the problem of legalism that Paul wrote his letter to the Galatians. In that letter he sums up his response to legalism:

> We who are Jews by birth and not 'Gentile sinners' know that a man is not justified by observing the law, but by faith in Jesus Christ. So we, too, have put our faith in Christ Jesus that we may be justified by faith in Christ and not by observing the law, because by observing the law no one will be justified.

However, there was such a sharp disagreement over this matter in the Church at Antioch that they couldn't settle the dispute themselves without ripping the Church apart. So what did they do? They appealed for help to the mother Church in Jerusalem. They sent Paul and Barnabas, along with some other believers, to go up to Jerusalem to see the apostles and elders to ask their advice about how to handle this problem.

So, Paul and Barnabas went to Jerusalem. And all along the way they raised support for their position. They shared with their Jewish-Christian brothers and sisters how the Gentiles had come to faith in Jesus as Messiah. When they got to Jerusalem they gave the same report to the apostles and elders. Then the circumcision party presented their side of the matter. "The Gentiles must be circumcised and required to obey the law of Moses."

The apostles and elders met together to consider the issue. Peter recounted once again how the Gentiles, like Cornelius, heard the Gospel through his lips and came to faith in Jesus. Peter clearly took Paul and Barnabas' side: "We believe it is through the grace of our Lord Jesus that we are saved, just as they are."

Then James, the brother of Jesus, stood up and turned to Scripture for the answer to the problem. He quoted from Amos 9:11-12. Based upon Scripture, and the accounts of Paul, Barnabas and Peter, James came to the conclusion:

> It is my judgment, therefore, that we should not make it difficult for the Gentiles who are turning to God.

Then James went on to spell out what ethical instruction should be given to the Gentile converts. The rest of the apostles and elders obviously agreed with James' advice because they sent a letter to the Gentile believers in Asia Minor laying out their position. And they sent Judas and Silas along with the letter to confirm their teaching on this matter by word of mouth.

What can we learn from this event about how to handle problems in our own time? When we have problems in the Church that can't be settled in an individual congregation we should appeal for help from other Christian brothers. We should take into account the experience of other Christians. But ultimately we should look to the Word of God for solutions to our problems.

In 1979 Verna Bowman of Telford, Pennsylvania, gave birth to her fourth child, Geoff, and quickly learned from doctors the frightening news: the baby had defective kidneys. Writing in *Guideposts*, she later told how the doctors ordered the child rushed to a children's hospital in Philadelphia, where he would receive dialysis.

Still hospitalized herself, Verna prayed and prayed for her son, and as she did so she soon felt God's presence with her. The words of John 11:4 started to reverberate in her mind: "This sickness is not unto death, but for the glory of God." She wrote the words down.

Later, Verna's husband called to report on Geoff's condition: "It's too soon to tell if he is going to make it."

"He's going to make it," Verna replied, and she read him the verse she believed the Lord had given to her. "I believe those words," she said.

"So do I, Verna," replied her husband. "So do I."

After three months of dialysis, Geoff's kidneys, though still defective, began to function on their own. Throughout his childhood Geoff took medication, but still he tired easily.

Throughout Geoff's childhood Verna collected in her journal other Scriptures she felt God was giving her to assure her that her son would be alright.

When Geoff was thirteen years old, the doctors reported that he would need a kidney transplant. Though this news was unsettling at first, it also turned out to be an answer to Verna's prayers. Verna herself provided the kidney, and the operation was a complete success. Geoff was able to live a normal life from that point on.

Later, Verna's daughter suggested they do something with the Scriptures which had meant so much to them during Geoff's long illness. Verna often made quilts and her daughter was skilled at cross-stitch, so they decided to make a quilt which displayed twelve of the cherished promises God had given to them from the Scriptures. Each Scripture was stitched on to white linen and bordered in a pattern of hunter green and burgundy. Three months later the quilt was finished and hung on the wall in their guest room. Friends admired it and so eventually the quilt was hung, for a time, in their church, and eventually for a period in other churches as well.

God's promises are often like a comforting quilt on a cold wintry night, they ward off soul-chilling fear. When we have problems and questions, the Word of God is the best place to turn for answers.

The second problem we read about in Acts 15 occurred when Paul and Barnabas decided to go on a second missionary journey together. Here we have the problem of *differing opinions* in the Church. Barnabas wanted to take his cousin John Mark along with them on the journey. Paul did not think it wise to take him because John Mark had deserted them on their first missionary journey.

Who was right in this situation? That is hard to say. From a distant vantage point one can see both points of view. Barnabas wanted to give his cousin a second chance. Paul didn't want to potentially sacrifice the success of their mission and the lives that could be won to Christ. This difference of opinion led to an impasse. Maybe if Barnabas had appealed to Scriptural precedence for a second chance, like the second chance that God gave Jonah to go to Ninevah, maybe Paul would have been won over. Or maybe if they had discussed the matter with others in the Church at Antioch Paul's heart could have been softened, or Barnabas could have compromised. But the only solution Paul and Barnabas came up with was to part company. Barnabas took Mark and sailed for his home country of Cyprus once again. Paul chose Silas and left, with the commendation of the Church in Antioch, for Syria and Cilicia.

What we need to see hear is that even when we face the problem of division in the Church, God can use those divisions to bring about his own good purposes. We shouldn't use this fact as an excuse to pursue divisiveness. Division is almost always the result of sin on someone's part. Jesus prayed for unity among his disciples and we need to pray for and aggressively pursue such unity. But when we can't see our way forward together—God can even use our divisions.

How did God use division in the case of Barnabas and Paul? Well, it was better for Paul and Barnabas to part peaceably rather than stay together and fight. And God used this division to reach more people with the Gospel. Instead of just one missionary team going out, two were sent. One to Cyprus, the other to Asia Minor and eventually to the European continent.

Within some twelve years, Paul had reconsidered his attitude toward John Mark. When Paul wrote to the Colossians and Philemon Mark was obviously with him for Paul sent greetings to the Colossians and Philemon *from* Mark. And he told the Colossians: "You have received instructions about him; if he comes to you, welcome him" (Colossians 4:10). Perhaps as much as five years later, when Paul was languishing in a dungeon in Rome, he wrote to his protégé Timothy and said: "Get Mark and bring him with you, because he is helpful to me in my ministry" (2 Timothy 4:11). This same John Mark became an associate of the Apostle Peter and was, most likely, the author of the second Gospel. There are times in our lives when we need to look back on previous problems and seek reconciliation and forgiveness just like Paul did.

Former president George Bush, Sr., was a Navy pilot during World War II. On one mission, after being hit by Japanese gunfire, Bush had to bail out of his burning torpedo bomber. The bail out did not go smoothly. As he jumped out of the plane he smashed his head against something, cutting and bruising himself badly, and partially tearing his parachute. Bush plummeted swiftly to the earth and might have been killed if he had not landed in the ocean.

George H. W. Bush received a Distinguished Flying Cross for his ordeal, but before he left the Navy he made a promise that he would jump out of an airplane again and get it right the next time. It took five decades and a term as President of the United States before he got around to it, but on March 25, 1997, George H. W. Bush, age 72, jumped from a plane at 12,500 feet above an army testing base in the desert of Arizona. With him were several professional jumpers from the Parachute Industry Association and the Army's Golden Knights demonstration team. The former president and his companions sailed without any glitches to the ground, and Mr. Bush made a feather-soft landing just forty yards away from the target X.

"It was wonderful," he told onlookers enthusiastically. "I'm a new man. I go home exhilarated."

It took fifty years, but in what had been termed "Operation Second Look" George Bush closed the book on a bad memory.

Bringing closure to past problems takes many forms. Sometimes it means asking for forgiveness which is long overdue, or fulfilling a promise, or finally taking on a frightening physical or spiritual challenge. Sometimes bringing closure to past problems means handling unfinished business with God. It is usually difficult, as I'm sure it was for Paul to change his mind and seek reconciliation with John Mark, but sometimes to be right with God and others such steps are absolutely essential.

Whatever closure we need on the problems of the past, God can help us with our own "Operation Second Look". And if we are facing problems in the present for which we have no solution, we can turn to The Good Book that has the ultimate answers to the greatest problems of life.

MENTORING

The Christmas after my father died my brother gave me a book entitled *Tuesdays with Morrie*. It is the true story of a sports writer, Mitch Albom, and his reunion with his former college professor who is dying of ALS. Albom is a multitasking workaholic, whose life is a series of hurried appointments, rushed phone calls, and last minute sprints to catch a flight. When he discovers that his former college professor and friend, Morrie Schwartz, is in the last stages of ALS, he honors a long-overdue promise to visit.

During these visits, Morrie teaches Mitch some important lessons about what matters most in life. On one particular visit, Morrie is very frail, lying in a recliner in obvious pain. He asks Mitch to rub his aching feet with salve. "When we're infants," says Morrie, "we need people to survive; when we're dying, we need people to survive; but here's the secret: in between, we need each other even more."

Mitch nods and responds with a quote that he has heard Morrie say many times: "We must love one another or die."

Morrie loses patience with Mitch. "Yeah, but do you believe that? Does it apply to you?"

Mitch is stunned and defensive as he confesses that he doesn't know what he believes. The world he lives in doesn't allow for the contemplation of spiritual things.

Morrie pushes a little further. "You hate that word, don't you—*spiritual*? You think it's just touchy-feely stuff, huh?"

"I just don't understand it," says Mitch.

"We must love one another or die," says Morrie. "It's a very simple lesson, Mitch."

It is a simple lesson, isn't it? But it is also so hard to learn it well. I think the essential lesson of life is that we will all die apart from the love of Jesus Christ. But if we discover that love and share it with others we can live forever.

The latter part of that equation is what I want to talk with you about in this chapter–sharing the love of Jesus Christ with others–and doing that in a very specific way. That way is often called *mentoring*. The word has its origin in ancient Greece and comes from the name of Odysseus' friend who was entrusted with the education of Odysseus' son Telemachus. The word itself can simply mean *enduring*. Thus one definition of mentoring is "a sustained relationship between a youth and an adult". Through continued involvement, the adult offers support, guidance, and assistance as the younger person goes through a difficult period, faces new challenges, or works to correct earlier problems.

There is natural mentoring and planned mentoring. Natural mentoring occurs through friendship, collegiality, teaching, coaching and counseling. By contrast, planned mentoring occurs through structured programs in which mentors and participants are selected and matched through formal processes. What I want to challenge you to consider doing is to enter into a mentoring relationship with another person.

Why would you want to be a mentor or seek out a mentor? Because, as Morrie says, we must love one another or die. And mentoring, I believe, is a biblical concept. It is a relationship which God is very much interested in. Biblically speaking, there are three different roles we might possibly play in a mentoring relationship.

PAUL

The first possibility is that God might want us to play the role of a Paul in someone else's life.

What do you think of when you think of the Apostle Paul? We often think of Paul as the great preacher and missionary who spread the Gospel across the Roman Empire. From the very moment of his dramatic conversion Paul was a preacher. (See Acts 9:20.) And Paul was such a firebrand, such a take-it-or-leave-it kind of guy that in one place the book of Acts tells us that the churches had more peace after Paul left the scene! (See Acts 9:31.)

Thus we often think of Paul as the great herald of the Good News of Jesus Christ. Less often do we think of Paul as one of the greatest mentors of all time. However, three of the New Testament letters which bear Paul's name are addressed to two of the most significant people whom he mentored: Timothy and Titus.

For the purpose of this chapter I want to focus on Paul's relationship with Timothy. Paul apparently met Timothy for the first time on his second missionary journey through Asia Minor. In Acts 16:1-5 we read:

> He came to Derbe and then to Lystra, where a disciple named Timothy lived, whose mother was a Jewess and a believer, but whose father was a Greek. The brothers at Lystra and Iconium spoke well of him. Paul wanted to take him along on the journey, so he circumcised him because of the Jews who lived in that area, for they all knew that his father was a Greek. As they traveled from town to town, they

delivered the decisions reached by the apostles and elders in Jerusalem for the people to obey. So the churches were strengthened in the faith and grew daily in numbers.

There are at least two interesting things we can learn from these brief verses. First of all, for some reason Paul was drawn to Timothy. Luke doesn't tell us exactly why, but Paul was drawn by the testimony of the believers in Lystra to want to take young Timothy along with him on his mission. This goes to show that mentoring relationships are, quite often, initiated by the "Pauls" in life.

The second thing we learn from these brief verses is that Timothy "owned" this mentoring relationship. Why else would he have submitted to circumcision as an adult? He wanted to be able to join the Apostle Paul in his work. Paul had fought for the fact that Gentiles did not need to be circumcised to become followers of Jesus. But Timothy had a Jewish mother. So, out of a desire to win Jews to Jesus, Paul had Timothy circumcised. Paul could fight valiantly for points of principle. But when it came to winning others to Christ, he was willing to become all things to all people that by all means he might win some. Apparently Timothy had the same desire.

Perhaps Timothy had been around during Paul's first visit to Lystra when Paul was stoned and left for dead outside the city. It was on that occasion that Paul got up and walked right back into the city where the Jews lived who had tried to kill him. Timid Timothy must have been inspired by the courage of the Apostle Paul to want to follow him in his ministry. Thus there was a mutual drawing together which happened in their relationship, and which happens in every good mentoring relationship.

A very deep relationship indeed was formed between Paul and Timothy. Paul later says of his young protégé,

> I have no one else like him, who takes a genuine interest in your welfare. For everyone looks out for his own interests, not those of Jesus Christ. But you know that Timothy has proved himself, because as a son with his father he has served with me in the work of the Gospel. (Philippians 2:20-22)

One of the most personal letters of the New Testament is Paul's second letter to Timothy. Toward the end of the letter Paul pleads with his son in the faith, from the darkness of a dingy Roman dungeon: "Do your best to come to me quickly."

Perhaps Paul and Timothy's relationship was similar in some ways to the relationship between a much later mentoring pair: Helen Keller and her teacher, Anne Sullivan. On the advice of Dr. Alexander Graham Bell, the parents of Helen Keller sent for a teacher from the Perkins Institution for the Blind in Boston, Massachusetts. Anne Sullivan, a 19 year old orphan, was chosen for the task of instructing 6 year old Helen. It was the beginning of a close and lifelong friendship between them. By means of a manual alphabet, Anne "spelled" into Helen's hand such words as *doll* or *puppy*. Two years later Helen was reading and writing Braille fluently. At 10 Helen learned different sounds by placing her fingers on her teacher's larynx and "hearing" the vibrations. Later Helen went to Radcliffe College where Anne spelled the lectures into Helen's hand. After graduating with honors, Helen decided to devote her life to helping the blind and deaf. As part of that endeavor, she wrote many books and articles and traveled around the world making speeches. Since Helen's speeches were not intelligible to some, Anne often translated them for her. Their nearly fifty years of companionship ended when Anne died in 1936. Helen wrote these endearing words about her lifelong mentor:

> My teacher is so near to me that I scarcely think of myself apart from her. I feel that her being is inseparable from my own, and that the footsteps of my life are in hers. All the best of me belongs to her—there is not a talent or an inspiration or a joy in me that has not been awakened by her loving touch.

The best of mentoring relationships can be very much like the relationship Anne had with Helen, or like that which Paul had with Timothy.

BARNABAS

However, there is another role that we can play in mentoring which is often overlooked. It is the role of Barnabas. Joseph was his real name. Barnabas was his nickname. He was given that nickname because Barnabas means "son of encouragement".

Barnabas was drawn to people he could encourage. Barnabas was one of the first to sell his possessions to help the poorer Christians of Jerusalem. (See Acts 4:36-37.) When Paul arrived in Jerusalem for the first time following his conversion, the local Christians were understandably reluctant to welcome him. After all, Paul had sought to kill Christians prior to his own conversion. Consequently, no one trusted his story. Only Barnabas proved willing to risk his life to meet with Paul and then convince the others that their former enemy was now a vibrant believer in Jesus. What would have happened if Barnabas had not encouraged Paul and introduced him to the apostles in Jerusalem? (See Acts 9:27.) Christianity may never have spread throughout the Roman Empire as it did or become a worldwide movement.

Barnabas was also an encourager to the Church in Antioch. He brought Paul to that Church to be a teacher there. (See Acts 11:23-26.) It was Barnabas who encouraged John Mark to accompany Paul and himself on their first missionary journey. However, in the middle of the trip, Mark deserted them. In spite of this, Barnabas later wanted to invite Mark to join himself and Paul on their second journey. He wanted to give his cousin a second chance. But Paul saw things differently. He did not want to take a chance on Mark. As a result, Paul and Barnabas went their separate ways. However, Barnabas' patient encouragement was confirmed by Mark's eventual effective ministry. So much so that Paul could even write at the end of his own life: "Get Mark and bring him with you, because he is helpful to me in my ministry." If it weren't for Barnabas' sustained encouragement of Mark we might not have the Gospel of Mark in the New Testament, or the Gospels of Matthew and Luke which were based, in part, on this earliest Gospel.

Thanks be to God, there are many "Barnabases" in the Church of Jesus Christ. Dr. Larry Crabb recalls an incident in the church he attended as a young man. It was customary in this church that young men were encouraged to participate in the communion services by praying out loud. Feeling the pressure of expectation, young Larry (who had a problem with stuttering) stood to pray. In a terribly confused prayer, he later recalled "thanking the Father for hanging on the cross and praising Christ for triumphantly bringing the Spirit from the grave." When Larry finished, he vowed he would never again speak or pray out loud in front of a group.

At the end of the service, not wanting to meet any of the church elders who might feel compelled to correct his theology, Larry made a beeline for the door. But before he could exit the building, an older man named Jim Dunbar caught him by the sleeve.

Having prepared himself for the anticipated correction, Larry was surprised to hear these words: "Larry, there's one thing I want you to know. Whatever you do for the Lord, I'm behind you one thousand percent."

Larry Crabb later reflected in one of his books: "Even as I write these words, my eyes fill with tears. I have yet to tell that story to an audience without at least mildly choking. Those words were life words. They had power. They reached deep into my being."

That's the power of the encourager, the one who comes alongside, the Barnabas.

TIMOTHY

A third role God might call us to play in a mentoring relationship is the role of Timothy.

Painful lessons are usually doorways to new opportunities. Even the Apostle Paul had much to learn. Shortly after his disappointing experience with John Mark, Paul recruited another eager young man, Timothy, to be his assistant. Paul's intense personality may have been too much for John Mark to handle. It could easily have created the same problem for Timothy. But Paul seems to have learned a lesson in patience from his old friend Barnabas. As a result, Timothy became like a son to Paul.

Timothy already had solid Jewish training in the Scriptures from his mother and grandmother. However, Timothy seemed to struggle with a naturally timid character and sensitivity to youthfulness. That is why the Apostle Paul later wrote to him, "For God did not give us a spirit of timidity, but a spirit of power, of love and of self-discipline." (2 Timothy 1:7) And Paul also wrote to him, "Don't let anyone look down on you because you are young, but set an example for the believers in speech, in life, in love, in faith and in purity." (1 Timothy 4:12)

Unfortunately, many who share Timothy's character traits are quickly written off as too great a risk to deserve much leadership responsibility. By God's grace, Paul saw great potential in Timothy. Paul was not deterred by Timothy's youthfulness and timidity, but instead demonstrated his confidence in Timothy by entrusting him with important responsibilities. Paul sent Timothy as his personal representative to Corinth during a particularly tense time. (See 1 Corinthians 4:14-17.) Later, Paul left Timothy in charge of the young Church in Ephesus, a church growing up in the midst of rampant pagan worship.

Perhaps you may feel like Timothy. You may long to have a more spiritually mature mentor in the Lord but you wonder if God could ever use you. The answer is: God can and God will use you if you allow God to have his way with you. If you are a Timothy, then the Lord wants you to seek out a Paul as a mentor so that one day you can be a Paul to someone else.

Paul wrote to Timothy at the end of his life:

> You then, my son, be strong in the grace that is in Christ Jesus. And the things you have heard me say in the presence of many witnesses entrust to reliable men who will also be qualified to teach others. (2 Timothy 2:1-2)

Paul was passing the spiritual baton to Timothy, asking him to multiply the ministry by mentoring others as he had been mentored. Such mentoring is a vital activity which can be practiced in many different settings.

Mr. Holland's Opus is a movie about a frustrated composer in Portland, Oregon, who takes a job as a high school band teacher in the 1960s. Although diverted from his lifelong goal of achieving critical fame as a classical musician, Glenn Holland (played by Richard Dreyfuss) believes his school job is only temporary.

At first he maintains his determination to write an opus or a concerto by composing at his piano after putting in a full day with his students. However, as family demands increase (including the discovery that his infant son is deaf) and the pressures of his job multiply, Mr. Holland recognizes that his dream of leaving a lasting musical legacy is merely a dream.

At the end of the movie we find an aged Mr. Holland fighting in vain to keep his job. The board has decided to reduce the operating budget by cutting the music and drama program. No longer a reluctant band teacher, Mr. Holland believes in what he does and passionately defends the role of the arts in public education. What began as a career detour became a thirty-five year mission, pouring his heart and soul into the lives of young people.

Mr. Holland returns to his classroom to retrieve his belongings a few days after school has let out for summer vacation. He has taught his final class. With regret and sorrow he fills a box with artifacts which represent the tools of his trade and memories of many meaningful classes. His wife and son arrive to lend him a hand.

As they leave the room and walk down the hall, Mr. Holland hears some noise in the auditorium. Because school is out, he opens the door to see what the commotion is. To his amazement he sees a capacity audience of former students and teaching colleagues and a banner which reads: "Goodbye Mr. Holland". Those in attendance greet Mr. Holland with a standing ovation while a band (consisting of past and present members) plays songs they learned under his direction.

The governor of Oregon arrives, who is none other than a former student Mr. Holland helped to believe in herself during his first year of teaching. As she addresses the room of well-wishers, she speaks for hundreds who fill the auditorium:

> Mr. Holland had a profound influence in my life (on a lot of lives, I know), and yet I get the feeling that he considers a great part of his life misspent. Rumor had it he was always working on this symphony of his, and this was going to make him famous and rich (probably both). But Mr. Holland isn't rich and he isn't famous—at least not outside our little town. So it might be easy for him to think himself a failure . . . but he'd be wrong. Because I think he's achieved a success far beyond riches and fame.

Looking at her former teacher the governor gestures with a sweeping hand and continues:

> Look around you. There is not a life in this room that you have not touched, and each one of us is a better person because of you. We are your symphony, Mr. Holland. We are the melodies and the notes of your opus. And we are the music of your life.

Meditations on the Acts of the Apostles

I wonder: Who are the notes of your opus? Who is the music of your life? You can make a difference by God's grace for Christ's Kingdom by being a Paul, a Barnabas or a Timothy. Which role will you take up with joy today?

PROVIDENCE

When Andy Griffith, star of the classic television series bearing his name, entered his fifties, he found it increasingly difficult to find work in Hollywood, and his personal finances became tighter and tighter. Years later he wrote about this experience in *Guideposts* magazine.

Andy and his wife Cindi finally decided life would be easier if they moved from Los Angeles back to Andy's home state of North Carolina; so they put their home up for sale and waited for a buyer. Unfortunately, the real estate market was in a slump, and no one gave the Griffiths a decent offer on their house. Months passed and Andy slipped into depression.

Then one day Cindi had this insight: "Maybe it's a good thing we couldn't sell the house. Maybe it was God showing us grace. If we moved to North Carolina now, you might indeed never work again. What we need to do is stay here and stoke the fire."

So that is exactly what they did. Every day Andy and Cindi went together to the office of Andy's agent. They sat in the lobby, talked with various people in the agency and went with them to lunch. Eventually the plan paid off; work started to come in: four TV movies that year, including a pilot for *Matlock*, a TV show that ended up running for nine years straight.

Sometimes a closed door is a signpost from God. Perhaps your closed door is a sign that God has a better way for you to go.

Such was the case for the Apostle Paul. We read about some of Paul's closed doors in Acts 16:6-10. . . .

> Paul and his companions traveled throughout the region of Phrygia and Galatia, having been kept by the Holy Spirit from preaching the word in the province of Asia. When they came to the border of Mysia, they tried to enter Bithynia, but the Spirit of Jesus would not allow them to. So they passed by Mysia and went down to Troas. During the night Paul had a vision of a man of Macedonia standing and begging him, "Come over to Macedonia and help us." After Paul had seen the vision, we got ready at once to leave for Macedonia, concluding that God had called us to preach the Gospel to them.

We learn from this passage that one of the keys to growth in the life of the individual Christian and in the life of the Church as a whole is learning to trust in God's providential guidance. And one of the ways God guides us is through closed doors. Here was Paul returning to the churches in Derbe, Lystra, Iconium and Pisidian Antioch where he had first preached the Gospel some years before. He had gone back to these churches along with his helper Silas, and now with his protégé Timothy in tow. Paul's purpose was to see how the churches were getting along and to encourage them in their growth.

But when Paul came to the end of this tour he must have felt a nudge from the Holy Spirit to go further, to venture beyond Pisidian Antioch in preaching the Gospel of Jesus Christ. We are not told specifically at this point what motivated Paul and his companions to venture west of Pisidian Antioch. Perhaps Paul had it in mind to travel to some of the major cities of the Roman Empire, like Ephesus on the coast of Asia Minor. Ephesus was in the province known as Asia.

At this point we read something curious. We are told that Paul was kept by the Holy Spirit from preaching the word in the province of Asia. He was kept from venturing into that physical territory where there would eventually be planted the seven churches mentioned in the book of Revelation. So prevented from traveling south, Paul tried to go north into the region of Bithynia, a route which would eventually have led him to Byzantium, the town which would later be renamed Constantinople, and renamed again–Istanbul. But again, "when they tried to enter Bithynia, the Spirit of Jesus would not allow them to."

What exactly prevented Paul and his companions, first, from going into the province of Asia and then from going into Bithynia? Some have suggested that since Silas had the gift of prophecy perhaps he had a word from the Lord which led Paul to avoid these regions. But the text mentions nothing of any prophecy.

One of the interesting things about this text is that it is the first of a number of "we" passages in Acts. In other words, someone joins Paul's traveling band in Troas, as recorded in Acts 16:10, and narrates some of the events of Paul's missionary travels as an eyewitness. By a process of elimination scholars have concluded that the person behind the "we" passages of Acts was none other than a man named Luke whom Paul mentions in Colossians 4:14 as being a physician.

Why does Luke suddenly emerge, behind the scenes, in Acts 16:10? Perhaps the reason is that Paul was struggling with his "thorn in the flesh" which some commentators have taken to be a case of poor eye-sight. And so, perhaps, Paul sought out the services of a doctor in Troas–and that doctor was Luke. Perhaps it was this severe problem with his eye-sight, or some other case of ill health, which barred Paul from traveling into the provinces of Asia and Bithynia. As William Barclay has written, "If this is so it is a great thought to think that Paul took even his weakness and his pain as a messenger from God." God often guides us by using closed doors in life, whether those doors are closed by ill health or some other immediate cause.

God has used closed doors in my life to guide me on a number of occasions. Some years ago it became evident, through a series of circumstances, that I needed to take an extended sabbatical from pastoral ministry. But what did God want me and our family to do instead? It was at this time that my friend Douglas Gresham, step-son of C. S. Lewis, gave me a helpful piece of advice. He said, "Pray that God will close all the doors he does not want you to go through, and open the one door he does want you to use. But while you are checking out different doors, make sure that you give the ones that are closed a good kick, just to make sure they are really closed by God!"

So that is what we did. We tried a number of different doors to see what God wanted us to do and discover where he wanted us to go. Finally, my wife Becky said to me one day, "What I would really like to do is go to Ireland and work with Doug and Merrie Gresham in their ministry." At that time the Greshams ran a ministry of hospitality and counseling out of their 12-bedroom house in County Carlow, Ireland. Following Becky's suggestion I e-mailed my friend Doug and asked him if they could use some help at Rathvinden House, the name of their home and ministry. He said "yes" and so we went off to Ireland as a family, planning to spend a year there, all because God opened that one door and closed all others.

In going to Ireland I should have been mindful of the verse in James 4:13-16 which says,

> Now listen, you who say, "Today or tomorrow we will go to this or that city, spend a year there, carry on business and make money." Why, you do not even know what will happen tomorrow. What is your life? You are a mist that appears for a little while and then vanishes. Instead, you ought to say, "If it is the Lord's will, we will live and do this or that." As it is, you boast and brag. All such boasting is evil.

We thought we were going to spend at least a year in Ireland, but God had other plans. After spending eight months in Ireland we were feeling a little bit homesick and we had used up a good bit of our financial resources. We wondered if God wanted us to stay in Ireland and perhaps plant a church there, or maybe he wanted us to return home to the United States. Again we prayed that God would open the one door he wanted us to go through and close all others. We soon found that we could not obtain a work visa to remain in Ireland past our year as guests of the Greshams. So we began to look at airfares to return home. (When we went to Ireland we went there on a one-way ticket. Something most missionaries never do!) When looking at airfares we found one day in the coming six months when we could fly at half the normal fare. It happened to be on December 21, just four days before Christmas. We were astonished. Even the airline could not tell us why they had that fare from Shannon Airport to Washington-Dulles on that particular day. But we didn't ask any more questions. With Doug and Merrie's blessing we bought our five tickets for a total of just one thousand dollars and we returned to the United States.

We decided to settle in Monterey, Virginia because we wanted to be near my family. My brother was leading a youth camp in Head Waters, Virginia at that time and he happened to be renting a house for staff people in Monterey, but he had no one occupying it. After looking at the house we concluded it was perfect for us and we moved in. Two weeks later my brother was diagnosed with cancer and five months later he went home to be with the Lord.

We never could have known what lay in the future as we were praying in Ireland about where God wanted us to be and to serve him. But once again God guided us through closing doors and opening the one he wanted us to go through. I believe he guided us to Virginia at that time, in part, so that we could be of comfort and encouragement to my family through a time of great trial.

So, God guides us by using closed doors and often opening just the one door he wants us to step through. But what happened to Paul and his companions after they arrived in Troas and met Dr. Luke? At that time God guided Paul in a different way, he guided Paul through a *vision*. During the night Paul had a vision of a man of Macedonia, that is a man from northern Greece, standing and begging Paul to come over to Macedonia and help them.

Who was this man of Macedonia in Paul's vision? Some have thought it was a vision of Alexander the Great. The full name of Troas was Alexandrian Troas. Philippi was named after Alexander's father. Alexander was the man whose vision was to marry the east to the west and so make one world. Paul wanted to make one world for Christ, marrying Asia in the east to Europe in the west.

Others have thought the man of Macedonia was Luke himself who may have been from that region. Others think the man of Macedonia in Paul's vision was the Philippian jailer whom Paul eventually led to faith in Christ. No one knows for certain who the man of Macedonia was because the text doesn't tell us.

What is certain is that God led Paul through a vision. And when Paul shared the contents of the vision with his companions they all concluded together that God was calling them to preach the Gospel in Macedonia.

Does God lead people through visions today? I think sometimes he does. It is important that we always subject our visions and supposed "words from the Lord" to the judgment of Scripture. God will never lead us to do something through a vision or prophecy which is contrary to his revelation in the Bible. Paul felt compelled by the love of Jesus Christ to share the good news of Christ with others (2 Corinthians 5:14). Paul's life and service were shaped by the revelation of God's Word in Jesus. As long as a vision is in line with the love of Christ revealed in Scripture, I think we can trust it.

I believe that God guides us providentially in many ways today, just as he guided Paul in many ways 2,000 years ago. He guides us primarily through his word in Scripture, the Bible. We need to soak ourselves in God's written revelation. This does not mean that we can just arbitrarily pick some passage of Scripture and expect that God will guide us through a single verse or passage in some magical way.

I'm sure you have all heard the story of the man who was following this "lucky dip" method of applying Scripture to his life. The man was contemplating an important decision and so he turned to Scripture for guidance. With his eyes closed, he opened the Bible and put his finger on a verse. The verse was about Judas and said, "Then he went away and hanged himself." Not liking that verse too much, the man closed his eyes, opened the Bible again and put his finger on another verse. That verse said, "What you are about to do, do quickly."

It should be evident from this example that we shouldn't use the Bible in this way! But when we soak ourselves in the overall message of Scripture, God will indeed use it to guide us in the small and large decisions of our lives.

God also guides us through circumstances, as we have seen in the case of Paul traveling through Asia Minor. God guides us through the wisdom of trusted and experienced Christian friends and counselors. God guides us through the gifts which he gives us that he wants us to use for his kingdom, and the desires he plants in our hearts to serve him.

In his book, *Take Another Look at Guidance*, Bob Mumford summarizes the ways God guides us by telling a story.

There was a certain harbor in Italy which could only be reached by sailing up a narrow channel between dangerous rocks and shoals. Over the years, many ships were wrecked on the rocks, and it became well-known that navigation into that Italian harbor was hazardous.

So to guide ships safely into port, three lights were mounted by the harbor master on three huge poles in the harbor. When the three lights were perfectly lined up and seen as one, a ship could safely proceed up the narrow channel. If the pilot saw two or three lights, he would know he was off course and in danger.

God has also provided basically three beacons to guide us. The same rules of navigation apply–the three lights must be lined up before it is safe for us to proceed. The three major harbor lights of God's guidance are:

- The Word of God (objective standard)
- The Holy Spirit (subjective witness)
- Circumstances (divine providence)

Together these three harbor lights assure us that the directions we've received are from God and will lead us safely along his way.

Learning to trust God's providential guidance through his Word, his Spirit and through everyday circumstances is one of the keys to growth in the life of the individual Christian and in the life of the Church.

WOMEN

In the mid 1960s the Reverend David Yonggi Cho was leading a church of some three thousand people in Seoul, South Korea. With the continued growth of the church, Pastor Cho was also required to lead the baptismal services even more often. One day, as he was baptizing several hundred people, he succumbed to overwork and exhaustion, and collapsed to the floor. As he was recovering in the hospital, a doctor recommended Pastor Cho change his profession. Brushing aside the doctor's advice, Pastor Cho discharged himself from the hospital to deliver the Sunday messages.

As he went forward to the pulpit, however, he dropped unconscious to the floor and was forced to return to the hospital once again. Then a wondrous thing happened as Pastor Cho began to read the Bible from his hospital bed. As he was reading in Exodus, a particular verse, Exodus 18:18 moved his heart. "You and these people who come to you will only wear yourselves out. The work is too heavy for you; you cannot handle it alone."

The next morning, Pastor Cho called a meeting with the elders and deacons to share with them the wisdom he had received from God through the Bible. This was the birth of small groups in Pastor Cho's church; they called them "cells". Although the elders and deacons realized the function and the necessity of the cell system, they were not yet trained to be able to implement the idea. Pastor Cho realized that there was a need for a training program for those who would become cell leaders. As Pastor Cho continued to search for solutions for the training of those who would be leaders, he learned another fact: that the men were reluctant to make home visits to other members. He realized that for this purpose, women were much more suited than the men. At the time, Korean society frowned upon women taking the role of leaders within groups containing both men and women. Even so, as the Holy Spirit moved the hearts of both women and men, such social obstacles were overcome and women played a critical role in the development and growth of the Yoido Full Gospel Church. The home visits by the cell leaders proved to be an effective method for drawing new members into the fold. And with the continued work of the Holy Spirit, these cells, and the cell system as a whole, worked effectively to promote fellowship between the members of the cells. In 1967, when the cell system was introduced, it consisted of 7,750 individuals of 2,267 families organized into 125 cells. Today Yoido Full Gospel Church has over one million members largely because of the cell groups led by the Christian women of Korea.

Throughout the two thousand year history of the Church of Jesus Christ, God has used women in a powerful way to grow the Church through the Holy Spirit. This insight was not lost on the chronicler of the growth of the apostolic church, Dr. Luke. Perhaps more than any other writer in the New Testament, Luke emphasizes the special role of women in God's plan for the Church.

William Barclay wrote in his introduction to Luke's Gospel: "In Palestine the place of women was low. In the Jewish morning prayer a man thanks God that he has not made him 'a gentile, a slave or a woman.' But Luke gives a very special place to women. The birth narrative is told from Mary's point of view. It is in Luke that we read of Elizabeth, of Anna, of the widow at Nain, of the woman who anointed Jesus' feet in the house of Simon the Pharisee. It is Luke who makes vivid the pictures of Martha and Mary and of Mary Magdalene. It is very likely that Luke was a native of Macedonia where women held a more emancipated position than anywhere else; and that may have something to do with it."

And so we come to Acts 16:11-15, Paul's entrance into Macedonia, and the story of the first Christian convert on the continent of Europe–a woman named Lydia....

> From Troas we put out to sea and sailed straight for Samothrace, and the next day on to Neapolis. From there we traveled to Philippi, a Roman colony and the leading city of that district of Macedonia. And we stayed there several days.
>
> On the Sabbath we went outside the city gate to the river, where we expected to find a place of prayer. We sat down and began to speak to the women who had gathered there. One of those listening was a woman named Lydia, a dealer in purple cloth from the city of Thyatira, who was a worshiper of God. The Lord opened her heart to respond to Paul's message. When she and the members of her household were baptized, she invited us to her home. "If you consider me a believer in the Lord," she said, "come and stay at my house." And she persuaded us.

In this brief passage Luke gives us *four characteristics of the woman God uses*. The first characteristic is that the woman God uses is a *worshiper of God*. The NIV says that Lydia was a worshiper of God, but in the Greek text the word is a verb: worship*ing*. After telling us that Lydia was from the city of Thyatira and a dealer in purple cloth, obviously a wealthy business woman, Luke tells us the most important thing about Lydia: she was worshiping God.

Now this phrase is a technical one which means that Lydia was believing and behaving like a Jew without actually becoming a full Jewish convert.

Paul was certainly hoping that there would be a synagogue in Philippi. It was his habit to preach the good news of Jesus Christ first in the synagogue, taking the message first to the Jews and then to the Gentiles. But there weren't even ten Jewish men in order to make up a synagogue in Philippi. I believe God was providentially circumventing Paul's normal missionary routine. Paul heard there was a place of prayer down by the river, outside the city gate, where a group of female followers of the Jewish faith gathered. So to that place of prayer Paul and his companions went. There they found this worshiper of God, Lydia, and several others.

The most important characteristic for a woman to have, in order to be used of God, is that she be worshiping God. The word in the Greek means to revere, to adore. That leads me to raise the question: Are you a worshiper of God? The Old English word for worship was "woerthshipe". This suggests that to worship God is to give him all he is worth. Do you worship God by giving him your life?

In his book *Imaginary Homelands* author Salman Rushdie writes of one of the family traditions of his home:

> In our house, whenever anyone dropped a book, it was required to be not only picked up but also kissed, by way of apology for the act of clumsy disrespect. I was as careless and butterfingered as any child, and accordingly I kissed a large number of books.
>
> Devout households in India still contain persons in the habit of kissing holy books. But we kissed everything. We kissed dictionaries and atlases. We kissed novels and Superman comics. If I'd ever dropped the telephone directory, I'd probably have kissed that too.

Is it any wonder that Salman Rushdie grew up to become an author? *What we worship defines us.* Lydia worshiped God and that worship defined her. To whatever or whomever you give your life, it will define you as well.

The second characteristic of the woman God uses is that she is a *listener*. Lydia listened to what Paul had to say about Jesus Christ. She gave Paul her undivided attention.

Have you ever been with someone who is a really good listener? A friend of our family, former United States Senator from Oregon, Mark Hatfield, is a good listener. When you are talking to him you feel like you are the most important person in the world to him. Other people may enter the room but his eyes stay focused on you.

My wife is a good listener like that. That's probably one reason why I married her. I like to talk. She likes to listen. It makes for a good match!

Meditations on the Acts of the Apostles

A few years ago I went to see a counselor because of some difficult things I was dealing with in my life at that time. This man was the greatest listener I have ever met. He listened so intensely I could feel him listening to me. By his listening, and asking deep questions, he drew things out of me I didn't even know were there.

The woman God uses is a good listener, not only to other people but to God.

In his book, *Directions*, James Hamilton writes:

> Before refrigerators, people used ice houses to preserve their food. Ice houses had thick walls, no windows, and a tightly fitted door. In winter, when streams and lakes were frozen, large blocks of ice were cut, hauled to the ice houses, and covered with sawdust. Often the ice would last well into the summer.
>
> One man lost a valuable watch while working in an ice house. He searched diligently for it, carefully raking through the sawdust, but didn't find it. His fellow workers also looked, but their efforts, too, proved futile. A small boy who heard about the fruitless search slipped into the ice house during the noon hour and soon emerged with the watch.
>
> Amazed, the men asked him how he found it.
>
> "I closed the door," the boy replied, "lay down in the sawdust, and kept very still. Soon I heard the watch ticking."

Often the question is not whether God is speaking, but whether we are being still enough, and quiet enough, to hear. The woman God uses has stillness, quietness in her life. Consequently she listens well to God and to other people.

A third characteristic of the woman God uses is that she has *an open heart*. We read that the Lord opened Lydia's heart to receive what Paul was saying about Jesus.

The heart represents not only the feelings but the thoughts of a person. The heart is the core of who we are as human beings. And the word in the Greek for "open" means to open *thoroughly*. God thoroughly opened Lydia's heart to the good news about Jesus Christ. And it is only God who can do such a work.

Someone whose heart is open to God is willing to invest time exploring his word in the Bible, like our friend Jennifer whom I mentioned in an earlier chapter. Someone whose heart is open to God is a great question-asker, a great learner, they are hungry to know more. Someone whose heart is open to God doesn't have to be pushed into the kingdom. When the fruit is ripe it falls off the tree. *Is your heart open to God?*

A fourth characteristic of the woman God uses is that she has *an open home*. After Lydia and her household were baptized she urged Paul and his companions: "If you consider me a believer in the Lord, come and stay at my house." And she persuaded them. I get the idea that Lydia was a woman who drove a hard bargain!

Homes were essential to the spread of the good news of Jesus Christ in the first century. The Church did not have its own buildings to meet in so it was incumbent upon the members of the various congregations in cities throughout the Roman Empire to open their homes for meetings of the Church for worship and other purposes.

Remember back in Acts 2:46 how the first believers in Jerusalem "broke bread in their homes and ate together with glad and sincere hearts"? The only way over three thousand new believers in Jerusalem could get to know each other was by meeting in small groups in one another's homes.

When Paul later wrote to the Church at Rome he said:

> Greet Priscilla and Aquila, my fellow workers in Christ Jesus. They risked their lives for me. Not only I but all the churches of the Gentiles are grateful to them. *Greet also the church that meets at their house* (Romans 16:3-5).

Hospitality was so essential to the growth of the Early Church that Paul made it a requirement for elders (1 Timothy 3:2; Titus 1:8). In Romans 12:13 Paul tells *all* Christians to "practice hospitality". And 1 Peter 4:9 says: "Offer hospitality to one another without grumbling."

Lydia's example goes to show us that an open heart leads to an open home. And as William Barclay has said, "A Christian home is a home with an ever-open door."

My wife is a wonderful woman of hospitality. She opens the door of our home sometimes when I would rather keep it closed. You see, I'm one of those people who gets concerned about whether the boys' rooms and the bathrooms are clean. What if people see the layer of dust on the tables in our house? Becky doesn't worry about those things, or what we have in the refrigerator, she just invites people over and makes them feel welcome. She is so good at it that people at her workplace often have her plan the parties. For a while she made every Friday "Pizza Day" at work. When she was going to be away from work one Friday one of her co-workers asked: "What do we do?" Becky said, "You call up and order the pizza!"

Years ago Becky discovered a wonderful book about hospitality which she has shared through classes with countless women in the various churches we have served. The book is entitled *Open Heart, Open Home* by Karen Burton Mains. In that book Mains makes the important distinction between hospitality and entertaining:

Entertaining says, "I want to impress you with my beautiful home, my clever decorating, my gourmet cooking." Hospitality, however, seeks to minister. It says, "This home is not mine. It is truly a gift from my Master. I am His servant and I use it as he desires." Hospitality does not try to impress, but to *serve*.

Entertaining always puts things before people. "As soon as I get the house finished, the living room decorated, my place settings complete, my housework done–then I will start having people in." "The So-and-so's are coming. I must buy that new such-and-such before they come." Hospitality, however, puts people before things. "We have no furniture; we'll eat on the floor." "The decorating may never get done. Please come just the same." "The house is a mess–but these people are friends. We never get to see them. Let's have this time together anyway."

We've literally done that "eating on the floor" thing too, and have the pictures to prove it! We learned even more about hospitality from the eight months we spent in Ireland with Doug and Merrie Gresham at their home, Rathvinden House. Doug and Merrie made a commitment to the Lord when they moved into their twelve bedroom Irish country house that they would welcome into their home whomever God sent to them. And so God began to send to them all sorts of people in need–people in need of counseling, full-time ministers in need of a holiday, non-Christians in need of a personal introduction to Jesus Christ. Doug and Merrie flung their doors wide open to one and all. During the eight months that we lived on the property of Rathvinden their home was seldom without visitors–some from as far away as America or even Australia. Some would drop in for a meal. Others would stay overnight. Some were there for weeks at a time. On countless occasions I would see Merrie stop what she was doing and make a cup of tea for someone who had just dropped in. And the cup of tea would usually lead to Merrie having an opportunity to share the Gospel or some bit of spiritual encouragement with her visitor. Doug showed hospitality in other ways. He developed the habit, following his mentor and step-father C. S. Lewis, of responding to each bit of correspondence he received by return of post. With the advent of the Internet and e-mail this meant a huge job for Doug. But I saw him do it day in and day out. His schedule was regularly "interrupted" by the commitment to respond to some spiritual inquirer who had just written to him. But Doug looked at those interruptions as part of his daily ministry.

What about you? Has your heart been opened to the Lord? And if so, is your home open to others? Would you dare to make the commitment to God which Doug and Merrie made, of opening your home to whomever God might send to you? Will you practice hospitality in the context of your local church for starters? How about inviting someone from church into your home for a meal or dessert, just to get to know them better. Remember it's not about entertaining—it's not about things—it's about people and loving them.

You may say, "But nobody else in my church is doing it." Then why don't you get the wheels of hospitality rolling in your church? The result may go far beyond what you might imagine. For as Karen Mains has written:

> I am firmly convinced that if Christians would open their homes and practice hospitality as defined in Scripture, we could significantly alter the fabric of society.

Hospitality shouldn't just be the ministry of women in the church, but it is a ministry which many women are gifted to perform. My hat is off to the women of the Church of Jesus Christ throughout the world, those of you who are true worshipers of God, great listeners, women of open heart and open home, because you are one major key to the growth of the Church. May God continue to bless you as you serve him!

ATTITUDE

Out West one day, a cowboy was driving down the road with his dog riding in the back of his pickup truck and towing his horse in a trailer behind. The cowboy took a turn in the road way too fast and ended up having a horrible accident.

After some time, a state trooper came upon the scene. Being an animal lover, the policeman noticed the horse first. The animal was obviously in great distress and beyond hope of recovery. So the trooper pulled out his pistol and put the beast out of his misery.

Then the trooper walked around the scene of the accident and noticed the dog. He too was critically injured. The trooper couldn't bear to hear the dog yelping in pain. So, mercifully, he shot him too.

Finally, the trooper located the cowboy who had been thrown from the vehicle. He was lying down in some weeds off to the side of the road and was obviously suffering from multiple injuries. The trooper called out, "Are you alright?"

The cowboy took one look at the smoking pistol in the officer's hand and quickly replied, "Never felt better in my life!"

That story just goes to show that attitude is everything in life!

In Acts 16:16-40 we see how having a proper attitude is a key to growth in the life of the individual Christian and in the life of the Church....

> Once when we were going to the place of prayer, we were met by a slave girl who had a spirit by which she predicted the future. She earned a great deal of money for her owners by fortune-telling. This girl followed Paul and the rest of us, shouting, "These men are servants of the Most High God, who are telling you the way to be saved." She kept this up for many days. Finally Paul became so troubled that he turned around and said to the spirit, "In the name of Jesus Christ I command you to come out of her!" At that moment the spirit left her.
>
> When the owners of the slave girl realized that their hope of making money was gone, they seized Paul and Silas and dragged them into the marketplace to face the authorities. They brought them before the magistrates and said, "These men are Jews, and are throwing our city

into an uproar by advocating customs unlawful for us Romans to accept or practice."

The crowd joined in the attack against Paul and Silas, and the magistrates ordered them to be stripped and beaten. After they had been severely flogged, they were thrown into prison, and the jailer was commanded to guard them carefully. Upon receiving such orders, he put them in the inner cell and fastened their feet in the stocks.

About midnight Paul and Silas were praying and singing hymns to God, and the other prisoners were listening to them. Suddenly there was such a violent earthquake that the foundations of the prison were shaken. At once all the prison doors flew open, and everybody's chains came loose. The jailer woke up, and when he saw the prison doors open, he drew his sword and was about to kill himself because he thought the prisoners had escaped. But Paul shouted, "Don't harm yourself! We are all here!"

The jailer called for lights, rushed in and fell trembling before Paul and Silas. He then brought them out and asked, "Sirs, what must I do to be saved?"

They replied, "Believe in the Lord Jesus, and you will be saved—you and your household." Then they spoke the word of the Lord to him and to all the others in his house. At that hour of the night the jailer took them and washed their wounds; then immediately he and all his family were baptized. The jailer brought them into his house and set a meal before them; he was filled with joy because he had come to believe in God—he and his whole family.

When it was daylight, the magistrates sent their officers to the jailer with the order: "Release those men." The jailer told Paul, "The magistrates have ordered that you and Silas be released. Now you can leave. Go in peace."

But Paul said to the officers: "They beat us publicly without a trial, even though we are Roman citizens, and threw us into prison. And now do they want to get rid of us quietly? No! Let them come themselves and escort us out."

The officers reported this to the magistrates, and when they heard that Paul and Silas were Roman citizens, they were alarmed. They came to appease them and escorted them from the prison, requesting them to leave the city. After Paul and Silas came out of the prison, they went to Lydia's house, where they met with the brothers and encouraged them. Then they left.

Meditations on the Acts of the Apostles

I believe this story in Acts addresses the issue of our attitude in at least four different dimensions. First of all: *What is our attitude toward interruptions?* When Paul was continually interrupted by the demon-possessed slave girl his attitude was one of *irritation*. The word in the Greek can be translated: grieved, troubled or annoyed.

This story shows us the great apostle Paul in all his humanity. One of the surest signs of the honesty of Luke as an author is that he paints the portraits of the great leaders of the early Christian movement showing warts and all. We might have expected verse 18 to read something like:

> While Paul was preaching the good news of Christ he was moved with compassion for the slave girl who had been crying out for several days. Paul laid hands on her, prayed for her healing, and sent her off with his blessings.

But it didn't happen that way! Paul was a focused, even a driven man. He was intent on doing one thing–the work of evangelism. This slave girl was becoming a nuisance and a distraction as far as Paul was concerned. I think he was ticked off. And in that spirit of irritation Paul commanded the evil spirit to come out of the girl. The truly amazing thing is that God honored that prayer even though it probably wasn't spoken in the right spirit.

What is our attitude toward interruptions? Bruce Larson has written: "We may sometimes welcome an interruption on a busy day. It might be a dear friend, and we sit and have coffee and share and pray together. The Spirit can use that encounter. But if you're like me, you're sometimes annoyed by interruptions, even feeling resentful about this person who is ruining your schedule."

C. S. Lewis once said this about interruptions in a letter to a friend:

> The great thing, if one can, is to stop regarding all the unpleasant things as interruptions of one's "own," or "real" life. The truth is of course that what one calls the interruptions are precisely one's real life–the life God is sending one day by day: what one calls one's "real life" is a phantom of one's own imagination. This at least is what I see at moments of insight: but it's hard to remember it all the time (*Letters to Arthur Greeves*, 20 December 1943).

Douglas Gresham, C. S. Lewis' stepson, often told me how Lewis, or Jack as he called him, if working on a bit of writing and called upon for some domestic help, would set down his pen without any sign of irritation whatsoever, attend to the need, and then resume his work as if the interruption had never come along in the first place. I think only Jesus can give us the kind of attitude toward interruptions which C. S. Lewis apparently had.

Secondly, what is our attitude toward circumstances? When Paul and Silas were put in prison they responded in prayer and singing hymns to God. God enabled them to have an attitude of *joy* in spite of their circumstances. Literally, Paul and Silas *celebrated* God in song while they were in chains.

My friend and fellow author, Tim Hansel, received a telegram one day which read simply: "UNTIL FURTHER NOTICE–CELEBRATE EVERYTHING!" How do you celebrate when life is not going the way you would like? The key to changing your attitude is changing your altitude.

On January 13, 1997 Steve Fossett climbed into the cockpit of a hot-air balloon in St. Louis, Missouri, and rose into the sky with the ambition of being the first to circle the globe in a balloon. After three days he had crossed the Atlantic and was flying at 24,500 feet eastward over Africa.

The prevailing wind carried him on a direct course for the country of Libya, and that was a problem. Libya had refused him permission to fly in its air space, which meant he could be shot down. Of course, hot-air balloons cannot turn. When a change of direction is called for, what they must do is change altitude. At a higher or lower altitude a balloonist can usually find a crosswind blowing in a different direction.

Fossett vented helium, and the balloon dropped 6,300 feet, where it came under the control of a wind blowing southeast. Fossett skirted safely south of Libya, then heated the balloon, rose almost 10,000 feet and caught an easterly wind, which carried him back on course.

Although Fossett, on that trip, only got as far as India, he still set dual records for the longest distance (10,360 miles) and duration (6 days, 2 hours, 44 minutes) in balloon flight. Eventually, Fossett was the first person to travel solo around the world in a balloon, on his sixth try in 2002.

Bertrand Piccard, the first man to travel with another team member nonstop around the world in a balloon, once remarked on the similarity between balloon flight and daily life. "In the balloon," says Piccard, "you are prisoners of the wind, and you go only in the direction of the wind. In life people think they are prisoners of circumstance. But in the balloon, as in life, you can change altitude, and when you change altitude, you change direction. You are not a prisoner anymore."

In life we change attitude by changing altitude. The closer you get to the Most High, the nearer you are to Jesus Christ, the more you will be enabled by his Spirit to rejoice in spite of your circumstances, because you will see your circumstances from a new perspective–God's vantage point.

Happiness is dependent on circumstances. The word for happiness comes from the same word for happenings. When what is happening around you is pleasant, happiness results. You get the job you have always wanted; you are happy. The person of your dreams says "yes" to your proposal of marriage; you exude happiness. Your children do well in school and get a scholarship to a top university—wow, that's happiness!

Joy, on the other hand, can thrive in any sort of circumstance—in prison, on welfare, in the cancer ward of a hospital. As Sheldon Kopp once said, "Life can be depended upon to provide all the pain any of us might need." That being the case, it behooves us all to discover the source of unending joy who can keep our attitude "up" in spite of the downers of life.

Thirdly, what is our attitude toward people? When the prison doors flew open and the Philippian jailer was about to kill himself, Paul and Silas could have cut and run. But they didn't because they had an attitude of *love* toward other people.

What would you have done if you were Paul or Silas in prison and there was an earthquake and the prison doors suddenly flew open? You don't have to be a rocket scientist to figure, "Now is the time to run!" But Paul and Silas didn't. In the darkness Paul and Silas probably figured what that jailer might do to himself if he lost all his prisoners. Rather than face a Roman tribunal and certain execution, the jailer might have decided to take his own life. Paul, caring more for the welfare of the Philippian jailer than his own freedom, called out through the darkness, "Don't harm yourself! We are all here!"

Can you imagine the response of the other prisoners? "Well Paul, it's one thing to sing hymns in prison, but to call out to the jailer when we could have escaped—what were you thinking?"

But that call of love made all the difference in the world to that jailer. He called for lights, rushed in and fell trembling before Paul and Silas, brought them out of their cell and humbly asked, "Sirs, what must I do to be saved?"

I don't think that jailer was moved so much by the earthquake. I don't think he was motivated by fear, so much as being motivated by the joy and the love he witnessed in Paul and Silas.

What about us? Do people see enough of the love of Christ in our life to make them ask, "How can I get what you have?" I believe God wants us to *love* people to Jesus, not beat them over the head with a Bible, not tell them how awful they are, just love them.

The following story comes from a Sunday school ministry in a part of New York City that has been rated the "most likely place to get killed". In this particular neighborhood, Pastor Bill Wilson has been stabbed, shot at, and had a member of his leadership team killed.

One Puerto Rican lady, after becoming a Christian through the ministry of the church, went to Pastor Bill with a request. She couldn't speak very much English, so through an interpreter she said, "I want to do something for God, please."

"I don't know what you can do," the pastor answered.

"Please, let me do something," she said in Spanish.

"Alright. I'll put you on one of our buses that picks up children for Sunday School. Ride a different bus every week and just love those children."

So every week this lovely Puerto Rican lady rode a different bus–the church had fifty of them–and she just loved the children. This lady would find the worst-looking child on the bus, put him on her lap and whisper over and over the only words she had learned in English: "I love you. Jesus loves you."

After several months, this woman became attached to one little boy in particular. "I don't want to change buses anymore. I want to stay on this one bus," she said. So they let her stay on that bus.

The boy didn't speak. He came to Sunday school every week with his sister and sat on the woman's lap, but he never made a sound. Each week the lady would tell him all the way to Sunday school and all the way home: "I love you and Jesus loves you."

One day, to this woman's amazement, the little boy turned to her and stammered: "I–I love you too." Then he put his arms around the Puerto Rican lady and gave her a great, big hug.

That was 2:30 on a Saturday afternoon. At 6:30 that night, that same boy was found dead in a garbage bag under a fire escape. His mother had beaten him to death and thrown his body in the trash.

"I love you and Jesus loves you." Those were some of the last words that little boy heard in his short life–from the lips of a Puerto Rican woman who could barely speak English.

Sometimes, some of us feel like we can't do very much for the Lord. But by his grace, we can love other people to Jesus.

Finally, let me ask: What is our attitude toward Jesus Christ? When the Philippian jailer asked Paul and Silas, "What must I do to be saved?" They said, "Believe in the Lord Jesus, and you will be saved–you and your household." Do we have an attitude of **faith** in Jesus Christ?

What does it mean to have faith in Jesus? It means believing certain facts about him, that's for certain. We must believe that Jesus is the Son of God. We must believe that he died on the cross for our sin and rose again from the dead. But faith is so much more than believing certain facts. Faith means trusting Jesus with our life, putting our life into his hands.

A friend of our family by the name of Ben Patterson once told this story in a book entitled *Waiting*:

> In 1988, three friends and I climbed Mount Lyell, the highest peak in Yosemite National Park. Our base camp was less than 2,000 feet from that peak, but the climb to the top and back was to take the better part of a day, due in large part to the difficulty of the glacier we had to cross to get to the top. The morning of the climb we started out chattering and cracking jokes.

Meditations on the Acts of the Apostles

As the hours passed, the two more experienced mountaineers opened up a wide gap between me and my less-experienced companion. Being competitive by nature, I began to look for shortcuts to beat them to the top. I thought I saw one to the right of an outcropping of rock—so I went, deaf to the protests of my companion.

Perhaps it was the effect of the high altitude, but the significance of the two experienced climbers not choosing this path did not register in my consciousness. It should have, for thirty minutes later I was trapped in a cul-de-sac of rock atop the Lyell Glacier, looking down several hundred feet of a sheer slope of ice, pitched at about a forty-five degree angle.... I was only about ten feet from the safety of a rock, but one little slip and I wouldn't stop sliding until I landed in the valley floor some fifty miles away! It was nearly noon, and the warm sun had the glacier glistening with slippery ice. I was stuck, and I was scared.

It took an hour for my experienced climbing friends to find me. Standing on the rock I wanted to reach, one of them leaned out and used an ice ax to chip two little footsteps in the glacier. Then he gave me the following instructions: "Ben, you must step out from where you are and put your foot where the first foothold is. When your foot touches it, without a moment's hesitation swing your other foot across and land it on the next step. When you do that, reach out and I will take your hand and pull you to safety."

That sounded real good to me. It was the next thing he said that made me more frightened than ever. "But listen carefully: As you step across, do not lean into the mountain! If anything, lean out a bit. Otherwise, your feet may fly out from under you, and you will start sliding down."

I don't like precipices. When I am on the edge of a cliff, my instincts are to lie down and hug the mountain, to become one with it, not to lean away from it! But that was what my good friend was telling me to do. For a moment, based solely on what I believed to be the good will and good sense of my friend, I decided to say no to what I felt, to stifle my impulse to cling to the security of the mountain, to lean out, step out, and traverse the ice to safety. It took less than two seconds to find out if my faith was well founded.

Faith is more than just believing that Jesus is the expert climber on the mountains of life. Faith is trusting him by putting our life in his hands and doing what he says. If we have that attitude of trust in Jesus Christ it will change our attitude toward everything else in life.

TROUBLE MAKING

Someone once said that Jesus promises us at least four things: peace, power, purpose and trouble. In John 16:33 Jesus said, "In this world you will have trouble. But take heart! I have overcome the world."

The church at Thessalonica was a church born in trouble, born in the midst of persecution. But what many people don't realize is that the church at Thessalonica was also started by one of the biggest trouble-makers this world has ever seen: the Apostle Paul.

Let's read together Acts 17:1-9 and I will show you what I mean. . . .

> When they had passed through Amphipolis and Apollonia, they came to Thessalonica, where there was a Jewish synagogue. As his custom was, Paul went into the synagogue, and on three Sabbath days he reasoned with them from the Scriptures, explaining and proving that the Christ had to suffer and rise from the dead. "This Jesus I am proclaiming to you is the Christ," he said. Some of the Jews were persuaded and joined Paul and Silas, as did a large number of God-fearing Greeks and not a few prominent women.
>
> But the Jews were jealous; so they rounded up some bad characters from the marketplace, formed a mob and started a riot in the city. They rushed to Jason's house in search of Paul and Silas in order to bring them out to the crowd. But when they did not find them, they dragged Jason and some other brothers before the city officials, shouting: "These men who have caused trouble all over the world have now come here, and Jason has welcomed them into his house. They are all defying Caesar's decrees, saying that there is another king, one called Jesus." When they heard this, the crowd and the city officials were thrown into turmoil. Then they made Jason and the others post bond and let them go.

"These men who have caused trouble all over the world have now come here." That's Paul and his companions, that's who the Jews of Thessalonica were talking about. They thought of Paul as one big troublemaker–literally one who was turning the world upside down for Jesus Christ. And that is exactly what Paul was doing. I think we can learn three things from Paul's example in

Meditations on the Acts of the Apostles

Thessalonica that will help us be trouble-makers, world-upside-down-turners for Jesus, too.

First of all, if we are going to cause trouble in the name of Jesus we must *reason with people from the Scriptures*. Paul and his companions traveled one hundred miles from Philippi to Thessalonica and that after being beaten and put in prison! There is no question that Paul was committed to the task of telling others about Jesus. He could not be deterred.

Once Paul got to Thessalonica he went straight for the synagogue, as was his custom. He spent three successive Sabbath days reasoning with the Jews from the Scriptures.

Now, if someone is not interested in the Bible then there is no sense reasoning with them from the Scriptures. You, your life, is the only Bible some people may ever read. So you better make it interesting reading.

But if someone is interested in the Bible, then to introduce them to Jesus Christ you need to reason from the Scriptures. Paul knew the Old Testament backwards and forwards. He was able to take numerous Old Testament passages and use them to prove that Jesus was the Messiah and that he had to suffer and rise from the dead.

My grandfather was a great expert at doing just what Paul did. He and my grandmother founded the Los Angeles Hebrew Mission. They devoted their lives to showing the Jewish people that Jesus was and is their Messiah. My grandmother was a Jewish Christian and so her very life was a convincing testimony. But my grandfather was a Gentile—a Gentile who knew the Hebrew Scriptures from cover to cover in their original language. He also taught Hebrew at the Bible Institute of Los Angeles. And in addition to starting a church to reach Jewish people for Jesus, he would often go out on to the beach in Santa Monica to do "chalk talks" about Christ. My grandfather was a Paul for his time and place.

But you know, it amazes me sometimes how few Christians today are able to reason with others from the Scripture. Maybe that is because fewer and fewer Christians really know their Bibles. I had a Jewish Christian professor once say to me in seminary, "You really have a great grasp on the theology of Paul. How did you get that?" I said, "By reading his letters." I thought the answer was obvious, but apparently it wasn't obvious to my professor. I think he was more accustomed to reading books about Paul than to reading Paul.

And there are probably more Christians today who read books about the Bible than those who actually read the Bible every day. But such regular soaking of oneself in the Scriptures is indispensable to growth in the Christian life.

One of my favorite praise songs, written by Lynn deShazo, is entitled *Ancient Words*:

Keys to Growth

Holy words long preserved
For our walk in this world,
They resound with God's own heart
Oh, let the ancient words impart.

Words of life, words of hope
Give us strength, help us cope
In this world, where'er we roam
Ancient words will guide us home.

Ancient words ever true
Changing me, and changing you.
We have come with open hearts
Oh let the ancient words impart.

Holy words of our faith
Handed down to this age.
Came to us through sacrifice
Oh heed the faithful words of Christ.

If we are going to turn the world upside down for Jesus Christ, as Paul did, then we need the ancient words of Scripture. We need to be able to reason from those Scriptures when we talk to others about Jesus.

And that leads to the second lesson we can learn from Paul about how to be trouble-makers. If we are going to turn the world upside down for Christ then we need to *focus on Jesus* in our witness. That's what Paul did in his witness; he focused on Jesus. He didn't get distracted enough to comment on the big social issues of his day; or even the political issues. Though it is clear from reading Paul that he recognized the Gospel has application to those issues. But in speaking to those outside the church Paul focused on the simple Gospel.

He didn't get wrapped up in discussions of how many days it took God to create the world, or even how God created the world. Personally I think many Christians today are wasting their time when it comes to trying to defend the Bible in the face of unbelievers. Why waste time trying to prove creation vs. evolution when talking to a non-Christian? When we have an opportunity to talk to non-Christians about spiritual matters we should focus on the simple Gospel which Paul summed up in 1 Corinthians 15:1-3,

> Now, brothers, I want to remind you of the Gospel I preached to you, which you received and on which you have taken your stand. By this Gospel you are saved, if you hold firmly to the word I preached to you. Otherwise, you have believed in vain.
>
> For what I received I passed on to you as of first importance: that Christ died for our sins according to the Scriptures, that he was buried,

> that he was raised on the third day according to the Scriptures, and that
> he appeared to Peter, and then to the Twelve.

Someone once said that our life in Christ can be compared to an aqueduct. I remember seeing an ancient Roman aqueduct in Israel when I went on a Holy Land tour in 1984. In days long ago these stone bridges would bring water from the mountains to the parched inhabitants of cities in the flat lands. In fact, these aqueducts built long ago are still in use in some countries today.

The Scriptures are like those huge stone aqueducts. The Scriptures are the objective conveyor of spiritual refreshment, but they are not that refreshment itself. Our daily experience of Jesus, that is like the fresh water flowing through the aqueduct.

Some Christians cast aside the Scriptures and seek out spiritual experiences. But without the aqueduct of the Scriptures to channel the experience of Jesus, our spiritual life would turn into puddles of error and waste.

Still other Christians have great aqueducts. They have done extensive study of the Bible, but they have no living experience of Jesus—no water in the aqueduct. And thus they have no spiritual refreshment for themselves or others.

Jesus once said to some of his fellow Jews:

> You diligently study the Scriptures because you think that by them
> you possess eternal life. These are the Scriptures that testify about me,
> yet you refuse to come to me to have life. (John 5:39-40)

If we are going to be trouble-makers, world-upside-down-turners like Paul, then we need both the aqueduct of the Scriptures and the living experience which is a relationship with Jesus Christ.

But if we are going to be trouble-makers like Paul we also need a third element. *We need to call people to surrender to the kingship of Jesus.* The Jews complained that Paul and his companions were "defying Caesar's decrees, saying that there is another king, one called Jesus."

Some years ago there was considerable debate among Christians as to whether a person could have Jesus as Savior without having him as Lord. I firmly believe that Jesus is both, Savior and Lord, forgiver and leader. But in my own Christian experience I can testify to the fact that I first understood Jesus as Savior, and only later did I begin to understand his Lordship.

I first understood the Gospel when listening to a preacher on television when I was twelve years old. That preacher made it very clear that Jesus had died for me, personally. The Gospel came to me as refreshing water for my soul. Finally I knew that I was forgiven and loved and rescued by the God of the universe who made himself known in Jesus. But it wasn't until a year later,

Keys to Growth

when I heard another pastor preaching about the Lordship of Christ that I made a public commitment of my life to follow Jesus.

We need to have Jesus as both Savior and Lord. But our discovery of Jesus as Savior and as Lord may not happen all at once. I am still learning what it means to have Jesus as both my leader *and* my forgiver.

My favorite illustration of this principle is a poem called *The Road of Life*:

> At first, I saw God as my observer,
> my judge,
> keeping track of the things I did wrong,
> so as to know whether I merited heaven
> or hell when I die.
> He was out there sort of like a president.
> I recognized His picture when I saw it,
> but I really didn't know Him.
>
> But later on
> when I met Christ,
> it seemed as though life were rather like a bike ride,
> but it was a tandem bike,
> and I noticed that Christ
> was in the back helping me pedal.
>
> I don't know just when it was
> that He suggested we change places,
> but life has not been the same since.
>
> When I had control,
> I knew the way.
> It was rather boring,
> but predictable . . .
> It was the shortest distance between two points.
>
> But when He took the lead,
> He knew delightful long cuts,
> up mountains,
> and through rocky places
> at breakneck speeds,
> it was all I could do to hang on!
> Even though it looked like madness,
> He said, "Pedal!"
> I worried and was anxious
> and asked,

MEDITATIONS ON THE ACTS OF THE APOSTLES

"Where are you taking me?"
He laughed and didn't answer,
and I started to learn to trust.

I forgot my boring life
and entered into the adventure.
And when I'd say, "I'm scared,"
He'd lean back and touch my hand.

He took me to people with gifts that I needed,
gifts of healing,
acceptance
and joy.
They gave me gifts to take on my journey,
my Lord's and mine.

And we were off again.
He said, "Give the gifts away;
they're extra baggage, too much weight."
So I did,
to the people we met,
and I found that in giving I received,
and still our burden was light.

I did not trust Him,
at first,
in control of my life.
I thought He'd wreck it;
but He knows bike secrets,
knows how to make it bend to take sharp corners,
knows how to jump to clear high rocks,
knows how to fly to shorten scary passages.

And I am learning to shut up
and pedal
in the strangest places,
and I'm beginning to enjoy the view
and the cool breeze on my face
with my delightful constant companion, Jesus Christ.
And when I'm sure I just can't do anymore,
He just smiles and says . . . "Pedal."

Keys to Growth

I hope that Jesus is on your tandem bike with you along the road of life, and that you have let him take the front seat. If you have then you too will be a trouble-maker, someone who turns your world upside down just like Paul.

SEEKING TRUTH

One *Peanuts* comic strip from many years ago shows a classroom on the first day of a new school year. The students are given an assignment to write an essay about returning to school after summer vacation. In her essay Lucy writes:

> Vacations are nice, but it's good to get back to school. There is nothing more satisfying or challenging than education, and I look forward to a year of expanding knowledge.

The teacher is quite pleased with Lucy's essay and compliments her appropriately. But then in the final frame of the comic strip, Lucy leans over and whispers to Charlie Brown in the seat next to her: "After awhile, you learn what sells."

I don't know if the Apostle Paul was ever tempted to say "what sells". But if he was, it is apparent from the New Testament that he never gave in to that temptation. Paul consistently and persistently preached what he believed to be the truth, no matter the cost. And at the next stop on his missionary tour, recorded in Acts 17:10-15, he met a group of people as committed to seeking the truth as he was to telling it. . . .

> As soon as it was night, the brothers sent Paul and Silas away to Berea. On arriving there, they went to the Jewish synagogue. Now the Bereans were of more noble character than the Thessalonians, for they received the message with great eagerness and examined the Scriptures every day to see if what Paul said was true. Many of the Jews believed, as did also a number of prominent Greek women and many Greek men.
>
> When the Jews in Thessalonica learned that Paul was preaching the word of God at Berea, they went there too, agitating the crowds and stirring them up. The brothers immediately sent Paul to the coast, but Silas and Timothy stayed at Berea. The men who escorted Paul brought him to Athens and then left with instructions for Silas and Timothy to join him as soon as possible.

Seeking truth is essential to growth in the Christian life and the life of the church. And in this passage we have three pointers for truth-seekers. The first pointer is that if we are committed to seeking the truth then we will be wise to *examine the Scriptures daily*. That's what the Jews in Berea did. They examined the Scriptures every day to see if what Paul was teaching about Jesus was true. That's what we should do with anything anyone tells us. Examine the Scriptures daily to see if what they are saying is true.

Obviously Luke thought that what the Bereans were doing was worthy of emulation. He said that the Jews of Berea were of more noble character than the Jews of Thessalonica. It is interesting to note what one twentieth century commentator had to say about a visit he paid to Berea:

> While the memory of St. Paul has almost vanished from its larger and more famous neighbour, Salonica [Thessalonica], little Beroea is intensely proud of its connexion with the Apostle. Any small child in Verria [modern day Berea] can lead you to a railed-off enclosure in the school playground and point out a flight of four massive steps, from which, he will tell you, the Apostle preached. On the top step it is just possible to trace the word 'Pavlos' in Greek letters. [H. V. Morton, *In the Steps of St. Paul* (New York: Dodd, Mead & Company, 1959), p. 293.]

As evidence of the Berean's nobility Luke pointed out that they were committed to searching the Scriptures for truth. Luke recognized, as I'm sure Paul himself did, that Paul was not the final authority for truth. God's Word in Scripture is our highest authority on earth.

It is amazing what authorities some people entrust themselves to. For example, in Denver, Pennsylvania, people used to set their clocks and watches by the sirens the hat factory would set off five days a week. At 5:30 a.m., the wake-up siren would begin the day followed by the starting, lunchtime, and quitting sirens at the designated times.

When the siren system was eventually disbanded, someone was reminiscing with the time-keeper about his job. The timekeeper was asked: "What did you use to determine the exact time?"

With a twinkle in his eye, the time-keeper reached into his pocket and pulled out a child's Mickey Mouse watch.

Some experts are not as authoritative as they seem. But there is no higher authority on earth than the Word of God in Scripture. Therefore when we are looking for truth that should be the first place we search.

The Jews at Berea had an eager response to Paul's message. And so I wonder: is that how we respond to the preaching of God's Word? Are we eager to hear it, test it by Scripture, and apply it to our lives? Or is preaching a ho-hum activity to sit through?

The eagerness of the Jews at Berea led them to examine the Scriptures daily. Literally, they embarked on an investigation. This process certainly involved asking questions in order to arrive at an answer.

I often like to compare Bible study to solving a murder mystery. I love murder mysteries, especially British murder mysteries. I love the settings in old English country towns. I enjoy trying to figure out who-done-it. We need to approach our study of the Bible with the same sense of eagerness and investigative spirit.

Here are some great questions to ask when seeking truth through Bible study:

- What does it say?
- What does it mean?
- What am I going to do about it?
- Is there a promise to claim?
- Is there a sin to forsake?
- Is there an example to follow?
- Is there a command to obey?

The great thing is that as we search the Scriptures for truth we also have the ultimate author of Scripture by our side–the Holy Spirit. At any time in our Bible study we can ask for the help of the Holy Spirit to understand and apply God's Word.

It is also of note that the Jews at Berea examined the Scriptures *every day*. There was nothing casual about their Scripture study. They gave it all they had.

Now I realize that there is no direct command in Scripture telling us that we must read it and study it every day. So I don't want to lay a guilt trip on you. That is the last thing I want to do. I realize also that many people have difficult circumstances or schedules which make daily Scripture study unrealistic. But I do think that the more we grow in Christ the more there will be a desire for daily Scripture reading and study. We will have a hunger for it.

In the summer of 1908-9, Sir Ernest Shackleton and three companions attempted to travel to the South Pole from their winter quarters in the Antarctic. The group set off with four horses to help carry the load. Weeks later, their horses dead, rations all but exhausted, they turned back toward their base; they failed to accomplish their goal. Altogether, they had traveled for 127 days.

On the return journey, as Shackleton recorded in *The Heart of the Antarctic*, the group spent a great deal of time talking about food–elaborate feasts, gourmet delights, sumptuous menus. As they staggered along, suffering from dysentery, not knowing whether they would survive, every waking hour was occupied with thoughts of eating.

Jesus, who also knew the ravages of food deprivation, said, "Blessed are those who hunger and thirst for *righteousness*." We can understand Shackleton's obsession with food, which offers us a glimpse of the passion Jesus intends for our quest for righteousness. And just as we should hunger and thirst for righteousness, so we should also hunger and thirst for the truth, and seek the truth of God in Scripture with every fiber of our being. For Jesus also said, "You shall know the truth and the truth shall set you free." Our study of Scripture should be sparked by a deep, burning desire for truth, and sustained by dutiful obedience to our Sovereign Lord.

A second pointer for truth-seekers which we see in this passage is that we should *expect opposition*. We read that "When the Jews in Thessalonica learned that Paul was preaching the word of God at Berea, they went there too, agitating the crowds and stirring them up."

I read an interesting book some time ago entitled: *Sailing Acts*. It was written by a professor at Eastern Mennonite University, Linford Stutzman, who took a sabbatical from teaching at the university, bought a sail boat in Greece, took his wife along, and navigated all the missionary journeys of the Apostle Paul. Stutzman had this to say about his visit to Berea, modern day Veria:

> In contrast to Thessaloniki, a bustling port city where memory of Paul is obscured by modern buildings and traffic-jammed streets, Veria is an inland town at the edge of a manufacturing and farming area, nestled against the mountains. A huge traffic sign above the main street in the town's center indicates the main route out of the town in one direction, and 'Paul's Altar' in the other. Following the signs, we found the little grotto with beautiful mosaics on the spot where Paul supposedly preached. There we read the story of Paul's short ministry in Berea....
>
> We sat in front of the mosaic depicting the scene. A balding Paul holds a document in one hand, and with the other, gives the sign of blessing to a group of serious, studious, and meek seekers. The seekers are seated around him, holding open scrolls on their laps, with a medieval-looking Berea in the background. Janet and I marveled at the disgruntled band of Paul's enemies from Thessalonica, who heard of the Bereans' positive response to Paul's message and trudged the same 45 miles from Thessalonica to incite a riot in Berea against him there. Paul wasn't the only highly motivated religious person in 51 A. D. The Roman roads made possible the movement of motivated people all throughout the Empire. [Linford Stutzman, *SailingActs* (Intercourse PA: Good Books, 2006) pp. 143-144.]

Meditations on the Acts of the Apostles

If we are going to be seekers of truth, and especially if we seek to pass on that truth to others, then we better expect opposition. And that opposition will not be merely of a human variety. In Ephesians 6:10-18 Paul wrote:

> Finally, be strong in the Lord and in his mighty power. Put on the full armor of God so that you can take your stand against the devil's schemes. *For our struggle is not against flesh and blood*, but against the rulers, against the authorities, against the powers of this dark world and against the spiritual forces of evil in the heavenly realms. Therefore put on the full armor of God, so that when the day of evil comes, you may be able to stand your ground, and after you have done everything, to stand. Stand firm then, with the belt of truth buckled around your waist, with the breastplate of righteousness in place, and with your feet fitted with the readiness that comes from the Gospel of peace. In addition to all this, take up the shield of faith, with which you can extinguish all the flaming arrows of the evil one. Take the helmet of salvation and the sword of the Spirit, which is the word of God. And pray in the Spirit on all occasions with all kinds of prayers and requests. With this in mind, be alert and always keep on praying for all the saints.

If we engage to be truth-seekers, and especially if we engage to pass on the truth of God to others, then we will be engaged in a spiritual battle. We will be opposed, not merely by human beings, both inside and outside the church, who may not like the truth we have to share, we will be opposed by the devil himself. So we better be ready for a fight. God does not leave us unequipped for the war, but we have to put our armor on.

Notice that Paul begins his list of the armor of God with the belt of truth. We must have the truth of God firmly buckled around our waist so that no enemy can rip it off of us. Then we must have the breastplate of righteousness in place—that is the righteousness of Christ, for we have no righteousness of our own. Then we must be ready to carry the truth of the good news of Jesus Christ to other people at all times.

In addition we must take up the shield of faith. When Paul wrote the letter to the church at Ephesus he would have known of the phalanx formation of the Roman army. When going into battle, Roman soldiers would stand shoulder to shoulder in a V-formation. Upon a signal from their commanding officer they would all raise their shields at one time. I think that may be the picture Paul had in mind when he wrote Ephesians 6:16.

When we confess our faith together Sunday by Sunday, using the form of The Apostles' Creed or The Nicene Creed, I like to think of that phalanx formation. When we say: "I believe in God the Father Almighty . . ." we are raising our shields together. When we do that it is very difficult for the enemy to penetrate our ranks. The shield of faith can extinguish all the flaming arrows of the evil one.

We also need to put on the helmet of salvation. Do you know for certain that you have been saved by Jesus Christ? Have you come to the point in your life where if you died tonight you know you would go to heaven? If you were to stand before God today and he was to ask you: "Why should I let you into heaven?" what would you say? I hope you would say: "I am trusting in Jesus Christ alone, his perfect life lived for me, his death on the cross which he died for my sins, and his resurrection from the dead." If you are trusting in Jesus then you can be as sure of heaven as if you were already there.

Finally, we need to take up the sword of the Spirit which is the word of God. The word of God in Scripture is our one offensive weapon in spiritual warfare. All the other elements of our armor are defensive. But God does not mean for us to always be on the defensive. We are to expect opposition, but we are also to give opposition to the enemy. We are to go on the offensive by sharing the word of God with others.

Furthermore, God never wants us to retreat in our battle with Satan and all his cohorts. That is why there is no armor for our backside. We are to face the enemy head-on and oppose him with the offensive weapon of the word of God, just as Jesus did when he was tempted in the desert.

And once we have the armor of God in place, then we should pray in the Spirit on all occasions for one another. Prayer is a powerful activity in spiritual warfare, perhaps the most powerful activity next to the exercise of the sword of the Spirit.

So if we are truth-seekers, and especially if we are truth-tellers, we should expect opposition. But the final pointer for truth-seekers which we see in this passage is that we should *keep on keeping on*. Just because Paul was opposed by the Jews at every turn of the road doesn't mean that he gave up. Far from it. Paul kept going no matter the odds which were against him.

What was it that kept Paul going no matter what? I think there were two things. First of all, Paul had the fellowship of other Christians to encourage him. When he was harassed by the Jews from Thessalonica it was the brothers in Berea who sent Paul to the coast where they caught a boat to Athens together.

The fellowship of other Christians is one key relationship which has helped individual Christians to endure spiritual warfare down through the ages. For years William Wilberforce, who lived from 1759 to 1833, pushed Britain's parliament to abolish slavery. At one point Wilberforce was so discouraged in his efforts that he was tempted to give up. It was at that critical juncture that his elderly friend, John Wesley, heard of Wilberforce's discouragement and from his deathbed Wesley called for pen and paper. With trembling hand,

Wesley wrote:

> Unless God has raised you up for this very thing, you will be worn out by the opposition of men and devils. But if God be for you, who can be against you? Are all of them stronger than God?
>
> Oh be not weary of well-doing! Go on, in the name of God and in the power of his might, till even American slavery shall vanish away before it.

Wesley died six days later. But Wilberforce fought for forty-five more years and in 1833, three days before his own death, he received the news that slavery was abolished in Britain. Even great Christians often need the encouragement of fellow Christians.

But the second thing that I believe helped Paul to endure in spiritual battle was his clear vision of Jesus Christ. He endured seeing him who is invisible. Right before his own death Paul wrote to Timothy:

> For I am already being poured out like a drink offering, and the time has come for my departure. I have fought the good fight, I have finished the race, I have kept the faith. Now there is in store for me the crown of righteousness, which the Lord, the righteous Judge, will award to me on that day—and not only to me, but also to all who have longed for his appearing.

Paul was able to endure hot and persistent opposition in spiritual battle because he never lost sight of the Lord, the righteous Judge, who would one day reward him for his troubles.

It was a fog-shrouded morning, July 4, 1952, when a young woman named Florence Chadwick waded into the water off Catalina Island. She intended to swim the channel from the island to the California coast. Long-distance swimming was not new to her; she had been the first woman to swim the English Channel in both directions.

The water was body-numbing cold that day. The fog was so pervasive that Florence could hardly see the boats in her group. Several times sharks had to be driven away with rifle fire. She swam more than fifteen hours before she asked to be taken out of the water. Her trainer tried to encourage her to swim on since they were so close to land, but when Florence looked, all she saw was fog. So she quit . . . only one-half mile from her goal.

Later she said, "I'm not excusing myself, but if I could have seen the land, I might have made it." It wasn't the cold or fear or exhaustion that got to Florence Chadwick. It was the pea-soup fog.

Many times we too fail, not because we're afraid or because of the pressure of other's opinions, or because of anything other than the fact that we lose sight of the goal—we lose sight of Jesus Christ. That's why Paul said, "Forgetting what is behind and straining toward what is ahead, I press on toward the goal to win the prize for which God has called me heavenward in Christ Jesus."

David Livingstone had the same spirit of pluck as the Apostle Paul. He once said, "I am prepared to go anywhere, so long as it is forward!" That's the spirit we all need to have.

And by the way, two months after her failure, Florence Chadwick walked off the same beach into the same channel and swam the distance, setting a new speed record, all because she could see the land that day.

Keep your eyes on Jesus. Keep on keeping on in the spiritual battle. Expect opposition and arm yourself with the word of God. With God's help, nothing and no one can defeat you.

BE A TRANSFORMER

Author R. C. Sproul tells the story of a visit to Washington, D.C. when he was taken on a guided tour of the Capitol building. He writes:

> I was moved by the understated elegance of the furnishings of the original Senate chambers and the Supreme Court. I enjoyed the wealth of art works that adorn this history-packed building. The legends, the lore of the great oratory of Henry Clay, of Webster and Calhoun, all came alive.
>
> My nostalgic and patriotic bubble burst, however, when we passed to the floor of the rotunda immediately beneath the vast dome that is the building's most recognizable feature. Our tour guide lifted her eyes toward the ceiling and pointed out the mural painted on the inside of the great Capitol dome. She told of the Herculean effort of the painter who created this masterpiece, rivaling the effort of Michelangelo in the Sistine Chapel. Then she announced the title of the painting: 'The Apotheosis of George Washington'.
>
> I was horror-stricken. Though I favor the separation of church and state, I was shocked to see the nation going this far in supporting a crass form of sheer idolatry. The principal meaning of apotheosis is 'deification' or 'elevation to divine status.' I am aware that many Americans have never heard the term apotheosis and are not the least bit troubled by it. Surely our tour guide had no problems with it.
>
> The mural displays George Washington being welcomed into the pantheon of gods by other pagan deities.... That this offensive painting is viewed daily by multitudes of Christians without any murmur or complaint underlines in red the prevailing cavalier attitude regarding idolatry.

In a similar fashion, the Apostle Paul was provoked when he was in Athens and he saw that the city was full of idols. Paul was distressed in his spirit, moved to action in response to the idolatry that lay before his eyes. Let us read from Acts 17 the account of what Paul did in response to this provocation ...

While Paul was waiting for them in Athens, he was greatly distressed to see that the city was full of idols. So he reasoned in the synagogue with the Jews and the God-fearing Greeks, as well as in the marketplace day by day with those who happened to be there. A group of Epicurean and Stoic philosophers began to dispute with him. Some of them asked, "What is this babbler trying to say?" Others remarked, "He seems to be advocating foreign gods." They said this because Paul was preaching the good news about Jesus and the resurrection. Then they took him and brought him to a meeting of the Areopagus, where they said to him, "May we know what this new teaching is that you are presenting? You are bringing some strange ideas to our ears, and we want to know what they mean." (All the Athenians and the foreigners who lived there spent their time doing nothing but talking about and listening to the latest ideas.)

Paul then stood up in the meeting of the Areopagus and said: "Men of Athens! I see that in every way you are very religious. For as I walked around and looked carefully at your objects of worship, I even found an altar with this inscription: TO AN UNKNOWN GOD. Now what you worship as something unknown I am going to proclaim to you.

"The God who made the world and everything in it is the Lord of heaven and earth and does not live in temples built by hands. And he is not served by human hands, as if he needed anything, because he himself gives all men life and breath and everything else. From one man he made every nation of men, that they should inhabit the whole earth; and he determined the times set for them and the exact places where they should live. God did this so that men would seek him and perhaps reach out for him and find him, though he is not far from each one of us. 'For in him we live and move and have our being.' As some of your own poets have said, 'We are his offspring.'

"Therefore since we are God's offspring, we should not think that the divine being is like gold or silver or stone—an image made by man's design and skill. In the past God overlooked such ignorance, but now he commands all people everywhere to repent. For he has set a day when he will judge the world with justice by the man he has appointed. He has given proof of this to all men by raising him from the dead."

When they heard about the resurrection of the dead, some of them sneered, but others said, "We want to hear you again on this subject." At that, Paul left the Council. A few men became followers of Paul and believed. Among them was Dionysius, a member of the Areopagus, also a woman named Damaris, and a number of others.

Are you provoked by the idolatry in our post-Christian society? If you are then let me challenge you to let that provocation lead you to be a transformer rather than a separatist. Many Christians, when they see the problems of our society choose to separate themselves to the extent that they never have any positive, transforming impact upon our culture.

That is not what Paul did. He didn't separate himself from the culture. And he didn't try to tear down the idols of Athens. Rather, he proclaimed the name of the One who should take the place of those idols. Paul took on the culture of Athens and their gods.

As a result of Paul's provocation he proceeded to go to the "turf" of the Athenians; "he reasoned in the synagogue with the Jews and the God-fearing Greeks, as well as in the marketplace day by day with those who happened to be there."

Do we spend time with non-Christians on their turf—at work, in our neighborhoods, at school? That is what Paul did. Not only did he contact non-Christians in the synagogue, but he was not afraid to encounter "un-churched" people in the marketplace. Do we run *from* or run *to* opportunities to encounter non-Christians on their turf? Perhaps for us today proceeding to the turf of "un-churched" people might mean joining a bowling league or community theater or a cooking class. I have led book discussion groups at Barnes & Noble bookstores in two different cities because that is a place where I can interact with some people outside of the church.

When we proceed to non-Christian turf we need to be prepared. As Peter wrote:

> But in your hearts set apart Christ as Lord. Always be prepared to give an answer to everyone who asks you to give a reason for the hope that you have. But do this with gentleness and respect, keeping a clear conscience, so that those who speak maliciously against your good behavior in Christ may be ashamed of their slander. (1 Peter 3:15-16)

We need to be prepared in at least two ways. First of all we need to know our Bibles. Paul knew the Scriptures, he had been brought up at the feet of the great Rabbi Gamaliel. He had studied and continued to study the Old Testament Scriptures intensely. Paul knew the Bible well enough that he was able to present the teaching of Scripture accurately without quoting it directly. Numerous Old Testament Scriptures form the basis of his speech on Mars Hill.

How well do we know the Bible? Have we read the whole Bible? Are we continuing to read large portions of Scripture? Are we memorizing key Scripture verses that we can use, either quoted or paraphrased in conversation with non-Christians?

Secondly, we need to be prepared by knowing our audience. Paul knew his audience in Athens. He had been brought up in Tarsus, a great educational center in Asia Minor. He was familiar with Epicurean and Stoic philosophy. Paul was familiar with Greek poetry and drama. In this passage he quotes the Cretan poet Epimenides who wrote, "In him we live and move and have our being," as well as the Cilician poet Aratus who wrote, "We are his offspring." Paul also quotes from a Greek comedy by Menander in 1 Corinthians 15:33.

How well do we know the culture in which we live, the audience to which the Lord wants us to address the Gospel? It is important not to assume anything about the people with whom we are trying to share the good news.

The importance of not making rash assumptions is illustrated by the following story. A traveler, between flights at an airport, went to a lounge and bought a small package of cookies. Then she sat down and began reading a newspaper. Gradually, she became aware of a rustling noise. From behind her paper, she was flabbergasted to see a neatly dressed man helping himself to her cookies. Not wanting to make a scene, she leaned over and took a cookie herself.

A minute or two passed, and then came more rustling. He was helping himself to another cookie! By this time, they had come to the end of the package, but she was so angry she didn't dare allow herself to say anything. Then, as if to add insult to injury, the man broke the remaining cookie in two, pushed half across to her, and ate the other half and left.

Still fuming some time later when her flight was announced, the woman opened her handbag to get her ticket. To her shock and embarrassment, there she found her pack of unopened cookies!

How wrong our assumptions can be! We shouldn't assume that the people with whom we are trying to share Jesus are stealing our cookies when in fact we may be stealing theirs.

How can we learn more about the culture within which we live so that we don't make any rash assumptions? One of the best ways is to read: the newspaper, news magazines, non-Christian books. Another way is to go to plays, movies, and watch television, but not just to be entertained. We need to think about the values that are being portrayed. We need to question what we are watching. We need to discuss the values and doctrines being taught.

Another way to learn more about our culture is to read what other Christians have written. We need to be prepared by knowing the Bible and knowing the culture within which we live in order to be able to present the reason for the hope that we have in Christ.

Paul was a man prepared, he was a man provoked, and he was a man who invaded the turf of non-Christians. But once there, what did he do? *He probed for a point of contact.* That is precisely what you and I need to do in our every day lives and relationships with non-Christians. We need to probe for a point of contact. Paul discovered an altar to an unknown God. He started from that point of contact, he began with his hearer's belief in an impersonal, divine essence, and from there he led them to the Living God revealed as Creator and Judge.

What are the points of contact that we have with non-Christians? We should not assume that non-Christians share any of our concepts of who God is. We need to explore, ask questions, find out what they believe. But our first point of contact with non-Christians, may not be a common belief at all. It takes time to find out what someone else believes. So our first point of contact may be a shared activity or a felt need on the part of our non-Christian friends.

A number of years ago when we lived in another town we had neighbors with a son around the same age as one of our boys. That boy was our point of contact with our neighbors. Raising children is something we had in common. From there we built a friendship which eventually gave us the opportunity to invite our neighbors to church and share the Gospel with them. This led to one of the parents making a profession of faith in Christ. We were not doing anything all that unusual. I believe many people come into a personal relationship with Jesus Christ through such friendship evangelism.

Having been provoked and prepared, and having proceeded to their turf, and having probed for a point of contact, Paul then went on to *present to the Athenians a personal God*. That is precisely what we need to do as well.

The growing belief in our culture today is that God is not personal but rather impersonal. "May the force be with you" could well be one of the most telling religious slogans of the past many years. People don't want to have a personal God who holds them accountable for their actions. We are living in what C. S. Lewis defined as a post-Christian culture.

The one significant difference between Paul's Athens and our culture is this: the people of Athens had not yet been exposed to the Gospel; they were pure pagans. People in our culture have been exposed to the Gospel and many have rejected it.

Against this backdrop we are called by the Lord to present him, as a personal God, to a culture that believes God is an impersonal force. As Charles Colson has said:

> Let's face it, friends, if we fail to articulate the reasoned defense of our faith, all of our witnessing, plans of salvation, and evangelistic efforts will be for naught. Secularization of Western culture is undermining the presuppositions absolutely essential for effective evangelization. In a society that has lost a common belief in moral absolutes, relativism reigns—thus the Bible is just another book and Jesus simply another superior teacher.

A number of years ago I worked a part-time job delivering pizzas for Pizza Hut. While there I got to know one of the drivers. Steve was unmarried, probably in his mid thirties. And he was the top driver with the most miles for this particular delivery unit. One day Steve discovered that I was a pastor. And then his first question to me was, "So are you one of those fundamentalist Christians?"

I replied, "What do you mean by fundamentalist?"

"Well, do you take the Bible literally?" he queried.

I proceeded to tell him that the Bible is made up of many forms of literature and that I try to read the Bible according to the rules of interpretation that apply to each particular form. "In other words, I read poetry as poetry and historical narrative as historical narrative."

That baffled him a little bit but he went on to ask: "So do you believe that the earth was really covered by a flood? That Jonah was really swallowed by a whale?" He went on and on.

Finally I said, "The most important thing about the Bible is that it points to Jesus of Nazareth who made some startling claims. Based upon my reading of the Gospels I have come to the conclusion that Jesus was and is Lord and God. Just as Jesus is fully human and fully God, so also the Bible is a human word, but a human word which God uses to communicate his divine word to me." That ended that conversation for the time being. But every time that I saw Steve after that, he would bring up the discussion of religion again.

Finally, I was getting tired of Steve asking me questions all the time, so I turned the tables on him. I asked him, "So what do you believe?"

He said, "Well I don't believe in a God who is out there. I believe that God is within each one of us and that we should try to live moral lives."

"What is your standard for morality?" I asked.

"The Ten Commandments," he replied.

"Well where did we get the Ten Commandments?"

"Oh, they were written by men."

"Well if the Ten Commandments are a merely human word why should we obey them?"

"Because it is what is right."

"But suppose I don't think it is right. Suppose I decide it is right to go out and kill someone."

"Well, the God who is within you wouldn't tell you to do that would he?"

"The God who was within Hitler obviously led him to commit all sorts of atrocities."

Steve finally admitted, "That is a problem I hadn't thought of before."

So there I found the point of contact with Steve. The point of contact was his own innate sense of right and wrong. The fact that every civilization down through the centuries has had very similar codes of right and wrong suggests that there must be some external standard. And in order to have right and wrong you must have a personal God. If God is impersonal, if he is just a force within each one of us, then there is no right and wrong. What I did was to force Steve to face up to the logical conclusions of his belief system and recognize that those conclusions were unacceptable. It was unacceptable to him that people should do whatever they want to do and violate his moral code. Thus he will have to recognize that there must be an objective standard and that therefore there must also be a personal God.

What I am suggesting is that we should all be "transforming Christians" not "separatist Christians". The Lord wants us to be knowledgeable about the culture within which we live and he wants us to "take on" the belief systems of our culture, challenge them and transform them by the power of the Holy Spirit. That's what Paul did in Athens. He took on the culture. Paul proclaimed a God who does not live in temples built by hands, in full view of the greatest temple ever built by human hands–The Parthenon. He proclaimed a personal creator in contrast with the views of pantheistic stoicism. Paul proclaimed God as Master Designer in contradistinction to the Epicurean god of chance. In challenge to the ethnic pride of the Athenians Paul enunciated the unity of the human race, that God made from one person every nation of people. In the midst of a culture that believed the greatest human good was eventually to be separated from the evils of the body and enjoy the pure repose of the immortality of the soul, Paul had the audacity to preach the resurrection of the body. Paul certainly did not declare a popular Gospel destined to be widely accepted among the Athenians. Yet he did proclaim a Gospel very powerful in its attraction because it was true and truth holds its own allure.

Paul in his speech on Mars Hill did not give a full blown presentation of the Gospel, but he did lay the groundwork for the Gospel to be proclaimed. He knew that a defense first had to be given of theism, the belief in a personal God, before the Athenians would be ready to hear the Gospel. The same thing is needed in our culture, where many people are returning to pantheism, believing that everything is God. In a culture where Shirley MacLaine can proclaim that she is God and gain a wide hearing, in a society that believes God is dead but Elvis is still alive somewhere, the tenets of theism must first be declared before the Gospel can make any sense.

Paul met with various responses to his preaching. Some of the people sneered. They totally rejected what Paul had to say. Others sincerely wanted to hear more. And then there were some who became believers, apparently after Paul explained more of the Gospel to them. However, Paul's efforts were not a waste. Some very influential people were won to Christ such as Dionysius and Damaris.

So we should not get discouraged as we seek to reason with non-Christians and present the truth about God to them. We should expect a positive response from some because the Gospel is powerful.

Sometimes we forget the Holy Spirit within us and how powerful our witness can be. The Gospel has supernatural power—when we speak it in confidence. In God's strength we can be transformers; we can take on the belief systems of the culture within which we live. We can present to others the personal God whom we know in Jesus Christ. And we can expect a positive response. Because through our witness, through our being transformers, God is going to cause his Church to grow.

GROWING RELATIONSHIPS

A series of articles entitled *Religion in the Workplace* appeared a number of years ago in the Harrisburg Pennsylvania Patriot-News. In one of those articles Suzanne Cassidy and Mary Warner wrote,

> Work and religion generally are thought to belong to quite separate realms. But, consciously or not, overtly or not, whether it is welcome or not, many people bring their faith to work every day. Though many may not discern it — and many may be indifferent to it — religious belief is a distinct thread in the fabric of working life . . .

This should come as no surprise to those of us who have a personal relationship with Jesus Christ. I do not believe that Jesus wants us to compartmentalize our lives in such a way that he is kept out of any part of it. The question is not, "Does Christ want us to bring our faith into the workplace?" but rather, "*How* does Christ want us to bring our faith into the workplace?"

Author Bruce Larson has written, "God wants us to be aware always of the people next to us. It's not enough to work honestly and industriously, for Christ calls us to be a priesthood of believers who willingly take responsibility for those who are our neighbors."

In short, I believe that God wants us to grow relationships with our co-workers that make a difference for Christ and his Kingdom. And I believe that we have a great example of this in action in Acts 18:1-3. . . .

> After these things he [Paul] left Athens and went to Corinth. And he found a certain Jew named Aquila, a native of Pontus, having recently come from Italy with his wife Priscilla, because Claudius had commanded all the Jews to leave Rome. He came to them, and because he was of the same trade, he stayed with them and they were working; for by trade they were tent-makers.

I think we can all learn at least three things from this passage about how to grow relationships with co-workers that make a difference for Christ. First of all, if we want to grow relationships that make a difference with co-workers, then we need to discover people at work with whom we have something in common.

Paul was a tentmaker. His work was closely connected with the chief manufacture of his native province, cilicium, a cloth of goat's hair, used for cloaks, curtains and other items.

Now most of us are probably familiar with the fact that Paul was also a Rabbi, raised in the Jewish traditions, who had also become a follower and teacher of Christ. So why did Paul labor as a tentmaker if he already had a job as a Rabbi? The reason is that all the teaching of the scribes and Rabbis had to be gratuitous. Therefore they had to make their living by practicing some trade. Paul probably learned tent-making as a youth since it was the Jewish custom to provide some kind of manual training for sons.

Paul had just come from Athens where he had taught about Christ to the philosophers who gathered near that great pagan temple, the Parthenon. It was Paul's custom to travel to the major cities of the Roman Empire in order to spread the message of Christ. So now he traveled to Corinth, which in many ways was the chief city of Greece. Corinth had a population of 250,000 free persons, plus as many as 400,000 slaves. Corinth was a crossroads for travelers and traders and the city had two harbors. It is, I think, interesting to note that tent-makers in Corinth were also sail-makers. So Paul would have much sail-making work in the winter when ships were laid up in the two harbors near Corinth.

Luke tells us that after Paul came to Corinth he discovered a Jew named Aquila who was a native of Pontus and a fellow tentmaker. We are not told exactly how Paul and Aquila met, but perhaps their meeting came about through their common work.

Aquila's home town of Pontus was in Bithynia, a Roman Province in the northeastern region of Asia Minor, modern day Turkey. Aquila had apparently moved from Pontus to Rome where he probably met his wife Priscilla. Priscilla and Aquila were expelled from Rome by the Roman Emperor Claudius probably in AD 49 or 50. Roman historians tell us that the expulsion order was given because of the Jews' "continual tumults instigated by Chrestus." Chrestus may have been a misspelling of "Christ," which means that Emperor Claudius may have expelled the Jews from Rome because of their riots with Jewish Christians regarding the person of Christ. In any case, these expulsions only had a partial and temporary effect, for later on Aquila and Priscilla returned to Rome.

Luke tells us that Paul *found* Aquila. The sense of the word in Acts 18:2 is that of finding someone without seeking them, to come upon someone accidentally. So Paul did not seek out Aquila. But there are no accidents with God. God, in his providence, put Paul and Aquila together. And God has providentially placed us in our various workplaces where we are now. He has put us together with our co-workers for a specific purpose. He wants us, as

Paul did, to form relationships with people in our workplace by discovering those with whom we have something in common.

Paul not only shared a common profession with Aquila, he shared a common religious background — Judaism, and they were both foreigners in Corinth. Aquila, being an exile, may have felt very alone and may have been looking for friendship.

I wonder who there might be in our workplaces with whom we might share something in common. Are there any lonely people looking for friendship? I believe the Lord wants us to discover them and build relationships with them.

The story is told of a Coloradan who moved to Texas and built a house with a large picture window from which he could view hundreds of miles of rangeland. "The only problem is," he said, "there's nothing to see."

About the same time, a Texan moved to Colorado and built a house with a large picture window overlooking the Rockies. "The only problem is I can't see anything," he said. "The mountains are in the way."

We have a way of missing what's right in front of us. We go to a city and see lights and glitter, but miss the lonely people. We hear a person's critical comments, but miss the cry for love and friendship. We go to work and do our jobs efficiently and well, but we miss the people all around us who are hungering for relationship.

Maybe you feel lost in your current job. You don't see why God has put you where you are right now. But he has a reason, if you would only open your spiritual eyes to see it. He wants you to reach out and discover the people he has placed around you at work. He wants you to begin to build relationships with them. If you want to grow relationships that make a difference with co-workers, then open your eyes and discover the people God has placed around you with whom you may have something in common.

The second principle we can learn from Paul's relationship with Aquila is that once we have discovered the people around us at work, we need to go to them to get to know them better.

Luke tells us that Paul went to Aquila. Literally, he found out where Aquila lived and he joined him in tent-making in his house because they were of the same trade.

What Paul was doing here was getting to know Aquila better. He could easily have worked on his own and never gotten to know Aquila, but he didn't do that. Paul knew that the Christian life is all about building loving relationships, so he reached out in friendship to Aquila.

Now Paul didn't stop at just getting to know Aquila, he got to know his wife Priscilla as well. Priscilla may not have been a tentmaker as was her husband. Throughout the rest of the New Testament whenever this couple is mentioned, Priscilla's name is usually mentioned first. This may indicate that she was of a higher social rank than her husband. In fact, Sir William Ramsey, among others, has held that Priscilla probably belonged to a noble Roman family. We don't know whether Priscilla was a Jew or not since Luke only tells us that Aquila was a Jew.

Paul got to know Priscilla and Aquila in the context of their home, and accepted their hospitality. Paul also got to know Priscilla and Aquila as they worked together. Sewing is a type of work which encourages thought and conversation. It may have been of Rome that Paul and Priscilla and Aquila talked, because Paul wanted to learn more about the capitol of the Roman Empire, as it was his hope one day to travel there. Perhaps for the first time in his life Paul had intimate contact with someone who could answer his questions about Rome, so I'm sure he made the most of the opportunity.

We can get to know our co-workers better by asking about their families, by socializing outside of work-time, and by asking them about subjects they are interested in. A number of years ago, my wife Becky worked as the office manager for a small firm. There were five other people who worked in Becky's office — her boss, who owned the company, and four others, three men and one woman. Becky got to know each of these people fairly well, and so did I whenever I went to Becky's workplace to have lunch with her. Their working situation was such that they could converse with one another frequently and informally. Becky got to know their family situations, their political opinions, as well as their religious backgrounds.

Her boss and his family were nominal Catholics. One of the men in the office was a Mormon elder. Another one was a self-professed ex-Mormon who had left the Mormon church when he got divorced. Then there was one woman in the office, who had grown up in the Presbyterian church, but who was, at the time, uninvolved in any church. And there was one man in the office who was "un-churched", but going through the motions of becoming Catholic because his fiancée was Catholic.

Becky became the social organizer for the office. She helped to plan birthday and Christmas parties among other things. And it was through the Christmas parties that we both got to know the other people at Becky's work and their families better.

Becky even developed a friendship with her boss' wife. They went out to lunch together on occasion. Becky's boss' wife was pregnant at the time and when it came time for her to deliver, Becky offered to stay at her boss' house and watch their kids for them because they really didn't have any close relationships with anyone else. So Becky ended up sleeping in her boss' bed overnight — but he wasn't there — he was at the hospital!

Becky also got to know her one female co-worker out of the group very well. They often ate lunch together and Becky's co-worker came over to our house for dinner on occasion. This co-worker fell in love with our cat, Papillon, and took care of him during some of our out-of-town trips. Becky invited this woman to visit our church, which she did off and on during the time she lived in San Diego.

The Mormon elder and his family came to our church on two occasions, once for a children's Christmas program and once for my ordination as a pastor. The latter event was also attended by Becky's boss and his wife.

We even had the ex-Mormon out of the group over to our house for dinner one night and had a very interesting conversation about Christ, the historicity of his resurrection, and the historical roots of Mormonism. The most pressing issue for this young man was how to raise his non-custodial child in a moral and religious vacuum, since he himself had no firm moral or religious convictions.

All of this I share to make the point that if you work at it, you can grow relationships with co-workers that make a difference for Christ. We saw no dramatic conversions among any of these friends during the time Becky had that job. But Becky stayed in touch with these people even after we moved away and we exchanged Christmas cards across the miles. The bottom line is that Becky was faithful to build no-strings-attached relationships with these co-workers, loving them for Christ's sake.

The third thing we can learn from Paul's relationship with Aquila and Priscilla is that if we want to grow relationships that make a difference for Christ we need to stay with people until they are grounded in Christ. Now I realize that job transfers and other life circumstances can often quickly separate us from co-workers. A person you build a relationship with today could move away tomorrow, or you could find yourself moving for one reason or another. But if God gives us the opportunity we need to stay in relationship with co-workers for the long haul.

Paul stayed with Priscilla and Aquila, literally he lived with them, until a very deep bond was formed. Luke tells us that Aquila was a Jew when he and Paul first met. We are not told exactly when Aquila and Priscilla became Christians. Perhaps Paul invited Aquila and Priscilla to go with him to the synagogue to hear him speak about Jesus to their fellow Jews. In any case, if Aquila was a devoted Jew he would surely have gone with Paul to the synagogue, and he would have heard from Paul's lips that Jesus was the Messiah.

The bond which Paul formed with Priscilla and Aquila was so deep in fact that when Paul moved from Corinth in Greece to Ephesus in Asia Minor, Priscilla and Aquila moved with him. The couple may have left Corinth for more profitable work in Ephesus, which was famous for the manufacture of luxurious tents. But whatever other reasons they had, clearly they had a strong attachment to Paul since they moved at the same time.

As I said, we are not told exactly when Priscilla and Aquila became believers in Jesus as their Messiah, but clearly they had become believers by their time in Ephesus. We read in Acts 18:26 that when a young man named Apollos "began to speak boldly in the synagogue . . . Priscilla and Aquila heard him [and] they invited him to their home and explained the way of God more adequately" to him. In other words, they heard Apollos talking about Jesus and realized he didn't have the full scoop, so they taught him more fully about Christ.

Later when Paul wrote a letter from Ephesus back to the church in Corinth in AD 55 he said, "Aquila and Priscilla greet you warmly in the Lord, and so does the church that meets at their house." (1 Corinthians 16:19) So not only had Priscilla and Aquila become Christians, they taught others, like Apollos, about Christ, and they provided a meeting place for the Ephesian church in their home. Priscilla and Aquila became reproducers who taught others about Christ, who in turn taught others.

When Paul wrote to the church of Rome a couple of years later in AD 57 he said, "Greet Priscilla and Aquila, my fellow workers in Christ Jesus. They risked their lives for me. Not only I but all the churches of the Gentiles are grateful to them. Greet also the church that meets at their house." (Romans 16:3-4) So by AD 57 Priscilla and Aquila had moved back to Rome and again the church was meeting in their house. Priscilla and Aquila had become such committed, sacrificial Christians and such good friends of Paul that they even had risked their lives for him in some way. And they were recognized leaders throughout the growing Christian Church across the Roman Empire.

In fact, Paul had formed a life-long friendship with Priscilla and Aquila, for when he wrote his last letter to Timothy around AD 66 or 67 he was still thinking of his old friends. When Paul wrote to Timothy in Ephesus from a cold dungeon in Rome, just before he was executed for his faith in Christ, he said, "Greet Priscilla and Aquila." Apparently these great friends of Paul had moved back to Ephesus where Timothy was, and as Paul came to the end of his life he was still thinking about their friendship.

In Rome today there stands a church by the name of St. Prisca on the Aventine. Tradition claims it as the sight of Priscilla and Aquila's home in which the early church met. In 1776 a subterranean oratory was discovered, the walls of which were decorated with 4th century frescoes. The discoverers walled up the oratory again, but there is little doubt that this was the ancient home of Priscilla and Aquila, two people who had become well-known warriors for the Christian faith, all because of one co-worker named Paul who befriended them.

The Lord wants us too to befriend co-workers for Christ's sake. He wants us to stay with them until they become grounded in Christ. Some people whom we befriend may never become believers in Christ, but God wants us to love them anyway. He wants us to form relationships of unconditional love, with no strings attached. But the most loving thing that any one of us can do for another human being is to lead them into a love-relationship with Jesus Christ.

How about you? Are you forming deep bonds with people in your workplace? Do you have people whom you have met through work with whom you stay in touch over the years, even when new jobs and moves may separate you? Are you at the point in some relationship where you might effectively invite a co-worker to come to church with you and hear the good news about Christ?

As Bruce Larson has said, "God calls the laity to do a job the clergy cannot do in many instances." You have contact with people through your work that would perhaps never come to church or want to listen to a preacher like me. But you, through your life and through your words, can communicate the love of Christ to these people.

Bruce Larson tells the story of a doctor whom he knew who became quite ill. Though Bruce visited him almost daily he saw no improvement and no benefit from his visits. However, one day Bruce went to visit this doctor and found him greatly improved and free from fear. He asked him what had happened. The doctor told Bruce of a visit he had a few hours before with a senior surgeon in the area who had prayed with him and given him a prescription. The prescription was to read Joshua 1:9 which says, "Have I not commanded you? Be strong and courageous. Do not be terrified; do not be discouraged, for the Lord your God will be with you wherever you go." Bruce's friend had been touched by God, and not through a clergyman but through a fellow physician.

Who is there in your line of work whom you can touch for Christ's sake this week? May God give you the power to reach out to them in love and make a difference for Christ and his kingdom.

CRISES

Charles Eerdman once wrote, "The experience through which Paul passed at Corinth was so serious and unusual that it is regarded as constituting a distinct crisis in his life. The causes of his discouragement were such as are common to Christians, particularly to workers on the foreign field. It may be helpful to enumerate these, and also the divine providences by which he was given relief; for thus some may find encouragement and help in hours of darkness."

I agree with Eerdman. I think we have a lot to learn from Paul about how to handle crises, especially from the crises he endured in Corinth which we read about in Acts 18:1-17. . . .

> After this, Paul left Athens and went to Corinth. There he met a Jew named Aquila, a native of Pontus, who had recently come from Italy with his wife Priscilla, because Claudius had ordered all the Jews to leave Rome. Paul went to see them, and because he was a tentmaker as they were, he stayed and worked with them. Every Sabbath he reasoned in the synagogue, trying to persuade Jews and Greeks.
>
> When Silas and Timothy came from Macedonia, Paul devoted himself exclusively to preaching, testifying to the Jews that Jesus was the Christ. But when the Jews opposed Paul and became abusive, he shook out his clothes in protest and said to them, "Your blood be on your own heads! I am clear of my responsibility. From now on I will go to the Gentiles."
>
> Then Paul left the synagogue and went next door to the house of Titius Justus, a worshiper of God. Crispus, the synagogue ruler, and his entire household believed in the Lord; and many of the Corinthians who heard him believed and were baptized.
>
> One night the Lord spoke to Paul in a vision: "Do not be afraid; keep on speaking, do not be silent. For I am with you, and no one is going to attack and harm you, because I have many people in this city." So Paul stayed for a year and a half, teaching them the word of God.
>
> While Gallio was proconsul of Achaia, the Jews made a united attack on Paul and brought him into court. "This man," they charged, "is

persuading the people to worship God in ways contrary to the law."

Just as Paul was about to speak, Gallio said to the Jews, "If you Jews were making a complaint about some misdemeanor or serious crime, it would be reasonable for me to listen to you. But since it involves questions about words and names and your own law—settle the matter yourselves. I will not be a judge of such things." So he had them ejected from the court. Then they all turned on Sosthenes the synagogue ruler and beat him in front of the court. But Gallio showed no concern whatever.

Crisis #1: Loneliness

While waiting for Silas and Timothy to arrive from Athens there was no one Paul knew in Corinth.

Tim Hansel has written in his book, *Dancin' Toward the Dawn*, "Loneliness is not the same as being alone. Loneliness is feeling alone . . . no matter how many people are around you."

Here was Paul in one of the biggest cities he had ever visited, hundreds of thousands of people milling about, but he didn't know a one of them. Certainly he felt lonely in those circumstances.

Someone once said that there are few things more emotionally draining than being in a crowd of people you don't know. You are looking into a sea of faces, but none of them are familiar, and so it is very tiring. Paul must have known the exhaustion of loneliness during his first days in Corinth.

But eventually God met Paul's need for companionship. The Lord answered this need in Paul's life by introducing him to Aquila and Priscilla. In the last chapter we saw how Paul had a profound influence on this couple. However, the fact is that they had no less an influence on Paul.

Don't misunderstand me. I don't think our need for love and friendship is ever fully met in this life. It is easy to look at people in the Bible, or people we read about in books, and think: Boy, they sure had it made. But when we meet real people, and really get to know them, we discover there is always a residual loneliness in their lives, and in ours, that is never fully taken away. As Tim Hansel has written: "God is not going to take all the loneliness away and patch every hole in our lives. He is just going to give it meaning and purpose. He doesn't promise to fix us–just make us whole and holy." Even Jesus, when he rose from the dead, still had the wounds from the cross. It has been said that when we get to heaven, God will not measure our lives according to our diplomas or our medals, but according to our scars and how we handled them.

How do you handle loneliness? Do you rush about trying to fill the emptiness with whatever or whomever is at hand? Or do you take time, as I'm sure Paul did, to embrace the stillness–the aloneness?

Keys to Growth

Writer, theologian and professor, Henri Nouwen, once broke away from his busy schedule to live for six months in a monastery. He later wrote about the experience and explained why he took this time out from his overcrowded life:

> I realized that I was caught in a web of strange paradoxes. While complaining about too many demands, I felt uneasy when none were made. While speaking about the burden of letter writing, an empty mailbox made me sad. While speaking nostalgically about an empty desk, I feared the day in which that would come true.
>
> In short, while desiring to be alone, I was frightened of being left alone. The more I became aware of these paradoxes, the more I started to see how much I had fallen in love with my own compulsions and illusions, and how much I needed to step back and wonder, "Is there a quiet stream underneath the fluctuating affirmations and rejections of my little world?"

Sometimes we need to embrace the loneliness of life and drink the cup of aloneness to the dregs. Other times we need to reach out for friendship but do it without grasping desperately. It is only as we get quiet before God that we will know which we need to do. It is only as we embrace our aloneness with him that he can begin to fill our empty cups.

Crisis #2: Poverty

The second crisis Paul faced in Corinth was the crisis of poverty. Paul was forced to make tents as a means of supporting himself. Later he wrote to the Church at Philippi:

> I know what it is to be in need, and I know what it is to have plenty. I have learned the secret of being content in any and every situation, whether well fed or hungry, whether living in plenty or in want. I can do everything, through him who gives me strength. . . . when I set out from Macedonia, not one church shared with me in the matter of giving and receiving, except you only; for even when I was in Thessalonica, you sent me aid again and again when I was in need.

Apparently by the time Paul got to Corinth even this support from the Philippians had dried up. But the fact that Paul was able to make money by tent-making in Corinth was also part of God's provision. Then when Silas and Timothy *did* show up, perhaps they brought financial support with them, for it was then that Paul devoted himself exclusively to preaching.

In the ups and downs, the ins and outs of everyday life, Paul learned to trust the Lord to provide for him and rest content in that provision, whether the Lord provided for Paul through tent-making or through the gifts of friends.

Jesus said, "But seek first his kingdom and his righteousness, and all these things will be given to you as well." (Matthew 6:33) If we put God first in our lives then we don't need to worry about provisions. As Paul wrote to the Philippians, "And my God will meet all your needs according to his glorious riches in Christ Jesus."

Dale Alan Robbins writes of an occasion early in his ministry when he and his wife were barely making ends meet:

> When I arrived home, my wife Jerri saw the worry on my face. I had $3 in my wallet and there was one can of soup in the cupboard. After our meager supper, I quietly leafed through my Bible in the dim light. Tears streamed from my eyes. I wondered whether we were really called by God. I felt like giving up. Then I thought, *What alternative do I have? Who else but God do I have to turn to?*
>
> I read the verse: "The effectual fervent prayer of a righteous man availeth much" (James 5:16). . . . Encouraged, yet still burdened, Jerri and I knelt at opposite ends of the little trailer to seek God. Into the night we prayed, until sleep finally overtook us.
>
> I was awakened by a pounding at the door. From the window I could see the brilliant orange sunrise behind the city skyline. A fresh, white blanket of snow now covered the ground. Again, the knocking came.
>
> "Who is it?" I asked.
>
> A mystery voice replied, "I've got something for you."
>
> Cautiously, I opened the door. There stood a short man with a grin on his face and two brown grocery bags in his arms. He quickly shoved the bags in the doorway, then turned, and walked away.
>
> Jerri joined me. Stunned, we began to look through the bags. There were bread, meat, canned goods, and several cans of my favorite soup. They were the same items and brands we normally purchased. There was also a can of shaving cream. Who knew I had just used my last ounce of shaving cream? On the bottom of one sack was an envelope with cash. (Later I discovered it was the precise amount needed to fill our gas tank to get us to our next destination.)
>
> On that wintry Saturday morning in Syracuse, my wife and I wept in our trailer and thanked God for hearing and answering our prayer. No one on the planet knew about our need, only our Lord God Almighty. And he dispatched a little grinning man to minister to us.

There is a time to pray and there is a time to work. Whether through the work of our own hands, or the gifts of others, the Lord provides for his own. You can go to the bank on that, just like Paul learned to go to the bank of heaven on it.

Crisis #3: Failure

The Jews whom Paul was trying to reach with the Gospel in Corinth opposed Paul and became abusive, so much so that Paul shook out his clothes in protest and said to them, "Your blood be on your own heads!" Later, the Jews made a united attack against Paul and brought him before the court of Gallio, the proconsul of Achaia and brother of Seneca, the philosopher and tutor of Nero. This must have been especially painful for Paul since he loved his own people and even wished that he himself could be damned if they could be saved (Romans 9:3). But God used the impartiality of Gallio to protect Paul from harm. And just when Paul was probably tempted to think that he had failed in Corinth, Crispus, the synagogue ruler, and his entire household became believers. Not only that, but many of the Corinthians who heard Paul believed and were baptized.

As Michael Green has noted in his book, *To Corinth with Love*: "We are not called to constant success. We are not called to instant glory now. We live between the ages; heirs to all the failure and frailty and fallenness of this age, heirs too to the power and life and love of the age to come. We live at the cross roads. The Master suffered . . . and rose. So will his apostolic church . . ."

Do you ever wonder why you seem to be failing so much in life? Do you ever feel like you are the worst Christian in the world because of your failures? Maybe you wonder if you are a Christian at all because you have gotten it into your head that Christians don't fail, they succeed all the time, don't they?

Maybe you better take another look at the heroes of faith in Hebrews 11. Do you think Abel felt successful when his brother Cain was about to kill him? Or what about Abraham when he was wandering through the desert without a home or an heir? Or Joseph when he was sold into slavery? He must have wondered if the dream God had given him would ever come true. Or how about Moses tending Jethro's sheep–do you think he felt like he had accomplished something in life? The writer to the Hebrews says that all of these heroes of the faith had their *weakness turned to strength*. They weren't known for their successes, but for their failures, and how God used those failures. Hebrews 11:35-38 reads:

> Others were tortured and refused to be released, so that they might gain a better resurrection. Some faced jeers and flogging, while still others were chained and put in prison. They were stoned; they were sawed in two; they were put to death by the sword. They went about

in sheepskins and goatskins, destitute, persecuted and mistreated–
the world was not worthy of them. They wandered in deserts and
mountains, and in caves and holes in the ground.

That is a description of the "normal" Christian life. It hardly sounds successful does it? However, only God can really count success or failure, for only he sees all our lives accurately, from an eternal perspective. Paul must have felt like a failure in the synagogue in Corinth when the Jews rejected his message. But he only needed to wait a little while to see the fruit the Lord was going to bring about in the midst of seeming failure.

As C. S. Lewis once said, "It is not your business to succeed but to do right: when you have done so, the rest lies with God."

Crisis #4: Alienation

Paul must have felt like he was in an alien land when he was in Corinth. It was the furthest distance he had ever traveled from his home in Tarsus, and the city presented many things which conflicted with his Jewish upbringing.

Corinth was on the main trade route between Rome and the eastern Mediterranean. It was the capitol of the province of Achaia. It was a wealthy and intellectual city, yet at the same time Corinth was notorious across the Roman Empire for her moral corruption.

Michael Green has written, "Corinth was the Vanity Fair of the ancient world. Aphrodite was worshiped there as *Porne* (prostitute), her temple on the Acrocorinth was given over to debauchery, and the very name of Corinth was used to denote fornication ("Corinthianizing"). The city was sex mad."

The temple of Aphrodite which once stood directly above the city was home to a thousand male and female temple prostitutes. Thus Corinth attracted worshipers of Aphrodite from all over the Roman Empire.

How did Paul handle the sense of alienation he must have felt in Corinth? The chief source of Paul's encouragement in the midst of an alien land was a fresh vision of Jesus Christ:

> One night the Lord spoke to Paul in a vision: 'Do not be afraid; keep on speaking, do not be silent. For I am with you, and no one is going to attack and harm you, because I have many people in this city.'

As a result of that vision Paul stayed for a year and a half in Corinth, longer than he had stayed anywhere else, and he taught them the word of God. Furthermore, from Corinth Paul wrote great letters of encouragement to the Church at Thessalonica. This should remind us that the place of many crises can also be the place where God uses us to comfort others. As Paul later wrote to the Church at Corinth:

> Praise be to the God and Father of our Lord Jesus Christ, the Father of compassion and the God of all comfort, who comforts us in all our troubles, so that we can comfort those in any trouble with the comfort we ourselves have received from God. (2 Corinthians 1:3-4)

Paul was able to thrive instead of just survive in the crises of loneliness, poverty, seeming failure and a sense of alienation because he had a clear vision of Jesus Christ. I have stood on the "bema", the raised judgment platform where Paul was brought before Gallio. Today, on that very spot, stands a large, square stone inscribed with these words of Paul from 2 Corinthians 4:17, written both in Greek and in English:

> For this slight momentary affliction is preparing for us an eternal weight of glory beyond all comparison.

Paul goes on in the next verse to say:

> So we fix our eyes not on what is seen, but on what is unseen. For what is seen is temporary, but what is unseen is eternal.

As Paul stood there on the "bema", the judgment platform, I imagine he thought of the judgment platform on which he would one day stand before God. As Paul stood on the bema before Gallio he could see plenty of temporary things: in the distance was the temple of Aphrodite on the Acrocorinth, right across the street was the temple of Apollo with its massive Doric columns, before Paul stood a beautiful Roman fountain, and to his left was a thriving marketplace. Paul saw all of this with his physical eyes, but he also had the God-given ability to close his physical eyes to what was temporary and open his spiritual eyes to the eternal.

The Lord's great word of comfort to us in the midst of an alien culture is: "I am with you." Paul was right: everything in Corinth was temporary; Corinth lies in ruins today. Paul certainly felt alienated in that city that was filled with things and activities completely foreign to his belief system. Paul was not at home in Corinth. He realized, as we all need to realize, that his home was with God. As Paul later wrote to the Philippians: "our citizenship is in heaven." (Philippians 3:20) And in the shadow of the goddess of love Paul told the Corinthians what real love was all about, a love that could heal humanity's greatest alienation–her alienation from God.

The movie, *Home Alone*, is about a family going on a European vacation for Christmas. The relatives all arrive to wish them *Bon Voyage*, but the little boy in the family is feeling slighted. He rebels, gets in trouble and is sent to his room. While there he wishes that everyone would just go away so he could be left alone.

In a bizarre plot twist the family forgets about the boy and leaves for the airport. They get on the plane thinking he is with them. When the boy wakes up the next morning he finds he is "home alone" and he is delighted. He does everything he ever wanted to do by himself. He watches movies ad infinitum, eats all the junk food he wants, and he doesn't have to answer to anyone.

Burglars try to break into the house but he is able to foil all of their plans. Finally, when that problem is solved, the boy realizes for the first time how lonely he is. Life on his own isn't what he thought it would be. He is sorry that he treated his parents so badly and he desperately wants them back.

Often we are like that little boy in our relationship with God. We resent God's authority and we long for our freedom. Then when we exercise our own autonomy we are happy for awhile, but in the end we realize we are desperately lonely. Without God, we are home alone.

The good news is that God can use our crises of loneliness, poverty, failure, and our sense of alienation in this world to draw us closer to himself. If that is the result of each of these crises then each one is worth going through, just so we can come out on the other side having grown closer to our Triune God.

PASSING THE TORCH

The Olympic Torch is a symbol of the Olympic Games. Commemorating the theft of fire from the Greek god Zeus by Prometheus, its origins lie in ancient Greece, when a fire was kept burning throughout the celebration of the ancient Olympics. The fire was reintroduced at the Olympics in 1928, and it has been part of the modern Olympic Games ever since. The modern torch relay was introduced for the Berlin Games of 1936.

The Olympic Torch today is ignited several months before the opening celebration of the Olympic Games at the site of the ancient Olympics in Olympia, Greece. By tradition, the Olympic flame is delivered to the officials of the host city in a ceremony taking place in the Athenian Stadium for the start of the relay by the city authorities of Athens.

The torch is then transported to the host city of the upcoming Olympics by a torch relay. Though traditionally, the flame is carried on foot, other means of transportation have been used as well. The runners have included athletes and celebrities, but many previously "unknown" people have also carried it, often chosen for their personal merits and achievements. Even my brother had the privilege of carrying the Olympic Torch in 1996, the year that the Summer Olympic Games were in Atlanta.

The Olympic Torch Relay ends on the day of the opening ceremony in the central stadium of the Games. The final carrier is often kept secret until the last moment, and is usually a sports celebrity of the host country. The final bearer of the torch runs towards the cauldron, usually placed at the top of a grand staircase, and then uses the torch to start the flame in the stadium. It is generally considered a great honor to be asked to light the Olympic Flame. After being lit, the flame continues to burn throughout the celebration of the Olympics and is extinguished at the end of the closing ceremony of the Games.

The Olympic Torch Relay is a symbol of passing on something vital. Jesus passed on a vital pattern of teaching and living by making disciples. The Apostle Paul adopted Jesus' method. In 2 Timothy 2:2 Paul wrote to one of his own disciples saying:

> And the things you have heard me say in the presence of many witnesses entrust to reliable men who will also be qualified to teach others.

MEDITATIONS ON THE ACTS OF THE APOSTLES

We have a vivid illustration in Acts 18 of how the torch of faith gets passed on. Paul left Athens for Corinth in order to pass the light of Christ on to others. Like an Olympic torchbearer, he handed the Gospel flame to other runners. Let us look for a moment at three Olympic-like runners in Acts 18. Watch as the flaming torch is passed from life to life....

> Paul stayed on in Corinth for some time. Then he left the brothers and sailed for Syria, accompanied by Priscilla and Aquila. Before he sailed, he had his hair cut off at Cenchrea because of a vow he had taken. They arrived at Ephesus, where Paul left Priscilla and Aquila. He himself went into the synagogue and reasoned with the Jews. When they asked him to spend more time with them, he declined. But as he left, he promised, "I will come back if it is God's will." Then he set sail from Ephesus. When he landed at Caesarea, he went up and greeted the church and then went down to Antioch.
>
> After spending some time in Antioch, Paul set out from there and traveled from place to place throughout the region of Galatia and Phrygia, strengthening all the disciples.
>
> Meanwhile a Jew named Apollos, a native of Alexandria, came to Ephesus. He was a learned man, with a thorough knowledge of the Scriptures. He had been instructed in the way of the Lord, and he spoke with great fervor and taught about Jesus accurately, though he knew only the baptism of John. He began to speak boldly in the synagogue. When Priscilla and Aquila heard him, they invited him to their home and explained to him the way of God more adequately.
>
> When Apollos wanted to go to Achaia, the brothers encouraged him and wrote to the disciples there to welcome him. On arriving, he was a great help to those who by grace had believed. For he vigorously refuted the Jews in public debate, proving from the Scriptures that Jesus was the Christ.

The first Olympic-like runner we see in this passage is the Apostle Paul. There are two activities vital in making disciples which we see portrayed in Paul's life. The first thing Paul did, which we have referred to over the past couple of chapters, is that he reasoned in the synagogue. The word for "reason" in Acts 18:19 is the word from which we get our modern English word: dialogue. In other words, Paul didn't just preach in the synagogue, he carried on discussions with the Jews who happened to be there. Paul's communication wasn't one way, it was two-way. He listened to the questions and objections the Jews had regarding Jesus as the Messiah, and he addressed those questions and objections; he tried to persuade the Jews that Jesus really was the Christ.

That makes me question: are we in dialogue with unbelievers about our faith in Jesus Christ? I don't believe the Lord wants us just to preach or hand out tracts. He wants us to be in dialogue with non-Christians. He wants us to introduce Jesus into our everyday conversation; he wants us to gently persuade others to accept Jesus as Savior and Lord.

In the last chapter we saw how Paul got discouraged in this process. Even he wasn't always successful at winning others to Christ. So we shouldn't get discouraged if we don't see any immediate fruit from our efforts to be witnesses for Jesus.

Robert and Mary Moffat, mother-in-law and father-in-law to David Livingstone, served as missionaries in one South African village for eight years. Seeing no one come to Christ, they changed their location and worked another four years. Still they saw no fruit. Their mission board prepared to call them home. But just before they were to return home the Moffats saw one young man receive Christ, then another, and before long a small church was formed.

Stories like that have been repeated over and over again through the history of the church. Hudson Taylor labored for twenty years in China before he saw anyone accept Christ as Lord and Savior. So if you have never seen anyone accept Jesus as a result of your witness you are in good company! But don't stop. Don't give up! Keep on dialoguing with others about the Savior.

The second thing Paul did to make disciples was that he *strengthened* them (Acts 18:23). That word in the Greek means to set fast, to confirm, to fix, to establish.

How did Paul strengthen disciples? Two chapters ago we saw how Paul did this with Aquila and Priscilla. He found them. He went to see them. He stayed with them. Paul worked with them. He passed the word on to them, probably through everyday conversation. Then Priscilla and Aquila traveled with Paul to Ephesus and Paul used them to plant a church there. The way we live our lives is always the best way of passing the torch of faith to others. Priscilla and Aquila liked so much what they saw in the life of Paul that they wanted to have the flame of Christ alight in their lives as well.

In his book, *Everyday Evangelism*, Tom Eisenman talks about being an everyday witness in his neighborhood. He talks about how it took four years living in their neighborhood and choosing to sink their roots deep before he saw relationships open up. His wife Judie had the opportunity to watch a neighbor's child while her neighbor was at work. This opened up the opportunity to invite the woman to church. She came to church and then started attending regularly.

Another relationship opened up when a woman down the block shared about a life-threatening illness. Eventually that woman started attending Tom and Judie's church and joined as a member.

Meditations on the Acts of the Apostles

In his book Tom talks about the need to develop small talk with our neighbors as a major ministry in our neighborhoods. It was during normal small talk that the woman down the street shared about her illness.

When another couple in the neighborhood experienced job loss Tom was able to arrange for help from the church. That led to that couple attending the church as well.

Bottom line, Tom says, is that we need to get to know our neighbors and take advantage of every opportunity to care for them in small, practical, down-to-earth sorts of ways. He says "If we remember the importance of salvation appeal—that we are dedicated to laying down our lives in service to others, sensitive and aware of their personal needs, and engaged in meeting those needs with second-mile living and loving—we will become appealing Christians who impact our neighborhoods for Christ today."

Tom and Judie Eisenman are a modern-day example of how to dialogue with neighbors about Christ, inviting them into the fellowship of the church, and establishing them in the faith. They are doing exactly what Paul described in his letter to the Thessalonians: "We loved you so much that we were delighted to share with you not only the Gospel of God but our lives as well, because you had become so dear to us." We need to love other people to Jesus and then keep on loving them to strengthen them in the faith.

Now let's look at the second runners in this Olympic-like relay: Priscilla and Aquila. They traveled with Paul from Corinth in Greece to Ephesus, on the coast of Asia Minor. After Paul left Ephesus, Priscilla and Aquila remained there. They attended the Jewish synagogue in Ephesus because they were modeling what Paul did. They knew the synagogue was a great place to make contacts with people whom they might love into the Kingdom.

One day in the synagogue Priscilla and Aquila heard a man named Apollos teaching about Jesus. But Priscilla and Aquila realized quickly that Apollos didn't have the whole story. He knew only about the baptism of John, not about Jesus.

Priscilla and Aquila followed Paul's example in another way. They reached out to Apollos relationally. They didn't speak up in the synagogue to correct his incomplete story. They invited Apollos into their home and in that comfortable setting they explained the way of God more adequately to him. Priscilla and Aquila did exactly what they had seen Paul doing. I'm sure they had to reason, they had to dialogue with Apollos. I imagine Apollos had a lot of questions because he was a learned man with a thorough knowledge of the Hebrew Scriptures. So Priscilla and Aquila reasoned with Apollos; that was the first step. But then once Apollos caught hold of the Gospel and wanted to take the Gospel to Achaia, we read that the brothers encouraged him and wrote to the disciples, most likely in Corinth and Cenchrea, to welcome him. So

Priscilla and Aquila followed Paul's pattern of disciple-making exactly. First they engaged Apollos in dialogue, then they encouraged and strengthened him in the faith.

And quite importantly, Priscilla and Aquila used the gift of hospitality in this process of disciple-making. As refugees in Corinth they opened their home to Paul. As missionaries in Ephesus they opened their home to Apollos, and as a meeting place for the church. Then later, when they moved back to Rome, they had church meetings in their house there too. Priscilla and Aquila were willing to risk drinks spilt on the carpet and broken dishes in order to open their home to be used by the Lord.

I wonder: are we willing to do that? The gift of hospitality can be powerfully used in disciple-making today, passing on the torch of faith, just as it was used in the time of Priscilla and Aquila. But we have to be willing to take the risk to really welcome people into our homes, no matter the consequences.

One mother tells the following story: "I remember one summer day when my ten-year-old son and a friend were getting a pitcher of lemonade from the refrigerator. I'd spent hours that morning scrubbing, waxing, and polishing the kitchen floor, so I warned the boys not to spill anything. They tried so hard to be careful that they innocently bumped a tray of eggs on the door shelf. Of course, it fell, splattering eggs all over my clean floor.

"The boys' eyes widened with alarm as I exploded angrily. 'Get out of here—now!' I shouted, while they headed for the door.

"By the time I'd finished cleaning up the mess, I had calmed down. To make amends, I set a tray of cookies on the table, along with the pitcher of lemonade and some glasses. But when I called the boys, there was no answer—they'd gone somewhere else to play, somewhere where my angry voice wouldn't reach them."

That sounds like me, I'm afraid! Sometimes I can be such a neat-nick, and so task-oriented that I miss the opportunity for relationship. Not so my wife—she is the one with the real gift of hospitality. Consequently we have had countless people in our home over 20 plus years of marriage. I have lost track of how many home Bible studies we have led. Because of Becky's God-given gift for hospitality the Lord has used our home to love people to himself and strengthen people in the faith. The Lord can do the same in your home if you offer it to him and not worry too much about spilt eggs!

Finally, let us look together at the third runner in this Olympic-like relay: his name is Apollos. Paul passed the torch of the faith to Priscilla and Aquila. Aquila and Priscilla passed the torch to Apollos. And Apollos passed the torch to others in Achaia.

Apollos passed on what he had experienced with Priscilla and Aquila. He did the same two things Paul did: he dialogued with the Jews and he strengthened believers. We read that on arriving in Achaia, Apollos "was a great help to those who by grace had believed. For he vigorously refuted the Jews in public debate, proving from the Scriptures that Jesus was the Christ."

So we see in Acts 18 a clear pattern for making disciples, for passing on the torch of the faith. Thus I have to ask: how are we doing at passing on the torch of the faith?

You say: "But I'm not a minister." Not so. Paul teaches that we are all ministers in the Body of Christ. The job of the pastor is to "prepare God's people for works of service" (Ephesians 4:12). "Works of service" *are* ministry. That's your job description. The pastor's job description is to prepare you for ministry.

And so I ask you: what is the argument of your life? You may not be a professional defender of the faith, or a professional evangelist, or a professional teacher of God's Word. But all of us can be in dialogue with unbelievers, and all of us can be used to strengthen and encourage other believers. And we do this best by the witness of our lives.

There was a couple who had a bakery in Dillenburg, Germany. After emigrating to the United States they opened another bakery in Fairlawn, New Jersey. As bakers they had a unique advantage in advertising. They didn't need to run any advertisements in the newspaper, or radio or television. All they had to do was open up the door of the bakery and let people smell the fresh baked goods.

They say the best way to sell a house is to bake some chocolate chip cookies when someone comes over to look with their real estate agent. The best way to attract others to Christ is to let them smell the aroma of our lives.

In 2 Corinthians 2:14-17 Paul says,

> But thanks be to God, who always leads us in triumphal procession in Christ and through us spreads everywhere the fragrance of the knowledge of him. For we are to God the aroma of Christ among those who are being saved and those who are perishing. To the one we are the smell of death; to the other, the fragrance of life. And who is equal to such a task? Unlike so many, we do not peddle the word of God for profit. On the contrary, in Christ we speak before God with sincerity, like men sent from God.

Are you opening the door of your life so that others in your home, your extended family, your neighborhood and your workplace can smell the sweet aroma of Christ? What could you do this week to strengthen other believers in the Lord. Maybe there is someone in your congregation who could use a letter of encouragement from you just as the brothers in Ephesus gave to Apollos.

As George Sweeting has written, "A Christian is by nature a disciple of

Jesus. And all disciples have a commission that is yet to be fulfilled: we are to be disciple-makers. Jesus commanded, 'Go . . . and make disciples of all the nations.' And He gives [twenty-first] century disciples the same comfort that He offered Peter, John, and Paul–that He will be with us always, 'even to the end of the age.'"

I encourage you to go forth from where you are today with the Olympic torch of the Gospel, the flame of the Holy Spirit, the light of Jesus Christ. And light up the lives of others with it, knowing that Jesus goes with you as you run your relay race for him.

CLAIMING THE POWER OF THE NAME

A woman by the name of June Cerza Kolk once told the following story:

> My family had gathered at my house for our yearly reunion. While we were in church singing the opening hymn, an earthquake hit. The building shook, and the overhead lights swung back and forth. In true California style we never missed a beat, even though we had to grab the pews in front to steady ourselves.
>
> Following the service, the pastor came over to greet my out-of-town relatives. My son-in-law grinned as he shook the pastor's hand and said, "I've been to a lot of church services in my life, but I can honestly say this was the most moving one I've ever attended."

It's too bad when there has to be an earthquake for us to have a "moving" experience in church! The power of God should be part of our everyday experience as Christians. In short, if we are going to claim the name of Jesus as our Lord, then we should see his power evident in our lives in a personal way. Claiming the power of the name is the key to growth we see in this next section of Luke's chronicle of the early church from Acts 19. . . .

> While Apollos was at Corinth, Paul took the road through the interior and arrived at Ephesus. There he found some disciples and asked them, "Did you receive the Holy Spirit when you believed?"
>
> They answered, "No, we have not even heard that there is a Holy Spirit."
>
> So Paul asked, "Then what baptism did you receive?"
>
> "John's baptism," they replied.
>
> Paul said, "John's baptism was a baptism of repentance. He told the people to believe in the one coming after him, that is, in Jesus." On hearing this, they were baptized into the name of the Lord Jesus. When Paul placed his hands on them, the Holy Spirit came on them, and they spoke in tongues and prophesied. There were about twelve men in all.
>
> Paul entered the synagogue and spoke boldly there for three months, arguing persuasively about the kingdom of God. But some of them

became obstinate; they refused to believe and publicly maligned the Way. So Paul left them. He took the disciples with him and had discussions daily in the lecture hall of Tyrannus. This went on for two years, so that all the Jews and Greeks who lived in the province of Asia heard the word of the Lord.

God did extraordinary miracles through Paul, so that even handkerchiefs and aprons that had touched him were taken to the sick, and their illnesses were cured and the evil spirits left them.

Some Jews who went around driving out evil spirits tried to invoke the name of the Lord Jesus over those who were demon-possessed. They would say, "In the name of Jesus, whom Paul preaches, I command you to come out." Seven sons of Sceva, a Jewish chief priest, were doing this. One day the evil spirit answered them, "Jesus I know, and I know about Paul, but who are you?" Then the man who had the evil spirit jumped on them and overpowered them all. He gave them such a beating that they ran out of the house naked and bleeding.

When this became known to the Jews and Greeks living in Ephesus, they were all seized with fear, and the name of the Lord Jesus was held in high honor. Many of those who believed now came and openly confessed their evil deeds. A number who had practiced sorcery brought their scrolls together and burned them publicly. When they calculated the value of the scrolls, the total came to fifty thousand drachmas. In this way the word of the Lord spread widely and grew in power.

After all this had happened, Paul decided to go to Jerusalem, passing through Macedonia and Achaia. "After I have been there," he said, "I must visit Rome also." He sent two of his helpers, Timothy and Erastus, to Macedonia, while he stayed in the province of Asia a little longer.

We see in this passage that if we are going to claim the power of the name of Jesus in our lives then we must receive the Holy Spirit and be filled with the Spirit. Apollos' incomplete preaching in Ephesus led to an incomplete spiritual experience on the part of the Ephesian people. It's like the saying goes: "Fog in the pulpit, fog in the pew!" Priscilla and Aquila had to explain to Apollos the way of God more adequately because he only knew the baptism of John. One can only pass on what one has. Thus Apollos had not passed on to the Ephesians the full message of Christianity. The result was that the people of Ephesus did not know anything about the power of the Holy Spirit.

But God sent Paul to Ephesus to correct this deficiency; he baptized people into the name of Jesus and laid his hands on them so they might receive the Holy Spirit. In a later letter to this same church Paul says:

> Having believed, you were marked in him with a seal, the promised Holy Spirit, who is a deposit guaranteeing our inheritance until the redemption of those who are God's possession—to the praise of his glory. (Ephesians 1:13-14)

In the same way as the Ephesians, if we have trusted in Jesus for our salvation, if we have come to the point of faith in him, then we have received the Holy Spirit. Believers in the Lord Jesus don't need to have a second work of grace in order to receive the Spirit. But we do need to work at being filled with the Spirit just as Paul commanded this same church in Ephesians 5:18, "Be filled with the Spirit." or literally: "Be being filled with the Spirit." Being filled with the Holy Spirit is an ongoing activity in the life of the Christian. Whenever we surrender to the Lordship and leadership of the Spirit in our everyday lives, then and there we are filled with the Spirit. Paul wrote about this to the church at Corinth:

> Now the Lord is the Spirit, and where the Spirit of the Lord is, there is freedom. And we, who with unveiled faces all reflect the Lord's glory, are being transformed into his likeness with ever-increasing glory, which comes from the Lord, who is the Spirit.

How are we supposed to surrender to the Lordship of the Spirit on a daily basis? Practically speaking, how does it happen? The Spirit exercises his Lordship in our lives through the Word of God in Scripture. As we saw a few chapters ago in Ephesians 6:17, we are to put on the armor of God which includes taking up "the helmet of salvation and *the sword of the Spirit*, which is the word of God." It is as we spend time daily reading God's word in Scripture that we will know what the Holy Spirit wants us to do with our lives. Hebrews 4:12 tells us,

> For the word of God is living and active. Sharper than any double-edged sword, it penetrates even to dividing soul and spirit, joints and marrow; it judges the thoughts and attitudes of the heart.

The monarch butterfly is a familiar sight in many places across our country and is a beautiful sign of spring. Few butterflies can compare with the striking beauty of the monarch's orange, yellow, and black wings. Each year people in many regions of the United States enjoy the unique pleasure of seeing thousands of these butterflies fill the sky as they begin to migrate south for the winter. These butterflies spend the winter months in forests of fir trees in the volcanic highlands of south-central Mexico. Environmentalists have identified nine areas where the monarchs cluster in colonies, and Mexico has designated five of these sites as sanctuaries of protection.

But these five sanctuaries are not enough to protect the monarch population; they only cover sixty-two square miles. Meanwhile poor farmers and commercial loggers are clearing fir forests, at times even in the restricted zones, putting increasing pressure on existing butterfly colonies. Some experts have predicted that we will not have a monarch migration in twenty years if sanctuaries aren't expanded and protected.

Like a beautiful, fragile monarch butterfly, God's Spirit usually fills the heart in a gentle way. But we must intentionally keep a sanctuary for him because there are many things that can encroach upon his home in us. Our sense of his presence, our ability to hear his voice, our awareness of his direction—all can be lost if we do not safeguard a place for him.

The second major thing we see in Acts 19 is that once we have the Spirit we can engage in all the ministries of the Spirit. Three are mentioned in this passage. The first is the ministry of evangelism—the ability to argue persuasively about the kingdom. In Acts 19:8 we read that Paul entered the synagogue in Ephesus and spoke boldly there for three months, arguing persuasively about the kingdom of God. When the Jews once again became obstinate, Paul took his teaching into the lecture hall of Tyrannus. Paul continued teaching there for two years so that all the Jews and Greeks who lived in the province of Asia heard the word of God. Amazing!

Some time ago as a family we watched the movie, *The End of the Spear*. It is the story of American missionaries, among them Jim and Elisabeth Eliot and Nate Saint and his family, who took the good news of Jesus Christ to the Auca tribe of South America. Jim Eliot, Nate Saint and three other men were killed by the Aucas even as they tried to share Christ with them. But that was not the end of the missionary work there. The very men who had killed these missionaries were won to Christ by the families of these slain missionaries who forgave them and loved them to Jesus. Who could have thought of a more unlikely scenario for building the kingdom of God in South America?

As a family we have also listened to *The Hiding Place* on CD and watched the movie. It is the story of Corrie ten Boom and her family who harbored Jews in their home in Holland during World War II. Corrie and her family were eventually sent to a prison camp because of their underground activities in helping the Jews. Corrie was the only member of her family to survive that ordeal. But she emerged from Ravensbruck concentration camp to become what she called a "tramp for the Lord" taking the good news of Jesus Christ to individuals and large groups around the world. In 1966 at the World Congress on Evangelism in Berlin, Corrie ten Boom was still an unknown name to most of the Christian world. Yet when this elderly woman stood up to speak among scholars and many well known leaders in the church you could have heard a pin drop.

God certainly has unusual ways of spreading the message of his Son. He uses people we might never suspect. After all, he started to build his church using a bunch of fishermen and a rabbi from Tarsus. Who could have guessed the results? God could. He knew what he was doing. And he still knows what he is doing. He can use you and me, as feeble as we think we are, to communicate the good news of Jesus to others.

St. Patrick, whose birthday we celebrate on March 17, was born of a Christian family in Britain. When he was sixteen he was taken captive by pirates and sold into slavery in Ireland. Six years later he escaped from his master and returned home. Later, in a dream, he heard the Irish people pleading with him to return to them: "Holy boy, we are asking you to come home and walk among us again." The suffering induced by his slavery led Patrick from nominal belief in Christ to a profound faith. He became convinced that God was calling him to convert the Irish. And so Patrick returned to the land of his captivity and turned Ireland upside-down for Jesus Christ.

Patrick was very self-conscious about his lack of education–greatly humbled by it. What he did not realize was that the very absence of refined rhetoric, which he so regretted, made his communication honest and direct.

If God could use the Eliots, the Saints, Corrie ten Boom, St. Patrick, then God can use you and me too. The secret of powerful evangelism is not us, but Christ *in* us. As it says in that famous prayer attributed to St. Patrick:

> Christ be with me,
> Christ within me,
> Christ behind me,
> Christ before me,
> Christ beside me,
> Christ to win me,
> Christ to comfort and restore me.
> Christ beneath me,
> Christ above me,
> Christ in quiet,
> Christ in danger,
> Christ in hearts of all that love me,
> Christ in mouth of friend and stranger.
>
> I bind unto myself the Name,
> The strong Name of the Trinity,
> By invocation of the same,
> The Three in One and One in Three.
> By Whom all nature hath creation,
> Eternal Father, Spirit, Word:
> Praise to the Lord of my salvation,

Salvation is of Christ the Lord.

The second ministry of the Spirit we see in this passage is the ministry of healing–being used by God to do miracles. "God did extraordinary miracles through Paul, so that even handkerchiefs and aprons that had touched him were taken to the sick, and their illnesses were cured . . ."

Have you ever heard a healing take place? On January 17, 1993 Duane Miller was teaching on Psalm 103 to his Sunday school class at First Baptist Church in Brenham, Texas. Duane had prematurely retired as a pastor three years earlier because of a virus which had destroyed his vocal chords reducing his speech to a raspy whisper.

As Duane taught his class that January day in 1993 he had a special microphone resting on his lips and he reaffirmed his belief in God's healing power which did not end with the book of Acts. If you were to listen to that tape today you could barely understand his words in certain spots. But a miracle happened when Duane got to Psalm 103:4. He said, "I have had and you have had in times past pit experiences." On the word "pit" Duane's voice changed–it was clear as a bell. He paused, startled. He began again and stopped. His voice was normal. The class erupted in shouts of joy. God completely healed Duane even as he was declaring the truth of Psalm 103:

> Praise the Lord, O my soul;
>   all my inmost being, praise his holy name.
> Praise the Lord, O my soul,
>   and forget not all his benefits--
>
> who forgives all your sins
>   and heals all your diseases,
> who redeems your life from the pit
>   and crowns you with love and compassion,

A third ministry we see in this passage which flows from the presence and power of the Holy Spirit is the ministry of exorcism–overcoming evil. We read that the Holy Spirit worked through Paul to cause evil spirits to leave many people, but when some Jews tried to cast out demons "in the name of Jesus whom Paul preaches" the demons turned on them and attacked them saying: "Jesus I know, and I know about Paul, but who are you?"

Exorcism is not a ministry we can exercise in our own strength. We must come under the protection of Jesus' blood and his name. That is the only way we have power over the enemy. But if you have a personal relationship with Jesus Christ even the demons will know your name and cower before you.

So many were amazed at the power of the Holy Spirit working through Paul that they openly confessed their evil deeds. Those who practiced sorcery brought their scrolls to be burned publicly.

Meditations on the Acts of the Apostles

I believe this stuff is as real today as it was in Paul's time. I know of a woman who spent her early life, from the time she was a teenager until she was in her thirties, in a mental institution. She was diagnosed as schizophrenic, homicidal and suicidal. She would set fires and even burn her own skin with cigarettes. But a female Methodist minister found this young woman in the mental ward and sought to help her out. She got her out of the hospital and set her up in her own apartment. One day as the minister was counseling this person the demons inside her started to manifest themselves. I know from conversation with this Methodist minister that she didn't even believe in demonic possession before that time, but her belief system was changed by her experience. She called in a Catholic priest to perform an exorcism. That didn't work. Then she called in a group of African American Christians who had a deliverance ministry. They prayed for days for this woman and finally she was delivered from her demonic oppression. She hasn't needed to be in a mental hospital for years now.

Christ's power over disease and death and the devil is as real today as it was 2000 years ago. But we must have a personal relationship with Jesus Christ if we are going to access that power.

There are many people today, even in the church, who have a form of godliness but deny its power. Paul says in 2 Timothy 3:1-5,

> But mark this: There will be terrible times in the last days. People will be lovers of themselves, lovers of money, boastful, proud, abusive, disobedient to their parents, ungrateful, unholy, without love, unforgiving, slanderous, without self-control, brutal, not lovers of the good, treacherous, rash, conceited, lovers of pleasure rather than lovers of God—*having a form of godliness but denying its power.* Have nothing to do with them.

We need a supernatural Christianity. We need to stop playing around with religion and get into a relationship of power and love with Jesus Christ.

The story is told of Ricardo Enamorado who set out on a jet ski one day from Chicago's Wilson Avenue boat ramp and headed north along the shoreline of Lake Michigan. After traveling several miles north he turned around to head back home, but his engine quit. Unable to restart it, he floated along thinking help would come sometime soon. But gradually the wind and waves pushed Enamorado further and further from shore. By dusk he was frantic. Dressed only in cut-offs, tennis shoes and a life preserver, Enamorado spent the night on the chilly waters of Lake Michigan.

The next day Coast Guard and fire department helicopters began searching for Enamorado. By the end of the day they still had not found the man on his jet ski. He was hungry and sun-burned and he resigned himself to spend another night on Lake Michigan.

Finally, the next morning, one of the search and rescue teams spotted a flash of light. Enamorado was signaling with a mirror. The two-day ordeal was over at last.

That story goes to show that a loss of power can be more dangerous than we think. We certainly don't want to run out of spiritual gas and become like the seven sons of Sceva—attacked by the power of the enemy. We need to come to Christ afresh today and every day. We need to ask him to fill us with his Spirit and then from us will flow the power of the Spirit in ministry to others who are lost, alone and powerless on the windy, storm-tossed seas of life.

RECOGNIZING THE WAY

On December 20, 1995, an American Airlines jet crashed into a mountainside in Colombia, South America killing 159 passengers. Months later, airline officials determined that the cause of the crash was an error by the captain of the plane along with a mix-up in computer coordinates.

As flight 965 approached Cali airport from the north, the control tower communicated to the pilot that he was to fly a straight path over the "Rozo" navigational radio beacon near the airport. The captain decided to use the plane's autopilot feature and punched the letter "R" into the computer, which he assumed would lead the plane over the right beacon. Unfortunately there was another radio beacon with a code name that also began with the letter "R," the "Romeo" beacon. This beacon was 132 miles to the left and behind the plane at the Bogota airport. The autopilot sent the plane crashing into a mountainside instead of safely to the Cali airport.

Accuracy and attention to detail are not only essential in navigation of an airplane but also in matters of faith. There are many people today who believe that all roads lead to heaven. But punching in the letter "R" for any old religion will not do, according to the Bible. If we are going to grow spiritually it is essential that we recognize the way which is right.

Recognizing the Way is the key to growth we learn about in this next section of the book of Acts, chapter 19, verses 23 to 41....

> About that time there arose a great disturbance about the Way. A silversmith named Demetrius, who made silver shrines of Artemis, brought in no little business for the craftsmen. He called them together, along with the workmen in related trades, and said: "Men, you know we receive a good income from this business. And you see and hear how this fellow Paul has convinced and led astray large numbers of people here in Ephesus and in practically the whole province of Asia. He says that man-made gods are no gods at all. There is danger not only that our trade will lose its good name, but also that the temple of the great goddess Artemis will be discredited, and the goddess herself, who is worshiped throughout the province of Asia and the world, will be robbed of her divine majesty."

When they heard this, they were furious and began shouting: "Great is Artemis of the Ephesians!" Soon the whole city was in an uproar. The people seized Gaius and Aristarchus, Paul's traveling companions from Macedonia, and rushed as one man into the theater. Paul wanted to appear before the crowd, but the disciples would not let him. Even some of the officials of the province, friends of Paul, sent him a message begging him not to venture into the theater.

The assembly was in confusion: Some were shouting one thing, some another. Most of the people did not even know why they were there. The Jews pushed Alexander to the front, and some of the crowd shouted instructions to him. He motioned for silence in order to make a defense before the people. But when they realized he was a Jew, they all shouted in unison for about two hours: "Great is Artemis of the Ephesians!"

The city clerk quieted the crowd and said: "Men of Ephesus, doesn't all the world know that the city of Ephesus is the guardian of the temple of the great Artemis and of her image, which fell from heaven? Therefore, since these facts are undeniable, you ought to be quiet and not do anything rash. You have brought these men here, though they have neither robbed temples nor blasphemed our goddess. If, then, Demetrius and his fellow craftsmen have a grievance against anybody, the courts are open and there are proconsuls. They can press charges. If there is anything further you want to bring up, it must be settled in a legal assembly. As it is, we are in danger of being charged with rioting because of today's events. In that case we would not be able to account for this commotion, since there is no reason for it." After he had said this, he dismissed the assembly.

Followers of the Way—that is one of the earliest names given to the followers of Jesus. We encountered this name for Christians all the way back in Acts 9:2 where we read that Saul "asked for letters to the synagogues in Damascus, so that if he found any there *who belonged to the Way*, whether men or women, he might take them as prisoners to Jerusalem."

This was and is an appropriate name for Christians because in John 14:6 Jesus is recorded as saying: "I am the way and the truth and the life. No one comes to the Father except through me." Jesus is *the* way, *the* truth, and *the* life. He is not just *a* way, *one* way among many. He is not just *one* possible truth. Jesus is not just *one* way of life to be chosen among many alternatives. Jesus himself asserts that he is the *only* way to the Father. And this claim is reiterated by his disciples. In Acts 4:12 Peter proclaimed before the Jewish ruling council in Jerusalem: "Salvation is found in no one else, for there is no other name under heaven given to men by which we must be saved."

This claim to exclusivity, while not popular in our day, is intriguing. I mean, if you had a choice of religions to follow and there was one religion which claimed to be the only way to God, wouldn't that intrigue you just a bit? Wouldn't you want to check out *that* religion first before possibly eliminating it as true and then moving on to examine the others? Christians get a bad rap these days because of their supposed exclusivity. People think we are being arrogant when we claim that our way is the only way. But we are just repeating what our Master said. Jesus claimed to be the only way to the Father. And is not such a claim worthy of our investigation?

Others complain and say: "Why would God give us just *one* way to come to him? Why doesn't he give us *many* ways?" This question seems to me to betray a sense of ingratitude. Shouldn't we rather be grateful that God has given us sinners *a* way, *any* way at all to come to him? And isn't it wonderful that he has made that way so clear and simple by there being *one* way?

C. S. Lewis very helpfully explains the exclusivity of Christianity in this way:

> If you are a Christian you do not have to believe that all the other religions are simply wrong all through. If you are an atheist you do have to believe that the main point in all the religions of the whole world is simply one huge mistake. If you are a Christian, you are free to think that all these religions, even the queerest ones, contain at least some hint of the truth. When I was an atheist I had to try to persuade myself that most of the human race have always been wrong about the question that mattered to them most; when I became a Christian I was able to take a more liberal view. But, of course, being a Christian does mean thinking that where Christianity differs from other religions, Christianity is right and they are wrong. As in arithmetic–there is only one right answer to a sum and all other answers are wrong: but some of the wrong answers are much nearer being right than others. (*Mere Christianity*, p. 43.)

Still, some people object and say, isn't it terribly unfair that eternal life should be given only to those who have heard of Jesus and been able to believe in him?

Once again, Lewis clarifies things. He says:

> But the truth is God has not told us what His arrangements about the other people are [those who haven't heard of Christ]. We do know that no man can be saved except through Christ; we do not know that only those who know Him can be saved through Him. But in the meantime, if you are worried about the people outside, the most unreasonable thing you can do is to remain outside yourself. Christians are Christ's

body, the organism through which He works. Every addition to that body enables Him to do more. If you want to help those outside you must add your own little cell to the body of Christ who alone can help them. Cutting off a man's fingers would be an odd way of getting him to do more work. (*Mere Christianity*, p. 65.)

So that is the first thing we see in this passage: Jesus is the way of salvation. But secondly, as a corollary, we hear about what Paul was teaching: *that man-made gods are no gods at all.*

Demetrius was a silversmith in Ephesus who made silver shrines of Artemis. To the Ephesians, Artemis was a mother-goddess, depicted with many breasts, in other words, a goddess of fertility. The Ephesians believed that Artemis' image had come down to them from heaven, possibly with a meteorite. The Temple of Artemis in Ephesus was one of the seven wonders of the ancient world. People came from great distances to see this temple which measured 425 feet long, 220 feet wide, and was four times the size of the Parthenon. The Temple of Artemis in Ephesus was the largest temple in the Ancient Greek empire. It had 127 white marble columns standing 62 feet high. According to Pliny, the ancient historian, the temple took 220 years to build. To people in Paul's day the temple must have seemed immortal. And yet Paul was apparently preaching that Artemis was no god at all.

Did Demetrius worship Artemis? If so, he only worshiped her tangentially. What Demetrius was really worshiping was money. Notice how he addresses the craftsmen of Ephesus: "Men, you know we receive a good income from this business." Demetrius was afraid that Paul's preaching was going to ruin his cash flow.

Not too different from today is it? Today there are plenty of people who worship money. Aristotle Onassis, at one time one of the richest men in the world, once said: "All that matters in this life is money. It is the people with money who are the royalty in our generation." Where is Onassis' wealth now? It certainly isn't in the same place where he is. When Onassis died his daughter was the only person by his side. I wonder if he realized even then that he had leaned the ladder of his life against the wrong wall?

Jesus said in Matthew 6:24, "No one can serve two masters. Either he will hate the one and love the other, or he will be devoted to the one and despise the other. You cannot serve both God and Money."

The god of Demetrius was money, but the city clerk in Ephesus had another god. The city clerk was afraid a riot was going to start in the amphitheater that day. I imagine the city clerk was afraid if that happened the Romans might come and take away his position of power and authority and replace him with another leader. The city clerk's god was self. He was determined to protect himself, to save his own skin at all cost by quieting the crowd.

MEDITATIONS ON THE ACTS OF THE APOSTLES

You might say that the city clerk's life motto was: "Safety first." Not so the Apostle Paul. Paul was willing to rush into the midst of that mob in the amphitheater to proclaim Christ. Paul's motto wasn't "Safety first" it was "Christ first".

Who or what is our god? Our god is whatever or whomever we put first in life.

This may sound crazy but many people in America have sports as their god. They give more of their time and money to worshiping sporting activities than to worshiping the one true god. I grew up in Southern California where people, even professing Christians, would easily give up a Sunday morning at church in favor of some sporting activity on a beautiful, sunny, Southern California Sunday.

The worship of sport in America was epitomized by a display at Lambeau Field in 1996, the year the Green Bay Packers won the Super Bowl in New Orleans and their quarterback Brett Favre was named the most valuable player. Some fans displayed a banner with the following words:

> Our Favre who art in Lambeau, hallowed be thy arm. The Bowl will come, it will be won, in New Orleans as it is in Lambeau. Give us this Sunday our weekly win. And give us many touchdown passes. But do not let others pass against us. Lead us not into frustration, but deliver us to Bourbon Street. For thine is the MVP, the best of the NFL, and the glory of the cheeseheads, now and forever. Go get 'em!

Apparently some fans in Wisconsin recognized their team support for what it really is: worship.

Maybe your god isn't sport. Maybe you are more like me and you worship food. I grew up in a family that worships food. We would be finishing one meal and already planning the next!

You don't have to have watched too much television to realize that on at least one occasion Oprah Winfrey lost a lot of weight. In fact, you don't have to be a television watcher at all–her picture continues to be emblazoned on magazine covers at the check out counter in most supermarkets.

Having tipped the scales at 237 pounds, Oprah tried one diet after another. She would lose weight and then put it right back on again, until in 1993 she found a new personal trainer. The most important thing that trainer did for Oprah was to help her understand *why* she wanted to eat so much. In *People* magazine Oprah said, "For me, food was comfort, pleasure, love, a friend, everything. I consciously work every day at not letting food be a substitute for my emotions."

When sad, lonely, feeling empty, eating is one way some people try to fill the void. Similar to using food as a substitute for love, people often use other things in this world to try to fill an emptiness that only God can fill.

As Blaise Pascal once said, "There is a God-shaped vacuum in the heart of every person."

To put things like sex, money, success, family, food, alcohol, drugs or anything else in God's place is to fight a losing battle. It just doesn't work. God has designed us to live in relationship with him. Jesus is the way to have that relationship. And as St. Augustine once said, "Our hearts are restless until they find their rest in God."

At first we may think we have a hard time relating to the worship of Artemis. But idolatry of all sorts continues all over the world today.

Several years ago a giant tree stood on the banks of the Awash River southeast of Addis Ababa, Ethiopia. This tree had stood there for generations, seemingly eternal.

For years the people who lived in the surrounding area had suffered from famine. In their suffering the people looked to the great tree for help. Believing that a great spirit gave the tree divine power, they worshiped this towering giant. Adults would kiss the tree trunk when they passed by. Children later said, "This tree saved us."

In 1989 World Vision began a development project in the same region providing an irrigation system for the surrounding countryside. But even as World Vision labored to build the system this great tree stood like an idol of the old order,

When World Vision workers saw how the people of that region worshiped the great tree they realized that the tree stood as a barrier between the people in that part of Ethiopia and Christ. One morning as the World Vision staff prayed together they were impressed with the words of Jesus in Luke 17:6, "If you have faith as small as a mustard seed, you can say to this mulberry tree, 'Be uprooted and planted in the sea,' and it will obey you." In faith the staff of World Vision began to pray that God would destroy this tree which stood as a barrier to the peoples' reception of Christ as Savior.

Soon the whole community knew the Christians were praying about the tree. Six months later, the tree began to dry up, its leafy foliage disappeared, and finally it collapsed like a stricken giant into the river.

The local villagers were astonished and said, "Your God has done this! Your God dried up the tree!" In the days and weeks which followed, about one hundred members of the village received Jesus Christ as Lord and Savior because they saw his power displayed in answer to Christian prayer.

What might happen in our own culture if we began to pray and ask Christ to display his power through us over against the gods of our culture?

I have been to the site of ancient Ephesus; it lies in ruins today. The ruins of Ephesus are among the most extensive and beautiful ruins of the ancient world—but the Temple of Artemis was wiped right off the map. There was little trace of it left in Ephesus.

The early Christians prayed and preached and worshiped the one true God who revealed himself in Jesus Christ and the worship of that God came to replace all the so-called gods of the Greek and Roman pantheon. Perhaps if we would pray and preach and worship as they did, God would do a similar work in our day.

ENCOURAGEMENT

Some time ago the world watched as three California gray whales, ice-bound off Point Barrow, Alaska, floated battered and bloodied, gasping for breath at a hole in the ice. Their only hope was somehow to be transported five miles past the ice pack to the open sea, so they could return to their winter home in Baja California.

Rescuers, many of them Eskimos, began cutting a string of breathing holes about twenty yards apart in the six-inch-thick ice. For eight days they coaxed the whales from one hole to the next, mile after mile. Along the way, one of the trio vanished and was presumed dead. Finally, with the help of the Soviet icebreaker ships, Admiral Makarov and Vladimir Arseniev, the whales Putu (which means ice hole) and Siku (which means ice) swam to freedom.

In a way, Christian fellowship is like a string of breathing holes the Lord provides his people. Battered and bruised in a world frozen over with greed, selfishness and hatred, we rise for air in the context of the church, the gathered body of believers, and we find a place to breathe freely again, to be loved and encouraged, until that day when the Lord forever shatters the ice cap with the ice-breaking event of Christ's return.

In Acts 20:1-6 we learn something about the ice-hole ministry of encouragement from the life of the Apostle Paul. . . .

> When the uproar had ended, Paul sent for the disciples and, after encouraging them, said good-by and set out for Macedonia. He traveled through that area, speaking many words of encouragement to the people, and finally arrived in Greece, where he stayed three months. Because the Jews made a plot against him just as he was about to sail for Syria, he decided to go back through Macedonia. He was accompanied by Sopater son of Pyrrhus from Berea, Aristarchus and Secundus from Thessalonica, Gaius from Derbe, Timothy also, and Tychicus and Trophimus from the province of Asia. These men went on ahead and waited for us at Troas. But we sailed from Philippi after the Feast of Unleavened Bread, and five days later joined the others at Troas, where we stayed seven days.

Paul encouraged the Ephesians before he left.

Following the riot in the Ephesian amphitheater, and before he left Ephesus, Paul sent for the disciples and encouraged them. As we saw in an earlier chapter, the Greek word for encouraging is παρακαλέσας; it means to call near, or alongside, to comfort or exhort. It refers to a word spoken when you come alongside someone and put your arm around them. The Holy Spirit is called, by John, the Paraclete, the ultimate One who comes alongside of us to wrap the arms of God around us and encourage us and lift us up. As Christians, having the Holy Spirit inside of us, we can also be encouragers, and Paul shows us how.

I think it is significant that Paul's last act in Ephesus on this occasion was to encourage the disciples. Paul didn't know for certain if he would see them again. As it turned out, this wasn't his last opportunity to speak to the disciples at Ephesus, but Paul didn't know for certain that he would have another opportunity.

Do you ever think about what the last word will be that you may speak to your loved ones in this life? You never know when you may be speaking your last word to someone. That's why we need to make all of our words encouraging.

So many of us speak "death words" to one another from day to day: "You're no good. You'll never amount to anything. You blew it again!" But what we all desperately need to hear is "life words" from other people. Will your family and friends remember your last words to them as being life words? Words that encourage and build up like: "I love you. You're the greatest! God loves you and has a wonderful plan for your life. There you go again, doing something fantastic! I love that about you!!" Those are the kind of words others need to hear from our lips.

Jason Tuskes was a 17 year old high school honor student in St. Petersburg, Florida. Jason was close to his mother, his wheel-chair bound father and his 13 year old brother, Christian. Jason was an excellent athlete who loved to scuba dive.

He left home on a Tuesday morning to explore a spring and underwater cave not far away. His plan was to be home in time to celebrate his mother's 42nd birthday by going out to dinner with his family that night.

However, Jason became lost in a cave where the water was murky at best. Then, in his panic, he apparently got wedged into a narrow passageway. When Jason realized he was trapped and almost out of air, he shed his yellow metal air tank and unsheathed his diver's knife. With the tank as a tablet and the knife as a writing instrument, he wrote one last message to his family: " I love you Mom, Dad and Christian." Then, sadly, Jason ran out of air and drowned.

The words we speak are so important, they reveal what is in our hearts. Jason knew those were going to be his last words, so he made them count. We don't often know when we may be speaking our last words–so we need to make *all* our words ones of encouragement and love.

Jesus' last words on the cross were words of love and encouragement: "Father, forgive them for they know not what they are doing."

What will your last words be?

Paul spoke many words of encouragement throughout Macedonia.

Paul didn't speak words of encouragement on just one occasion, we read that he was speaking *many* words of encouragement as he traveled throughout Macedonia and Greece.

It is interesting to note that the first time the word "encouraging" is used in this passage Luke doesn't specifically tell us that Paul used *words* to encourage the disciples. But this second time it is specific: he encouraged God's people *with many words*.

There are many ways we can encourage others, but encouraging words are often the most powerful. In her book, *The Whisper Test*, Mary Ann Bird writes:

> I grew up knowing I was different, and I hated it. I was born with a cleft palate, and when I started school, my classmates made it clear to me how I looked to others: a little girl with a misshapen lip, crooked nose, lopsided teeth, and garbled speech.
>
> When schoolmates asked, "What happened to your lip?" I'd tell them I'd fallen and cut it on a piece of glass. Somehow it seemed more acceptable to have suffered an accident than to have been born different. I was convinced that no one outside my family could love me.
>
> There was, however, a teacher in second grade whom we all adored– Mrs. Leonard. She was short, round, happy–a sparkling lady.
>
> Annually we had a hearing test. . . . Mrs. Leonard gave the test to everyone in the class, and finally it was my turn. I knew from past years that as we stood against the door and covered one ear, the teacher sitting at her desk would whisper something, and we would have to repeat it back–things like "The sky is blue" or "Do you have new shoes?" I waited there for those words that God must have put into her mouth, those seven words that changed my life. Mrs. Leonard said, in her whisper, "I wish you were my little girl."

Sometimes it doesn't take many words. In seven words, or even less, you could change someone's life for the better.

Paul kept encouraging others despite persecution.

The truly amazing thing about Paul is that he kept encouraging others even when he was facing very discouraging circumstances. It seems like Paul couldn't travel anywhere or say anything without upsetting someone. In Ephesus it was the manufacturers of Artemis shrines. Now it is the Jews who are plotting against him again as he is about to set sail for Syria.

Since this was around the time of the biggest Jewish festival, Passover, the ship Paul wanted to take to Syria, near Palestine, was probably filled with pilgrims headed to Jerusalem. It would have been the easiest thing in the world for some of the Jews on that ship, who were against Paul, to simply slip him overboard one night on the way to Syria. So instead of taking that ship Paul decided to go back through Macedonia.

Why did Paul catch so much flak, so much hatred from some Jews? Because he was a change agent, he was upsetting their religion, and it just made them too uncomfortable. Paul was a lightening rod and some people just didn't want to face the light.

Jackie Robinson was such a lightening rod. He was the first African American to play major league baseball. While breaking baseball's color barrier he faced jeering crowds in every stadium where he played.

While playing one day in his home stadium in Brooklyn, New York, Robinson committed an error. Even his own fans began to ridicule him. Robinson stood at second base, humiliated, while the fans jeered.

Suddenly, shortstop "Pee Wee" Reese came over and stood next to Jackie Robinson. He put his arm around his fellow player and faced the crowd. A hush fell over the stadium. Robinson later said that arm around his shoulder saved his career.

Is there someone you know who may be having a hard time of it just now? Perhaps they are suffering unjustly the meanness of other people. Is there someone in your life who could use your arm around their shoulder today?

Paul received encouragement from a band of brothers.

As Paul traveled through Macedonia he was accompanied by Sopater son of Pyrrhus from Berea, Aristarchus and Secundus from Thessalonica, Gaius from Derbe, Timothy also, and Tychicus and Trophimus from the province of Asia. These were all people whom Paul had won to Christ by preaching the good news about Jesus in their cities. Now these men surround Paul and are even willing to travel with him, and possibly suffer persecution with him, just to be an encouragement. Gaius and Aristarchus were seized during the riot in Ephesus (Acts 19:29) but apparently were set free. Aristarchus was later among those brothers who journeyed with Paul, the prisoner, to Rome. In fact, according to Paul's letter to the Colossians, Aristarchus became a prisoner with Paul in Rome (Colossians 4:10).

Acts 20:5 says: "These men went on ahead and waited for *us* at Troas." That *us* clues us into the fact that Luke has once again joined Paul's company in Philippi. Luke is also one of the band of brothers. And at the end of Paul's life he specifically mentions Luke as the only brother who stayed with him as he was awaiting execution (2 Timothy 4:11).

At different times in my life I have gotten together maybe once a week or once per month with at least one other man or a group of men to share a meal and prayer and Scripture together. Those small bands of brothers have meant the world to me. My wife has experienced the same thing in various women's groups in the many churches we have served. We all need groups to belong to like that, where there is no sense of competition, where everyone speaks words of encouragement and hope and blessing to one another. When we leave such a group meeting we depart feeling lifted up! Every one of us needs a band of brothers or sisters like that to encourage us on a regular basis.

In fact, we all need to be more like sandhill cranes. In his book, *Wind and Fire*, Bruce Larson points out some interesting facts about sandhill cranes:

> These large birds, who fly great distances across continents, have three remarkable qualities. First, they rotate leadership. No one bird stays out in front all the time. Second, they choose leaders who can handle turbulence. And then, all during the time one bird is leading, the rest are honking their affirmation. That's not a bad model for the church. Certainly we need leaders who can handle turbulence and who are aware that leadership ought to be shared. But most of all, we need a church where we are all honking encouragement.

Paul received encouragement from the Lord through worship.

Finally, in verse 6, Luke tells us that Paul and his companions "sailed from Philippi after the Feast of Unleavened Bread, and five days later joined the others at Troas, where we stayed seven days."

The Feast of Unleavened Bread began with Passover and lasted a week. Paul had originally hoped to be in Jerusalem sooner (Acts 19:21). Now it became his goal to reach Jerusalem by the Feast of Pentecost (Acts 20:16). As a Jew, Paul's life had been ordered by and structured around the Jewish Feast Days. As we will see in the next chapter, Paul's life came to have a new significant day—Sunday—the Lord's Day, the first day of the week, the day on which Jesus rose from the dead. This became the most significant day for Paul. And I believe it became a significant day for Paul because he received encouragement from the Lord through worship with other believers in Jesus.

Meditations on the Acts of the Apostles

Is worship an upper or a downer for you? If it is a downer, maybe you need to change your place of worship, or perhaps change your own attitude in worship, because I believe worship of the Lord is meant to be an upper–a great source of encouragement.

In Bill Moyers' book *A World of Ideas II*, Jacob Needleman remembers being an observer at the launch of Apollo 17 in 1975:

> It was a night launch, and there were hundreds of cynical reporters all over the lawn, drinking beer, wisecracking, and waiting for this 35-story-high rocket.
>
> The countdown came, and then the launch. The first thing you see is this extraordinary orange light, which is just at the limit of what you can bear to look at. Everything is illuminated with this light. Then comes this thing slowly rising up in total silence, because it takes a few seconds for the sound to come across. You hear a "WHOOOOOSH! HHHH-MMMM!" It enters right into you.
>
> You can practically hear jaws dropping. The sense of wonder fills everyone in the whole place, as this thing goes up and up. The first stage ignites this beautiful blue flame. It becomes like a star, but you realize there are humans on it. And then there's total silence.
>
> People just get up quietly, helping each other. They're kind. They open doors. They look at one another, speaking quietly and interestedly. These were suddenly moral people because the sense of wonder, the experience of wonder, had made them moral.

Worship of our Triune God should be like that. It should fill us with a sense of wonder, a sense of awe and up-lift, a sense of encouragement that should transform our behavior toward others. That's what worship did for Paul. I believe it was in the context of worship, in the celebration of the Jewish Feast Days and in the Christian celebration of Christ's resurrection, that Paul received encouragement from the Lord to be an encourager to others. May it be so for you and me as well.

WORSHIP

Years ago a woman entered a Haagen-Dazs ice cream shop in Kansas City in order to buy an ice cream cone. After placing her order she happened to turn around and suddenly realized she was staring into the face of actor Paul Newman who was also waiting in line for some ice cream. Newman happened to be in town filming a movie. Newman smiled and said "hello" to this woman who was so overcome by Newman's blue eyes that her knees started to shake.

The woman managed to turn back around, pay for her ice cream and leave the ice cream shop when suddenly she realized she didn't have her ice cream. Pulling herself together, the woman turned back and re-entered the shop just as Newman was exiting.

"Are you looking for your ice cream?" he asked. The woman nodded, totally unable to even get a word out of her mouth.

Then Newman said, "You put the ice cream in your purse with your change."

I wonder, when was the last time we were so overcome by the presence of the Lord that our pulse quickened?

I think Acts 20:7-12 has some things to teach us about worship of our Triune God as a key to growth in the Christian life....

> On the first day of the week we came together to break bread. Paul spoke to the people and, because he intended to leave the next day, kept on talking until midnight. There were many lamps in the upstairs room where we were meeting. Seated in a window was a young man named Eutychus, who was sinking into a deep sleep as Paul talked on and on. When he was sound asleep, he fell to the ground from the third story and was picked up dead. Paul went down, threw himself on the young man and put his arms around him. "Don't be alarmed," he said. "He's alive!" Then he went upstairs again and broke bread and ate. After talking until daylight, he left. The people took the young man home alive and were greatly comforted.

I don't know about you, but I get excited when I read a passage like this in the New Testament. My pulse quickens just a bit, because I think in this passage we are invited to be like flies on the wall, sitting in on a worship service in the Early Church. And something within me tells me that if we could just get back to being more like the Early Church, especially in our worship, the Church would be revolutionized. So, let's see what we can learn from this passage.

First of all, we learn something about the day of worship: Sunday. Paul and his companions had traveled from Philippi to Troas en route to Jerusalem. This band of brothers spent a week in Troas and we read, literally, that on the first day after the Sabbath, the followers of Jesus in Troas came together to break bread.

Something remarkable had happened to change the day of worship for these early followers of Jesus, many of whom were Jewish. For many of them Saturday had been the Sabbath, the correct day to worship the Lord. But since Jesus rose from the dead on the first day of the week the early Christians began to worship on Sunday. And this text in Acts 20 is one of the earliest reflections of that fact.

Paul also says in 1 Corinthians 16 that the members of the church in Corinth should set aside a sum of money in keeping with their income *on the first day of the week*. This implies that the Church at Corinth also gathered for worship on Sunday.

Then in Revelation 1:10 we read that John was "in the Spirit" on the Lord's Day. That was the new name that the Early Christians gave to this special day on which Jesus rose.

In fact, there is even the suggestion of Sunday worship in the Gospel of John. The appearances of the risen Jesus all happen in the presence of the disciples as they are gathered together on the first day of the week, first on the day Jesus rose, then again on the next Sunday (John 20:26).

The sad thing is that in our own day many Christians have lost any sense of Sunday being a special day to be set aside for rest and worship. I'm not suggesting that we need to keep Sunday like the Jews of old kept the Sabbath on Saturday. But I do think we could benefit by recapturing some of their enthusiasm for the Sabbath and apply it to our worship of the Lord on Sunday.

Many years ago Becky and I read together Karen Mains' book *Making Sunday Special* and we were enchanted by it. At the beginning of the book Mains talks about taking a trip to Israel with a Jewish tour group....

> On Wednesday we began to hear comments such as "Oh, Shabbat will be in Tel Aviv. Shabbat will be in Tel Aviv." Sure enough, on Friday afternoon, we checked into a hotel in Tel Aviv and joined some new Orthodox Jewish friends to participate in the evening Sabbath meal. I will never forget the lovely linen cloths on the dining tables, the yarmulkes on the men's heads, the Hebrew blessing over the wine, the prayer over the broken bread, the lighting of the candles.

Then later on in the book Mains writes:

> Shabbat is the high point of the Jewish week. There is the rhythm of anticipation, participation and reflection–three days to look forward, then Shabbat, then three days to look back. Some Jewish writers interpret the different wording in the Deuteronomy and Exodus passages to reflect this cycle. Deuteronomy 5:12 says, "Observe . . ." and Exodus 20:8 says, "Remember . . ." Both nuances are captured in the sacred rhythm of the Jewish week, not a one-time but a lifetime renewal of a commitment to God. (Karen Burton Mains, *Making Sunday Special*, pp. 18, 24)

Somehow, as Christians, we need to recapture that Jewish delight in the Sabbath and apply it to our worship of the Lord's Day. We need to make Sunday special by looking forward to it, preparing for it, celebrating it when it comes, and then remembering the joys of the Lord's Day as we head into a new week.

Some time ago a member of one of the churches I serve sent me an e-mail on a Tuesday to tell me that she was still "enjoying" the sermon from Sunday. That should be our attitude to the whole of Sunday worship and rest; we should continue enjoying it, by reflecting on it from Monday to Wednesday. And then beginning with Thursday we should look forward to, pray about, be filled with anticipation of the good things God is going to do in our lives on the next Lord's Day.

The next thing we see in Acts 20:7-12 is something about the content of worship. There are three elements mentioned in this passage: The Supper, The Sermon and The Sign.

First of all we have the Supper. We read that on the first day of the week the Jesus-followers in Troas came together to break bread. "To break bread" is Luke's terminology for Holy Communion. Back in Acts 2:42 we read about how the first disciples in Jerusalem devoted themselves to the breaking of the bread. And in Luke 24 Luke relates how Jesus' identity was made known to the two on the road to Emmaus when Jesus broke bread with them in the house.

The Lord's Supper, Jesus' transformation of the Passover meal into a meal commemorating and communicating his own death for sins, became one of the most meaningful aspects of the worship services in the Early Church. In fact, Communion was probably celebrated as part of a larger "agape" feast in a home, since the early Christians didn't have "church buildings" as such, and Communion was probably celebrated every Sunday.

Somehow as Christians we need to recapture the intimacy and joy those early Christians must have experienced in their celebration of the Lord's

Meditations on the Acts of the Apostles

Supper. Of course one good step in that direction, for many of us, would be to celebrate the Lord's Supper more frequently. But mere frequency will not necessarily impart to us the right attitude in taking Communion; what we need is for the Holy Spirit to do an overhaul on our spirits as well.

I love the story told by Henri Nouwen in the March 1994 issue of the New Oxford Review. He wrote:

> A few years ago Bob, the husband of a friend of mine, died suddenly of a heart attack. My friend decided to keep her two young children away from the funeral. She thought it would be too hard for them to see their father put in the ground. For years after Bob's death, the cemetery remained a fearful and a dangerous place for them.
>
> One day, my friend asked me to visit the grave with her, and invited the children to come along. The elder one was too afraid to go, but the younger one decided to come with us. When we came to the place where Bob was buried, the three of us sat down on the grass around the stone engraved with the words, A KIND AND GENTLE MAN.
>
> I said: "Maybe one day we should have a picnic here. This is not only a place to think about death, but also a place to rejoice in our life. Bob will be most honored when we find new strength, here, to live."
>
> At first it seemed a strange idea: having a meal on top of a tombstone. But isn't that similar to what Jesus told his disciples to do when he asked them to share bread and wine in his memory?
>
> A few days later my friend took her elder child to the grave, the younger one having convinced his sister that there was nothing to fear. Now they often go to the cemetery and tell each other stories about Bob.

I think that story hints at what Communion should be all about: a place to tell stories about Jesus, our Savior who died for our sins; a place to remember his death, but also a place to rejoice in his life—because Jesus is alive and can come afresh into our hearts as we partake of the bread and the wine in faith. Communion ought to be like a frequent, joyful picnic in a graveyard rather than a fearful, too solemn thing we keep our distance from for fear that we will defile it.

The second element we see in the content of worship at Troas is the sermon. "Paul spoke to the people and, because he intended to leave the next day, kept on talking until midnight!"

I love what Bruce Larson says about this story: "Paul, the great evangelist, put part of his audience to sleep. . . . It's comforting to know that on at least one occasion Paul was guilty of dull preaching." Then Bruce goes on to tell the story of the stranger who wandered into a Sunday evening service in a little church in a small Southern town. The preacher was going on and on and on. Turning to someone in the pew behind him the stranger asked: "How long has this man been preaching?" And the other man responded, "Oh, about ten years!" To which the stranger said, "Well, in that case, I guess I'll stay because he must be about done by now!"

Seriously speaking, we don't know for certain that it was a dull sermon that put Eutychus to sleep. It may just have been the fact that he had worked hard that day, it was late on Sunday night, the room was warm because of all the oil lamps burning, and so the combination of exhaustion, the smell of oil, the warmth and the lateness of the hour put the young man, or boy, gradually to sleep.

I get a kick out of the fact that Paul didn't seem to learn anything from the experience. Even after the boy falls out of the window and dies, and Paul raises him from the dead, Paul continues on preaching until morning!

To give Paul his due, it should be noted that Paul's speaking was not a sermon as we would think of it today, but rather a dialogue. What Paul was probably doing was taking questions from the congregation about the Christian life and passing on what wisdom he had in a discussion format. I imagine it was pretty engaging. At least I know I would have liked to have been there that night, though I wouldn't like to have been Eutychus!

Of course many people have poked fun at sermons and preachers over the years. Many years ago in *The British Weekly* the following letter to the editor was published:

> Dear Sir:
>
> It seems ministers feel their sermons are very important and spend a great deal of time preparing them. I have been attending church quite regularly for thirty years, and I have probably heard 3,000 of them. To my consternation, I discovered I cannot remember a single sermon. I wonder if a minister's time might be more profitably spent on something else?

For weeks a storm of letters to the editor followed that first one. Finally the whole controversy was settled with this one:

> Dear Sir:
>
> I have been married for thirty years. During that time I have eaten 32,850 meals–mostly my wife's cooking. Suddenly I have discovered I cannot remember the menu of a single meal. And yet . . . I have the distinct impression that without them, I would have starved to death long ago.

Whatever you or I may think of preaching, what is much more important is what God thinks of preaching. The Apostle Paul wrote in 1 Corinthians 1:21, "For since in the wisdom of God the world through its wisdom did not know him, God was pleased through the foolishness of what was preached to save those who believe."

The final element in the content of worship which we see in this passage is a spontaneous one, and that is a *sign*—the sign, wonder, or miracle of Paul raising from the dead this young man, this boy who fell out of the window. There is no doubt that the young man was dead because the Greek text quite clearly says that he was dead. And Paul laid on top of the young man's body, or embraced him, just as Elijah and Elisha both did, as recorded in the Hebrew Scriptures, and each of them raised a boy from the dead (1 Kings 17:19 ff.; 2 Kings 4:32-33). I suppose it was rather good of Paul to do this. I mean, after all, if you are going to put your listeners to sleep and cause them to fall out of windows, then it is only fitting that you should then raise them from the dead.

I had a similar experience once when I was preaching in Latvia. It was a Sunday evening service in an upper room of a Baptist church, and all the while that I was preaching there was a young man sitting on the window sill of this packed room; and the window was open, I believe, because it was a warm summer night. You'll be glad to know the young man didn't fall asleep during my sermon, nor did he fall out of the window, so I didn't have to raise him from the dead!

As we have seen throughout the book of Acts, the healing ministry of the Early Church is not something which we can separate out of these historical accounts. Healing was very much a vital ministry then, and it can be again now, if we would put our faith in the Lord who does the healing.

I call this element of worship in the Early Church *a sign*, because it is a pointer to a greater reality. Paul's healing of this young man is a pointer to the reality of Christ's triumph over death, that victory which will one day be communicated to all of us when we receive our resurrected bodies at Christ's Second Coming.

The story is told of a boy and his father who were driving down a country road on a gorgeous spring day, when suddenly a bee flew in the car window. The little boy, who was allergic to bee stings, was quite frightened. And so the father reached out quickly, grabbed the bee and then released it.

The boy became even more petrified as the bee continued to buzz around him. So the father once again reached out his hand, but this time he showed the boy his palm. There, stuck in his skin, was the stinger from the bee. "Do you see this?" the father asked his son. "You don't need to be afraid anymore. I've taken the sting for you."

And that is just what Jesus has done for us through his death and resurrection. He has taken the sting out of death.

> Where, O death, is your victory?
> Where, O death, is your sting?

The sting of death is sin, and the power of sin is the law. But thanks be to God! He gives us the victory through our Lord Jesus Christ (1 Corinthians 15).

Through celebrating the Supper, the Sermon and the Sign every Sunday the Lord communicates that victory to us. Thanks be to God!

LEADERSHIP

The story is told of a church that had several pastors. Each had a specific title such as Senior Pastor, Pastor of Caring and Fellowship, and so on. One day a woman came into the church office wanting to see the Pastor of Missions. But as she approached the receptionist she suddenly became a bit confused. Searching her mind for the exact title of the person she wanted to see, she blurted out: "May I see the Minister of Passion?"

Perhaps we have all heard of certain ministers who have been passionate in the wrong way. But the story reminds me of the fact that we are all called to be ministers of passion. Is it merely coincidental that we call Jesus' final suffering and death: "The Passion of the Christ"? We are all called to be ministers, or servants of, that Passion. And we need to be servants of the suffering Christ in a passionate way.

The section of the book of Acts which we are going to talk about in this chapter has a lot to say about what is needed in such ministers of passion, or passionate leaders. You say, "Well I'm not a leader in the church so I guess I can skip this chapter." I hope not. I believe that every Christian is called to be a leader in some way.

I define leadership as *influencing others in a positive direction*. Every one of us, by the power of the Holy Spirit, has the opportunity to influence others in a positive direction. So let us each watch for what the Spirit has to say to us in this passage from Acts 20:13-38. . . .

> We went on ahead to the ship and sailed for Assos, where we were going to take Paul aboard. He had made this arrangement because he was going there on foot. When he met us at Assos, we took him aboard and went on to Mitylene. The next day we set sail from there and arrived off Kios. The day after that we crossed over to Samos, and on the following day arrived at Miletus. Paul had decided to sail past Ephesus to avoid spending time in the province of Asia, for he was in a hurry to reach Jerusalem, if possible, by the day of Pentecost.
>
> From Miletus, Paul sent to Ephesus for the elders of the church. When they arrived, he said to them: "You know how I lived the whole time I was with you, from the first day I came into the province of Asia. I

served the Lord with great humility and with tears, although I was severely tested by the plots of the Jews. You know that I have not hesitated to preach anything that would be helpful to you but have taught you publicly and from house to house. I have declared to both Jews and Greeks that they must turn to God in repentance and have faith in our Lord Jesus.

"And now, compelled by the Spirit, I am going to Jerusalem, not knowing what will happen to me there. I only know that in every city the Holy Spirit warns me that prison and hardships are facing me. However, I consider my life worth nothing to me, if only I may finish the race and complete the task the Lord Jesus has given me—the task of testifying to the Gospel of God's grace.

"Now I know that none of you among whom I have gone about preaching the kingdom will ever see me again. Therefore, I declare to you today that I am innocent of the blood of all men. For I have not hesitated to proclaim to you the whole will of God. Keep watch over yourselves and all the flock of which the Holy Spirit has made you overseers. Be shepherds of the church of God, which he bought with his own blood. I know that after I leave, savage wolves will come in among you and will not spare the flock. Even from your own number men will arise and distort the truth in order to draw away disciples after them. So be on your guard! Remember that for three years I never stopped warning each of you night and day with tears.

"Now I commit you to God and to the word of his grace, which can build you up and give you an inheritance among all those who are sanctified. I have not coveted anyone's silver or gold or clothing. You yourselves know that these hands of mine have supplied my own needs and the needs of my companions. In everything I did, I showed you that by this kind of hard work we must help the weak, remembering the words the Lord Jesus himself said: 'It is more blessed to give than to receive.'"

When he had said this, he knelt down with all of them and prayed. They all wept as they embraced him and kissed him. What grieved them most was his statement that they would never see his face again. Then they accompanied him to the ship.

I believe this passage has a number of things to say about the kind of leaders we need in the church today. You may not see yourself in all of these characteristics, but I hope you see yourself in at least one or more of these.

First of all, we need church leaders who take time to be alone with God. When Paul and his companions set out from Troas, the companions went by ship to Assos, but Paul went on foot. The text doesn't tell us why Paul did this, but I imagine he wanted to take the time to be alone with the Lord. Paul had a sense, expressed in this passage, of what lay in store for him in the future. He knew a bit about the suffering he might have to endure in Jerusalem. And so to prepare himself, just as Jesus prepared himself in the Garden of Gethsemane, Paul took the time to be alone with his Lord.

Do you take time every day to be alone with your Lord? I know each of us has different schedules and different opportunities. But every one of us needs to take time alone with the Lord, even if it is only for a few minutes every day. Without that time alone with Jesus we can never effectively lead others to Jesus or influence others in a positive direction.

A number of years ago *National Geographic* magazine published an article about the Alaskan bull moose. The male moose battle for dominance during the autumn breeding season; they go head-to-head with antlers crunching together as they compete. If one bull moose hasn't prepared properly, his antlers may be broken, and that will insure defeat.

The heaviest moose, with the largest and strongest antlers, wins. Therefore, the battle fought in the autumn is really won in the summer, when the moose eat continually. The bull-moose that consumes the best diet for growing antlers and gaining weight will be the heavyweight in the fight. Those who eat a poor diet display weaker antlers and less bulk.

There is a lesson in this for every Christian. Spiritual battles await us, just as they awaited the Apostle Paul. Satan will choose what he thinks the best season to attack. Will we defeat the devil, or will he defeat us? The answer depends in large part on what we do before the actual fight. The bull-moose principle is: enduring faith, strength and wisdom for the battle are best developed before we face our opponent. Paul knew this, and that's why he took time to be alone with his Lord before going up to Jerusalem.

A second thing we see about leaders in this passage is that they serve. Paul says, "I served the Lord with great humility and with tears, although I was severely tested by the plots of the Jews."

Notice who Paul says he was serving–the Lord. The Christian must always keep the Lord first. As the saying goes, the way to spell JOY is:

> **J**esus first
> **O**thers second
> **Y**ourself last

Paul tells us that he served the Lord in humility; he put himself last. And he served the Lord with tears; there's the passion. And he also served the Lord in spite of trials. Every place Paul went he wasn't welcomed with a brass band, but rather with brass knuckles ready to kill him. Are you ready to serve the

Lord and keep him first, no matter what?

Personally I have great admiration for former President Jimmy Carter. He could have retired to a life of ease after leaving the White House. Instead he began working for Habitat for Humanity and busied himself with many diplomatic peacekeeping missions. Carter explained his reasons for this in *The New Yorker* magazine:

> When Rosalynn and I left the White House, we decided since I was one of the youngest survivors of the office and we had a lot of years ahead of us, and I was deeply interested in human rights, and I didn't want to just build a library and go back to farming—we would do things that others wouldn't or couldn't do.
>
> To me, this is part of my duty as a human being. It is part of my duty to capitalize on my reputation and fame and influence as a former President of a great nation. And it's exciting. It's unpredictable. It's gratifying. It's adventurous. I just enjoy it.

You are not a former president of the United States. Neither am I. But whether someone is a former president or a teenager working at McDonald's, we each have a sacred duty and opportunity to use to the fullest whatever talents and opportunities God has given us. That is not a grim duty. It can be a great joy to serve the Lord and do whatever he wants us to do.

A third thing we learn about Christian leaders from this passage is that we need leaders who will teach God's people. Paul says, "You know that I have not hesitated to preach anything that would be helpful to you but have taught you publicly and from house to house."

We see three important things here about Paul's teaching. First of all, he held back nothing. He didn't hesitate to teach whatever he thought would be profitable for the people in Ephesus. Later on in verse 27, he says that he has not hesitated to proclaim the whole will of God. We need more Christian teachers today who will teach God's people the *whole* counsel of God and not just spoon feed bits and pieces of Scripture.

Secondly, Paul taught publicly. That is of primary importance. We need teachers in the church today who will devote themselves to study and preparation of public messages with excellence. I remember the pastor who baptized me once saying, "You have no right to speak it out in the sanctuary unless you have sweat it out in the study!" We need more preachers who will take that to heart in our day.

Thirdly, Paul went from house to house, teaching the Christians in the house churches, and most likely, teaching individuals and families. Richard Baxter was a pastor in 17th century England. He personally made a habit of going from house to house in his town of Kidderminster. When he visited each home he made sure that each family was learning their catechism, which was a question and answer method of learning Christian doctrine. It is said that by that method Baxter won all 800 households in Kidderminster to the Lord. He later wrote about his experiences in a book entitled: *The Reformed Pastor.*

Whether one uses Baxter's method or not, we need more Christian leaders today who will teach God's people from house to house. But it is not only the pastor who can do this. Laypeople can form small house groups, just as they did in the Early Church, and learn from God's Word together.

A fourth thing we need Christian leaders to do today is to testify. Paul says, "I have declared to both Jews and Greeks that they must turn to God in repentance and have faith in our Lord Jesus." Then in verse 24 Paul says, "However, I consider my life worth nothing to me, if only I may finish the race and complete the task the Lord Jesus has given me–the task of testifying to the Gospel of God's grace."

Acts 20:24 has been a life verse for me for a number of years. I think every Christian ought to have a life verse–a verse of Scripture that characterizes your life goal or purpose–something to meditate on frequently–a verse you can seek to understand and apply more deeply with every passing year. For me, Acts 20:24 is such a verse. I want more than anything else in my life to complete the task the Lord Jesus has given me–the task of testifying to the Gospel of God's grace. That means being a witness. And as we have seen already in the book of Acts, we get our modern English word–martyr–from the Greek word for witness. To be a witness of Jesus Christ is to be a martyr. It is something to which you must give your whole life.

Have you come to the place where you can say your life is worth nothing to you if only you can be a witness for the Lord Jesus Christ–whether that is a witness to your family, your friends, your community, or even to the whole world? I can think of nothing more important.

I think of the Greeks who came to Philip in John 12:21 and said, "Sir, we would see Jesus." I well remember those words being emblazoned on the pulpit at the Montreat Presbyterian Church in Montreat, North Carolina–placed there so that every person who would preach from that pulpit would have Jesus as their focus. I can think of nothing better than to come to the end of my life here on earth and have my family, my friends, my church, and everyone who knows me say, "We saw Jesus in Will's life and words." That is what being a witness is all about.

What is your one goal in life? If you don't have a goal, any road will get you there. What would you like people to say about you in your obituary? What would you want emblazoned on your tombstone? What few words would summarize what you want your life to be about? Life definition is crucial to life direction. And if you don't already have a life definition I think Acts 20:24

offers a great one that will give you direction every day of your life.

A fifth word in this passage which characterizes what Christian leaders need to be about today is the word: shepherd. Paul says to the elders at Ephesus: "Keep watch over yourselves and all the flock of which the Holy Spirit has made you overseers. Be shepherds of the church of God, which he bought with his own blood."

That is especially the job of elders in the church, to shepherd the people of God. But to be good shepherds we must first keep watch over ourselves. We must first tend to our own souls. If you are an elder in a church you need to be feeding yourself every day on the Word of God. Only then can you feed the sheep and properly care for the sheep.

Being a shepherd of God's flock also involves protecting the flock from wolves—wolves who bring false teaching. Elders need to be willing to stand up and say: "That's not what the Word of God teaches. Here is the truth!" Having the guts to say "NO" to false teaching is not popular in our day. We are taught to be tolerant of everyone and everything. But the Lord obviously doesn't want us to tolerate false teaching. That would be like tolerating cancer. If you tolerate cancer it will eat you up–it will eventually destroy every good cell in your body. The same is true of false teaching–it will kill every good cell in the Body of Christ.

A sixth word in this passage which is vital to Christian leadership is the word: commit. Paul says, "Now I commit you to God and to the word of his grace, which can build you up and give you an inheritance among all those who are sanctified."

We need more Christian leaders today who will recognize that the people of God are not their people. I have never had a congregation that belonged to me. Every Christian belongs to God through his Son Jesus Christ.

Sometimes as Christian leaders we have to be willing to let go, as Paul did in Ephesus, and move on to another part of God's flock. It was hard for Paul to leave the Ephesian Christians. Paul had invested a lot of his life in Ephesus and so I am sure he shed a few tears as he knelt on the beach with the elders and told them he would never see them again.

This act of the Christian leader committing God's people back to God is so important. Sometimes people get so attached to their pastor they confuse their pastor with God. The pastor is not God. God alone is able to build up each individual Christian by the word of his grace and give us an inheritance among all those who are sanctified. I can't do that for anyone. No pastor can do that. Only God can do that.

A final word which should characterize every Christian leader and every Christian is the word: prayer. After Paul gave this admonition to the elders of Ephesus "he knelt down with all of them and prayed."

Meditations on the Acts of the Apostles

I will never forget one morning, very early, when I left my parents' home in California to drive across the country and attend seminary. My father laid his hand upon my shoulder and prayed for me. That is the act of a Christian leader influencing someone in a positive direction.

I will also never forget the pastor who did the most to train me for Christian ministry: Calvin Thielman. Calvin was a praying pastor, a praying man. He would often stop in mid sentence and say, "We need to pray for . . ." and then he would begin praying. Prayer permeated Calvin's life. Prayer just naturally flowed out of him all the time. And that is the way everyone of us needs to be in our relationship with God. Prayer should just naturally flow out of us.

Leighton Ford, another one of my mentors, once wrote:

> When our daughter, Debbie, was about sixteen, Corrie Ten Boom, that wonderful Dutch lady of "The Hiding Place" fame, came to our city. She and I were to be co-speakers at a meeting. I took Debbie with me to the home at which she was staying for a brief visit. At the close of our conversation, Corrie said very simply, "Let's talk to the Father."
>
> With no change of voice or posture or inflection she closed her eyes and began talking to God just as naturally as she had been talking to us.
>
> On the way home, Debbie was quiet, then said, "Dad, I have the most weird feeling. While Corrie was praying, I almost think I had a vision.
>
> "There was this long dark hall and Corrie was walking down it. At the end were these large doors with a sliver of light showing underneath. As she got to the doors, some guards swung the doors open and welcomed her with a smile.
>
> "Past the doors there was this large brilliantly lighted room with a throne in the center. I could see Corrie walk up to God's throne.
>
> "And as she approached, I imagined God saying, 'Well, hello, Corrie, what can I do for you today?'"
>
> My daughter had an insight into the life of this wonderful woman, a person of prayer, whose life was filled with a sense of God's presence. And when she prayed, it was the speaking part of their relationship.

One of the great privileges of knowing Jesus Christ personally is that through his death for us, weak, sinful humans can also have that same intimate relationship.

As Oswald Chambers once wrote: "Prayer is not getting things from God . . . prayer is getting into perfect communion with God. I tell him what I

Keys to Growth

know he knows in order that I may get to know it as he does."

TENACITY

Tenacious means:

- Not easily pulled apart, cohesive, tough.
- Tending to adhere or cling, especially to another substance.
- Persistent in maintaining or adhering to something valued as habitual.

Tenacity is a key to spiritual growth, a key which the Apostle Paul used to unlock God's purposes for his life. Let us examine what is essential to such spiritual tenacity in Acts 21:1-16.

> After we had torn ourselves away from them, we put out to sea and sailed straight to Cos. The next day we went to Rhodes and from there to Patara. We found a ship crossing over to Phoenicia, went on board and set sail. After sighting Cyprus and passing to the south of it, we sailed on to Syria. We landed at Tyre, where our ship was to unload its cargo. Finding the disciples there, we stayed with them seven days. Through the Spirit they urged Paul not to go on to Jerusalem. But when our time was up, we left and continued on our way. All the disciples and their wives and children accompanied us out of the city, and there on the beach we knelt to pray. After saying good-by to each other, we went aboard the ship, and they returned home.
>
> We continued our voyage from Tyre and landed at Ptolemais, where we greeted the brothers and stayed with them for a day. Leaving the next day, we reached Caesarea and stayed at the house of Philip the evangelist, one of the Seven. He had four unmarried daughters who prophesied.
>
> After we had been there a number of days, a prophet named Agabus came down from Judea. Coming over to us, he took Paul's belt, tied his own hands and feet with it and said, "The Holy Spirit says, 'In this way the Jews of Jerusalem will bind the owner of this belt and will hand him over to the Gentiles.'"
>
> When we heard this, we and the people there pleaded with Paul not

to go up to Jerusalem. Then Paul answered, "Why are you weeping and breaking my heart? I am ready not only to be bound, but also to die in Jerusalem for the name of the Lord Jesus." When he would not be dissuaded, we gave up and said, "The Lord's will be done."

After this, we got ready and went up to Jerusalem. Some of the disciples from Caesarea accompanied us and brought us to the home of Mnason, where we were to stay. He was a man from Cyprus and one of the early disciples.

People can pull us this way and that. Paul knew it. I am sure the elders in Ephesus would have liked it very much if Paul had remained there. But Paul knew the Holy Spirit had other purposes for him. And so he pulled himself away from there and he set his face toward Jerusalem. Why? The reason lies back in Acts 20:22-23 where Paul said:

And now, compelled by the Spirit, I am going to Jerusalem, not knowing what will happen to me there. I only know that in every city the Holy Spirit warns me that prison and hardships are facing me.

Paul felt compelled, literally "bound", by the Holy Spirit of God to go to Jerusalem to deliver the offering he had collected for the Christians there. At the same time the Holy Spirit was warning Paul of what was awaiting him.

So here we see the first principle of spiritual tenacity, spiritual stick-to-it-iveness: *obey the Holy Spirit no matter what.*

But based upon a surface reading it seems like the guidance of the Holy Spirit is confusing. As I have just pointed out, in Acts 20, Paul felt compelled by the Holy Spirit to go up to Jerusalem despite the warnings of the same Spirit that prison and hardship were awaiting him there. But then in Acts 21:4 the disciples in Tyre urge Paul, *through the Spirit*, not to go on to Jerusalem. Was the Holy Spirit changing tack or what?

I think John Stott explains this best when he says that Luke's statement in Acts 21:4 "is a condensed way of saying that the warning was divine while the urging was human. After all, the Spirit's word to Paul combined the compulsion to go with a warning of the consequences."

But this raises the question: *How can we know God's will for our lives when the word of the Holy Spirit and the words of our friends can be in such conflict?* I think there are at least four steps to knowing the will of God for our lives:

1. We must first have the Holy Spirit in our hearts to guide us. We must surrender our lives to the Spirit of Christ if we want him to guide us.
2. We must read God's Word in the Bible and be willing to obey it. Scripture is where we find the will of God expressed in principle.

3. We must pray and earnestly ask the Holy Spirit to take the Word of God and use it to guide us.
4. We must listen to the Spirit.

In her book, *A Slow and Certain Light*, former missionary Elisabeth Eliot tells of two adventurers who stopped by to see her one day. They were all loaded down with equipment for traveling through the rain forests of South America. Interestingly enough they didn't seek advice from Elliot; they just wanted a few phrases to use to converse with the natives.

Eliot makes this application to our spiritual lives: "Sometimes we come to God as the two adventurers came to me—confident and, we think, well-informed and well-equipped. But has it occurred to us that with all our accumulation of stuff, something is missing?"\Eliot suggests that we often ask God for too little. "We know what we need—a yes or no answer, please, to a simple question. Or perhaps a road sign. Something quick and easy to point the way.

"What we really ought to have is the Guide himself. Maps, road signs, a few useful phrases are good things, but infinitely better is Someone who has been there before and knows the way."

It is our privilege to have the Guide himself living inside of us when we invite the Holy Spirit of God to live in our hearts. That is the first essential to spiritual tenacity.

The second principle of spiritual tenacity is to *be willing to suffer*. When Paul's friends tried to dissuade him from going up to Jerusalem he said, "Why are you weeping and breaking my heart? I am ready not only to be bound, but also to die in Jerusalem for the name of the Lord Jesus." (Acts 21:13) Paul was willing to suffer whatever was necessary for the sake of the Gospel. Are we?

Hundreds of years ago, Thomas a Kempis wrote in his book, *The Imitation of Christ*:

> Jesus hath now many lovers of his heavenly kingdom, but few bearers of his cross. He hath many desirous of comfort, but few of tribulation. He findeth many companions of his table, but few of his abstinence. All desire to rejoice with him, few are willing to endure anything for him. Many follow Jesus unto the breaking of bread; but few to the drinking of the cup of his passion. . . . Many love Jesus so long as adversities do not happen. Many praise and bless him, so long as they receive comforts from him. (*The Imitation of Christ*, Chicago: Moody, 1980, pp. 114-115.)

Those words are just as true today as ever.

There are at least three ways that suffering comes to Christians:

1. *By persecution.* This is the kind of suffering Paul had endured everywhere he went and he would endure again in Jerusalem. Paul later wrote to Timothy, "In fact, everyone who wants to live a godly life in Christ Jesus will be persecuted." (2 Timothy 3:12) And he wrote to the Church at Philippi: "For it has been granted to you on behalf of Christ not only to believe on him, but also to suffer for him." (Philippians 1:29) And Jesus himself said to his disciples: "If you belonged to the world, it would love you as its own. As it is, you do not belong to the world, but I have chosen you out of the world. That is why the world hates you." There is no beating about the bush in this: if you are a Christian you will most likely face some persecution in this life.

2. But a second way suffering comes to some Christians is simply *by bodily decay and death*. Face it: all of us are going to die unless Christ comes back first. And dying is not pleasant. In fact, the body starts deteriorating, moving toward disorganization and death very early on in the human life span. Paul says in Romans 8:22, "We know that the whole creation has been groaning as in the pains of childbirth right up to the present time." That is true of us as human beings and of all creation: we groan. And in 2 Corinthians 5:2 Paul says the same thing again: "Meanwhile we groan, longing to be clothed with our heavenly dwelling."

3. *Suffering is a part of growth.* Suffering comes to every Christian seeking to grow in the Christian life. In Colossians 3:5 Paul says, "Put to death, therefore, whatever belongs to your earthly nature: sexual immorality, impurity, lust, evil desires and greed, which is idolatry." There are things we have to put off in order to grow, as well as things we have to put on. And the putting off often hurts. The Sacraments which help us to grow remind us of the role of suffering in the Christian life. Baptism symbolizes dying to the old life and rising to the new in Christ. Communion symbolizes the death of Christ which must be applied to us every day.

However, in the midst of suffering there is also good news: there is the comfort of God. Paul says in 2 Corinthians 1:3-5,

> Praise be to the God and Father of our Lord Jesus Christ, the Father of compassion and the God of all comfort, who comforts us in all our troubles, so that we can comfort those in any trouble with the comfort we ourselves have received from God. For just as the sufferings of Christ flow over into our lives, so also through Christ our comfort overflows.

In fact, it is in the midst of suffering that we grow closer to Christ, and that sort of intimacy is worth any price.

In his book, *The Problem of Pain*, C. S. Lewis explains why pain is necessary in this sinful world to help us grow closer to Christ:

> My own experience is something like this. I am progressing along the path of life in my ordinary contentedly fallen and godless condition, absorbed in a merry meeting with my friends for the morrow or a bit of work that tickles my vanity today, a holiday or a new book, when suddenly a stab of abdominal pain that threatens some serious disease, or a headline in the newspapers that threatens us all with destruction, sends this whole pack of cards tumbling down. At first I am overwhelmed, and all my little happinesses look like broken toys. Then, slowly and reluctantly, bit by bit, I try to bring myself into the frame of mind that I should be in at all times. I remind myself that all these toys were never intended to possess my heart, that my true good is in another world and my only real treasure is Christ. And perhaps, by God's grace, I succeed, and for a day or two become a creature consciously dependent on God and drawing its strength from the right sources. But the moment the threat is withdrawn, my whole nature leaps back to the toys: I am even anxious, God forgive me, to banish from my mind the only thing that supported me under the threat because it is now associated with the misery of those few days. Thus the terrible necessity of tribulation is only too clear. God has had me for but forty-eight hours and then only by dint of taking everything else away from me. Let Him but sheathe that sword for a moment and I behave like a puppy when the hated bath is over–I shake myself as dry as I can and race off to reacquire my comfortable dirtiness, if not in the nearest manure heap, at least in the nearest flower bed. And that is why tribulations cannot cease until God either sees us remade or sees that our remaking is now hopeless. (*The Problem of Pain*, New York: Macmillan, 1986, pp. 106-107.)

Three principles of spiritual tenacity: (1) Obey the Holy Spirit no mater what, (2) Be willing to suffer for the Lord. And the third principle of spiritual tenacity is to *keep your eye on the prize*.

The reason why Paul was willing to endure suffering and even die in Jerusalem for the name of the Lord Jesus was because he had his eye on the prize. This isn't spelled out in Acts 21, but this focus was certainly present in Paul's mind and it enabled him to be tenacious, to hold on and not give up. Paul says in Philippians 3:10-14 . . .

> I want to know Christ and the power of his resurrection and the fellowship of sharing in his sufferings, becoming like him in his death,

and so, somehow, to attain to the resurrection from the dead.

Not that I have already obtained all this, or have already been made perfect, but I press on to take hold of that for which Christ Jesus took hold of me. Brothers, I do not consider myself yet to have taken hold of it. But one thing I do: Forgetting what is behind and straining toward what is ahead, I press on toward the goal to win the prize for which God has called me heavenward in Christ Jesus.

When Jewish psychiatrist Victor Frankl was arrested by the Nazis during World War II, he was stripped of everything—property, family, possessions. He had spent years researching and writing a book on the importance of finding meaning in life—concepts which would later be known as logo-therapy. When he arrived in Auschwitz, that infamous concentration camp, even Frankl's manuscript, which he had hidden in the lining of his coat, was taken away.

"I had to undergo and overcome the loss of my spiritual child," Frankl later wrote about the incident. "Now it seemed as if nothing and no one would survive me; neither a physical nor a spiritual child of my own! I found myself confronted with the question of whether under such circumstances my life was ultimately void of meaning."

Frankl was wrestling with that question when the Nazis forced the prisoners to give up their clothes: "I had to surrender my clothes and in turn inherited the worn out rags of an inmate who had been sent to the gas chamber," says Frankl. "Instead of the many pages of my manuscript, I found in the pocket of the newly acquired coat a single page torn out of a Hebrew prayer book, which contained the main Jewish prayer, *Shema Yisrael* (Hear, O Israel! The Lord our God is one God. And you shall love the Lord your God with all your heart and with all your soul and with all your might.)

"How should I have interpreted such a 'coincidence' other than as a challenge to live my thoughts instead of merely putting them on paper?"

Later, as Frankl reflected on his ordeal, he wrote in his book, *Man's Search for Meaning*, "There is nothing in the world that would so effectively help one to survive even the worst conditions, as the knowledge that there is a meaning in one's life. . . . He who has a *why* to live for can bear almost any *how*."

Paul had a great "why" to live for—Jesus Christ—and so he was able to bear any "how"—even persecution, suffering and finally death. Do you know that great "why"?

COMPROMISE

In November 2002 *Time* magazine printed a photograph of the back of Washington Redskins quarterback Jeff George (his helmet off, revealing a big, white-skinned bald spot) sitting on the bench flanked by two African-American teammates, each with a hand on his shoulder.

The caption read, "What counts most in creating a successful team is not how compatible its players are, but how they deal with incompatibility."

In Acts 21:17-26 we see how two great Christian leaders, James (the representative of Jewish Christianity) and Paul (the representative of mission to the Gentiles), dealt with incompatibility. . . .

> When we arrived at Jerusalem, the brothers received us warmly. The next day Paul and the rest of us went to see James, and all the elders were present. Paul greeted them and reported in detail what God had done among the Gentiles through his ministry.
>
> When they heard this, they praised God. Then they said to Paul: "You see, brother, how many thousands of Jews have believed, and all of them are zealous for the law. They have been informed that you teach all the Jews who live among the Gentiles to turn away from Moses, telling them not to circumcise their children or live according to our customs. What shall we do? They will certainly hear that you have come, so do what we tell you. There are four men with us who have made a vow. Take these men, join in their purification rites and pay their expenses, so that they can have their heads shaved. Then everybody will know there is no truth in these reports about you, but that you yourself are living in obedience to the law. As for the Gentile believers, we have written to them our decision that they should abstain from food sacrificed to idols, from blood, from the meat of strangled animals and from sexual immorality."
>
> The next day Paul took the men and purified himself along with them. Then he went to the temple to give notice of the date when the days of purification would end and the offering would be made for each of them.

The great Scottish Bible commentator, William Barclay, wrote about this passage: "There is a time when compromise is not a sign of weakness but of strength." And so I suggest to you today that *godly compromise is a key to growth in the Church and in the Christian life.* We are not talking here about compromise on essential doctrines or practices of the Christian faith. We are talking about compromise in a non-essential. As Rupert Meldenius once wrote:

> In essentials unity;
> In non-essentials liberty;
> In all things charity.

That is what we see practiced here by James and Paul. There is a settlement of difference reached by mutual concession.

What was the difference between James and Paul? James, as a Jew, believed in continuing to follow the ceremonial laws from the Hebrew Scriptures. Paul was wrongly accused by the Jews of Jerusalem of teaching Diaspora Jews to turn away from Moses. Paul taught no such thing. Paul taught that the Gentile believers in Jesus were not under obligation to follow Jewish law. To Paul, the question of whether a Jewish believer in Jesus should continue to follow Jewish customs was a matter of indifference. Paul himself felt free to abandon such customs, but when it was important to the forward movement of the Gospel, Paul could compromise and practice Jewish customs, as he did in the case of having Timothy circumcised.

Once again, Paul makes a concession on this occasion, for the purpose of keeping the Jewish and Gentile branches of the Christian Church united. It is not a concession on an essential, but rather on a non-essential.

James has the same purpose in mind. He praised God for what God had done through Paul's ministry. James wanted to see that ministry continue. He was afraid that the Jews in Jerusalem might bring a halt to Paul's ministry. So he asked Paul to join in the Jewish purification rites of four believers among them who had made a vow. James also asked Paul to pay for their expenses, which could be pretty hefty. Paul agreed to this concession.

The principle practiced by Paul in Acts 21 is taught by him in Romans 14:1-15:13. Paul's answer to the problem of incompatibility in the Church is that we all need to become servant leaders, people who would lead others closer to Jesus by serving. And in Romans 14 he tells us how to be servant leaders. Paul teaches the delicate art of Christian compromise. The first step is that we need to accept one another. "Accept him whose faith is weak without passing judgment on disputable matters." (Romans 14:1)

Paul talks about the weak and the strong in the church. Who are these people? From the context of the passage in Romans we can discern that the weak were, for the most part, as John Stott says, "Jewish Christians, whose weakness consisted in their continuing conscientious commitment to Jewish regulations regarding diet and [holy] days." The strong then are, for the most part, Gentile Christians who have developed an educated conscience and are rejoicing in their Christian freedom from having to observe a special diet or holy days in order to please God. So the distinction between weak and strong in Romans applies in Acts as well. Paul is the strong one who knows he is free from having to obey the Jewish ceremonial law. The Jewish Christians in Jerusalem were the weak ones who thought they were still bound by the law.

But how does Paul say strong Christians should act toward weak ones? Paul's message to the strong in the church is to accept those whose faith is weak without passing judgment on disputable matters. In the Roman Church the disputable matters in Paul's day were the following of a kosher diet and the observance of Jewish holy days. In our day the issues may be different (the advisability of Christians drinking alcohol or gambling, for example) but the principle for dealing with differences is the same; *we need to accept each other.* Paul says that one person's faith allows them to do one thing, while another person's faith in Christ allows them to do another. The one who abstains from the questionable activity and the one who does not must not condemn the other person.

It should be noted, once again, that we need to accept each other in the Church when there are differences over *non-essentials*. Paul is not saying that it is no big deal when we differ over essentials, such as the doctrines which today we have summarized in The Apostles' Creed. When core doctrine is at stake we can't just accept false teaching. But when we differ over non-essential matters to which all the answers may not be clearly revealed in the Bible or clearly understood by all Christians, then we need to learn to accept each other.

"Why should we accept one another?" That is the big question. Paul, in the letter to the Church at Rome, gives us four reasons for accepting one another. First of all, we should accept each other because God has accepted us. That is an amazing thing isn't it? That God has accepted us in Christ in spite of our sin is phenomenal. And not only did he accept us once, he continues to accept us.

The only way the Father can accept us, as a holy God, is because he gave his Son to live for us and die for us and rise again for us. That leads to the second reason why we should accept each other– because Christ died and rose again from the dead that we might belong to him. We are each *his* servants, primarily, and Paul says a servant should be judged by his own master. Therefore we should not judge one another in non-essential matters.

Thirdly, we should accept one another because we are all brothers and sisters in Christ. We are all part of one family in Jesus.

Back in the hippie days of the early 1970s a long-haired young man wearing blue jeans and a T-shirt with holes in it walked into a well-dressed, very conservative church. The young man was a new believer and recognized his need to get involved in a Christian fellowship. That's why he went to church. But he arrived late for the service on Sunday morning and found that the sanctuary was packed. He headed down the center aisle looking for a seat. Nobody moved to make room for him. Reaching the front of the church, right near the pulpit, and finding no seat available, he squatted down and sat on the floor.

By this time the congregation was feeling uncomfortable. But then, from the back of the church, came a grey-haired elder in a three-piece suit. He started walking toward the young man using his cane as an aid. When the elderly man reached the young college student, he dropped his cane on the floor, and, with some difficulty, lowered himself to sit next to the young man.

As the minister started into his sermon he said, "What I'm about to preach, you'll never remember. What you've just seen, you'll never forget."

Point taken: We are all brothers and sisters in Christ, so we need to accept each other.

Fourth, we should accept one another because God is our judge. Ultimately God will judge each one of us for what we have done in the body. Each of us will give an account to God. So why waste time now judging each other in disputable matters?

The second major step of Christian compromise, Paul says in Romans, is that we need to edify one another. "Let us therefore make every effort to do what leads to peace and to mutual edification." (Romans 14:19)

Paul says that when we have differences in the church over non-essential matters we need to do what will lead to peace and mutual edification. We need to edify each other, build each other up.

Why should we build each other up? Paul again gives four reasons.

First of all, we need to build each other up because we affect one another. Paul notes how easy it is for each one of us to put a stumbling block in each other's way. He says that he is convinced that no food is unclean in itself (the "strong" position) but if anyone is convinced that something is unclean (the "weak" position) then for him it is unclean and he shouldn't eat it. He says that if our brother is distressed because of what we eat then we shouldn't eat it either, at least not in front of the person, because to do so is to not act in love.

Secondly, we need to build each other up because the kingdom needs to be our priority not our own selfish agendas. Paul says that the strong should not allow what they consider to be good to be spoken ill of. This suggests that maybe some educating of the weak needs to happen. But the most important thing is not what we eat or don't eat, not what we drink or don't drink. What is most important is Christ's kingdom and building each other up. For example, it is more important that I should build you up in your relationship with Christ than that I should ever drink another glass of wine. And if my drinking a glass of wine impedes the Christian growth of another brother or sister, then I should forego having that glass of wine.

This leads to the third reason why we should build each other up: because we must help each other grow. Should I destroy God's work in your life just so that I can eat and drink what I want? "No way!" Paul says.

Finally, Paul says we should focus on building each other up rather than forcing our own opinions on each other. Whatever we believe about disputable matters, Paul says we should keep between ourselves and God. But the man who doubts whether a certain disputable activity is right is condemned if he participates. Not condemned by God, but by his own uneducated conscience.

For example, we can take the issue of music in the church. There are some Christians who believe that contemporary music in worship services is wrong. I do not believe that is the case. I do not believe there is a Scriptural case that can be made out to show that it is wrong. But I should not force my opinion on those who do believe it is wrong. I should not force them to sing songs that they think are evil. I may want to try and educate, but I should not force.

Finally, the third major step that Paul says we need to take in order to practice the Christian art of compromise is that we need to please one another. "Each of us should please his neighbor for his good, to build him up." (Romans 15:2)

Now, let me make clear what it means to please your neighbor. John Stott says,

> Neighbour-pleasing, which Scripture commands, must not be confused with 'men-pleasing', which Scripture condemns. In this pejorative sense, to 'please men', usually in antithesis to pleasing God, means to flatter people in order to curry favour with them, to win their approval by some unprincipled compromise.

Again, Paul gives us reasons to focus on pleasing each other. First of all, he says, the strong ought to bear with the failings of the weak. It only makes sense in other areas of life that the strong should take care of and bear with the weak. So when it comes to disputable matters in the church we should do the same.

Secondly, Paul says we should not focus on pleasing ourselves. We spend enough time focused on ourselves. Focusing on pleasing others is healthy for us. It draws us out of ourselves.

Thirdly, Paul says we should please our neighbor because it is good for him. It can build him up in the Lord.

Then Paul gives us four reasons based upon Christ, four reasons why we should please others because of who Christ is. Paul says that we should focus on pleasing others because Christ didn't please himself. He took the insults that were due to us, and the punishment that was due to us, upon himself. If he did that for us, then certainly we should live for him and for others, rather than living to please ourselves.

Secondly, Paul shows us that Christ is the way to united worship. Jesus is the one who brings Jew and Gentile together. He is the one who gives a spirit of unity to his Church. He can bring black and white together, teetotalers and wine-bibbers, as well as Christians of every denomination across the spectrum.

Third, we should focus on pleasing others because Christ has accepted us. We should please and accept each other because that is what Jesus has done for us. And when we do so it brings praise to God.

Finally, we should focus on pleasing others because Christ has become a servant. I have found it true in life that the greatest people I have met are the most humble servants; their whole goal in life seems to be, not to draw attention to themselves, but to bring out the best in others.

Frank Darabont, director of *The Green Mile*, reflects on Tom Hanks' selfless commitment to helping rising actor Michael Duncan achieve his best:

> Fifteen, twenty years from now, what will I remember [about filming *The Green Mile*]? There was one thing–and I'll never forget this: When [Tom] Hanks was playing a scene with Michael Duncan....
>
> As we're shooting, [the camera] is on Michael first, and I'm realizing that I'm getting distracted by Hanks. Hanks is delivering an Academy Award-winning performance, *off-camera*, for Michael Duncan–to give him every possible thing he needs or can use to deliver the best possible performance.
>
> He wanted Michael to do *so* well. He wanted him to look *so* good. I'll never forget that.

In 1999, Michael Clarke Duncan was nominated for an Academy Award in the Best Actor in a Supporting Role category. Tom Hanks, however, was not nominated.

The only way we can be servant leaders like that, people who practice the Christian art of compromise by accepting one another, edifying one another, and living to please one another, not just on one occasion, but every day, is if we have Jesus at the center of our lives, because he is the ultimate servant leader. That servant heart led Jesus to the cross. That servant heart will lead each one of us to the cross. And as we will see in our continuing study of Acts, that servant heart led Paul to the cross as well. . . .

CLOSED DOORS

Have you ever prayed for God to open a door in your life? I'm sure you have. How about closed doors? Have you ever prayed for a closed door? We don't like closed doors do we? And yet, as I mentioned in the chapter on Providence, a few years back when I was facing a change in life, my friend Douglas Gresham encouraged me to pray for closed doors.

Beginning in Acts 21:27 we read about a door that was slammed in the face of the Apostle Paul. Let's read together about Paul's closed door, and the new windows of opportunity God opened for him. . . .

> When the seven days were nearly over, some Jews from the province of Asia saw Paul at the temple. They stirred up the whole crowd and seized him, shouting, "Men of Israel, help us! This is the man who teaches all men everywhere against our people and our law and this place. And besides, he has brought Greeks into the temple area and defiled this holy place." (They had previously seen Trophimus the Ephesian in the city with Paul and assumed that Paul had brought him into the temple area.)
>
> The whole city was aroused, and the people came running from all directions. Seizing Paul, they dragged him from the temple, and immediately the gates were shut. While they were trying to kill him, news reached the commander of the Roman troops that the whole city of Jerusalem was in an uproar. He at once took some officers and soldiers and ran down to the crowd. When the rioters saw the commander and his soldiers, they stopped beating Paul.
>
> The commander came up and arrested him and ordered him to be bound with two chains. Then he asked who he was and what he had done. Some in the crowd shouted one thing and some another, and since the commander could not get at the truth because of the uproar, he ordered that Paul be taken into the barracks. When Paul reached the steps, the violence of the mob was so great he had to be carried by the soldiers. The crowd that followed kept shouting, "Away with him!" As the soldiers were about to take Paul into the barracks, he asked the commander, "May I say something to you?"

"Do you speak Greek?" he replied. "Aren't you the Egyptian who started a revolt and led four thousand terrorists out into the desert some time ago?"

Paul answered, "I am a Jew, from Tarsus in Cilicia, a citizen of no ordinary city. Please let me speak to the people."

The Closed Door of Paul's Arrest

I find this one brief statement in our text today to be very dramatic and evocative: ". . . and immediately the gates were shut." From Acts 9 all the way through to this point we have been reading about Paul's virtually unhindered witness throughout the Roman Empire. Yes, Paul has been persecuted by the Jews on numerous occasions. Yes, he has been arrested before. Yes, he has even been stoned and left for dead. But on this occasion when Paul is arrested he doesn't get out of it. In fact, we will see Paul under arrest throughout the rest of the book of Acts. So let us carefully examine exactly how this happens to Paul.

You will remember from the last chapter that Paul agreed with James to join in the purification rites of four other Jewish believers and pay for their expenses. This godly compromise which Paul made is what led him into the temple in Jerusalem in the first place. Now it also got him into hot water!

Some Jews from the province of Asia saw Paul in the temple. These were apparently some of the same Jews who had given Paul trouble as he traveled throughout Galatia. They stirred up the crowd with claims that Paul had been teaching against the Jewish people, the Jewish law and the Jewish temple. Ironic isn't it, that just when Paul had made a godly compromise in order to win the Jews of Jerusalem over, he is accused of doing just the opposite? Sometimes you just can't win! These Jews also made a second untrue accusation. They accused Paul of bringing a Greek into the temple area. The temple precincts were divided into different areas. Non-Jews could only enter into a certain part of the temple area. In fact there was a dividing wall between the area where the Gentiles could be and the area only Jews could enter. And there were signs posted all along this wall threatening the Gentiles with death if they violated the barrier. This is what Paul is referring to in Ephesians 2:14-15 when he writes: "For he [Christ] himself is our peace, who has made the two [Jew and Gentile] one and has destroyed the barrier, the dividing wall of hostility, by abolishing in his flesh the law with its commandments and regulations."

The reaction to these accusations was that the whole city was aroused. A mob formed and they seized Paul, dragging him out of the more sacred portion of the temple precincts, and the gates to that portion of the temple were shut. While this mob was trying to kill Paul news of the lynching reached the commander of the Roman troops, stationed in the Antonia fortress adjacent to the temple. The commander immediately brought a contingent of soldiers to check out what was going on, and when the mob saw the Roman soldiers they stopped beating Paul.

Bruce Larson describes the rest of the scene this way:

> Imagine, if you will, that you are a film director doing the story of the life of Paul and shooting this scene. There is the legendary cast of thousands, crowded on Solomon's Porch, the courtyard of the temple, yelling, 'Kill Paul! Kill Paul!' As this is about to happen, a group of Roman soldiers who are there to keep the peace, form a flying wedge and move into the crowd to rescue the source of the trouble, this wild little evangelist. They pick him up, carry him over their heads on their shields, and hustle him through the mob, who are all the while yelling, 'Kill him! Kill him!' Meanwhile, Paul is lying up there on the shield trying to converse with the tribune in charge of this rescue operation. He addresses him in good Greek, which makes a very positive impression. The tribune thought he was an Egyptian, a well-known revolutionary. As they are carrying him up the stairs to the guardhouse, followed still by the angry crowd, Paul says, 'Put me down. I've got to talk to them.' From the steps of the barracks, he begins to give his personal witness. Our imaginary director would have a hard time making this scene credible on film. Paul's holy boldness can only be accredited to God's own Spirit in and with him.

What do you do when a door slams shut in your face, when you lose your job, or your spouse walks out on you, when all your hopes and dreams come crashing down? Do you sit there and cry about the closed door? Yes, we all do because we are human. But then if you are trusting in Christ you should be looking, even through tears, for the new door that God is opening for you, because, as the Reverend Mother says in *The Sound of Music*, "God never closes a door without opening a window somewhere."

The story is told of an Irish boy who often roamed the hills outside his village. One day the path he was following led to a tall gate. The boy found the gate locked so that there was no going through. The gate was part of a high stone wall and there was no way the boy could go around the wall. The boy either had to forsake his journey or figure out a way to climb over the wall. To build up his own inner sense of commitment to the task the boy threw his much-loved cap over the wall.

Next, using his Irish common sense, the boy creatively found some foot-holds and hand-holds in the stone wall. He climbed over the obstacle, retrieved his cap and continued on his journey. The locked gate had forced him to consider another way of accomplishing his purpose.

That story reminds me of The Possibility Thinker's Creed which I memorized as a child:

> When faced with a mountain I will not quit!
> I will keep on striving
> until I climb over,
> find a pass through,
> tunnel underneath,
> or simply stay and turn the mountain into a gold mine
> with God's help!

That's a good creed to make your own. I think, in a sense, that was Paul's creed. When he was faced with the slammed door of his own arrest, he immediately started looking around for another open door for witness to his Savior Jesus Christ. And Paul found that open door, first in the very mob in front of him who had tried to kill him moments before.

The Open Door to the Mob

Listen to how Paul used the open door that was before him in Acts 22.

> Having received the commander's permission, Paul stood on the steps and motioned to the crowd. When they were all silent, he said to them in Aramaic: "Brothers and fathers, listen now to my defense."
>
> When they heard him speak to them in Aramaic, they became very quiet.
>
> Then Paul said: "I am a Jew, born in Tarsus of Cilicia, but brought up in this city. Under Gamaliel I was thoroughly trained in the law of our fathers and was just as zealous for God as any of you are today. I persecuted the followers of this Way to their death, arresting both men and women and throwing them into prison, as also the high priest and all the Council can testify. I even obtained letters from them to their brothers in Damascus, and went there to bring these people as prisoners to Jerusalem to be punished.
>
> "About noon as I came near Damascus, suddenly a bright light from heaven flashed around me. I fell to the ground and heard a voice say to me, 'Saul! Saul! Why do you persecute me?'
>
> " 'Who are you, Lord?' I asked.
>
> " 'I am Jesus of Nazareth, whom you are persecuting,' he replied. My companions saw the light, but they did not understand the voice of him who was speaking to me.
>
> " 'What shall I do, Lord?' I asked.

Meditations on the Acts of the Apostles

" 'Get up,' the Lord said, 'and go into Damascus. There you will be told all that you have been assigned to do.' My companions led me by the hand into Damascus, because the brilliance of the light had blinded me.

"A man named Ananias came to see me. He was a devout observer of the law and highly respected by all the Jews living there. He stood beside me and said, 'Brother Saul, receive your sight!' And at that very moment I was able to see him.

"Then he said: 'The God of our fathers has chosen you to know his will and to see the Righteous One and to hear words from his mouth. You will be his witness to all men of what you have seen and heard. And now what are you waiting for? Get up, be baptized and wash your sins away, calling on his name.'

"When I returned to Jerusalem and was praying at the temple, I fell into a trance and saw the Lord speaking. 'Quick!' he said to me. 'Leave Jerusalem immediately, because they will not accept your testimony about me.'

" 'Lord,' I replied, 'these men know that I went from one synagogue to another to imprison and beat those who believe in you. And when the blood of your martyr Stephen was shed, I stood there giving my approval and guarding the clothes of those who were killing him.'

"Then the Lord said to me, 'Go; I will send you far away to the Gentiles.'"

Paul had learned something from his experience in Athens. He doesn't engage in any fancy intellectual discourse on this occasion. He simply tells the Jewish mob his story. As William Barclay has said, ". . . personal experience is the most unanswerable argument on earth."

Paul starts basically by saying: "A funny thing happened to me on the way to Damascus...." He trots out his credentials as a very religious Jew. He notes how he studied under Gamaliel, one of the most respected rabbis in Jerusalem. Paul reminds his audience that he was just like they are, so zealous for the law that he persecuted the Christians.

But then Paul goes on to tell his audience how he has changed, how he has become different from them. The reason is his personal encounter with Jesus Christ on the road to Damascus. Since meeting Jesus Paul has come to realize that Christ is the Savior of all people and God is the lover of all people, whereas he used to believe that God was the lover of the Jews only.

In verse 14 we have a wonderful summary of what the Christian life is all about. God has chosen us, as he chose Paul, *to know his will, to see the righteous one* [Jesus], and *to hear the voice of his mouth*. It was said of some great preacher that he often paused in his preaching as though he were listening for another voice. The Christian is one who must always listen for the voice of God behind him or her saying, "This is the way, walk ye in it." Paul listened for the voice of God even as he faced the closed door of his arrest, and so he immediately saw a new, open door of opportunity for witness.

In Paul we see a great example of how to utilize an open door for evangelism. *First of all, Paul identified with his audience.* He showed them how he was a Jew just like them. We too need to identify with our audience. If we don't love the people around us with God's love, and find things we have in common with them, then they will never want to hear what we have to say about Jesus.

Secondly, Paul talked to the Jews of Jerusalem in a language they could understand, in this case, Aramaic. Often as Christians we develop our own language that no one else understands. We talk about "getting saved", "walking with Jesus" and we use a host of other terms that non-Christians can't relate to. We have to learn how to translate our experience into language that non-Christians can understand.

Thirdly, Paul shared, very simply, what Jesus had done in his life. Paul's life had been dramatically changed from a persecutor of Christians to a herald of the Christ. Your story may not be as dramatic as Paul but every Christian has a story to tell of how Christ is working in his or her life.

The Response of Paul's Audience

How did Paul's audience respond to his speech? Listen to what happened from Acts 22:22-29....

> The crowd listened to Paul until he said this. Then they raised their voices and shouted, "Rid the earth of him! He's not fit to live!"
>
> As they were shouting and throwing off their cloaks and flinging dust into the air, the commander ordered Paul to be taken into the barracks. He directed that he be flogged and questioned in order to find out why the people were shouting at him like this. As they stretched him out to flog him, Paul said to the centurion standing there, "Is it legal for you to flog a Roman citizen who hasn't even been found guilty?"
>
> When the centurion heard this, he went to the commander and reported it. "What are you going to do?" he asked. "This man is a Roman citizen."
>
> The commander went to Paul and asked, "Tell me, are you a Roman citizen?"

"Yes, I am," he answered.

Then the commander said, "I had to pay a big price for my citizenship."

"But I was born a citizen," Paul replied.

Those who were about to question him withdrew immediately. The commander himself was alarmed when he realized that he had put Paul, a Roman citizen, in chains.

Luke shows us two responses to Paul's message, that of the crowd and that of the Roman commander. The Jewish mob rejected both Paul and his message. As soon as he mentioned his ministry to the Gentiles they were ready to lynch him again. They believed that God loved the Jews pretty exclusively; they didn't want to hear anything of Paul's mission to the Gentiles.

We too must be prepared to accept the fact that some people will reject what we have to say about Jesus, maybe not for the same reasons the Jews rejected Paul, but they may reject us and our message nonetheless. As Jesus himself said, "In this world you will have trouble. But take heart! I have overcome the world." (John 16:33)

Rejection wasn't the only response Paul received to his message. The Roman commander wanted to know more. He wanted to know why the people were crying out for Paul's death. Of course the commander did not go about getting an answer out of Paul in the right way. He was ready to have Paul flogged until he learned that Paul was a Roman citizen, and to flog a Roman citizen before trial was illegal.

In the same way, if we faithfully share the message of Jesus with others, rejection won't be the only response. We won't always face a closed door. God will give us open doors of opportunity with some people whom he has prepared to respond positively to his offer of salvation. God had more open doors of opportunity in store for Paul, and he will for each one of us as well. As it says in Revelation 3:7-8....

> These are the words of him who is holy and true, who holds the key of David. What he opens no one can shut, and what he shuts no one can open. I know your deeds. See, I have placed before you an open door that no one can shut. I know that you have little strength, yet you have kept my word and have not denied my name.

These are God's words of hope for each one of us today.

GOD'S SOVEREIGNTY

The only survivor of a shipwreck landed on a deserted island. He prayed desperately to God for rescue and every day he looked out to sea for help, but every day he was disappointed.

Finally, the man decided to settle in to life on his lonely island. He built a shelter for himself, as best he could with his limited skills in that area, and he put his few possessions, which had washed up on shore, in the hut. Then one day, after going out hunting for food, the man returned "home" only to find his shelter going up in smoke. He sat down on the sand feeling utterly defeated.

In the midst of that defeat, early the next day, a boat arrived at the man's island and rescued him.

Flabbergasted, the man asked his rescuers, "What drew you to the island?"

His rescuers replied: "We saw your smoke signal, of course."

Oftentimes God uses what seems like our greatest defeat to bring about his good purposes. In the last chapter we saw what seemed to be the great defeat of all Paul's plans. He was arrested in Jerusalem. But in Acts 23 we will begin to see how God, in his sovereign goodness, used this seeming defeat to bring about his purpose....

> The next day, since the commander wanted to find out exactly why Paul was being accused by the Jews, he released him and ordered the chief priests and all the Sanhedrin to assemble. Then he brought Paul and had him stand before them.
>
> Paul looked straight at the Sanhedrin and said, "My brothers, I have fulfilled my duty to God in all good conscience to this day." At this the high priest Ananias ordered those standing near Paul to strike him on the mouth. Then Paul said to him, "God will strike you, you whitewashed wall! You sit there to judge me according to the law, yet you yourself violate the law by commanding that I be struck!"
>
> Those who were standing near Paul said, "You dare to insult God's high priest?"
>
> Paul replied, "Brothers, I did not realize that he was the high priest;

for it is written: 'Do not speak evil about the ruler of your people.'"

Then Paul, knowing that some of them were Sadducees and the others Pharisees, called out in the Sanhedrin, "My brothers, I am a Pharisee, the son of a Pharisee. I stand on trial because of my hope in the resurrection of the dead." When he said this, a dispute broke out between the Pharisees and the Sadducees, and the assembly was divided. (The Sadducees say that there is no resurrection, and that there are neither angels nor spirits, but the Pharisees acknowledge them all.)

There was a great uproar, and some of the teachers of the law who were Pharisees stood up and argued vigorously. "We find nothing wrong with this man," they said. "What if a spirit or an angel has spoken to him?" The dispute became so violent that the commander was afraid Paul would be torn to pieces by them. He ordered the troops to go down and take him away from them by force and bring him into the barracks.

In Acts 23 we see several truths which flow naturally out of the sovereign rule of God. By God's sovereignty I mean God's good rule over all of his creation and his ability to bring about whatever he so desires. Paul talks about God's sovereignty in Ephesians 1:11 where he mentions ". . . the plan of him who works out everything in conformity with the purpose of his will." God has given to human beings freedom. We are free to reject God's plan for our lives or to accept it by his grace. Yet, at the same time, God works in and through and beyond the free choices of human beings to bring about his purposes. So let's examine how God's sovereignty and our human freedom work in a specific situation by examining Acts 23. The first thing we see here is that *because of God's Sovereignty we can be bold.*

Paul knew that God was in charge of his situation and that no one was going to harm him unless God allowed it for some good reason. So Paul dared to be bold in his testimony before the Jewish ruling council, the Sanhedrin. Ananias didn't like Paul's boldness and so in his human freedom he had Paul struck on the mouth.

What did Ananias not like about what Paul was saying? Ananias probably didn't think it was possible for anyone to have a clear conscience as Paul was claiming. And he certainly didn't think that Paul was in the right. After all, Paul was a Christian, he was claiming that Jesus was the Son of God, and to Ananias that was blasphemy.

But Paul didn't let a little blood on his lip stop him from testifying about his Savior. Not realizing it was the high priest who ordered him struck (remember Paul suffered from some sort of impairment of sight) he condemned Ananias' action. He called Ananias a white-washed wall.

What did Paul mean by this statement? The Jews, believing that they would be defiled if they touched anything having to do with a dead body, white-washed the walls of their tombs so they would be warned not to touch them. So Paul was basically saying that Ananias was like a white-washed tomb—he looked good on the outside but on the inside he was spiritually dead.

Once Paul realized his error in referring to the high priest in this fashion he decided to take another approach. Paul knew that the Sanhedrin was made up of Sadducees who did not believe in the resurrection of the body (that is why they are "sad you see"!) and Pharisees like himself who did believe in the resurrection. So Paul very cleverly divided his accusers in their opinion of him.

At the same time Paul probably spoke of the resurrection for a more important reason. Notice that Paul doesn't waste time arguing with the Sanhedrin about the reasons for his arrest. What he is more eager to do is witness to them about the central belief of the Christians: the belief in the resurrection of the body and the fact that part of God's resurrection plan had already taken place in Jesus of Nazareth. Paul was always thinking about how he could share the good news about Jesus with anyone with whom he came in contact. And he was bold in his witness.

The response of the Sanhedrin to Paul's witness was that the Sadducees and Pharisees were bitterly divided. So much so that the Roman commander was afraid they were going to tear Paul to pieces. So he had Paul removed from the assembly.

I wonder: are we like Paul? Do we realize that God is fully in charge of our lives and that therefore we can dare to be bold for him? I'm not talking about being obnoxious in our witness for Jesus and purposely offending other people. I'm just talking about being clear. When I highlight something in bold print on my computer that word stands out more than all the rest. The print is darker, clearer, easier to read. It jumps out from the paper. That's the way we need to be in our witness for Christ. And we can afford to be bold because in Jesus we have nothing to lose.

Several years ago a high school valedictorian in Florida by the name of Shannon Spaulding used her speech at graduation to tell about her faith in Jesus Christ. Her speech drew a mixed reaction in the crowd that was present as well as garnering national media attention. Many people questioned whether it was appropriate or not for a valedictorian to turn her speech into what some thought was a sermon. Apparently the statement in Spaulding's speech which was most offensive to some people was this one: "I want to tell you that Jesus Christ can give you eternal life in heaven. If we die with that sin on our souls, we will immediately be pulled down to hell to pay the eternal price for our sins ourselves."

We might be tempted to argue about whether *all* of Shannon Spaulding's words in her speech were appropriate or not for the context in which she was speaking. Sometimes as Christians we give offense in our witness when we don't need to. But my hat is off to Shannon Spaulding for her boldness and her willingness afterwards to stand by what she said when questioned by the news media.

We don't all have the same opportunities or even abilities that Shannon Spaulding has or that the Apostle Paul had, but by God's grace we can all be more bold in our witness for Jesus Christ, knowing that ultimately we have nothing to lose because of his sovereign rule over our lives.

After Paul gave his bold testimony to his faith in the resurrection of the body before the Sanhedrin, we read in Acts 23:11,

> The following night the Lord stood near Paul and said, "Take courage! As you have testified about me in Jerusalem, so you must also testify in Rome."

The missionary Jim Elliot, who gave his life trying to reach the Auca tribe of South America once said: "Your life is immortal until your job is done." *Because of God's sovereignty our lives really are immortal until our job is done.*

No one could take Paul's life away from him until God's purposes for his life were fulfilled. Part of God's purpose and plan for Paul was for him to testify to Jesus Christ in Rome, the capitol of the empire. How encouraging it must have been for Paul, after enduring the abuse of the Sadducees, to hear this comforting word from the Lord! He was finally going to get to go to Rome and testify to his faith in Christ just as he had long desired to do.

I believe the Lord wants to speak a comforting word to you today as well. Take courage! Take heart! God's purpose for your life will be fulfilled if you allow him to work in you. As Paul said in Philippians 1:6, "he who began a good work in you will carry it on to completion until the day of Christ Jesus." Salvation doesn't mean we will always be safe, in physical terms, but it does mean God's purposes will be fulfilled in our lives.

On April 28, 1996, a gunman walked into a crowded café in Port Arthur, Australia, and started firing his weapon. Tony Kistan, a member of the Salvation Army from Sydney, and his wife Sarah were in the restaurant when the crazed man began his rampage. Courageously Tony stepped in front of his wife to protect her from the bullets that were flying, so he was one of the first of thirty-four victims to be gunned down. As he lay dying in his wife's arms Tony said to her, "I'm going to be with the Lord."

Those final words of faith in Christ were quoted by the Australian media and carried to the world. At a press conference following the shooting, Tony's son Nesan, who was 24 years old at the time, explained to reporters how his father had assurance of eternal life through Christ and he went on to describe his father's dedication to serving the Lord. Hardened journalists and photographers wept openly. During his life on earth Tony had been one to witness openly to strangers and friends alike about his faith in Christ. So it was appropriate that in death Tony witnessed to others through his simple, dying words to his wife.

Being a witness for Christ in this fallen world brings eternal purpose to even the most tragic and painful events. And because God is sovereign, your life is immortal until your job is done.

A third result which flows from God's sovereignty is that: *because God is sovereign, human beings cannot foil his plan.* Let's see what happened with Paul after God gave him his word of assurance. . . .

> The next morning the Jews formed a conspiracy and bound themselves with an oath not to eat or drink until they had killed Paul. More than forty men were involved in this plot. They went to the chief priests and elders and said, "We have taken a solemn oath not to eat anything until we have killed Paul. Now then, you and the Sanhedrin petition the commander to bring him before you on the pretext of wanting more accurate information about his case. We are ready to kill him before he gets here."

The Jews were determined that Paul should pay with his life for taking the good news about Jesus to the Gentiles. One almost feels sorry for these Jews in their misguided religious zeal. I mean, what were these forty men to do who had taken the oath not to eat anything until they killed Paul? Little did they know that God had other plans and that there was no way they were going to take Paul's life. If they truly carried out their vow these men were destined to die of hunger!

This little true story just goes to show that no one can thwart God's plan. As it says in Isaiah 14:27,

> For the Lord Almighty has purposed, and who can thwart him?
> His hand is stretched out, and who can turn it back?

The Lord was determined that Paul should testify to Jesus Christ in Rome, and there was no human being that was going to be able to foil God's plan.

A fourth aspect of God's sovereignty which we see exercised in Acts 23 is that *God uses people to make certain his plan is carried out.* Listen to the rest of Paul's story and see the unique people God used to carry out his plan for Paul.

> But when the son of Paul's sister heard of this plot, he went into the barracks and told Paul.
>
> Then Paul called one of the centurions and said, "Take this young

man to the commander; he has something to tell him." So he took him to the commander.

The centurion said, "Paul, the prisoner, sent for me and asked me to bring this young man to you because he has something to tell you."

The commander took the young man by the hand, drew him aside and asked, "What is it you want to tell me?"

He said: "The Jews have agreed to ask you to bring Paul before the Sanhedrin tomorrow on the pretext of wanting more accurate information about him. Don't give in to them, because more than forty of them are waiting in ambush for him. They have taken an oath not to eat or drink until they have killed him. They are ready now, waiting for your consent to their request."

The commander dismissed the young man and cautioned him, "Don't tell anyone that you have reported this to me."

Then he called two of his centurions and ordered them, "Get ready a detachment of two hundred soldiers, seventy horsemen and two hundred spearmen to go to Caesarea at nine tonight. Provide mounts for Paul so that he may be taken safely to Governor Felix."

He wrote a letter as follows:

Claudius Lysias,

To His Excellency, Governor Felix:

Greetings.

This man was seized by the Jews and they were about to kill him, but I came with my troops and rescued him, for I had learned that he is a Roman citizen. I wanted to know why they were accusing him, so I brought him to their Sanhedrin. I found that the accusation had to do with questions about their law, but there was no charge against him that deserved death or imprisonment. When I was informed of a plot to be carried out against the man, I sent him to you at once. I also ordered his accusers to present to you their case against him.

So the soldiers, carrying out their orders, took Paul with them during the night and brought him as far as Antipatris. The next day they let the cavalry go on with him, while they returned to the barracks. When the cavalry arrived in Caesarea, they delivered the letter to the governor and handed Paul over to him. The governor read the letter and asked what province he was from. Learning that he was from Cilicia, he said, "I will hear your case when your accusers get here." Then he ordered that Paul be kept under guard in Herod's palace.

God used quite a number of different people and each had their different motives, but God used each of them to carry out his purposes for Paul's life.

First of all, there was *Paul's nephew*. I'm sure he had the best of motives for wanting to protect the life of his uncle. And he was in the right place at the right time, under the sovereignty of God, to render great service to his uncle Paul. This just goes to show the truth of the statement once made by Francis Schaeffer: "There are no little people and no little places." Paul's nephew may have seemed to others like an insignificant person, but he wasn't insignificant in God's plan. And neither are we.

Secondly, God used *Claudius Lysias* to protect Paul more than once. At least four times in Acts 21 through 23 the Roman commander Claudius Lysias rescued Paul from almost certain death. As we gather from the letter Claudius wrote to Governor Felix, he had mixed motives at best. He lied about the order of events, for he only learned *after* he was about to flog Paul that Paul was a Roman citizen. To be sure, Claudius would do whatever was necessary to make himself look good and to save his own skin. But God used him, nonetheless, to protect his servant Paul. And that just goes to show that God can use all sorts of people in his plan, those we think wicked as well as those we think good.

Thirdly, God used *the Roman army* to protect Paul. Paul's travel insurance was provided by the Roman government! Imagine it–200 soldiers, 70 horsemen and 200 spear-men. That's pretty heavy-duty travel insurance!

I believe there are at least two ways people can look at these events in the life of Paul. We can look at it and say: "Oh, Paul's life just worked out naturally, according to his own free will and the free will of other people." Or we can look at Paul's life and say, "There is obviously another hand involved here."

Many years ago the following story appeared in *The London Observer*,

> Imagine a family of mice who lived all their lives in a large piano. To them in their piano-world came the music of the instrument, filling all the dark spaces with sound and harmony. At first the mice were impressed by it. They drew comfort and wonder from the thought that there was Someone who made the music–though invisible to them–above, yet close to them. They loved to think of the Great Player whom they could not see.
>
> Then one day a daring mouse climbed up part of the piano and returned very thoughtful. He had found out how music was made. Wires were the secret; tightly stretched wires of graduated lengths which trembled and vibrated. They must revise all their old beliefs: none but the most conservative could any longer believe in the Unseen Player.

Later, another explorer carried the explanation further. Hammers were now the secret, numbers of hammers dancing and leaping on the wires. This was a more complicated theory, but it all went to show that they lived in a purely mechanical and mathematical world. The Unseen Player came to be thought of as a myth.

But the pianist continued to play.

Were the events of Paul's life merely the product of wires and hammers or was there really an unseen piano player "behind the scenes"? And what about your life and mine?

I'll tell you what I believe. I believe God, the great pianist, in his sovereignty, will continue to play beautiful music using the keys, the hammers and the strings of our lives, if we allow him to do so. He will add line upon line until the concerto is complete in the day of Christ Jesus. No one will be able to stop his music in our lives until the symphony reaches its triumphant conclusion.

HOLY BOLDNESS

On July 15, 1986, Roger Clemens, the renowned pitcher for the Boston Red Sox, played in his first All-Star Game. During the second inning Clemens actually stepped into the batter's box, something he hadn't done in a long while due to the American League's designated hitter rule. Clemens took a few tentative practice swings and then looked right in the eye of the opposing pitcher, Dwight Gooden, winner of the Cy Young award the previous year.

Gooden started off with a sizzling fast ball fired right over the plate. Strike one! Clemens smiled, stepped out of the batter's box, turned to catcher Gary Carter and asked, "Is that what my pitches look like?"

Carter replied, "You bet it is!"

Clemens quickly struck out, but he went on to pitch three perfect innings. At the end of the day he was named the game's MVP. From that day on, Clemens pitched with greater boldness than ever before. Why? Because of a fresh reminder of how overwhelming a white hot fast ball can be.

Sometimes we forget how powerful the Gospel really is. Paul said, "I am not ashamed of the Gospel, because it is the power of God for the salvation of everyone who believes: first for the Jew, then for the Gentile." (Romans 1:16) If we would only remember how powerful the good news of Jesus Christ truly is, then I think we would be more bold in sharing it with others.

Let's look together at the holy boldness of Paul in Acts 24. . . .

> Five days later the high priest Ananias went down to Caesarea with some of the elders and a lawyer named Tertullus, and they brought their charges against Paul before the governor. When Paul was called in, Tertullus presented his case before Felix: "We have enjoyed a long period of peace under you, and your foresight has brought about reforms in this nation. Everywhere and in every way, most excellent Felix, we acknowledge this with profound gratitude. But in order not to weary you further, I would request that you be kind enough to hear us briefly.
>
> "We have found this man to be a troublemaker, stirring up riots among the Jews all over the world. He is a ringleader of the Nazarene sect and even tried to desecrate the temple; so we seized him. By examining him yourself you will be able to learn the truth about all these charges we are bringing against him."

The Jews joined in the accusation, asserting that these things were true.

Paul's Audience

Let's examine who was in Paul's audience. First of all there was Ananias, the high priest. Ananias was noted for his cruelty, gluttony, thievery and violence. When the Jewish revolt broke out in the 60s of the first century he was eventually assassinated by his own people.

Secondly, there was the lawyer, Tertullus. He began his speech with what William Barclay once called "nauseating flattery". Every word Tertullus spoke, he knew to be untrue. Tertullus thanked the Roman procurator, Felix, for the peace ushered in under his rule. In reality Felix had crushed Jewish rebellion with such brutality, the people were horror-stricken. Not only did Tertullus flatter the judge, he distorted the charges against the defendant. He accused Paul of stirring up riots, being part of a sect, and dishonoring the temple. As we will see in a few moments, Paul denied all of these false charges. Finally, Tertullus lied about how Paul was apprehended. He suggested that the Jews arrested him while in fact the Jews were intent on lynching Paul and it was the Roman commander Claudius Lysias who arrested Paul and thereby spared his life.

That leads us to the third major character in this narrative, the Roman procurator, Felix himself. The Roman historian Tacitus wrote of him, "Felix reveled in cruelty and lust and wielded the power of a king with the mind of a slave." Felix had, in fact, been a slave and was set free because his brother, Pallas, was a favorite of the emperor, Claudius. It was for this same reason that Felix was appointed governor of Judea in AD 52. Felix was on his third marriage, having married three princesses in succession. His current wife, Drusilla, daughter of Herod Agrippa I, we will meet in a moment. Two years hence Felix will be recalled by Rome due to misrule.

Finally, in Paul's audience there were the other Jewish leaders who had come from Jerusalem to press charges. They joined in the accusations against Paul even though they knew these accusations were untrue.

It's hard to imagine a tougher audience than that for a hearing of the good news about Jesus Christ.

Who is our audience? What are they like? And how do we handle our audience?

In *Today's Christian Woman*, contemporary Christian singer Susan Ashton told how God arranged for her to sing about Christ before an audience she never would have imagined having the opportunity to perform before. At the time, country singer Garth Brooks's brother, Kelly, was dating a woman who liked Ashton's music. One day, after this woman played Ashton's recordings for Kelly, he called his brother Garth on the phone and told him he should take Susan Ashton on the road. Garth Brooks did just that.

Once Ashton got to know Brooks better he admitted he hadn't heard Ashton sing until they were on stage in Spain. That night Garth Brooks said he was overwhelmed by the beauty of Ashton's voice and the moving nature of her lyrics.

At first, Ashton was afraid to tour with Brooks. She was afraid she would be booed off the stage with calls for "Garth! Garth!". But an unusual thing happened. Ashton received a standing ovation her first time out on stage opening for Garth Brooks. Ashton later said she was overcome with the openness of the audience to hearing her witness for Christ.

Neither you nor I may ever witness for Christ on stage as a country music singer. But the Lord will put each of us in situations we never would have dreamed of, just as Paul was thrust before an audience he never would have imagined speaking to. Your stage may be your cubicle at work, or an athletic banquet at school (like one I attended where I was invited to pray), or you may meet a stranger on the street and have an opportunity to share about Jesus with him or her. The Lord who arranges such divine appointments will also give you boldness to speak for him. As Jesus said in Matthew 10:18-20,

> On my account you will be brought before governors and kings as witnesses to them and to the Gentiles. But when they arrest you, do not worry about what to say or how to say it. At that time you will be given what to say, for it will not be you speaking, but the Spirit of your Father speaking through you.

Let's look next at what Paul said when he was brought before the governor.

> When the governor motioned for him to speak, Paul replied: "I know that for a number of years you have been a judge over this nation; so I gladly make my defense. You can easily verify that no more than twelve days ago I went up to Jerusalem to worship. My accusers did not find me arguing with anyone at the temple, or stirring up a crowd in the synagogues or anywhere else in the city. And they cannot prove to you the charges they are now making against me. However, I admit that I worship the God of our fathers as a follower of the Way, which they call a sect. I believe everything that agrees with the Law and that is written in the Prophets, and I have the same hope in God as these men, that there will be a resurrection of both the righteous and the wicked. So I strive always to keep my conscience clear before God and man.
>
> "After an absence of several years, I came to Jerusalem to bring my people gifts for the poor and to present offerings. I was ceremonially clean when they found me in the temple courts doing this. There was no crowd with me, nor was I involved in any disturbance. But there are

some Jews from the province of Asia, who ought to be here before you and bring charges if they have anything against me. Or these who are here should state what crime they found in me when I stood before the Sanhedrin—unless it was this one thing I shouted as I stood in their presence: 'It is concerning the resurrection of the dead that I am on trial before you today.'"

Paul's Witness

What can we learn from Paul's witness before Felix? Paul got straight to the point and answered the charges brought against him by Tertullus. He didn't waste any time flattering Felix. He was polite, but to the point.

Paul answered the charge of being a rabble-rouser by pointing out that he did not stir up the crowd in the temple, but that he was simply there to worship God. Secondly, Paul admitted the charge of being part of the Nazarene sect, but he pointed out that his belief in the resurrection was in agreement with the Law and the Prophets which all the Jews accept. Thirdly, in regard to desecrating the temple, Paul pointed out that he was simply there to present offerings.

Paul's public confession of faith before Felix really had four points:

1. I worship the God of our fathers.
2. I believe everything that agrees with the Law and the Prophets.
3. I have the same hope in God as these men.
4. I strive always to keep my conscience clear.

I wonder, if you or I were asked today by someone on the street to defend our faith in Jesus Christ, could we do it as succinctly, as pointedly, as Paul? 1 Peter 3:13-16 says:

> Who is going to harm you if you are eager to do good? But even if you should suffer for what is right, you are blessed. "Do not fear what they fear; do not be frightened." *But in your hearts set apart Christ as Lord. Always be prepared to give an answer to everyone who asks you to give the reason for the hope that you have.* But do this with gentleness and respect, keeping a clear conscience, so that those who speak maliciously against your good behavior in Christ may be ashamed of their slander.

Paul gave his answer to Felix with gentleness and respect. Do we present Christ to others with the same spirit? Paul was prepared to give an answer to those who asked him to give a reason for his hope. Are we so prepared?

When Jeff Van Gundy, later coach of the New York Knicks basketball team, was a student at Yale University, he learned an important life lesson the hard way.

When Van Gundy was a student in New Haven, Connecticut he lived in a dormitory across the quad from actress Jodie Foster, who was also a Yale freshman. All twelve male students on Van Gundy's dorm floor put $100 each into a pot with the promise that if one of them could get a legitimate date with Jodie Foster that guy would get the $1200.

Van Gundy, recounting the incident years later, said: "I had seen Jodie Foster around but I was too shy to go engage her in conversation, let alone, ask her out on a date."

One evening on his way back to the dormitory Van Gundy walked by a store that made popcorn. He stopped to look in the window and suddenly heard a voice behind him say: "Geez, that popcorn smells really good." Van Gundy turned around and found himself staring into the eyes of Jodie Foster. The only words he could get out of his mouth were: "Yeah it does." That was it.

Finally, one of the other guys on Van Gundy's floor got up the gumption to ask Jodie Foster out on a date. And she said, "Yes." So that guy got the $1200.

Van Gundy vowed that he would never be that flustered or unprepared again!

Many opportunities in life come along suddenly, including the opportunity to tell others about Jesus Christ. We need to be prepared like Paul was.

Now let's look at the response to Paul's defense. . . .

> Then Felix, who was well acquainted with the Way, adjourned the proceedings. "When Lysias the commander comes," he said, "I will decide your case." He ordered the centurion to keep Paul under guard but to give him some freedom and permit his friends to take care of his needs.
>
> Several days later Felix came with his wife Drusilla, who was a Jewess. He sent for Paul and listened to him as he spoke about faith in Christ Jesus. As Paul discoursed on righteousness, self-control and the judgment to come, Felix was afraid and said, "That's enough for now! You may leave. When I find it convenient, I will send for you." At the same time he was hoping that Paul would offer him a bribe, so he sent for him frequently and talked with him.
>
> When two years had passed, Felix was succeeded by Porcius Festus, but because Felix wanted to grant a favor to the Jews, he left Paul in prison.

The Response

Felix's response to Paul's witness was to put him off. First, Felix put off judgment regarding Paul's case until he got a report from Claudius Lysias. But even after Felix had all the facts, he left Paul in prison for two years, just to please the Jews. Felix was clearly a corrupt bureaucrat as well as a cruel tyrant. One moment he could brutally crush a Jewish rebellion; the next moment he was trying to curry favor with the Jews, hoping not to lose his power and position. Felix sent for Paul frequently and listened to what Paul had to say, but really his only desire was that Paul would perhaps pay him a bribe to get out of jail.

We may seldom, if ever, have an audience for our Christian witness like Paul had. But by the power of the Holy Spirit each of us can be just as persistent as Paul was. Notice that Paul doesn't allow the fact that he is being treated unjustly deter him from his primary goal in life. We read about that goal back in Acts 20:24,

> However, I consider my life worth nothing to me, if only I may finish the race and complete the task the Lord Jesus has given me—the task of testifying to the Gospel of God's grace.

Despite how Paul was being treated by Felix, Paul remained focused on the good news of Jesus Christ. He longed for Felix not only to hear and understand that good news but also to embrace it. And notice how Paul tailored his message to meet the needs of Felix and Drusilla. Paul talked to them about faith in Christ, righteousness, self-control and the judgment to come. These were the very topics Felix and Drusilla most needed to hear something about. Felix had seduced Drusilla away from her first husband, Azizus, king of Emesa, by use of a magician. So we see here how Paul boldly warned Felix and Drusilla about their sin and the coming judgment, while at the same time he clearly showed them the way of hope through faith in Jesus Christ.

Can you imagine being as bold as Paul if you were in the same situation? What allowed Paul to be so bold? I think it is the fact that Paul had tunnel vision. What mattered to him most in life and in death was that he should be a faithful witness to Jesus Christ above all else. That desire was planted in his heart by the Holy Spirit who had transformed his life on the road to Damascus.

How about you? What is your response to the good news of Jesus' death on the cross for your sins and his resurrection from the dead? Not a one of us can afford to put God off like Felix did. Felix said, "That's enough for now! You may leave. When I find it convenient, I will send for you." Who knows if Felix or Drusilla ever had another opportunity to respond to the Gospel? As Paul says in 2 Corinthians 6:2, "I tell you, now is the time of God's favor, now is the day of salvation." And as it says in Hebrews 3:15, "Today, if you hear his voice, do not harden your hearts."

We shouldn't ever say to God, "If it's convenient, I will send for you." I remember one woman I witnessed to about Christ many years ago saying to me, "I'll think about becoming a Christian after I've had some fun and done what I want to do in life." That is a dangerous thing to say. As James 4:15 says, "What is your life? You are a mist that appears for a little while and then vanishes."

If you have put off a decision about this, don't waste any more time just playing around with God, playing around with religion. Come to Christ and do business with him today. Surrender your life to him while there is still something to surrender. You will never regret that decision.

Back in 1949 my father was working in organized crime. He was supposed to go to St. Louis on November 10 to set up a system to control all of the illegal off-track betting on the horse races in the western half of the United States. But he never made that meeting, because on the 6th of November he happened to attend a tent meeting in Los Angeles where Billy Graham was preaching. That night in the tent Mr. Graham said, "There is a man in this audience tonight who has heard this message many times before, but he has never given his life to Christ, and this may be his last opportunity."

I am so grateful for Billy Graham's boldness. And I am so glad my father surrendered his life to Christ that night. If he hadn't done so he would not have lived and I would never have been born. For as my father subsequently found out, there was a rival gang set up to kill him in St. Louis.

If you haven't given your life to Jesus Christ before now, you do not know if you will ever have another opportunity like this one. Don't hold back. Don't put God off. Give your life to him today.

A LIVING SAVIOR

Our family has a game we have created to play in the car in order to make the time pass more quickly on long trips. We haven't ever given it a name, but if it had a name it might be: *Guess Who?* One person in the family picks someone who they are going to be—either a person from a book, a movie, or real life. The person could be anyone from all of human history, though we each try to pick people whom all family members will recognize.

One day in the car my son Jonathan picked who he was going to be and we all tried to guess who he was, but he picked a real stumper. The first questions we usually ask in this game are:

- Are you male or female?
- Child or adult?
- Living or dead?
- Real or fictitious?

These questions yielded the answer that Jonathan's identity was that of a real, living, adult, male. When we asked if this person lived in the United States, Jonathan said "yes". After we exhausted all of the people we could think of in the United States, both people known personally by us and those known to many, we finally gave up. And Jonathan revealed that he was . . . Jesus.

At that point we all cried "foul". I wanted to say, "Jonathan, you led us astray by saying that you were alive and living in the United States." But as Jonathan's preacher father I couldn't say that, because he was, in fact, right. Jesus *is* alive and *living* in the United States, just as he lives in every part of our world by his Spirit.

And that fact, when embraced by a person's heart, mind and will, makes all the difference in the world. That fact made all the difference to the Apostle Paul. So much so that Paul's faith in the living Lord Jesus Christ was the major defining characteristic of his life.

Listen to what the Roman governor Festus had to say about Paul in Acts 25 and you will see what I mean. . . .

> Three days after arriving in the province, Festus went up from Caesarea to Jerusalem, where the chief priests and Jewish leaders appeared before him and presented the charges against Paul. They

urgently requested Festus, as a favor to them, to have Paul transferred to Jerusalem, for they were preparing an ambush to kill him along the way. Festus answered, "Paul is being held at Caesarea, and I myself am going there soon. Let some of your leaders come with me and press charges against the man there, if he has done anything wrong."

After spending eight or ten days with them, he went down to Caesarea, and the next day he convened the court and ordered that Paul be brought before him. When Paul appeared, the Jews who had come down from Jerusalem stood around him, bringing many serious charges against him, which they could not prove.

Then Paul made his defense: "I have done nothing wrong against the law of the Jews or against the temple or against Caesar."

Festus, wishing to do the Jews a favor, said to Paul, "Are you willing to go up to Jerusalem and stand trial before me there on these charges?"

Paul answered: "I am now standing before Caesar's court, where I ought to be tried. I have not done any wrong to the Jews, as you yourself know very well. If, however, I am guilty of doing anything deserving death, I do not refuse to die. But if the charges brought against me by these Jews are not true, no one has the right to hand me over to them. I appeal to Caesar!"

After Festus had conferred with his council, he declared: "You have appealed to Caesar. To Caesar you will go!"

A few days later King Agrippa and Bernice arrived at Caesarea to pay their respects to Festus. Since they were spending many days there, Festus discussed Paul's case with the king. He said: "There is a man here whom Felix left as a prisoner. When I went to Jerusalem, the chief priests and elders of the Jews brought charges against him and asked that he be condemned.

"I told them that it is not the Roman custom to hand over any man before he has faced his accusers and has had an opportunity to defend himself against their charges. When they came here with me, I did not delay the case, but convened the court the next day and ordered the man to be brought in. When his accusers got up to speak, they did not charge him with any of the crimes I had expected. Instead, they had some points of dispute with him about their own religion and about a dead man named Jesus who Paul claimed was alive. I was at a loss how to investigate such matters; so I asked if he would be willing to go to Jerusalem and stand trial there on these charges. When Paul made his appeal to be held over for the Emperor's decision, I ordered him held until I could send him to Caesar."

Then Agrippa said to Festus, "I would like to hear this man myself." He replied, "Tomorrow you will hear him."

The next day Agrippa and Bernice came with great pomp and entered the audience room with the high ranking officers and the leading men of the city. At the command of Festus, Paul was brought in. Festus said: "King Agrippa, and all who are present with us, you see this man! The whole Jewish community has petitioned me about him in Jerusalem and here in Caesarea, shouting that he ought not to live any longer. I found he had done nothing deserving of death, but because he made his appeal to the Emperor I decided to send him to Rome. But I have nothing definite to write to His Majesty about him. Therefore I have brought him before all of you, and especially before you, King Agrippa, so that as a result of this investigation I may have something to write. For I think it is unreasonable to send on a prisoner without specifying the charges against him."

I want to focus with you in this chapter on one phrase from Acts 25: *a dead man named Jesus who Paul claimed was alive.* This text demands that we ask the question: Is Jesus dead or alive to us?

To Festus, as to many people today, Jesus was simply a dead man from the past. Is that what Jesus is to you? I recognize that there are many dead people from the past whom we admire, want to emulate, and we are grateful for their lives—but they are still dead. They do not have any real effect on our daily lives—not like the effect of someone we live with day in and day out. To many people, as to Festus, Jesus is just like that.

Such people, like Festus, may have even heard the reports of Jesus' resurrection from the dead. But they consider such reports to be mere fables. After all, dead people don't come to life again. I'm sure that is what Festus thought.

What explanations do such people give for the accounts of the resurrection of Jesus which we have in the New Testament?

Some say, "Well maybe Jesus didn't really die on the cross. Maybe he merely swooned, then woke up in the tomb and came out to be greeted by his grateful disciples. Then Jesus went on to die just like everyone else." The problem with such a theory is that it was the job of the Roman soldiers to make sure that the people they hung on crosses were really dead when all was said and done. That's why the soldiers came along and broke the legs of the men hanging on either side of Jesus—to hasten their death. Then when the soldiers came to Jesus to break his legs, they found he was already dead. And just to make sure, one of them thrust a spear through his side, and out came blood and water. As any doctor will tell you, the fact that the blood had separated in such a way shows that Jesus was already, very much, dead.

And even if such a "swoon" theory could be supported, how could such a "risen" Jesus have inspired such great faith in the disciples that they would go to their death for him? That seems rather incredible to me.

Another theory some people come up with, in order to explain the resurrection accounts, is to say that someone stole the body of Jesus from the tomb and put it elsewhere. But who would do such a thing? The Jewish leaders wouldn't have done it. And if they did they certainly would have produced the body when the disciples started going around and saying that Jesus had risen. The Jewish leaders would have done everything in their power to squash this movement.

The Romans would have had no reason to move Jesus' body. And they were obviously intent on pleasing the Jewish leaders by putting Jesus to death. So if the Romans had moved the body, once the disciples started proclaiming their faith in their risen Lord, the Roman leaders would have produced the body to please the Jewish leaders and curry their favor.

Some say that perhaps the disciples themselves stole the body of Jesus in order to foist a hoax on the world. But that doesn't make sense either. Many of these first disciples gave up their lives because of their belief that Jesus had risen from the dead. Why would they give up their lives for something they knew was a lie?

Along the same lines, still others today maintain that the New Testament accounts are legends created long after the death of Jesus. The problem with that theory is that all of the resurrection accounts we have in the New Testament were written down within a generation of the life and death of Jesus. There was not enough time for a legend about him to develop. It isn't until the second century and later that such legendary tales about Jesus are told and written down. This story was being told and written down while there were still people walking around who knew the facts. When Paul wrote 1 Corinthians 15, within twenty years or so of Jesus' death, he notes that there were five hundred people who saw Jesus risen from the dead at one time, and he states emphatically that many of those five hundred were still alive at the time of his writing. Clearly the accounts we have in the New Testament are not legends. And if someone or a group of people made up the story of Jesus' resurrection in the first century, others certainly would have come along to deny the tale and it would have put an end to the whole Christian movement.

1 Corinthians 15 also negates another popular theory regarding the resurrection of Jesus. Some people claim that the first disciples experienced a hallucination. They were experiencing such deep grief, and they so longed to see Jesus again, that they imagined they saw him alive again after his crucifixion. But as Paul points out in 1 Corinthians 15, over 500 people, at one time, saw Jesus risen from the dead. Hallucinations like that simply do

not happen to masses of people at one time in one place. And even if the individual accounts of Jesus' appearances were hallucinations, they were the strangest hallucinations on record in human history. On a number of occasions the disciples did not, at first, recognize the hallucination as being Jesus. So I think we can safely wipe out the hallucination theory; it simply doesn't make sense of the facts.

Still other people today say that those who believe in the bodily resurrection of Jesus have got it all wrong. They say that what the New Testament teaches is that Jesus rose spiritually. But this doesn't jive with the Gospel accounts or the subsequent proclamation of Paul. The Gospel of Luke records that on one occasion when Jesus appeared to his disciples they thought he was a ghost. In other words, they were prone to believe that Jesus had "risen" in some spiritual fashion. But Jesus was at pains to prove to them that he had risen in a physical body. He asked his disciples to bring him something to eat. They brought him a piece of broiled fish and he ate it in their presence. If the author of the Gospel of Luke was trying to teach some sort of spiritual resurrection of Jesus he certainly went about it in a strange fashion.

Or what shall we make of the proclamation of Paul? Many of the Greeks to whom Paul preached were only too ready to believe in the immortality of the soul. Some of the philosophers in Athens certainly would have agreed with Paul about some sort of after-life. But what did the Areopagites say? "We want to know what this new teaching is that you are bringing before our ears." They thought Paul was preaching about two new divinities—Jesus and Anastasis (the Greek word for resurrection). The Greeks knew that Paul was teaching something other than the immortality of the soul.

And what if Jesus didn't rise from the dead? Why does it matter? The bottom line is this: if Festus was right and Jesus was and is dead—then there are certain things which follow from that fact which must be faced. Paul faces us with these facts in 1 Corinthians 15:12-19. He says,

> But if it is preached that Christ has been raised from the dead, how can some of you say that there is no resurrection of the dead? If there is no resurrection of the dead, then not even Christ has been raised. And if Christ has not been raised, our preaching is useless and so is your faith. More than that, we are then found to be false witnesses about God, for we have testified about God that he raised Christ from the dead. But he did not raise him if in fact the dead are not raised. For if the dead are not raised, then Christ has not been raised either. And if Christ has not been raised, your faith is futile; you are still in your sins. Then those also who have fallen asleep in Christ are lost. If only for this life we have hope in Christ, we are to be pitied more than all men.

If Jesus is dead then we must face these facts:

1. Our Christian faith is futile.
2. We are still in our sins.
3. Christians who have died are lost.
4. If our Christian hope is only for this life here and now, then we are to be pitied.

Those are sobering facts to face. Yet, thankfully, Paul does not end 1 Corinthians 15 on that note. He continues and says, "But Christ has indeed been raised from the dead, the firstfruits of those who have fallen asleep."

You see Paul, as a Pharisee, held to faith in the resurrection of the body *before* he became a follower of Jesus. Belief in the resurrection was a fairly new idea among the Jews. The Sadducees held to the old belief in Sheol–that at death all people go to some sort of shadowy underworld from which no one will ever return. But the Pharisees held to a new idea–that at the end of time all believers in the Lord would be raised bodily–to live in God's new kingdom forevermore.

Paul held to this belief before he became a follower of Jesus. But what no Jew of the first century ever expected was that one person would be raised from the dead in the middle of human history. And this is what Paul and the other early Christians had come to believe had happened to Jesus.

Why was Paul so sure that Jesus had risen bodily from the grave? Because he met him on the road to Damascus in some fashion more similar to Jesus' other resurrection appearances than it was similar to a vision. It was on this basis that Paul claimed to be an apostle just like Peter, James and all the rest. As Paul himself will testify in Acts 26, "I saw a light ... I heard a voice ... I was not disobedient to the vision from heaven." As a result, to Paul, Jesus was a living presence in the present. And that living presence made all the difference to Paul. The living Jesus gave to Paul:

1. *Forgiveness for the past.* On the road to Damascus Paul realized how wrong he had been, and that he needed the Lord to put his life right again.

2. *A purpose for living in the present*–to proclaim the good news of Christ's death for our sins and his resurrection from the dead.

3. *Hope for the future.* Paul could "be of good cheer" because he knew that Jesus had overcome the world and therefore he, Paul, would be more than a conqueror in Christ.

The only questions which remain are these: have *we* met Jesus on our own "road to Damascus"? Is Jesus a living presence in our life today? If we can say yes to these two questions, then we, like Paul, have forgiveness for the past, a purpose in the present, and a hope for the future.

A number of years ago I took my family on a trip to England. One of our most special times during that trip was our visit to St Paul's Cathedral in London. St Paul's is of course the cathedral with the huge dome designed by Sir Christopher Wren some 400 years ago. Amazingly this beautiful church survived the bombing of London by the Germans during World War II. One of the things my three boys wanted to do was to climb to the top of the dome and enjoy the spectacular view of London which can be had from the gallery atop the dome, outside in the open air. Part way through our climb up the hundreds of steps (there is no elevator) my youngest son, Joshua, who was three years old at the time, pooped out. So I had to carry him up the dizzying heights inside of the dome of St. Paul's.

Toward the bottom of the inside of the dome there is what is called a whispering gallery. We tested it out, by the way. One of us stood on one side of the dome and whispered something as we faced the wall of the dome itself. Another one stood all the way on the other side of the dome and could hear what was whispered.

Many great events have taken place in St Paul's Cathedral over the past 400 years. Many around the world remember it as the site of the wedding of Prince Charles and Lady Diana Spencer. St Paul's was also the site of the state funeral for Sir Winston Churchill, Prime Minister of the United Kingdom during World War II, and again, from 1951 to 1954. Interestingly enough, Churchill planned his own funeral, including many of the great hymns of the Church and the incomparable Anglican liturgy. But the most unique part of the service of worship came at the end. After the benediction, Churchill had instructed that a trumpeter, positioned up in the whispering gallery, high inside the dome of St Paul's Cathedral, should play *Taps*, that great military song indicating the end of the day. And then when *Taps* was finished, another trumpeter played *Reveille*, that other great military tune signaling the beginning of the day–"It's time to get up. It's time to get up. It's time to get up in the morning."

That was Sir Winston Churchill's final testimony to his faith in the resurrection, his belief that at the end of history the final song will not be *Taps* but rather *Reveille*.

It is only because of the risen Lord Jesus Christ that we can have such a hope for the end of history. It is because of the Jesus who was raised in the middle of history that we have hope for our resurrection at the end of all things.

Tyrants down through the ages have wielded power over their subjects with the threat of death. That threat is what many religious and political leaders in the first century hoped would put an end to the followers of Jesus of Nazareth. But what they didn't count on was the power of faith in a living Lord. Because Paul believed in a risen Lord Jesus Christ, a living Lord who had forgiven his past, lived with him in the present, and would raise his own body in the future, Paul was no longer afraid of death. And therefore Paul and the other early Christians could no longer be bullied by the tyrants of the world. It was this faith in a living Lord which mystified Festus, intrigued Agrippa, and propelled Paul to testify for Christ unto his dying breath.

If we have faith in a living Jesus then we too have forgiveness for the past, a living Lord with us in the present, and a hope for the future.

TELLING YOUR STORY

Dr. Paul Brand was speaking to a medical college in India on the Gospel text: "Let your light so shine before men that they may behold your good works and glorify your Father." In front of the lectern was an oil lamp, with its cotton wick burning from the shallow dish of oil. As he preached, the lamp ran out of oil, the wick burned dry, and the smoke made him cough. He immediately used the opportunity.

"Some of us here are like this wick," he said. "We're trying to shine for the glory of God, but we stink. That's what happens when we use ourselves as the fuel of our witness rather than the Holy Spirit.

"Wicks can last indefinitely, burning brightly and without irritating smoke, if the fuel, the Holy Spirit, is in constant supply."

The wick of your own life story can be a powerful light to someone else's life if the Holy Spirit is your fuel. That's the way it was with the Apostle Paul's life story. Paul tells that story before King Agrippa in Acts 26. . . .

> Then Agrippa said to Paul, "You have permission to speak for yourself."
>
> So Paul motioned with his hand and began his defense: "King Agrippa, I consider myself fortunate to stand before you today as I make my defense against all the accusations of the Jews, and especially so because you are well acquainted with all the Jewish customs and controversies. Therefore, I beg you to listen to me patiently.
>
> "The Jews all know the way I have lived ever since I was a child, from the beginning of my life in my own country, and also in Jerusalem. They have known me for a long time and can testify, if they are willing, that according to the strictest sect of our religion, I lived as a Pharisee. And now it is because of my hope in what God has promised our fathers that I am on trial today. This is the promise our twelve tribes are hoping to see fulfilled as they earnestly serve God day and night. O king, it is because of this hope that the Jews are accusing me. Why should any of you consider it incredible that God raises the dead?
>
> "I too was convinced that I ought to do all that was possible to oppose the name of Jesus of Nazareth. And that is just what I did in Jerusalem. On the authority of the chief priests I put many

of the saints in prison, and when they were put to death, I cast my vote against them. Many a time I went from one synagogue to another to have them punished, and I tried to force them to blaspheme. In my obsession against them, I even went to foreign cities to persecute them.

"On one of these journeys I was going to Damascus with the authority and commission of the chief priests. About noon, O king, as I was on the road, I saw a light from heaven, brighter than the sun, blazing around me and my companions. We all fell to the ground, and I heard a voice saying to me in Aramaic, 'Saul, Saul, why do you persecute me? It is hard for you to kick against the goads.'

"Then I asked, 'Who are you, Lord?'

" 'I am Jesus, whom you are persecuting,' the Lord replied. 'Now get up and stand on your feet. I have appeared to you to appoint you as a servant and as a witness of what you have seen of me and what I will show you. I will rescue you from your own people and from the Gentiles. I am sending you to them to open their eyes and turn them from darkness to light, and from the power of Satan to God, so that they may receive forgiveness of sins and a place among those who are sanctified by faith in me.'

"So then, King Agrippa, I was not disobedient to the vision from heaven. First to those in Damascus, then to those in Jerusalem and in all Judea, and to the Gentiles also, I preached that they should repent and turn to God and prove their repentance by their deeds. That is why the Jews seized me in the temple courts and tried to kill me. But I have had God's help to this very day, and so I stand here and testify to small and great alike. I am saying nothing beyond what the prophets and Moses said would happen—that the Christ would suffer and, as the first to rise from the dead, would proclaim light to his own people and to the Gentiles."

At this point Festus interrupted Paul's defense. "You are out of your mind, Paul!" he shouted. "Your great learning is driving you insane."

"I am not insane, most excellent Festus," Paul replied. "What I am saying is true and reasonable. The king is familiar with these things, and I can speak freely to him. I am convinced that none of this has escaped his notice, because it was not done in a corner. King Agrippa, do you believe the prophets? I know you do."

Then Agrippa said to Paul, "Do you think that in such a short time you can persuade me to be a Christian?"

Paul replied, "Short time or long—I pray God that not only you but all who are listening to me today may become what I am, except for these chains."

The king rose, and with him the governor and Bernice and those sitting with them. They left the room, and while talking with one another, they said, "This man is not doing anything that deserves death or imprisonment."

Agrippa said to Festus, "This man could have been set free if he had not appealed to Caesar."

Certainly, Paul's story was unique. He actually saw the Lord Jesus after he was risen from the dead. Paul's story of his conversion in Acts 26 is also unique in that it is a type of legal testimony. Paul was not testifying, in this case, in a court of law, but it was an official investigation. So his presentation of his conversion story is rather formal. However, there are several things which I think we can learn from Paul's story which will enable us to tell our own story of relationship with Christ effectively.

First of all, when sharing our story of what Christ has done to change our lives we need to *be patient*. You may remember from Acts 24:27, "When two years had passed, Felix was succeeded by Porcius Festus, but because Felix wanted to grant a favor to the Jews, he left Paul in prison." So Paul spent two years in prison before he had the opportunity to again share his testimony before an official of the Roman government. But I doubt that Paul sat around doing nothing during those two years. I imagine he spent a good bit of time in prayer, and perhaps some of his "prison letters" were written from Caesarea. Certainly, Paul spent these two years in prison thinking through what he wanted to say, should he ever have another opportunity after the one with Felix, to share his story of faith in Christ.

We too need to be patient in our life of witness for Christ. Sometimes we can go for long periods without any opportunity to be a witness, then suddenly another opportunity will come along, God will bring someone into our lives and we need to be ready to speak a word for Christ.

Once there was a prison warden who asked a man on death row what he would like to eat for his last meal. The prisoner said, "I would like to have a large watermelon."

The warden replied, "You've got to be kidding! This is December. Watermelons have not even been planted, let alone harvested."

The prisoner said, "That's alright. I don't mind waiting."

Sometimes we would rather wait than face the inevitable. But for Paul I imagine it was hard to wait in that Caesarean prison in Herod's palace, not knowing for certain what his future held. I'm sure Paul learned to have greater patience than ever before. And I'm sure he learned to use the time to prepare for his next opportunity to be a witness for Jesus Christ.

A second thing we can learn from Paul's witness is to *be polite*. Notice what Paul's attitude was when he shared his story with King Agrippa. Paul was polite, he addressed Agrippa with respect. He honored Agrippa by recognizing Agrippa's familiarity with the Jewish religion and customs. Paul was polite to Agrippa even though Agrippa was living in an incestuous relationship with his sister Bernice.

Remember again what Peter had to say on this very subject of politeness,

> But in your hearts set apart Christ as Lord. Always be prepared to give an answer to everyone who asks you to give the reason for the hope that you have. *But do this with gentleness and respect*, keeping a clear conscience, so that those who speak maliciously against your good behavior in Christ may be ashamed of their slander. (1 Peter 3:15)

We must honor and respect all people, for all, including those whom we think to be the most immoral, are bearers of God's image.

Thirdly, there should be a note of *passion* as we talk to non-Christians about the Savior. There was a note of pleading in all that Paul said. Paul "begged" Agrippa to listen to him. Now, that doesn't mean that Paul got down on his hands and knees, but the note of pleading is woven throughout his speech. He was concerned for Agrippa's welfare and his relationship with God. Paul couldn't let things go at just relating the facts about Christ without also communicating his passion for Christ, and his compassion for Agrippa who was without Christ.

Fourthly, we need to *be plain* and honest in the telling of our story. The Apostle Paul told the story of his life very plainly and honestly. He didn't embellish it in any way. He began by telling Agrippa that he had grown up as a very religious Jew.

This gives an important pointer: we shouldn't feel that we have to make our story sound like someone else's. If you grew up in a religious home, don't try to make it sound like you didn't, just to make your story sound "better".

I grew up in the shadow of a famous father. I heard my Dad tell his story countless times to many audiences. It would be easy for me to think that I'm not as great a Christian because I don't have a spectacular conversion story. It would be tempting to embellish my story and make myself out to be someone other than who I am, in order to "measure up" to my father's story. It would also be easy for me to hide behind my father's story and not tell my own, simple as it may be.

The importance of not embellishing our story is borne out by the following example. A guy named Sam survived the great flood in Johnstown,

Pennsylvania when a dam broke and took hundreds of lives. He spent the rest of his life telling the story of how he escaped. When the Lord took him to heaven at the age of 95, he was ready to go home. St. Peter met him at the entrance.

"Sam, as a newcomer, you can have anything you ask for — one time!" St. Peter said.

Sam only wanted to tell everyone about his flood experience. St. Peter told him he could have the chance to share his story in the prayer meeting that night. But just as Sam was getting up to speak to an audience of millions, St. Peter whispered in his ear, "Just remember that Noah is sitting in the front row."

It's important to be plain when telling your story. The guy you're talking to may have a better story than yours!

Paul told:

1. What his life was like before he became a Christian,
2. How he became a Christian and
3. How he had changed since becoming a Christian.

We each need to stick to the same plain facts.

Be patient, be polite, be passionate, be plain in the way that you communicate your story. Also—*put it in the present tense.* Paul told Agrippa, "I have had God's help to this very day."

When you tell others how your life changed when you became a Christian don't just leave it in the past tense. Tell others how Christ is continuing to change your life in the present. This will make what you have to share more meaningful and more accessible to the person hearing your story. As Sam Shoemaker once asked: "Is your Christianity ancient history or current events?"

In his book *Don't Park Here*, C. William Fisher likens many a Christian to a piano player. For many Christians, their story never changes. Instead of drawing on the full range of their journey with Christ, they concentrate on just one or two "notes". They "play middle C" again and again. In a "testimony meeting" or during a sharing time, they say the same old thing–"I was saved 40 years ago, and I know I'm going to heaven." Others get the feeling that person has made little progress in all that time. Yet there's so much to the Christian life. Fisher commented, "Why, with all the rich, wide range of the keyboard of spiritual insight and truth, do so many Christians play on only one note?... Why should anyone be content to be a dull monotone when God intends his life to be a rich, harmonious symphony?" The psalmist said, "I will tell of *all* your marvelous works."

While you are putting your story in the present tense, don't forget to *be personal* as well. Remember that your story is not a static thing. Paul communicated his Christian experience in different ways to different people. Paul adapted the telling of his story to address and appeal to people in a personal way. In Acts 22:12 when Paul was defending himself before a Jewish audience he emphasized the role of Ananias, a devout observer of the law, in his conversion.

Being personal also means not being afraid to share about what has been wrong in our lives and how Christ has put it right. Many years ago there was a well known preacher named Brownlow North. He was a man who, in his younger years, had led a bit of a rough life. One day, just before he was to preach in a church in Aberdeen, Scotland, Brownlow North received a piece of correspondence. The author of the note told him that he had evidence of some shameful thing North had done many years before. The letter went on to say that he was planning to interrupt the church service and tell the whole congregation of the disgraceful act if North went ahead and preached there.

Do you know what Brownlow North did? He took that letter with him to church and he read it to the assembly. Then he proceeded to tell the group exactly what he had done, which the author of the note had threatened to reveal. He confessed that the charge against him was absolutely true but that Jesus Christ had changed his life and that Jesus could do the same thing for each person assembled there. Brownlow North used the evidence of his own sin to lead people to Jesus as Savior.

We should never be afraid to get personal in our testimony like Brownlow North did. With Christ as our Savior we have nothing to prove and nothing to lose.

Also remember, the telling of our story is not complete until we have asked for our hearer's response. In communicating Christ to others we must always *be pointed*. We always need to come to the point of asking others what their response to Christ is. This is what Paul did with Agrippa, and doing this can turn our story from being a monologue into a dialogue about the Christian faith. Be prepared for the other person to give you their honest response; give them room to poke you and prod you a little for more detail on certain points if they need to do so. Let there be a free give-and-take, but always bring the conversation back to the most important issue: *What are you going to do with Christ?* You need to ask for their response, not just to your story, but to the big story about Jesus' death for our sins and his resurrection from the dead.

Finally, we must *be prayerful* in all our encounters with non-Christians, especially as we share with them about our relationship with Christ. At the end of his address to King Agrippa, Paul hinted at the life of prayer which lay behind the sharing of his story. Paul said, "Short time or long–I pray God that not only you but all who are listening to me today may become what I am, except for these chains." Any other prisoner might have prayed for his captors that they would become what he was "*with* these chains"! Instead, Paul indicated that he was praying for the conversion of all those who would hear his story. He wanted them to connect their story with God's story.

The role of prayer in evangelism is essential, because only God can change people's hearts. If people could change their own hearts then we wouldn't need to pray to God, we could focus all our time on pleading with people to change. However, that is not the case, and so we should focus considerable, concentrated time on praying for non-Christians. Paul wrote to his young disciple Timothy that this kind of prayer was of first importance in the church:

> I urge, then, first of all, that requests, prayers, intercession and thanksgiving be made for everyone—for kings and all those in authority, that we may live peaceful and quiet lives in all godliness and holiness. This is good, and pleases God our Savior, who wants all men to be saved and to come to a knowledge of the truth. For there is one God and one mediator between God and men, the man Christ Jesus, who gave himself as a ransom for all men--the testimony given in its proper time. And for this purpose I was appointed a herald and an apostle—I am telling the truth, I am not lying—and a teacher of the true faith to the Gentiles. (1 Timothy 2:1-7)

As Charles Spurgeon once said,

> You cannot bring souls to God if you do not go to God yourself.... If you are much alone with Jesus, you will catch His Spirit. You will be fired with the flame that burned in His breast and consumed His life. You will weep with the tears that fell upon Jerusalem when He saw it perishing; and if you cannot speak so eloquently as He did, yet shall there be about what you say somewhat of the same power which in Him thrilled the hearts and awoke the consciences of men.

A missionary in India was once teaching the Bible to a group of Hindu ladies. Halfway through the lesson, one of the women got up and walked out. A short time later, she came back and listened more intently than ever. At the close of the hour the leader inquired, "Why did you leave the meeting? Weren't you interested?"

"O yes," the Hindu lady replied. "I was so impressed with what you had to say about Christ that I went out to ask your carriage driver whether you really lived the way you talked. When he said you did, I hurried back so I wouldn't miss out on anything."

Don't underestimate the power of your own life story to lead people to Jesus. Many people are searching for a faith that works. When they see that faith in Christ is working in your life, that may be just what they need to push them over the edge of commitment to Christ. Let God use the telling of your story to draw others to himself.

STORMY WEATHER FAITH

Many Christians probably do not realize that the founder of Methodism, John Wesley, tried to serve the Lord before he became a Christian, but it didn't work too well. At Oxford University Wesley led a religious group called the Holy Club. They were devoted to confessing their sins to one another and working hard for the Lord, but Wesley knew little, if anything, of God's grace in Christ. John Wesley even sailed on a missionary adventure to America without Christ in his heart. The mission was not successful, but Wesley learned an important lesson while on board the ship en route to the colonies.

Two storms disrupted the three and a half month journey. During one of them Wesley wrote in his journal, "The sea broke over us from stem to stern, burst through the windows of the state cabin . . . and covered us all over." However, a third storm, on January 25, 1735, was even worse. In the midst of the storm what really struck Wesley with spiritual force was the calm and peace he saw on the faces of some Moravian Christians. Wesley wrote in his journal that it was as if "the great deep had already swallowed us up." But in the midst of this the Moravians read the Psalms and sang hymns. Panic spread among the rest of the passengers but the German Christians had a stillness about them at the center of the storm.

After the storm had passed Wesley asked one of the Germans, "Weren't you afraid during the storm?" The German replied, "I thank God, no."

"But weren't your women and children scared?"

"No," the Moravian quietly explained, "Our women and children are not afraid to die."

The peace in that Moravian's eyes disturbed Wesley in the core of his being because he knew that *he was* afraid to die. Eventually Wesley found his own peace with God through Christ at a Christian meeting in Aldersgate Street, London, where a small group was reading Martin Luther's preface to Paul's letter to the Church at Rome. That night Wesley's heart was "strangely warmed".

Do you have a faith that can handle stormy weather? The Apostle Paul did. We read about his stormy weather faith in Acts 27. . . .

> When it was decided that we would sail for Italy, Paul and some other

prisoners were handed over to a centurion named Julius, who belonged to the Imperial Regiment. We boarded a ship from Adramyttium about to sail for ports along the coast of the province of Asia, and we put out to sea. Aristarchus, a Macedonian from Thessalonica, was with us.

The next day we landed at Sidon; and Julius, in kindness to Paul, allowed him to go to his friends so they might provide for his needs. From there we put out to sea again and passed to the lee of Cyprus because the winds were against us. When we had sailed across the open sea off the coast of Cilicia and Pamphylia, we landed at Myra in Lycia. There the centurion found an Alexandrian ship sailing for Italy and put us on board. We made slow headway for many days and had difficulty arriving off Cnidus. When the wind did not allow us to hold our course, we sailed to the lee of Crete, opposite Salmone. We moved along the coast with difficulty and came to a place called Fair Havens, near the town of Lasea.

Much time had been lost, and sailing had already become dangerous because by now it was after the Fast. So Paul warned them, "Men, I can see that our voyage is going to be disastrous and bring great loss to ship and cargo, and to our own lives also." But the centurion, instead of listening to what Paul said, followed the advice of the pilot and of the owner of the ship. Since the harbor was unsuitable to winter in, the majority decided that we should sail on, hoping to reach Phoenix and winter there. This was a harbor in Crete, facing both southwest and northwest.

When a gentle south wind began to blow, they thought they had obtained what they wanted; so they weighed anchor and sailed along the shore of Crete. Before very long, a wind of hurricane force, called the "northeaster," swept down from the island. The ship was caught by the storm and could not head into the wind; so we gave way to it and were driven along. As we passed to the lee of a small island called Cauda, we were hardly able to make the lifeboat secure. When the men had hoisted it aboard, they passed ropes under the ship itself to hold it together. Fearing that they would run aground on the sandbars of Syrtis, they lowered the sea anchor and let the ship be driven along. We took such a violent battering from the storm that the next day they began to throw the cargo overboard. On the third day, they threw the ship's tackle overboard with their own hands. When neither sun nor stars appeared for many days and the storm continued raging, we finally gave up all hope of being saved.

After the men had gone a long time without food, Paul stood up before them and said: "Men, you should have taken my advice not to sail from Crete; then you would have spared yourselves this damage and loss. But now I urge you to keep up your courage, because not one of you will be lost; only the ship will be destroyed. Last night an angel of the God whose I am and whom I serve stood beside me and said, 'Do not be afraid, Paul. You must stand trial before Caesar; and God has graciously given you the lives of all who sail with you.' So keep up your courage, men, for I have faith in God that it will happen just as he told me. Nevertheless, we must run aground on some island."

On the fourteenth night we were still being driven across the Adriatic Sea, when about midnight the sailors sensed they were approaching land. They took soundings and found that the water was a hundred and twenty feet deep. A short time later they took soundings again and found it was ninety feet deep. Fearing that we would be dashed against the rocks, they dropped four anchors from the stern and prayed for daylight. In an attempt to escape from the ship, the sailors let the lifeboat down into the sea, pretending they were going to lower some anchors from the bow. Then Paul said to the centurion and the soldiers, "Unless these men stay with the ship, you cannot be saved." So the soldiers cut the ropes that held the lifeboat and let it fall away.

Just before dawn Paul urged them all to eat. "For the last fourteen days," he said, "you have been in constant suspense and have gone without food—you haven't eaten anything. Now I urge you to take some food. You need it to survive. Not one of you will lose a single hair from his head." After he said this, he took some bread and gave thanks to God in front of them all. Then he broke it and began to eat. They were all encouraged and ate some food themselves. Altogether there were 276 of us on board. When they had eaten as much as they wanted, they lightened the ship by throwing the grain into the sea.

When daylight came, they did not recognize the land, but they saw a bay with a sandy beach, where they decided to run the ship aground if they could. Cutting loose the anchors, they left them in the sea and at the same time untied the ropes that held the rudders. Then they hoisted the foresail to the wind and made for the beach. But the ship struck a sandbar and ran aground. The bow stuck fast and would not move, and the stern was broken to pieces by the pounding of the surf.

The soldiers planned to kill the prisoners to prevent any of them from swimming away and escaping. But the centurion wanted to spare Paul's life and kept them from carrying out their plan. He ordered those who could swim to jump overboard first and get to land. The rest were to get there on planks or on pieces of the ship. In this way everyone reached land in safety.

This passage is probably the most detailed description of navigation in all of ancient literature. We have here definite signs of an eyewitness account. At this point in Acts we resume the "we" passages. Luke has once again joined Paul, and Aristarchus the Thessalonian is also with them.

But what I find most intriguing in this chapter is the display of three different approaches to life. First of all, there is the *self-centered approach*. This approach to life is taken by the person who seeks to anchor all their hopes and dreams in the self. You can imagine what would happen if you were sailing on the Mediterranean and you hit a storm and you lodged your anchor in your own boat. You probably would not survive the storm. The same is true in life. The self is not a sufficient center in which to anchor your existence.

The self-centered approach to life is seen in a few different characters in this chapter. The first one is the owner of the ship from Alexandria, Egypt. He is intent on getting his cargo of grain to Rome. Merchants in those days could make more money if they took the chance of sailing in the autumn months. We are told in verse 9 that sailing had already become dangerous on the Mediterranean because it was after the Fast, that is, the Jewish Day of Atonement, which took place in late September or early October. Sailing after mid September was a dubious operation. After mid-November it was suicidal. So this merchant, on whose ship Paul was being transported to Rome, was taking a big chance with 276 people on board. The merchant ignored the advice of Paul, who was a seasoned traveler on the Mediterranean, having made some eleven previous voyages. The merchant owner of the ship was taking other lives into his own hands just so he could make some extra profit that year.

Then there were the sailors on the ship, the ones responsible for carrying out the captain's orders and getting the ship with its cargo and passengers safely to its destination. After encountering a rather terrible storm on the open sea, these seasoned sailors were, understandably, frightened. But we see their self-centered approach to life displayed in the fact that, afraid of shipwreck, they seize the first opportunity to escape from the ship by letting down the lifeboat into the sea. Duty is out the window. All these sailors care about at this point is saving their own necks. Paul catches wind of the sailors' plan and warns the centurion and the soldiers that if these sailors do not stay with the ship they will be putting everyone else's lives in danger. I can just imagine the response of the sailors to Paul's intervention! However, the centurion and the soldiers heed Paul's warning at this point and cut the ropes to the lifeboat, letting it drift away.

The soldiers as well as the sailors had a self-centered approach to living. When the captain of the ship seeks to run the vessel aground in order for the passengers to be able to disembark on the island of Malta, the soldiers want to kill the prisoners on board. Why? Because they know that if any of the prisoners escape in the course of the shipwreck, they will be responsible for their lives and will have to pay with their own lives as a result. These soldiers are obviously not concerned about the lives of their prisoners; their only object is self-preservation.

The self-centeredness displayed in this story reminds me of another famous shipwreck. On April 15, 1912, the Titanic struck an iceberg in the North Atlantic tearing a 300-foot gash in its hull. Two hours and forty minutes later the Titanic sunk 12,000 feet to the bottom of the ocean.

There were only twenty life-boats and rafts on the Titanic, too few to save the number of passengers on board. Most of the passengers struggled to stay afloat in the icy waters while the life boats, only partially filled, waited a safe distance away.

Lifeboat number fourteen was the only one to row back to the spot where most of the survivors were shivering to death. That one life boat was only able to save a few more people. Why did no other life boat join in the rescue operation? Some were already overloaded, but many still had room for more survivors. Why didn't the people with more room in their boats try to help their fellow passengers who were drowning? They feared that they would be swamped by so many swimmers that their own craft would sink.

That's what the self-centered approach to life looks like. In our sinful nature we naturally look out for #1. Fear often prevents us from putting others first. Scripture foretells the end of those who are anchored in the self. Long before he ever boarded the ship bound for Rome, Paul wrote to the Church at Rome, "To those who by persistence in doing good seek glory, honor and immortality, he [God] will give eternal life. But for those who are self-seeking and who reject the truth and follow evil, there will be wrath and anger." (Romans 2:7-8)

A second approach to life which we see in Acts 27 is the *other-centered approach*. The example of the other-centered approach to life is seen in Julius, the centurion in charge of Paul and the other prisoners. At the beginning of Paul's voyage, when the first ship lands at Sidon, Julius, in kindness to Paul, allows him to visit some friends so that they might meet his needs. Then when the second ship runs aground on the island of Malta, it is Julius who prevents the soldiers from killing Paul and the other prisoners. Julius was obviously a man who cared about others and showed them kindness whenever he could.

Being other-centered is much better than being self-centered. But there is a problem with the other-centered approach to life. When you sink your life's anchor into the lives of other people you can often be swayed by those others in the wrong direction. When Paul warned the centurion that it would be disastrous to sail from Crete at that time of year, Julius did not listen to what Paul said, but instead followed the advice of the captain and owner of the ship. That wrong choice led to a storm and a shipwreck.

It is a good thing to serve others and do what is best for them. That is love. And God wants us to love others in that way. But when the anchor of our life is in other human beings alone, that can lead to trouble. There is no human being on planet earth of sufficient ballast to provide eternally secure anchorage for your life.

C. S. Lewis tells us where a certain kind of other-centeredness can end up:

> In the end, you will either give up trying to be good, or else become one of those people, who, as they say, 'live for others' but always in a discontented, grumbling way–always wondering why the others do not notice it more and always making a martyr of yourself. And once you have become that you will be a far greater pest to anyone who has to live with you than you would have been if you had remained frankly selfish. (*Mere Christianity*, Book IV, chapter 8, paragraph 4.)

The third lifestyle presented in Acts 27 is the *God-centered approach to life*. We see this in the attitude of the Apostle Paul. Here he is a prisoner, but he isn't living life "under the circumstances".

Have you ever caught yourself saying that? Someone asks you, "How are you doing?" And you respond, "Not bad, under the circumstances." We see in the life of the Apostle Paul that no Christian has to live *under* the circumstances. By God's grace we can always live on top of our circumstances.

When the ship and its passengers were facing the worst possible circumstance, a violent storm at sea, it was Paul who brought them encouragement. And that encouragement came directly from Paul's relationship with God.

Paul was human. He wasn't above saying, "I told you so." when the crew didn't listen to him about not sailing from Crete and they ended up facing a disastrous storm. But Paul didn't stop at saying, "I told you so." He encouraged the passengers saying, "Not one of you will lose your lives. Only the ship will be destroyed." How did Paul know this? An angel had appeared to him the night before and told him that he would indeed stand trial before Caesar and that God had given him the lives of those sailing with him. Obviously Paul had been praying that the Lord would spare all of their lives.

Paul was also a man of practicality, not just a man of vision. Later on, he encouraged all of the passengers to eat something. They had all been living their lives in suspended animation as the storm rocked them this way and that. The simple act of Paul breaking bread and praying over the meal encouraged everyone in the midst of the storm. A God-centered person, conducting his or her normal life, living out a relationship with Jesus, can positively effect the entire atmosphere in which he or she lives.

When complimented on her homemade biscuits, the cook at a popular Christian conference center once told the famous preacher and Bible commentator Harry Ironside:

> Just consider what goes into the making of these biscuits. The flour itself doesn't taste good, neither does the baking powder, nor the shortening, nor the other ingredients. However, when I mix them all together and put them in the oven, they come out just right.

Think of all that Paul went through in his earthly journey with Christ: in prison frequently, flogged, exposed to death again and again. Five times he received from the Jews thirty-nine lashes with a whip. Three times he was beaten with rods. Once he was stoned. He says he was shipwrecked three times (2 Corinthians 11:25). He spent a night and a day in the open sea. He lived his life in danger from rivers, bandits, his own countrymen, the Gentiles, and false brothers. He was often without the daily necessities of life: food, shelter, clothing, all because of his commitment to Christ. I'm sure that each of those ingredients in Paul's life were not exactly delicious to him. But God combined all those ingredients to make something tasteful of Paul's life.

Paul was able to deal with all the negative circumstances in his life because his anchor was in Christ Jesus who died for him and rose again. The Lord told Paul, "My grace is sufficient for you, for my power is made perfect in weakness." And Paul's response to that was,

> Therefore I will boast all the more gladly about my weaknesses, so that Christ's power may rest on me. That is why, for Christ's sake, I delight in weaknesses, in insults, in hardships, in persecutions, in difficulties. For when I am weak, then I am strong. (2 Corinthians 12:9-10)

Can you say that when you are weak you are strong? You can if your anchor is in Christ. He can give you a faith to withstand any stormy weather.

A man once witnessed a bird clinging tenaciously to the branch of a tree in the midst of a ferocious storm. The man said it was as if the bird was saying, "Do your worst, Storm! You can even knock me off this branch if you want to. Go ahead, knock me off! I still have wings!!"

Because of Christ's death and resurrection, Paul had wings in the midst of the storm, and so can you and I.

PREACHING

If you were to choose the words to be written on your tombstone, what would they be? Perhaps you have heard of the hypochondriac who had the following epitaph on his tombstone: "I told you I was sick!" My mother has told me what she wants on her tombstone: "Alive and well!"

Acts 28 gives us a fitting epitaph for the Apostle Paul. . . .

> Once safely on shore, we found out that the island was called Malta. The islanders showed us unusual kindness. They built a fire and welcomed us all because it was raining and cold. Paul gathered a pile of brushwood and, as he put it on the fire, a viper, driven out by the heat, fastened itself on his hand. When the islanders saw the snake hanging from his hand, they said to each other, "This man must be a murderer; for though he escaped from the sea, Justice has not allowed him to live." But Paul shook the snake off into the fire and suffered no ill effects. The people expected him to swell up or suddenly fall dead, but after waiting a long time and seeing nothing unusual happen to him, they changed their minds and said he was a god.
>
> There was an estate nearby that belonged to Publius, the chief official of the island. He welcomed us to his home and for three days entertained us hospitably. His father was sick in bed, suffering from fever and dysentery. Paul went in to see him and, after prayer, placed his hands on him and healed him. When this had happened, the rest of the sick on the island came and were cured. They honored us in many ways and when we were ready to sail, they furnished us with the supplies we needed.
>
> After three months we put out to sea in a ship that had wintered in the island. It was an Alexandrian ship with the figurehead of the twin gods Castor and Pollux. We put in at Syracuse and stayed there three days. From there we set sail and arrived at Rhegium. The next day the south wind came up, and on the following day we reached Puteoli. There we found some brothers who invited us to spend a week with them. And so we came to Rome. The brothers there had heard that we were coming, and they traveled as far as the Forum of Appius and the

Three Taverns to meet us. At the sight of these men Paul thanked God and was encouraged. When we got to Rome, Paul was allowed to live by himself, with a soldier to guard him.

Three days later he called together the leaders of the Jews. When they had assembled, Paul said to them: "My brothers, although I have done nothing against our people or against the customs of our ancestors, I was arrested in Jerusalem and handed over to the Romans. They examined me and wanted to release me, because I was not guilty of any crime deserving death. But when the Jews objected, I was compelled to appeal to Caesar—not that I had any charge to bring against my own people. For this reason I have asked to see you and talk with you. It is because of the hope of Israel that I am bound with this chain."

They replied, "We have not received any letters from Judea concerning you, and none of the brothers who have come from there has reported or said anything bad about you. But we want to hear what your views are, for we know that people everywhere are talking against this sect."

They arranged to meet Paul on a certain day, and came in even larger numbers to the place where he was staying. From morning till evening he explained and declared to them the kingdom of God and tried to convince them about Jesus from the Law of Moses and from the Prophets. Some were convinced by what he said, but others would not believe. They disagreed among themselves and began to leave after Paul had made this final statement: "The Holy Spirit spoke the truth to your forefathers when he said through Isaiah the prophet:

> " 'Go to this people and say,
> "You will be ever hearing but never understanding;
>   you will be ever seeing but never perceiving."
> For this people's heart has become calloused;
>   they hardly hear with their ears,
>   and they have closed their eyes.
> Otherwise they might see with their eyes,
>   hear with their ears,
>   understand with their hearts and turn,
>   and I would heal them.'

"Therefore I want you to know that God's salvation has been sent to the Gentiles, and they will listen!"

For two whole years Paul stayed there in his own rented house and welcomed all who came to see him. Boldly and without hindrance he preached the kingdom of God and taught about the Lord Jesus Christ.

Keys to Growth

A lot happens in Acts 28. Paul is shipwrecked on the island of Malta. He is attacked by a viper but emerges from the incident unharmed. Paul heals a number of people and then sets sail for Rome. Upon arriving at the capitol of the empire Paul is greeted by a number of Christian brothers. He is allowed to live, under guard, in his own rented house, which he uses as an outpost for preaching and teaching.

Acts 28:31 would have been a fitting epitaph for the Apostle Paul's tombstone if he had one. "Boldly and without hindrance he preached the kingdom of God and taught about the Lord Jesus Christ." Those few words serve as the ending to the book of Acts. Many have wondered why the book ends so abruptly. The answers are varied. However, this much we can say, Luke set out to write about the Gospel being taken to Jerusalem, Judea, Samaria, and the ends of the earth (Acts 1:8). Having set forth the fact that Paul preached the Gospel in Rome, the center of the empire, Luke achieved his purpose. It is significant that Luke ends his second volume on the note of preaching. The preaching of the word has been the dominant subject of his history and is thus presented as one of the primary keys to the growth of the Church. The abrupt ending to the book of Acts also suggests that we are to continue living out the Acts of the Holy Spirit in our day as well.

So what application does this last verse of this ancient history book have for us today, we who live in an apathetic, anti-authority, anti-preaching age? Is preaching still relevant after all these years, or are we free to discard it and adopt wholly new methods for communicating the good news about Jesus Christ? Furthermore, what is your role in preaching, those of you who sit in the pews Sunday after Sunday?

Let me offer at least one application of this Scripture to your life today, and that is that the Lord wants you to pray for the preaching of the word. Paul wrote to the church at Ephesus:

> Pray also for me, that whenever I open my mouth, words may be given me so that I will fearlessly make known the mystery of the Gospel, for which I am an ambassador in chains. Pray that I may declare it fearlessly, as I should. (Ephesians 6:19-20)

Paul may have written these words while he was in prison at Rome. And so we may presume that it was the prayers of God's people in Ephesus that made the effective preaching in Rome possible by God's grace.

What should you pray for when you pray for the preaching of God's word? Let me suggest you follow Acts 28:31 as an outline for what to pray.

First of all, as you pray for all Christian preachers, *PRAY FOR BOLD PREACHING*. The word means outspokenness, frankness, plainness of speech, that conceals nothing and passes over nothing. The word is used several times in the book of Acts. The believers pray in Acts 4:29, "Now, Lord, consider their threats and enable your servants to speak your word with great boldness." And we read that "After they prayed, the place where they were meeting was shaken. And they were all filled with the Holy Spirit and spoke the word of God boldly." (Acts 4:31)

When you pray for the bold preaching of God's Word, you should pray not only for pastors, but for yourself as well, that the Lord would enable you to speak boldly about him to non-Christians.

In Acts 9:28 we find the Apostle Paul, shortly after his conversion, moving freely about Jerusalem "speaking boldly in the name of the Lord." Bold preaching is not just the activity of older believers but of new believers as well, for the boldness comes not from ourselves, but from God. The same word is used again in Acts 13:46, 14:3, 18:26, and in 19:8. Each time it refers to the communication of God's word.

If I want to be certain that someone reads something which I have written in a letter or an article, I put it in bold print. Bold preaching is the kind of preaching that makes God's word absolutely clear to the hearer. It also captures the attention of the hearer.

Peter Cartwright, a nineteenth-century, circuit riding, Methodist preacher, was an uncompromising man. One Sunday morning when he was to preach, he was told that President Andrew Jackson was in the congregation, and was warned not to say anything out of line.

When Cartwright stood to preach, he said, "I understand that Andrew Jackson is here. I have been requested to be guarded in my remarks. Andrew Jackson will go to hell if he doesn't repent."

The congregation was shocked and wondered how the President would respond. After the service, President Jackson shook hands with Peter Cartwright and said, "Sir, if I had a regiment of men like you, I could whip the world."

That's bold preaching! But bold preaching doesn't have to be unnecessarily offensive. It just has to be clear.

In his book, *The Power of Little Words*, author John Beckley, former business editor of *Newsweek* magazine, observes:

> The emphasis in education is rarely placed on communicating ideas simply and clearly. Instead, we're encouraged to use more complicated words and sentence structures to show off our learning and literacy . . . instead of teaching us how to communicate as clearly as possible, our schooling in English teaches us how to fog things up. It even implants a fear that if we don't make our writing complicated enough, we'll be considered uneducated.

You know what they say about fog? "If there's fog in the pulpit, there will be fog in the pew." And you know what some people say about preachers? "Six days invisible, one day incomprehensible!" Pray for preaching in the church of Jesus Christ to be clear and comprehensible.

Secondly, this passage suggests we should *PRAY FOR UNHINDERED PREACHING*. What are the hindrances to effective preaching of God's word today? There are many hindrances but basically three *sources* of hindrance: the preacher, the audience, and Satan.

What are the hindrances to effective preaching which stem from the preacher? There are probably many. But the one that many un-churched people mention today is that the preachers they have heard are boring and irrelevant.

Calvin Miller has written a book entitled *The Empowered Communicator*. In that book he has several imaginary letters written from audience to speaker. One of my favorites is this one:

> Dear Speaker:
>
> The world has never gotten over its likin' of the truth. I've been a member of a church now for more'n fifty years. We must have had twenty pastors or more. I don't know for sure. None of 'em stayed very long. Every one of them told the truth. There was only one out of the whole bunch that we ever really wanted to keep. He told the truth interestingly. One time he put on his bathrobe and played like he was King David. Sure was interesting. Another time he played like he was the inn keeper in Bethlehem. Then one time he smeared his face with soot — sure looked strange — and told us he was Job. We all knew better and he knew we did, but I never really understood the Book of Job till that sermon. One time he dressed up in a white robe and came in the back of the auditorium carrying a sign. He told us he was an Archangel. He seemed so convinced, we believed him. Darndest thing, he'd do per't near't anything to keep our attention. He always did. Big church down in Chattanooga hire him away from us. The good'uns always seem to get away.
>
> They arrested a man over by Greenville the other day. They threw him in jail. He was walking around town in a white robe, carrying a sign that said "THE WORLD IS COMING TO AN END." I don't know why they arrested him. Most everybody believed he was right. As I saw it, he was telling the truth interestingly. Last week my preacher preached on that very thing. The way he told that same truth wasn't all that interesting. They might have locked up the wrong man.
>
> It sure seems important to me to tell the truth interestingly. Not too many people do it. A bunch of us who listen to your sermons are

wishing you'd do it. You might try the white robe and sign routine. Just don't go outside.

Your Audience

Pray for preachers to keep the preaching of God's word interesting!

What are the hindrances to effective preaching which stem from the audience? I have heard people say they just don't get anything out of preaching. Karen Mains suggests a wonderful solution to that problem in her book *Making Sunday Special*. It is called "The Sunday Search." The idea is to participate in Sunday worship by searching for how Christ will *speak to* and *through* you. David and Karen Mains would remind their children before going to church to look for ways that Christ might speak to them and through them. Then when they came home from church they would share as a family how Christ spoke to them and through them. Christ might speak to you in ways other than through the sermon. But I think this is an especially great way to approach listening to a sermon. As one anonymous author has said,

> At least one time in every sermon God breaks through the words of the preacher and speaks directly to the people. It may be in a single sentence or in just one phrase. . . . So many of us miss that one special word from God because we are comparing the preacher's manner with that of some other preacher we have heard recently. From now on, just listen intently for that one portion God intends to be applied specifically to your heart!

You can also go to church looking for ways that God will speak *through you* to others. It may be through a word of encouragement or a pat on the back. In any case, getting involved in the Sunday Search can keep us from having the consumer mentality that all we do is come to church to get something. God also wants to give something through us. Try the Sunday Search on for size and help remove another hindrance to effective preaching.

A third hindrance to the effective preaching of God's Word is Satan. Jesus told a parable once about a farmer who sowed seed. In Jesus' parable the seed that the farmer sowed represented the word of God. Jesus said that some people are like seed sown along a path, as soon as they hear the word, Satan comes like a bird and takes away the word that was sown in them.

C. S. Lewis once wrote in *The Screwtape Letters*, "There are two equal and opposite errors into which our race can fall about the devils. One is to disbelieve in their existence. The other is to believe, and to feel and excessive and unhealthy interest in them. They themselves are equally pleased by both errors, and hail a materialist or a magician with the same delight."

So we must be careful not to ignore the hindrance that Satan can pose to effective preaching. But we must also be careful not to exaggerate the power that he has. If anything would appear to be a hindrance to the preaching of the word, Satan would seem to be the greatest hindrance. But in fact, Satan can only do what God allows him to do. When the Lord wants to open a door for the preaching of his word to take place, nothing can stop him, not you, not the preacher, and not Satan. Jesus said to the church in Philadelphia in the book of Revelation, chapter 3, verses 7 and 8:

> These are the words of him who is holy and true, who holds the key of David. What he opens no one can shut, and what he shuts no one can open. I know your deeds. See, I have placed before you an open door that no one can shut. I know that you have little strength, yet you have kept my word and have not denied my name. I will make those who are of the synagogue of Satan, who claim to be Jews though they are not, but are liars—I will make them come and fall down at your feet and acknowledge that I have loved you.

There is nothing that can stop the children of God from declaring the good news about Jesus when God opens the door!

The Lord opened a door for the church in Philadelphia; the Lord opened a door for Paul in Rome and he preached the Gospel unhindered. Pray that the Lord will open a door for me and for you where we each live.

Thirdly, when you pray for the preaching of God's Word, *PRAY FOR EDUCATIONAL PREACHING*. We read that the Apostle Paul "*preached* the kingdom of God and *taught* about the Lord Jesus Christ."

What is the difference between preaching and teaching? The word translated as "preached" in this sentence means "to announce". Paul was a herald, an announcer of the kingdom of God. What did he announce about the kingdom of God? He announced that God's kingdom had drawn near to us in the coming of the King— Jesus. His teaching about the Lord Jesus Christ was explanatory of his announcement of the kingdom. Thus preaching and teaching are not completely separate activities; they go together.

Author and theologian, J. I. Packer has written of our time and culture:

> The general populace is well-nigh abysmally ignorant of Bible history and Bible doctrine, as well as Bible ethics. In consequence, evangelistic preaching must today be first of all instructive. Paul spoke of "the Gospel, for which I was appointed a preacher ... and a teacher" (II Timothy 1:10 f.), and said of Christ, "we proclaim him ... teaching every man with all wisdom" (Col. 1:28). In both texts the reference to teaching is explanatory of the reference to preaching; Paul saw himself as a teaching preacher, an educational evangelist, and it is vitally important at the present time that we should confine ourselves to patterns of evangelistic practice which allow for thorough instruction,

after Paul's example. For there is in fact a good deal to be conveyed. (James I. Packer, "What Is Evangelism?", *Theological Perspectives On Church Growth*, pp. 100-101.)

But educational preaching does not have to be dry; it can be entertaining. The dictionary defines "entertainment" as holding a person's attention or interest. Certainly good preaching ought to do that. I don't want to be like the young pastor who was given a tape recorder by his church to help him in a program he had devised for self-improvement. At the first opportunity he used it during a Sunday morning service. When he got home, he settled down in his easy chair and began to listen carefully. He was quite pleased with what he heard. The prayers, Scripture reading and announcements all went very well. Then came the message. Some time later he awoke from a sound sleep, startled to hear the congregation singing the closing hymn!

This incident reminds of what someone said about a certain Bible teacher: "He goes down deeper, stays under longer, and comes up dryer than anyone I've ever heard."

But educational preaching does not have to be arid and dull. One of the most arid regions on earth is found along the Persian Gulf. Because little rain ever falls, fresh water is not readily available. The people survive because divers with great goatskin bags plunge to the bottom of the sea where copious springs exist. Returning to the surface with these huge containers filled with crystal-clear water, they supply refreshment for the thirsty inhabitants. Please pray for the preaching of God's word to be like that–supplying refreshment for spiritually thirsty people.

Finally, when we pray for the preaching of God' Word, I think we need to *PRAY FOR FOCUSED PREACHING*. Pray that Christian preaching today would be like the Apostle Paul's, pray that the preaching of God's word would focus on the Kingdom and the King–the Lord Jesus Christ.

It is so tempting for preachers to want to please people. I think most pastors love their people and want to be loved by them. But there is no way any one pastor can ever fulfill all of the expectations in any one congregation.

Perhaps you have heard of "The Model Preacher":

> He preaches exactly 20 minutes and then sits down. He condemns sin, but will never hurt anyone's feelings. He works from 8 a.m. to 10 p.m. in every type of work, from preaching in the pulpit to custodial services ... he is 26 years old and has been preaching for 30 years. He has a burning desire to work with teenagers and spends all of his time with older folks. He smiles all the time with a straight face because he has a sense of humor that keeps him seriously dedicated to his work. He makes 15 calls a day on church members, spends all his time evangelizing the un-churched, and is never out of his office.

Obviously, no pastor can meet everyone's expectations all of the time. But there is a solution to the problem of improper expectations on the part of the congregation, and the temptation to try to please everyone on the part of the pastor. We all need to get our eyes off of ourselves and on to the Lord. Jesus said, "But seek first his kingdom and his righteousness, and all these things will be given to you as well." (Matthew 6:33) The most important thing in preaching is not whether it pleases us but whether it pleases the Lord.

I love what John Maxwell says about his first time preaching:

> It was in the little Methodist Church in Walpole, Mass. I was a seminary student at the time, and I wanted that sermon to be a gem of scholarly eloquence. So I tried to put into writing all that I knew of theology and literature. But it just wouldn't jell, and I became confused and discouraged. In despair I telegraphed my father, a Methodist district superintendent, asking help. He replied: 'JUST TELL THE PEOPLE THAT JESUS CHRIST CAN CHANGE THEIR LIVES. Love Dad.' That message has been engraved in my memory ever since.

Pray for us preachers that we would maintain that focus on the Kingdom and on the King, the Lord Jesus Christ. Pray for our preaching, that it would be educational; pray that it would go unhindered; pray that it would be bold, clear and captivating to believer and seeker alike.

CONCLUSION

When I first became a pastor I thought I only needed one key to unlock growth for the little congregation I was serving. I figured all I needed was good preaching. So I focused a lot of time and energy on producing the best sermons I could create at that time. Interestingly enough, the congregation didn't grow in numbers. It actually declined. I think God was trying to teach me something: that I needed more than one key on my key-chain.

We have examined no less than forty-one keys to growth in our study of *The Acts of the Apostles*. All of these keys are important to use at one time or another to unlock growth in our individual lives, in specific congregations, and in the Church as a whole. But perhaps the most important key is the first one we looked at in this book: Jesus the Christ, who was sent by the Father and who continues to send his Holy Spirit into hearts that are open. At the beginning of Acts we heard Jesus say,

> But you will receive power when the Holy Spirit comes on you; and you will be my witnesses in Jerusalem, and in all Judea and Samaria, and to the ends of the earth. (Acts 1:8)

I believe Jesus' promise is as good today as it was two thousand years ago. If we ask the Father and his Son Jesus Christ to send the Holy Spirit into our hearts, then we *will be* good and effective witnesses for Jesus, beginning in our own "Jerusalem", then in our own "Judea and Samaria", and to the ends of the earth, for the glory of our Triune God.

ACKNOWLEDGEMENTS

I am indebted to PreachingToday.com for many of the illustrations in this book. I have been collecting illustrations of the book of Acts for so long that in some cases I have forgotten where they came from. Where I have failed to provide proper attribution I will be happy to correct my errors in future editions of this book.

SELECT BIBLIOGRAPHY

Barclay, William, *The Acts of the Apostles*, Philadelphia: The Westminster Press, 1955.
Bruce, F. F. *The Acts of the Apostles*, Grand Rapids: Eerdmans, 1970.
Erdman, Charles, *The Acts*, Philadelphia: The Westminster Press, MCMXIX.
Larson, Bruce, *Living Out The Book of Acts*, Dallas: Word Publishing, 1984.
Lewis, C. S. *Mere Christianity*, London: Geoffrey Bles, 1952.
Morton, H. V. *In The Steps of St. Paul*, New York: Dodd, Mead & Company, 1959.
Phillips, J. B. *The Young Church in Action*, New York: Macmillan, 1955.
Stott, John R. W. *The Message of Acts*, Downers Grove, Illinois: InterVarsity Press, 1990.
Stutzman, Linford, *Sailing Acts*, Intercourse, PA: Good Books, 2006.
Sweeting, George & Sweeting, Donald, *The Acts of God*, Chicago: Moody Press, 1986.
The Holy Bible, New International Version, International Bible Society, 1973, 1978, 1984.

WILL VAUS

- was born outside of New York City and grew up in Southern California.
- is the son of Jim Vaus, former organized crime wiretapper who came to Christ through the ministry of Billy Graham in 1949.
- holds a Bachelor of Arts degree in drama from the University of California at San Diego and a Master of Divinity degree from Princeton Theological Seminary.
- has served as a pastor in California, South Carolina and Pennsylvania.
- is the president of Will Vaus Ministries, through which he has communicated the love of Christ around the world since 1988.
- is the author of *Mere Theology: A Guide to the Thought of C. S. Lewis*, *My Father Was a Gangster: The Jim Vaus Story*, *The Professor of Narnia: The C. S. Lewis Story*, *Speaking of Jack: A C. S. Lewis Discussion Guide*, and *The Hidden Story of Narnia: A Book-by-Book Guide to Lewis' Spiritual Themes*
- and his wife, Becky, have been married since 1988 and have three sons: James, Jonathan and Joshua.
- has a website you can visit: www.willvaus.com

OTHER BOOKS OF INTEREST

C. S. Lewis

C. S. Lewis: Views From Wake Forest - Essays on C. S. Lewis
Michael Travers, editor

Contains sixteen scholarly presentations from the international C. S. Lewis convention in Wake Forest, NC. Walter Hooper shares his important essay "Editing C. S. Lewis," a chronicle of publishing decisions after Lewis' death in 1963.

"Scholars from a variety of disciplines address a wide range of issues. The happy result is a fresh and expansive view of an author who well deserves this kind of thoughtful attention."
     Diana Pavlac Glyer, author of *The Company They Keep*

The Hidden Story of Narnia:
A Book-By-Book Guide to Lewis' Spiritual Themes
Will Vaus

A book of insightful commentary equally suited for teens or adults – Will Vaus points out connections between the *Narnia* books and spiritual/biblical themes, as well as between ideas in the *Narnia* books and C. S. Lewis' other books. Learn what Lewis himself said about the overarching and unifying thematic structure of the Narnia books. That is what this book explores; what C. S. Lewis called "the hidden story" of Narnia. Each chapter includes questions for individual use or small group discussion.

Why I Believe in Narnia:
33 Reviews and Essays on the Life and Work of C. S. Lewis
James Como

Chapters range from reviews of critical books, documentaries and movies to evaluations of Lewis' books to biographical analysis.

"A valuable, wide-ranging collection of essays by one of the best informed and most accute commentators on Lewis' work and ideas."
     Peter Schakel, author of *Imagination & the Arts in C. S. Lewis*

C. S. Lewis Goes to Heaven: A Reader's Guide to The Great Divorce
David G. Clark

This is the first book devoted solely to this often neglected book and the first to reveal several important secrets Lewis concealed within the story. Lewis felt his imaginary trip to Hell and Heaven was far better than his book *The Screwtape Letters*, which has become a classic. Clark is an ordained minister who has taught courses on Lewis for more than 30 years and is a New Testament and Greek scholar with a Doctor of Philosophy degree in Biblical Studies from the University of Notre Dame. Readers will discover the many literary and biblical influences Lewis utilized in writing his brilliant novel.

C. S. Lewis & Philosophy as a Way of Life
Adam Barkman

C. S. Lewis is rarely thought of as a "philosopher" per se despite having both studied and taught philosophy for several years at Oxford. Lewis's long journey to Christianity was essentially philosophical – passing through seven different stages. This 624 page book is an invaluable reference for C. S. Lewis scholars and fans alike

C. S. Lewis: His Literary Achievement
Colin Manlove

"This is a positively brilliant book, written with splendor, elegance, profundity and evidencing an enormous amount of learning. This is probably not a book to give a first-time reader of Lewis. But for those who are more broadly read in the Lewis corpus this book is an absolute gold mine of information. The author gives us a magnificent overview of Lewis' many writings, tracing for us thoughts and ideas which recur throughout, and at the same time telling us how each book differs from the others. I think it is not extravagant to call C. S. Lewis: His Literary Achievement a tour de force."
       Robert Merchant, *St. Austin Review*, Book Review Editor

Mythopoeic Narnia:
Memory, Metaphor, and Metamorphoses in The Chronicles of Narnia
Salwa Khoddam

Dr. Khoddam, the founder of the C. S. Lewis and Inklings Society (2004), has been teaching university courses using Lewis' books for over 25 years. Her book offers a fresh approach to the Narnia books based on an inquiry into Lewis' readings and use of classical and Christian symbols. She explores the literary and intellectual contexts of these stories, the traditional myths and motifs, and places them in the company of the greatest Christian mythopoeic works of Western literature. In Lewis' imagination, memory and metaphor interact to advance his purpose – a Christian metamorphosis. *Mythopoeic Narnia* helps to open the door for readers into the magical world of the Western imagination.

Speaking of Jack: A C. S. Lewis Discussion Guide
Will Vaus

C. S. Lewis societies have been forming around the world since the first one started in New York City in 1969. Will Vaus has started and led three groups himself. *Speaking of Jack* is the result of Vaus' experience in leading those Lewis societies. Included here are introductions to most of Lewis' books as well as questions designed to stimulate discussion about Lewis' life and work. These materials have been "road-tested" with real groups made up of young and old, some very familiar with Lewis and some newcomers. *Speaking of Jack* may be used in an existing book discussion group, to start a C. S. Lewis society, or to guide your own exploration of Lewis' books.

George MacDonald

Diary of an Old Soul & The White Page Poems
George MacDonald and Betty Aberlin

The first edition of George MacDonald's book of daily poems included a blank page opposite each page of poems. Readers were invited to write their own reflections on the "white page." MacDonald wrote: "Let your white page be ground, my print be seed, growing to golden ears, that faith and hope may feed." Betty Aberlin responded to MacDonald's invitation with daily poems of her own.

"Betty Aberlin's close readings of George MacDonald's verses and her thoughtful responses to them speak clearly of her poetic gifts and spiritual intelligence."
    Luci Shaw, poet

George MacDonald: Literary Heritage and Heirs
Roderick McGillis, editor

This latest collection of 14 essays sets a new standard that will influence MacDonald studies for many more years. George MacDonald experts are increasingly evaluating his entire corpus within the nineteenth century context.

"This comprehensive collection represents the best of contemporary scholarship on George MacDonald."
    Rolland Hein, author of *George MacDonald: Victorian Mythmaker*

In the Near Loss of Everything: George MacDonald's Son in America
Dale Wayne Slusser

In the summer of 1887, George MacDonald's son Ronald, newly engaged to artist Louise Blandy, sailed from England to America to teach school. The next summer he returned to England to marry Louise and bring her back to America. On August 27, 1890, Louise died, leaving him with an infant daughter. Ronald once described losing a beloved spouse as "the near loss of everything". Dale Wayne Slusser unfolds this poignant story with unpublished letters and photos that give readers a glimpse into the close-knit MacDonald family.

A Novel Pulpit: Sermons From George MacDonald's Fiction
David L. Neuhouser

"In MacDonald's novels, the Christian teaching emerges out of the characters and story line, the narrator's comments, and inclusion of sermons given by the fictional preachers. The sermons in the novels are shorter than the ones in collections of MacDonald's sermons and so are perhaps more accessible for some. In any case, they are both stimulating and thought-provoking. This collection of sermons from ten novels serve to bring out the 'freshness and brilliance' of MacDonald's message."
    From the author's introduction

Through the Year with George MacDonald: 366 Daily Readings
Rolland Hein, editor

These page-length excerpts from sermons, novels and letters are given an appropriate theme/heading and a complementary Scripture passage for daily reading. An inspiring introduction to the artistic soul and Christian vision of George MacDonald.

Behind the Back of the North Wind:
Critical Essays on George MacDonald's Classic Children's Book
John Pennington and Roderick McGillis, editors

The unique blend of fairy tale atmosphere and social realism in this novel laid the groundwork for modern fantasy literature. Sixteen essays by various authors are accompanied by an instructive introduction, extensive index, and beautiful illustrations.

Shadows and Chivalry:
C. S. Lewis and George MacDonald on Suffering, Evil, and Death
Jeff McInnis

Shadows and Chivalry studies the influence of George MacDonald, a nineteenth-century Scottish novelist and fantasy writer, upon one of the most influential writers of modern times, C. S. Lewis – the creator of Narnia, literary critic, and best-selling apologist. This study attempts to trace the overall affect of MacDonald's work on Lewis's thought and imagination. Without ever ceasing to be a story of one man's influence upon another, the study also serves as an exploration of each writer's thought on, and literary visions of, good and evil.

Christian Living

The Living Word of the Living God:
A Beginner's Guide to Reading and Understanding the Bible
Rev. Tom Furrer

This book is based on over 20 years experience of teaching the Bible to confirmation classes at Episcopal churches in Connecticut. Chapters from Genesis to Revelation.

Keys to Growth: Meditations on the Acts of the Apostles
Will Vaus

Every living things or person requires certain ingredients in order to grow, and if a thing or person is not growing, it is dying. *The Acts of the Apostles* is a book that is all about growth. Will Vaus has been meditating and preaching on *Acts* for the past 30 years. In this volume, he offers the reader forty-one keys from the entire book of Acts to unlock spiritual growth in everyday life.

Called to Serve: Life as a Firefighter-Deacon
Deacon Anthony R. Surozenski

Called to Serve is the story of one man's dream to be a firefighter. But dreams have a way of taking detours – so Tony Surozenski became a teacher and eventually a volunteer firefighter. And when God enters the picture, Tony is faced with a choice. Will he give up firefighting to follow another call? After many years, Tony's two callings are finally united – in service as a fire chaplain at Ground Zero after the 9-11 attacks and in other ways he could not have imagined. Tony is Chief Chaplain's aid for the Massachusetts Corp of Fire Chaplains and Director for the Office of the Diaconate of the Diocese of Worcester, Massachusetts.

Harry Potter

The Order of Harry Potter: The Literary Skill of the Hogwarts Epic
Colin Manlove

Colin Manlove, a popular conference speaker and author of over a dozen books, has earned an international reputation as an expert on fantasy and children's literature. His book, *From Alice to Harry Potter*, is a survey of 400 English fantasy books. In *The Order of Harry Potter*, he compares and contrasts *Harry Potter* with works by "Inklings" writers J.R.R. Tolkien, C.S. Lewis and Charles Williams; he also examines Rowling's treatment of the topic of imagination; her skill in organization and the use of language; and the book's underlying motifs and themes.

Harry Potter & Imagination: The Way Between Two Worlds
Travis Prinzi

Imaginative literature places a reader between two worlds: the story world and the world of daily life, and challenges the reader to imagine and to act for a better world. Starting with discussion of Harry Potter's more important themes, *Harry Potter & Imagination* takes readers on a journey through the transformative power of those themes for both the individual and for culture by placing Rowling's series in its literary, historical, and cultural contexts.

Repotting Harry Potter: A Professor's Guide for the Serious Re-Reader
Rowling Revisited: Return Trips to Harry, Fantastic Beasts, Quidditch, & Beedle the Bard
James W. Thomas

In *Repotting Harry Potter* and his sequel book *Rowling Revisited*, Dr. James W. Thomas points out the humor, puns, foreshadowing and literary parallels in the Potter books. In *Rowling Revisted*, readers will especially find useful three extensive appendixes – "Fantastic Beasts and the Pages Where You'll Find Them," "Quidditch Through the Pages," and "The Books in the Potter Books." Dr. Thomas makes re-reading the Potter books even more rewarding and enjoyable.

The Deathly Hallows Lectures:
The Hogwarts Professor Explains Harry's Final Adventure
John Granger

In *The Deathly Hallows Lectures*, John Granger reveals the finale's brilliant details, themes, and meanings. *Harry Potter* fans will be surprised by and delighted with Granger's explanations of the three dimensions of meaning in *Deathly Hallows*. Ms. Rowling has said that alchemy sets the "parameters of magic" in the series; after reading the chapter-length explanation of *Deathly Hallows* as the final stage of the alchemical Great Work, the serious reader will understand how important literary alchemy is in understanding Rowling's artistry and accomplishment.

Sociology and Harry Potter: 22 Enchanting Essays on the Wizarding World
Jenn Simms, editor

Modeled on an Introduction to Sociology textbook. this books is not simply about the series, but also used the series to facilitate reader's understanding of the discipline of sociology and a development of a sociological approach to viewing social reality. It is a case of high quality academic scholarship written in a form and on a topic accessible to non-academics. As such, it is written to appeal to Harry Potter fans and the general reading public. Contributors include professional sociologists from eight countries.

Harry Potter, Still Recruiting:
Essays on Harry Potter and Pop Culture
Valerie Frankel, editor

Chapters include a wide variety of topics such as social networking, Pottermore, college quidditch, fan art, fan fiction, conferences, exhibitions, Wizard Rock, websites, and fan locations such as the Wizarding World of Harry Potter. Includes interviews with prominent Harry Potter community members such as Muggle Net, Harry and the Potters, and Whimsic Alley. Frankel emphasizes the recent effects on society ranging from the Simpsons to Facebook.

Hog's Head Conversations: Essays on Harry Potter
Travis Prinzi, editor

Ten fascinating essays on Harry Potter are divided into five sections: Conversations on 1) Literary Value, 2) Eternal Truth, 3) Imagination, 4) Literary Criticism, and 5) Characters. Contributors include the following popular Potter writers and speakers: John Granger, James W. Thomas, Colin Manlove, and Travis Prinzi.

Fiction

The Iona Conspiracy (from The Remnant Chronicles book series)
Gary Gregg

Readers find themselves on a modern adventure through ancient Celtic myth and legend as thirteen year old Jacob uncovers his destiny within "the remnant" of the Sporrai Order. As the Iona Academy comes under the control of educational reformers and ideological scientists, Jacob finds himself on a dangerous mission to the sacred Scottish island of Iona and discovers how his life is wrapped up with the fate of the long lost cover of *The Book of Kells*. From its connections to Arthurian legend to references to real-life people, places, and historical mysteries, *Iona* is an adventure that speaks to eternal truths as well as the challenges of the modern world. A young adult novel, *Iona* can be enjoyed by the entire family.

Poets and Poetry

Remembering Roy Campbell: The Memoirs of his Daughters, Anna and Tess
Introduction by Judith Lütge Coullie, editor
Preface by Joseph Pearce

Anna and Teresa Campbell were the daughters of the handsome young South African poet and writer, Roy Campbell (1901-1957), and his beautiful English wife, Mary Garman. In their frank and moving memoirs, Anna and Tess recall the extraordinary, and often very difficult, lives they shared with their exceptional parents. The book includes over 50 photos, 344 footnotes, a timeline of Campbell's life, and a complete index.

In the Eye of the Beholder: How to See the World Like a Romantic Poet
Louis Markos

Born out of the French Revolution and its radical faith that a nation could be shaped and altered by the dreams and visions of its people, British Romantic Poetry was founded on a belief that the objects and realities of our world, whether natural or human, are not fixed in stone but can be molded and transformed by the visionary eye of the poet. Unlike many of the books written on Romanticism, which devote many pages to the poets and few pages to their poetry, the focus here is firmly on the poems themselves. The author thereby draws the reader intimately into the life of these poems. A separate bibliographical essay is provided for readers listing accessible biographies of each poet and critical studies of their work.

The Cat on the Catamaran: A Christmas Tale
John Martin

Here is a modern-day parable of a modern-day cat with modern-day attitudes. Riverboat Dan is a "cool" cat on a perpetual vacation from responsibility. He's *The Cat on the Catamaran* – sailing down the river of life. Dan keeps his guilty conscience from interfering with his fun until he runs into trouble. But will he have the courage to believe that it's never too late to change course? (For ages 10 to adult)

"Cat lovers and poetry lovers alike will enjoy this whimsical story about Riverboat Dan, a philosophical cat in search of meaning."
    Regina Doman, author of *Angel in the Water*

The Half Blood Poems
Inspired by the Stories of J.K. Rowling
Christine Lowther

Like Harry Potter, Christine's poetry can soar above the tragic to discover the heroic and beautiful in such poems as "Neville, Unlikely Rebel," "For Our Wide-Armed Mothers," and "A Boy's Hands." There are 71 poems divided into seven chapters that correspond to the seven books. Fans of Harry Potter will experience once again many of the emotions they felt reading the books – emotions presented most effectively through a poet's words.

Pop Culture

To Love Another Person: A Spiritual Journey Through Les Miserables
John Morrison

The powerful story of Jean Valjean's redemption is beloved by readers and theatergoers everywhere. In this companion and guide to Victor Hugo's masterpiece, author John Morrison unfolds the spiritual depth and breadth of this classic novel and broadway musical.

Through Common Things: Philosophical Reflections on Popular Culture
Adam Barkman

"Barkman presents us with an amazingly wide-ranging collection of philosophical reflections grounded in the everyday things of popular culture – past and present, eastern and western, factual and fictional. Throughout his encounters with often surprising subject-matter (the value of darkness?), he writes clearly and concisely, moving seamlessly between Aristotle and anime, Lord Buddha and Lord Voldemort.... This is an informative and entertaining book to read!"
    Doug Bloomberg, Professor of Philosophy, Institute for Christian Studies

Above All Things: Essays on Christian Ethics and Popular Culture
Adam Barkman

"Whether discussing Winnie the Pooh or The Walking Dead, this book digs up buried philosophical treasure. Those who don't normally think of themselves as philosophically inclined will be surprised and delighted as Barkman rescues philosophy from dry classroom abstractions and reveals how it fills the glorious messiness of everyday life."
    Dr. Kevin Flatt, Assistant Professor of History, Redeemer University College

Spotlight:
A Close-up Look at the Artistry and Meaning of Stephenie Meyer's Twilight Novels
John Granger

Stephenie Meyer's *Twilight* saga has taken the world by storm. But is there more to *Twilight* than a love story for teen girls crossed with a cheesy vampire-werewolf drama? *Spotlight* reveals the literary backdrop, themes, artistry, and meaning of the four Bella Swan adventures. *Spotlight* is the perfect gift for serious *Twilight* readers.

Virtuous Worlds: The Video Gamer's Guide to Spiritual Truth
John Stanifer

Popular titles like *Halo 3* and *The Legend of Zelda: Twilight Princess* fly off shelves at a mind-blowing rate. John Stanifer, an avid gamer, shows readers specific parallels between Christian faith and the content of their favorite games. Written with wry humor (including a heckler who frequently pokes fun at the author) this book will appeal to gamers and non-gamers alike. Those unfamiliar with video games may be pleasantly surprised to find that many elements in those "virtual worlds" also qualify them as "virtuous worlds."

www.ingramcontent.com/pod-product-compliance
Lightning Source LLC
Chambersburg PA
CBHW030219100526
44584CB00014BA/1020